EXPLORATIONS IN COLONIAL BENGAL

Explorations in Colonial Bengal

Essays on Religion, Society, and Culture

Remembering Ramakanta Chakrabarty

Edited by

Achintya Kumar Dutta

With a Foreword by

Amiya P. Sen

Orient BlackSwan

EXPLORATIONS IN COLONIAL BENGAL: ESSAYS ON RELIGION, SOCIETY, AND CULTURE

ORIENT BLACKSWAN PRIVATE LIMITED

Registered Office
3-6-752 Himayatnagar, Hyderabad 500 029, Telangana, India
e-mail: centraloffice@orientblackswan.com

Other Offices
Bengaluru, Chennai, Guwahati, Hyderabad, Kolkata,
Mumbai, New Delhi, Noida, Patna

First published by Orient Blackswan Private Limited 2023

ISBN 978-93-5442-513-4

040345

Typeset in
Adobe Jenson Pro 11.5/13.5
by Le Studio Graphique, Gurgaon 122 007

Printed in India at
Replika Press Pvt. Ltd.

Published by
Orient Blackswan Private Limited
3-6-752 Himayatnagar, Hyderabad 500 029, Telangana, India
e-mail: info@orientblackswan.com

Contents

Tables and Figure

Tables

Figure

Images

FOREWORD

Ramakanta Chakrabarty: The Modern Historian of Bengal Vaishnavism

AMIYA P. SEN

It is naturally difficult to write of a fellow scholar whom one has never met in person, nor heard speaking from a public platform. My acquaintance with Professor Ramakanta Chakrabarty is based entirely on his writings on the cultural history of Bengal. Even this has been rather selective, inasmuch as my reading was confined to his researches on Vaishnavism in Bengal. It was only recently that I became aware of his astonishing range of intellectual interests, stretching from music and folklore to astronomy and science fiction, from local and provincial history to the study of historiography. Arguably, Ramakanta Babu remains in essence a historian of ethnic Bengal in all its staggering cultural breadth and complexity. This, one has to say, has been the source of both his strength and weakness. The weakness many of us have exhibited as well, but rarely the strength. My own research interests have hinged on modern Bengal and Hindu Bengalis almost exclusively, further beset by the disadvantage of not being able to write in Bengali as fluently or copiously as did Professor Chakrabarty. When writing in his first language, Ramakanta Babu wrote with the felicity and grace of a native speaker who had imbued the best of both Sanskrit and the vernacular traditions. His English prose, by comparison, was a trifle taut and unentertaining and, more often than not, he adopted a narrative style that was more anecdotal and descriptive than engagingly analytical or argumentative. Thankfully, though, he refrained from the use of words, expressions, or syntax, now quite commonplace in academic writing, which befuddles and leaves the reader both gaping and groping. Ramakanta Babu himself did not appear to consider opacity the mark of semantic excellence. There was simplicity, not naivete, in his English-language writings. Such writings were neither ebullient nor evocative, and yet rested solidly on an unambiguously framed and adequately annotated argument. They chose to inform more than to entertain, to humbly present a case rather than pompously pontificate.

I imagine Professor Chakrabarty's linguistic and cultural training in Sanskrit qualitatively enriched his Bengali as the eminent educator and writer from nineteenth-century Bengal, Pundit Iswarchandra Vidyasagar, had once believed it would. His connection with Vidyasagar is more than simply fortuitous. Professor Chakrabarty graduated from Vidyasagar College in north Kolkata, an institution once established by the Pundit himself under a different name, and subsequently went on to edit commemorative volumes on him which I have had the pleasure of consulting. It is not common knowledge that although a professional historian by training, Ramakanta Babu taught Sanskrit for nearly ten years at Rabindra Bharati University, Kolkata. It is a pity, therefore, that none of his erstwhile students from that University, or more generally, Sanskritists, could be approached to contribute to this timely volume.

Although he has written widely on the cultural history of Bengal, Professor Chakrabarty's forte was indeed Gaudiya Vaishnavism, and perhaps I am right in assuming that the intellectual foundations thereof were principally three. First, there is the matter of his ancestry. I am reliably informed that some of his ancestors were professional *pathaks*, a fact that would have had a bearing on both his interest in local Vaishnavism and continuing passion for music. Second, there is his cultural location in Bardhaman, an important seat of Vaishnava piety and learning in the late medieval era. In my own fleeting forays into Vaishnava culture and history, I was introduced to a work that was appropriately called *Srikhander Prachin Vaishnava*, which details the life histories of Vaishnava poets and saints based in the famed *sripat* (theological centre) of Srikhanda, located in the district of Bardhaman. In the course of my researches, I also recall having consulted a catalogue of Vaishnava manuscripts that the Bardhaman University holds, a majority of them being drawn from Srikhanda and from neighbouring Katwa and Nabadwip. For a man who belonged to a quasi-Vaishnava lineage, this was a location whose cultural importance could not have been lost or ignored. Third, and perhaps most importantly, there was the personal idiosyncrasy of the man himself. To my mind, Ramakanta Babu inherited the historicism of the two Majumdars (Ashok Kumar and Bimanbihari), the literary curiosity of Dineshchandra Sen, and the textual scholarship of Sushil Kumar De. I would like to speculate that he was also aware of the literary scholar Sukumar Sen who, I am given to understand, was educated at the Burdwan Raj College and showed a lifelong passion for Vaishnava culture.

Looking back at his work, it would now appear as though Professor Chakrabarty successfully navigated through the pioneering but complexly formulated work of such scholars and arrived at his own niche which, I think, was a careful mix of sheer empiricism and cultural imagination. Professor Achintya Dutta, a student of Ramakanata Babu and the editor of this volume, informs me that Professor Chakrabarty was averse to the use of abstruse and undifferentiated theoretical labels and chose to ground his work in established facts more than improvised theory. He was also not given to the use of interdisciplinary tools or methods, which differentiates his work from that of scholars like Hitesh Ranjan Sanyal and Joseph T. O'Connell. I am not sure, though, if for his readers and researchers, this has been something of a disadvantage. It has generally been my impression that people who preferred to work within a chosen cultural-literary-anthropological framework were not always meticulously attentive to matters of temporal and historical detail. Professor Chakrabarty, by comparison, remained a Rankean, although his archives comprised not merely state-owned repositories of dust-laden documents, but also zealously guarded private manuscripts and vernacular songs and poetry which had a life of their own. In that sense, at least, he was as much an anthropologist as he was a historian.

It was Ramakanta Babu who took Gaudiya Vaishnavism beyond the conventionally accepted dates and figures. Unlike the works of Melville Kennedy, Sushil Kumar Dey, and A. K. Majumdar, his own writings go beyond the study of both the cosmopolitan Sanskrit textual culture of the Vrindavan Goswamis or the foundational figure of Chaitanya himself and the movement that developed around him. It might be no exaggeration to say that his magnum opus, *Vaishnavism in Bengal: 1486–1900* (1985), is the first work to treat Vaishnavism as a social and historical force or movement in the post-Chaitanya age, and beyond select events, episodes, and personalities. To him also goes the credit of making available in the English language a fascinatingly rich history of Bengal Vaishnavism, as culled from an overwhelmingly large body of religious and poetic literature. In terms of its general sweep, nothing comparable had been produced prior to Chakrabarty, nor since his time.

One may justly fault Professor Chakrabarty for somewhat unimaginatively determining the chronological framework of his magnum opus. Gaudiya Vaishnavism did not commence with the birth of Chaitanya (in 1486), nor did it cease to exist in 1900. Thanks to a team of dedicated young scholars committed to detailed cultural interrogation, we now know of many important issues and debates within the Vaishnava community of Bengal concerning critical issues of community formation and identity, which actually surfaced after 1900. These touched upon questions of how to run an active Vaishnava press, the veracity of certain Vaishnava texts, evangelism both at home and abroad, and controversies surrounding the birthplace of Chaitanya. Ramakanta Babu appears to be in error in somewhat conflating Vaishnavism in Bengal with Chaitanya Vaishnavism, even though the confusion did not originate with him and still persists in many quarters. For one, he does not sufficiently accept the possibility of Bengal Vaishnavism being a category apart from Bengali Vaishnavism. It was Joe O'Connell (whom I had the pleasure of meeting during my academic tenure at Santiniketan) who first alerted me to this problem. I have found it fit to pursue his line of argument, albeit not as effectively or persuasively. It has been left to contemporary scholars like June McDaniel to demonstrate that there was indeed a vibrant folk Vaishnavism in ethnic Bengal that drew upon the Radha–Krishna mythology, but stayed outside the religious domains controlled by the Goswamis. Perhaps this is where Professor Chakrabarty's methodological presuppositions and the relative lack of active fieldwork would have proved a disadvantage. Unlike Sashibhushan Dasgupta, Ramakanta Babu does not appear to have been interested in quotidian and esoteric religious cults which represented a dissenting voice in relation to mainstream Vaishnavism. This is a trifle surprising, given that one of his own forebears had joined the cult of the Kishoribhajas, a sub-community of Vaishnavas known to have originated in Sylhet, and which adopted certain Sahajiya ideas and practices that mainstream Gaudiya Vaishnavism strongly opposed. On the other hand, I am reliably informed that Ramakanta Babu disliked the use of typological slots such as 'High' Hinduism and the 'Low', 'elite' and the 'popular', and presumably, his critique evolved from his ability to see the fluid and porous nature of cultural thought and practice which often collapsed synthetically constructed boundaries. Perhaps unknown to himself, he too was discouraging the use of un-problematised certitudes through recourse to anthropological exceptionalism which has now come to deeply influence contemporary history-writing.

Personally, I would have preferred to know more about Ramakanta Babu as a man, outside the world of scholarship. I found quite interesting the allusion to his habitual use of snuff and the slightly nasal intonation to his voice that this reportedly produced. This was a description that promptly produced some distinctive images of the man himself, at least in his more unguarded but self-indulgent moments. How did he carry himself, I have wondered, and just what were his other peculiarities or proclivities which could readily catch one's attention? Was he an indulgent teacher or an unrelenting disciplinarian? Miserly or generous with the marks that he awarded his students? A rigorously methodical researcher or someone lazy, laidback, and relying more on flashes of intuitive truth? Ideologically, did he lean to the Left or Right? We know that he was deeply religious, but was he a Vaishnava in his dietary preferences too? Or was he a Vaishnava of the kind Bankimchandra was, who attempted to re-establish Krishna as an ideal god and avatar but relished fowl curry? I raised these questions, stirred by the feeling that sometimes memories of an individual as an individual, founded even on casual or sundry descriptions, endure more than carefully measured professional assessments.

I commend Professor Dutta on his decision to put together this commemorative volume in honour of one of our prominent cultural historians and thank all contributors for positively responding to his call. There is a personal debt that I owe to Ramakanta Babu which needs to be expressed here. His engagement with religious history manifested itself at a time when any discussion on religion was virtually taboo, at least in the reputedly 'progressive' institutions of learning. I distinctly remember being mocked by one of my left-leaning teachers at the Delhi University for sporting a rosary made of *rudraksha* beads on my person. As I recall, that was a time when students were carefully groomed to appreciate how, without Karl Marx, there could be no realistic hope of securing marks! I am happy to have survived that challenging ordeal. Looking back at those years, I can say that two individuals, in their own ways, gave me the courage and conviction to pursue my interest in religion: Professors Ramakanta Chakrabarty and Joseph T. O'Connell. Together, they have pushed me to the edge of a precipice from where I can only fling myself with abandon into the deeper ravines of religious studies.

Gurgaon, May 2023

Preface

The idea of publishing a volume to pay tribute to my departed teacher and historian, Ramakanta Chakrabarty (1932–2019), came to my mind in 2019 when I was invited to deliver a talk on his contribution to the sociocultural history of Bengal at a seminar jointly organised by the Departments of History and Bengali of Vivekananda Mahavidyalaya, Burdwan and the Bardhaman Itihas Sandhan, a public body interested in researching the local history of Burdwan. I am happy to say that the talk was well-received by the learned audience and, thereafter, the idea of developing this into a larger project seized me. I pondered over this question for long and came to the conclusion that publishing a collection of essays on the society and culture of Bengal in memory of my departed teacher, the late Professor Ramakanta Chakrabarty, would be a befitting attempt to pay public homage to him. The present project was launched in the middle of 2019. The core of this volume lies in the study of Bengali society, religion, and culture, and other aspects of Bengal's history in which Professor Chakrabarty himself specialised. Some leading scholars in the fields of social and cultural history of Bengal were approached for this purpose. I take this occasion to express my gratitude to all of them for agreeing so readily and with great enthusiasm.

A good-looking person with a robust physique, Ramakanta Chakrabarty was always very smart and confident. He was very polite, soft-spoken, friendly, and easy to talk to. It was his natural elegance that always struck me. He was proud to be a Bangal (a resident of the erstwhile East Bengal), and his Bangal accent and penetrating laugh had a pleasant ring to them. I can still picture him in my mind.

Ramakanta Chakrabarty was an open-hearted teacher whose affection for students, disarming simplicity, and dedication to teaching impressed me very much. In our MA class at The University of Burdwan, he could teach a variety of subjects covering Indian history, European history, International Relations, and so on, and he was very popular amongst the students. I have learnt a lot from his fascinating classroom discourses as well as from the discussions I had with him outside of class. As a student, I benefitted immensely from his advice and suggestions on how to build my career. I remember how he was always willing to extend help to sincere students. I cannot restrain myself from offering one instance of his affection: He taught the History of International Relations to my MA class and had once asked me to prepare a note on Sino-America relations during the Cold War, giving me the book *From Yalta to Vietnam: American Foreign Policy in the Cold War* by David Horowitz for the purpose. I found the book, which was of a very high standard, difficult, and failed to grasp the subject. When Professor Chakrabarty came to know about this, he prepared the note for me. I was quite amazed at this gesture and it brought us closer.

His style of correcting our notes was very interesting. He looked at the note very meticulously and gave insightful comments on it, indicating the marks that the note could carry. As an examiner, he was very generous in awarding marks to good answers, but could be very harsh to bad answers. I consider myself fortunate for having had the opportunity to sit in his class and win his affection. It gave me immense pleasure to work with him as a colleague at The University of Burdwan, albeit for a mere month, because he retired from service shortly afterwards. I still cherish the memory of an academic discussion with him in our department during this short period.

He also worked in institutions in Calcutta, such as The Asiatic Society and Bangiya Sahitya Parisat. His distinguished career in teaching and research earned him several prestigious awards, including the Sir Jadunath Sarkar Gold Medal (2018) and the Manas Roychaudhury Smriti Puraskar (2004), for his significant contributions to the study of history and religion. He also received the Ananda Puraskar (1996) for his book, *Bange Baisnab Dharma*.

In the early years of his academic career, Professor Chakrabarty conducted studies on the social and cultural history of medieval and modern Bengal. He published a great deal on the history of music, especially the *tappa* songs of Ramnidhi Gupta (1741–1838), commonly known as Nidhu Babu, one of the reformers of Bengali tappa music. His research on religion, particularly Gaudiya Vaishnavism, earned him recognition as a pioneer in this subject. Aside from this, he also wrote on numerous facets of Bengali life and culture, including studies on Hinduism, Bengali peasants, Bengal's emerging culture in the nineteenth century, and Iswarchandra Vidyasagar's educational goals.

Political history was of less importance to Professor Chakrabarty than social and cultural studies. In a pamphlet titled *Freedom Movement in Burdwan* (1985), which he co-authored with Professor Bhaskar Chattopadhyay of the Department of History, The University of Burdwan, he argued that political history, and more specifically the history of India's freedom movement at the national, regional, and local levels, cannot be properly perceived without a complete understanding of the society and culture of a given place.

He had a strong command over Bengali and Sanskrit, as is evident from his writings. His proficiency in Sanskrit facilitated his access to the Sanskrit texts that might possibly have helped him study Vaishnavism. He seems to have imbibed the true spirit of Vaishnava philosophy and the essence of the Vaishnava ideal was reflected through his humanity, humility, and simplicity, which endeared him greatly to his pupils, friends, colleagues, and well-wishers. His work, *Vaisnavism in Bengal 1486–1900* (1985), based on literary sources and fieldwork, is a tremendous 555-page treatise comprising twenty-three chapters that evoked a sensation amongst scholars, researchers, and academics. Unlike many other scholars who were well-disposed to the study of the Renaissance or political or economic history, Professor Chakrabarty ventured to study the cultural history of Bengal for his own academic interest. He had a splendid understanding of the different facets of cultural history, as is evident from many of his publications. Interestingly, despite leaning towards the political Left, he showed how cultural history in general, and the history of religion in particular, could be presented in a rational and objective manner. Professor Chakrabarty had a soft spot in his heart for Nabadwip, the birthplace of Chaitanya (the exponent of Gaudiya Vaishnavism), and its glorious academic heritage, which is evident from his enthusiastic participation in the programme of the Banga Bibudha Janani Sabha, an old scholars' body of Sanskritic studies of Nabadwip. Despite the plethora of work done in this field, Professor Chakrabarty is regarded as an authority in the study of Vaishnavism in Bengal, and is remembered with admiration for his seminal contribution to the field.

He was not in favour of neatly thematic divisions of Indian history into its conventional periods. He could really see how they were related. He taught me that no historical event can be considered unique and that there cannot exist a vacuum between historical events in ancient India and modern India. However, Ramakanta Chakrabarty preferred empirical studies based on facts and evidence over theoretical propositions relating to a particular model. He was averse to the models of structuralism, postmodernism, deconstruction, or any such model deemed to be complex, as none of these could reconstruct the history of the people in a fascinating manner. Professor Chakrabarty was very methodical in his study of any field, be it social, cultural, economic, or political history. I had the opportunity to listen to his learned talk on the necessity of a regional and local history of Bengal, which he delivered at a seminar on 'Bardhaman Itihas Sandhan' ('Quest for Burdwan's History'), held in 2004 at Rajbati, Burdwan, organised by 'Sourav', a cultural association of Burdwan, in collaboration with Victoria Memorial, Kolkata. It was an enthralling lecture that reflected both his investigative methodology and his meticulous scholarship. I remember his rigorous and analytical review of my book, *Economy and Ecology in a Bengal District: Burdwan 1880–1947* (2004), in a Bengali daily, *Anandabazar Patrika*.

Interestingly, Ramakanta Chakrabarty was well-versed in music and had an innate ability to sing. What is fascinating to note is that he could sing both *kirtans* and *bhaoaiya* songs (folk songs of north Bengal) well, occasionally demonstrating his ability as a performing artist, albeit an amateur one. Before the Partition of India (in 1947), he had migrated from his ancestral place in Bikrampur Pargana, Dacca to Coochbehar, staying there with his elder sister for a few years, and his familiarity with bhaoaiya songs might possibly have developed during this period. He organised an amateur team and sometimes, when requested by close friends, relatives, or neighbours, also performed. I still recall how he held the audience's attention by singing a folk song while delivering a lecture on this subject at a seminar at Jadavpur University sometime in the early 1990s.

It is now time to acknowledge my indebtedness to those who have helped me in different ways and lent their support to this plan. I am grateful to Amiya P. Sen, former Professor of History, Jamia Millia Islamia, New Delhi for his continued support, encouragement, and valuable advice while bringing out this volume. This book could not have seen the light of day without his help. I express my sincere gratitude to Professor Suranjan Das for his valuable suggestions that helped me immensely in completing this work. I am particularly indebted to Dr Santanu Dey, Associate Professor of History, Ramakrishna Mission Vidyamandira, Belur Math for his unstinting support in making this project a success. I owe a great debt of thanks to Anuradha Roy, former Professor of The University of Burdwan for contributing reminiscences of Ramakanta Chakrabarty. I express my deep gratitude to all the contributors who helped enrich this volume with their learned contributions, despite their busy schedules. I appreciate the energy and labour they invested in contributing to this work. My thanks are also due to Sujata Mishra and Kanchan Kamilla, Deputy Librarians of the Asiatic Society, Kolkata and The University of Burdwan, respectively, for their help and cooperation in the making of this volume.

I am also very thankful to Saktikanta Chakrabarty, former Professor of Mathematics, The University of Burdwan and a close relative of Ramakanta Chakrabarty, and Subrata Roychowdhury, Associate Professor of Bengali, Mrinalini Dutta Mahavidyapith,

Birati, Kolkata and an honourable member of the Executive Committee of the Bangiya Sahitya Parisat, who provided me with valuable information on Professor Chakrabarty's academic and extra-academic achievements. I acknowledge my indebtedness to Giridhari Sarkar, an aficionado of the history of Burdwan and an admirer of Ramakanta Chakrabarty, and Sanjoy Mukherjee, Associate Professor of History, Saldiha College, Bankura who always encouraged me to complete this work. I would also like to express my thanks to my wife and daughter for sharing their joy in the making of this volume. I am grateful to the anonymous referee for his/her insightful comments and incisive suggestions.

Lastly, Orient BlackSwan has earned my deep gratitude for expressing an interest in its publication. I hope that the essays contained in this book will engender further interest amongst scholars and researchers interested in this field, and will be useful to teachers and students at the university level.

Burdwan, July 2023 **Achintya Kumar Dutta**

RAMAKANTA CHAKRABARTY

A Tribute

ANURADHA ROY

It was 1982. I had just completed my Masters and was contemplating doctoral research. I wanted to study cultural history, which was yet to catch on in our country. In those days, history meant mostly political and economic history and also perhaps social history in a very narrow sense. I was told that the only academic who specialised in cultural history in Kolkata was Professor Ramakanta Chakrabarty of The University of Burdwan. This took me to his third-floor flat in north Kolkata. I had decided to work on the earliest phase of the Communist-inspired cultural movement in Bengal. Professor Chakrabarty helped me considerably in grasping the subject. Had I done the work at Burdwan University, I would have done it under his supervision. But I received a fellowship at Calcutta University and decided to do it there. However, I continued to consider myself lucky for having got to know Professor Chakrabarty and for having won his affection, too, although I could not keep in regular touch with him. Many years later, in 1994, I joined the Department of History, Burdwan University as his junior colleague, and workplace proximity (we also travelled together in the same train sometimes) brought me closer to him. But he remained, and still remains, a teacher to me, above everything else.

So I came to know Professor Chakrabarty primarily as a pioneering cultural historian of Bengal. Since then, cultural history has made rapid strides, and the vast interdisciplinary field of cultural studies, with its stress on critical theory, has developed too. But this does not take away from Professor Chakrabarty's distinction as a pioneer insofar as the history of Bengali culture is concerned. In this obituary, I will try to reflect on his role as a historian, particularly a cultural historian, but I cannot help including some personal remembrances as well.

When I met him first, Professor Chakrabarty was immersed in his work on Vaishnavism in Bengal. We used to talk about it sometimes, and I realised that this was going to be a history of human beings rather than a mere history of religion. He had already written his book on Nidhubabu (Ramnidhi Gupta), the famous reformer of Bengali *tappa* music in early modern Bengal. I was to read this book, titled *Bismrita Darpan* (2001), later, to my benefit. His research on Vaishnavism won him the degree of D.Litt. from Calcutta University, and was published in 1985 under the title *Vaishnavism in Bengal 1486–1900*. About ten years later, he published *Bange Vaishnav Dharma* in Bengali, which won him the prestigious Ananda Puraskar in 1996. His knowledge and understanding of different aspects of cultural history, and also history in a broad sense, was remarkable, as is borne out by his many publications, which include *A Short History of Vidyasagar College 1872–1972* (published in 1975; he had taught at this college before joining Burdwan University) and *Freedom Movement in Burdwan* (1985, authored jointly with Professor Bhaskar Chattopadhyay), and edited volumes such as *Mutinies and the People* (by an anonymous writer, 1969), Nishikanta Chattopadhyay's *The Yatras or the Popular Dramas of Bengal* (1976), and Beveridge's *Warren Hastings in Bengal* (1977).

A collection of essays in Bengali, titled *Bangalir Dharma, Samaj o Samskriti* ('Religion, Society, and Culture of Bengalis'), came out in 2002. It covered wide-ranging themes—Brahmins in ancient India, religion in the medieval period (of course with special reference to Vaishnavism), the spiritual songs of Bauls (a group of mystic minstrels hailing from the Bengal countryside), as well as Bankimchandra, Vidyasagar, Bengali peasants in relation to the Bengal Renaissance, Bengali songs of past centuries, *Haridaser Guptakatha* (a very popular novel of nineteenth-century Bengal, which was, however, looked down upon by the proponents of 'high culture'), *kathakata* (the professional practice of narrating scriptural or mythological stories), and the Quit India Movement. He has to his credit many more articles and essays published in different learned journals—*Journal of Indian Philosophy, Journal of Comparative Literature* (Jadavpur University), *Journal of Asiatic Society, Journal of Museological Society, Journal of Vaishnava Studies*—as well as in Bengali, which are yet to be compiled in book form. He wrote regular book reviews in the Bengali daily *Anandabazar Patrika* for many years, which highlighted the range of his knowledge and interests. I remember once being fascinated by a Bengali article on ghost stories written by Professor Chakrabarty. There were many more subjects that interested him, although perhaps he never wrote on them. (Astronomy is just one example.) He was fond of science fiction written by Isaac Asimov.

Professor Chakrabarty did not subscribe to the usual periodisation of history into ancient, medieval, and modern, and was well-versed in all three. He possessed the most important key to ancient Indian history, that is, a knowledge of the Sanskrit language and literature. Even though a professor of history, he also taught at the Department of Sanskrit, Rabindra Bharati University, from 1989–1998. He translated a number of Sanskrit plays into Bengali. Another forte was the history of modern Europe, which he taught for many years.

Within cultural history, he could move elegantly from elite to popular culture; for example, from Bankim to Baul, as we have noted above. Indeed, unlike most scholars, he refused to make a strict distinction between the two. I once presented a paper at a seminar with Professor Chakrabarty in the chair. The paper was on the religious culture of the Bengal countryside and the songs related to it. I used jargon like 'great tradition' and 'little tradition' in my presentation. Professor Chakrabarty praised my paper, but at the same time cautioned me that in Bengal villages, 'little tradition' was, more often than not, 'great tradition.'

Professor Chakrabarty was averse to fashionable theories, which often impede our understanding rather than facilitating it. He did not have to resort to theories because of the depth of his empirical knowledge, thanks to his grasp on language and literature and his intimate relationship with indigenous culture. In a sense, his was a kind of old-style research based on solid data (although perhaps not so much archival as literary). Indeed, he used rare historical sources in his writings—he had many such sources in his personal collection. But he was also open to new ideas and had a sharp analytical vision.

His style of writing was also engrossing. The essay 'Unish Shataker "Kolikata Sabhyata" o Bangal' ("The Civilisation of Nineteenth-century Kolkata and Bangal'), in his book *Bangalir Dharma, Samaj o Samskriti,* opened with the following lines: 'Bangal has two lexical meanings—1) a resident of East Bengal, 2) a rustic. In the latter sense, Scots are Bangals of Britain, Ukrainians are Bangals of Russia, people of south Germany are Bangals of Germany, etc.' Thus, the essay at the very outset compels the attention of the reader. To my mind, it was like opening an innings with an over-boundary. I cite another line, this one from the very first paragraph of the essay 'Bangali Krishak o Bangali Renaissance' ('Bengali Peasants and Bengali Renaissance'), included in the same book: "The Company deployed the zamindars to exploit the peasants following the policy "*Pap hobe to Kasem Alir*."' The punch line here is an oft-quoted one from Rajsekhar Basu's famous story, 'Siddheswari Limited', meaning, 'If this is a sin, it is Kasem Ali who must pay for it' (uttered by a character in the story, who was masterminding and funding a corrupt business enterprise, but doing so indirectly, through someone else). Thus, a familiarity with literature not only increased the literary weight of his writings, but also heightened their aesthetic value. At least, a literature buff like myself would often be bowled over.

As I write this tribute, so many things are coming to mind. I remember his habit of taking snuff and the resultant nasal tone of his voice, his sense of humour, his remarkable dignity in situations of conflict. He was a deeply religious man, and yet above all bigotry and obscurantism. I will ever treasure the memory of my association with Ramakanta Chakrabarty and also the books he gifted me—a couple of his own books as well as a beautiful compilation of English short stories by assorted authors. He was reading it on the train. I took it from him, glanced through it, and expressed my liking. He instantly gave it to me. Such was his affection and generosity! My deepest respect for him!

Glossary

Adimula	the Supreme Creator, as the cause or source of all creation
Adya Sradh	first ceremony for the benefit of the departed soul
Agraharika	supervisor of *devottar* lands
akhara	a congregational settlement of practising Vaishnavas of various kinds, living under the spiritual supervision of a mahant/guru
Antyaja	people belonging to the lowest strata in the caste hierarchy
aratdar	grain dealer
asat	unclean
Atibadi	literally, one given to verbosity and self-conceit; a particular Vaishnava sect originating from Jagannath Das, an Odia associate of Chaitanya in the sixteenth century, reprimanded by the latter for his boastful approach
atmashakti	self-prowess
baiji	female professional entertainer specialising in singing and dancing, patronised by the rich and the aristocracy
baishnabi	female Vaishnava mendicant, or associate of a male Vaishnava mendicant
bakunathanti	speaking (in Odia)
beshya	female sex-worker
bhadralok	prosperous and well-educated person

bhadramahila	women belonging to the genteel, cultured classes; equally applied to Hindu and Muslim communities in Bengal
Bhagavatakara	composer of Bhagavata (text)
bhakti	devotion
Bhakti Rasa Sastra	Vaishnava theory of aesthetics and devotion; also, the name of a particular genre of Vaishnava texts
bhek	initiation into Vaishnava monasticism
Chaturdasakshyari	poetical line having fourteen letters
Chatuspathi	centre of Sanskrit education
darpatnidar	those who took the lease of *patni* taluqs from the patnidar
deuthanti kahi	speaking or clarifying
devottar land	land dedicated to the deity
Dewan	chief treasury official
Dhama	sacred abode or dwelling place in Hinduism where the earthly and the divine aspects of Gods' acts (*lila*) are believed to eternally coexist
Dutibodha	a text on the feelings of a female follower, or *gopi*
ektara	a single-stringed musical instrument made out of the hollowed and dried cavity of a gourd
Gaurapramayavada	a theory which projects Gaur (Chaitanya) as the supreme principle and object of worship
Gopis	female cowherd, both married and unmarried, associated with the Mathura-Vrindavan region; in Vaishnava literature and mythology, they are depicted as the earliest devotees and lovers of Lord Krishna

Gosain	a colloquial variant of the term Goswamin
Goswamin	literally, it refers to 'the lord of the cows', a term ascribed to Vaishnava figures of eminence
Harinama	singing the name of Hari
Jari	a dirge popular in pre-independence eastern and northern Bengal
jobba	long flowing garment worn by Bauls
jote	agricultural land
jotedars	holder of estates
Kadcha	Indigenous Bengali literary narrative genre akin to the form of diary, notes, or sketches
karma	profession
Kamar/Karmakar	Bengali caste of metal workers, especially ironsmiths
Kartabhaja	Vaishnava sect of southern Bengal, engaged in radical social and cultural practices
khanjani	a small, hand-held metallic percussion instrument, used in devotional singing
khanqah	Sufi hospice
kirtan	devotional songs sung either individually or in a group, with the accompaniment of one or more musical instruments
Lilamrita	nectar of life activities, or divine sport
Madhura Rasa	erotic mood or manifestation
mahanta	administrative and spiritual head of a monastic establishment or a religious shrine
mahotsavs	grand Vaishnava feast/festivity
manush-bandha	binding human beings
math	monastery

mukti	a concept of liberty that is to be achieved inwardly and that leads to realisation of human essence
munsif	judge
Nabasakh	nine branches of clean Sudras
nabakshyari	a poetical line with nine letters
nagdee	soldier who was paid in cash
Nirguna Tattva	the Hindu theory of the Supreme creator of the Ultimate Reality as being 'formless' and 'without qualities'
Nur-i-Muhammadi	the Light of Muhammad
padas	rhymed poetic meter with lyrical verses
padhunathanti	continued reading (in Odia)
Pancha Sakha	This is a collective name for the famed five saints or associates of medieval Odisha, namely Balarama Das, Jagannath Das, Achyutananda Das, Yashobanta Das, and Sisu Ananta Das
Pancha Tirtha	five religious centres
panda	priests at the Jagannath temple, Puri
parakiya	a doctrine identified with Gaudiya Vaishnavism representing intense transgressive love, going beyond ordinary social ties of marriage and conjugality
patita	literally, a women falling from social virtues; commonly used for female sex worker
patitpavan	one who absolves the sinner or purifies the fallen one
patni taluq	lot of land leased at a fixed rent
Premapanchamrita	a text in Odia on the five nectars of love
prithulakaya	plump or fat
Priti Sandarbha	a treatise on love
pundits	traditional Sanskrit scholars

raganuga bhakti	Vaishnava devotional practice inculcating passionate love towards the object of one's worship
raiyats	peasants
sad Gosain	six Gosains (Vaishnava figures of eminence)
sadhana	spiritual practices involving both the body and mind under the supervision of a guru
sahajiya	a term describing individuals who adopted dissenting and esoteric social and spiritual practices, historically found among both Buddhists and Vaishnavas
sampradaya	sect, or the followers of a particular religious congregation
sannyas	renunciation from the familial and social worlds
Sarvatma	one who dwells in everyone's heart or one who is all-pervasive
sat	clean
sevadasis	female servitors, usually attached to a mahant or a guru
shalgramsheela	a sacred stone
shripat	Vaishnava sacred place or centre
siddha	a spiritual practitioner who has achieved perfection
siddha-rupa	the state of perfected spiritual consciousness; a term used in Gaudiya Vaishnava theology
swadesh	one's own country
swadeshi	nationalist
tilak	a mark on the forehead, made usually from sandalwood paste
tol	centre of Sanskrit education
upacharya	assistant minister/priest

Introduction

Achintya Kumar Dutta

The present volume is a humble tribute to the renowned scholar and historian, Ramakanta Chakrabarty (1932–2019), whose contribution to the reconstruction of the sociocultural history of modern Bengal is both brilliant and crystalline. The life and culture of Bengal in the nineteenth and twentieth centuries have attracted the attention of scholars, perhaps because of the fact that Bengal was the primary centre of interaction between the East and the West, and the first region in India to be deeply influenced by British culture and resonate with it. This volume sheds light on some important yet relatively less-explored aspects of the sociocultural changes that took place in Bengal in the colonial milieu. Before going into the details of the structure of this volume, it would not be out of place to say a few words about the unfolding of research on the social and cultural history of modern Bengal.

Evolution of the Sociocultural History of Bengal

Scholarly exercises on cultural history are a relatively new development. Even in the 1980s, historical study focussed mainly on political and economic history, and maybe social history in a narrow sense. Until the 1950s, professional historians of India concentrated more on the political, military, or diplomatic history of a given region at a specified time. Various economic issues, issues related to the life and activities of the people, and particularly the history of the growth and development of society and culture hardly gripped their attention, with a few exceptions like D. D. Kosambi and S. B. Chaudhuri (see Chaudhuri 1955; Kosambi 1956).

Although in the succeeding decades a shift in this direction was noticed and academics departed from this traditional method of writing history, largely discarding the British Indian traditions of cultivating political narratives and attempting to uncover some new, previously unexplored aspects of modern Indian history (Banerjee 1987, 108–13), it would be unreasonable to state that the subsequent researchers kept themselves completely away from doing political history. Historian Sumit Sarkar argues that modern Indian historical research of that time was dominated by nationalist historiography and inclined towards the anti-colonial movement at the national and regional levels, and this led to the subordination of social history (Sarkar 1997, 38–39).

A significant departure from the traditional pattern of research can be found in Pradip Sinha's *Nineteenth Century Bengal: Aspects of Social History* (1965), which is considered a 'study in some new pressures on society and a peep into the relationship between tradition and change' (Banerjee 1987, 116–117). In a learned essay titled 'Social Changes' in *The History of Bengal,* he delineated certain aspects of a historical situation and the forces of change that exerted pressure on traditional society, putting into context the growth of a new urban society in Calcutta known as a metropolitan society, which exhibited a major departure from traditional urban life (Sinha 1996, 384–428). Thereafter, some other works on fundamental aspects of the social history of Bengal, such as Amitabha Mukherjee's *Reform and Regeneration in Bengal, 1774–1823* (1968), Chittabrata Palit's *Tensions in Bengal Rural Society* (1975), Ratnalekha Ray's *Change in Bengal Agrarian Society c1760–1850* (1979), and Tarasankar Banerjee's *Various Bengal: Aspects of Modern History* (1985), have enriched the sub-discipline of the social history of Bengal.

The sociocultural history of Bengal has undeniably experienced changes in approaches to sources and themes over the decades since India's Independence, and many new areas, including new social classes and marginal groups of all kinds—which include criminals or sex workers—relatively unknown religious sects, print and publishing, language, literature, intellectuals, gender, sport, scientific changes, and disease and health have been brought within its purview. Potential scholars have explored such new areas of research, thus adding to a better understanding of sociocultural transformation in modern Bengal. In this context, we may refer to some significant works published in the last four decades. Chittabrata Palit's collection of essays, *New Viewpoints on Nineteenth Century Bengal* (1980), presented some sociocultural issues concerning the problem of Bengali identity through biographical studies. Amiya P. Sen's *Hindu Revivalism in Bengal, 1872–1905: Some Essays in Interpretation* (1993) re-examines facets of Bengal's intellectual life, portraying the life and work of some eminent personalities and examining certain developments centred in and around Calcutta to study Hindu identity through Hindu revivalism in nineteenth-century Bengal. In his *Explorations in Modern Bengal, c1800–1900* (2010), Sen studies the religion, history, and culture of modern Bengal, analysing the important and interrelated aspects of Hindu-Bengali intellectual life in the nineteenth century. Sekhar Bandyopadhyay's edited volume, *Bengal: Rethinking History Essays in Historiography* (2001), also focuses on social identities and politics, or 'the politics of identity formation' that deals with the 'cultural processes related to patterns of political mobilisation' (p. 26). In his *Caste, Culture and Hegemony: Social Dominance in Colonial Bengal* (2004), Bandyopadhyay also shows the complex interplay between caste, culture, and power, and reveals how Bengali Hindu society maintained the essentials of caste discrimination in colonial times.

Unish Shataker Bangali Jiban O Sanskriti (*Life and Culture of Nineteenth-century Bengalis*, 2003), a collection of perceptive essays edited by Swapan Basu and Indrajit Chaudhuri, highlights the notable changes that occurred in the urban and rural life of Bengal and focuses on the new thoughts and ideas of the educated intelligentsia. An innovative cultural history of marriage practices in colonial Bengal is presented in *Marriage and Modernity: Family Values in Colonial Bengal* by Rochona Majumdar (2009). How the history of sport can be viewed as an inseparable part of cultural history is illustrated in Kausik Bandyopadhyay's *Scoring off the Field: Football Culture in Bengal, 1911–80* (2011), which explains the way football represented a unique cultural identity of the Bengali people. Tapti Roy's *Print and Publishing in Colonial Bengal: The Journey of Bidyasundar* (2018) reconstructs the history of printing and publishing in nineteenth-century Bengal. She studies how, after the introduction of the printing press in Bengal, indigenous people participated in the business of producing, selling, purchasing, acquiring, and consuming books and journals, thus disseminating knowledge and leading to an enrichment of culture. *A Comprehensive History of Modern Bengal, 1700–1950*, Vol. II, edited by Sabyasachi Bhattacharya (2020), is a collection of essays on the sociocultural history of Bengal, throwing light on the middle-class intelligentsia, castes in Bengal, Bengali language and literature, popular culture, and the growth of journalism.

More importantly, the culture of Bengal has also been the subject of international scholarship. For instance, the cultural ethos and vernacular discourse of colonial Bengal as presented through the ideas and works of Ishwarchandra Vidyasagar and the 'dynamics of a cultural encounter' in Bengal during the mid-nineteenth century have been explored by Brian A. Hatcher (1996). In the recent past, international scholars have attempted to contextualise Bengal studies in the broader global perspective. Andrew Sartori explores the emergence of Bengali culturalism in a way that can 'grasp its local specificity and the global resonance of its major themes'. In other words, he locates 'Bengali culturalism within a global framework'. In the course of the nineteenth and twentieth centuries, culture, as Sartori points out, achieved the status of a truly global concept, and he attempts to view it through a sociohistorical framework (Sartori 2008, 21). In doing so, he focuses on some of the great personalities of nineteenth and twentieth-century Bengal, such as Rammohan Roy and Rabindranath Tagore. To him, the intellectual history of modern Bengal is an entry point to 'grasping the historicity of modern Bengali society' (ibid., 232–233).

Milinda Banerjee's ambitious study on intellectual history, *The Mortal God: Imagining the Sovereign in Colonial India*, depicts the changing meanings of 'kingship, rulership, and sovereignty' in late colonial Bengal and in that context, focuses on political and social movements in that period. Referring to such movements in north Bengal, Banerjee showed how modern Rajvanshi politics is 'embedded in histories and memories of state formation', and how the Rajvanshis fought for their identity, claiming Kshatriya ancestry for the community as a whole (Banerjee 2018, 313). In his fascinating work *Recasting the Region: Language, Culture and Islam in Colonial Bengal* (2014), Neilesh Bose uncovers the history of Bengali Muslim literary culture in the first half of the twentieth century. By literary culture, he refers to the 'literal texts that Bengali Muslim writers and critics were creating as well as the relationships between their social contexts and the worldviews of politicians, public intellectuals, and their audiences', and examines the Bengali Muslim's 'relationship to changing perceptions of regional identity, folklore and enrichment of language alongside Hindus in the late colonial period' (Bose 2014, xxi–xxii).

These studies added a new dimension to the cultural history of Bengal, which made it more discursive. This volume will highlight some of these recent trends in writings on the cultural history of Bengal. We thought this would be an apt way to commemorate the contributions of Ramakanta Chakrabarty to our understanding of the sociocultural history of modern Bengal.

Ramakanta Chakrabarty and His Works

Professor Chakrabarty has left an indelible mark on the understanding of the social history of Bengal. His writings on religious movements, on ethnic music, and many other themes from Bengali culture, more specifically on Bengal Vaishnavism, have deeply influenced scholars and laymen alike. The history of the life and culture of Bengali people that he has reconstructed has added to the historiography of Bengal's culture. He is justly acclaimed as one of the pioneering scholars and historians of the cultural history of Bengal, and more specifically of Gaudiya Vaishnavism. His work on Vaishnavism is regarded as not only a history of religion but also as a history of the people, and it has inspired scholars in India and overseas to consider this subject and further explore this area, undoubtedly through the use of novel approaches. Following this, academics have focused on specificity rather than an overgeneralisation of this topic. Unlike other scholars, he laid equal stress on both literary sources and fieldwork in the writing of cultural history. His articles and books in the vernacular are also fascinating, and enable the general Bengali readers to understand the activities of the Vaishnavas and the significance of Gaudiya Vaishnavism in the life and culture of Bengal. He is held in great esteem by scholars for his original contributions, which have enriched the sociocultural history of Bengal. All of this made me think it would be appropriate to honour such a scholar and historian by bringing out a commemorative volume. Unfortunately, we could not felicitate him in a befitting manner during his lifetime.

Ramakanta Chakrabarty's scholarship is evident from his command over the exposition, argument, and synthesis of historical facts. Several fascinating areas of cultural history, such as Hinduism and Hindu revivalism in Bengal, Bengali songs in the nineteenth century, *baul* songs, Bengali peasants, the culture and civilisation of nineteenth-century Calcutta, and the educational ideals of Ishwarchandra Vidyasagar formed the subjects of his meticulous scholarship. A compilation of several essays on these themes can be found in his *Bangalir Dharma, Samaj O Sanskriti* (*Religion, Society and Culture of the Bengali*, 2002). Ramakanta Chakrabarty's academic pursuits on another aspect of cultural history is reflected in his *Bismrita Darpan: Nidhubabu, Babu Bangla O Gitratna* (*Forgotten Mirror: Nidhubabu, the Bengal of Babus*, and *Gitratna* [a book of songs authored by Nidhubabu], 1971), which delves into the legacy of Ramnidhi Gupta (commonly known as Nidhubabu), an important figure in the history of music in nineteenth-century Bengal, and the impact of his *tappa* songs (a type of court music) on Bengali society and culture in the nineteenth century.[1] Thus, Chakrabarty's works can be divided into two broad categories: studies on Vaishnavism and on general Bengali culture and society.

In keeping with the nature of his interests, this volume is divided into two parts.

Professor Chakrabarty had a special interest in the study of Gaudiya Vaishnavism. His family connection with Gaudiya Vaishnavism might have evoked this interest to study various Vaishnava sects, Vaishnava theology, and so on. His uncle, Shashimohan Smritibhushan, a *Smarta* pundit (famous for his knowledge of jurisprudence and code of law), embraced Vaishnavism and eventually became a guru (master or guide, Goswami) belonging to the popular Vaishnava sect 'Kishoribhaja', branded by some as 'Sahajiya Vaishnavas', and had many Shudra disciples (Chakrabarty 1996, 135, 139). While studying Sanskrit texts, he grew familiar with Gaudiya Vaishnava literature and religion. This might possibly have attracted him to the study of Gaudiya Vaishnavism and its characteristics. He was deeply influenced by Surendranath Dasgupta and Sushil Kumar De's *A History of Sanskrit Literature: Classical Period* (2013), Nihar Ranjan Ray's *Bangalir Itihas: Adi Parba* (*History of the Bengali: The Beginning*, 2019 [1949]), Sukumar Sen's *Bangla Sahityer Itihas* (*History of Bengali Literature*, 2016 [1940]), and Sashibhusan Dasgupta's *Obscure Religious Cults as Background of Bengali Literature* (1946). More specifically, the learned works of Sukumar Sen, a pioneer in the study of Vaishnavism in Bengal, greatly inspired Chakrabarty to learn more about religious traditions (Chakrabarty 1985, viii; 2005, 5–6). Significantly, he was based in Burdwan during his teaching career at The University of Burdwan from the 1970s when he was drawn to the nearby centres of Vaishnava culture—Srikhanda, Katwa, and Nabadwip. His visits to these places might have enhanced his enthusiasm to study Gaudiya Vaishnavism.

His *Vaisnavism in Bengal, 1486–1900* (1985) is considered a classic and has been widely acclaimed. This tremendous work is an outcome of Professor Chakrabarty's untiring effort and painstaking research of more than a decade. The book deals with the socio-historical context and consequences of the Vaishnava bhakti movement in Bengal, delineating how Vaishnavism was inseparably connected with the Bengali way of life. He was of the view that man is the central figure in Gaudiya Vaishnavism, and laid stress on the culture of the common people to understand the impact of the Chaitanya movement. The work undeniably has certain limitations, as some recent works have pointed out. Although he has discussed the revival of Gaudiya Vaishnava traditions in the nineteenth century, he offered no analysis of the origins, processes, and modalities of this revival, and the deliberation suffers from oversimplification (Dey 2015, 28). It is also argued that Ramakanta Chakrabarty was arbitrary in selecting the dates of his monograph (1486–1900). Neither date refers to any significant event related to the history of Vaishnavism in Bengal, barring the fact that Chaitanya was born in 1486. The Gaudiya Vaishnava movement did not end in the year 1900, but continued well into the beginning of the twentieth century. His work did not address the social implications of the Chaitanya Vaishnava tradition in the colonial period either (Dey 2015, 28; O'Connell and Sen 2020, 112–122; Sen 2019, 3–4). However, despite the dearth of critical focus on particularity in his work, the study of Gaudiya Vaishnavism was motivated by his fundamental research in this field. Scholars would hardly have considered studying such a subject at the time when Professor Chakrabarty was pursuing his research. To Ramakanta Chakrabarty, of all the cultural movements in modern Bengal, Vaishnavism was found to be the dominant force. Herein lies his contribution to the study of Vaishnavism. It has undoubtedly inspired subsequent students and researchers, who concentrated more on the analytical study of a particular sub-theme rather than narrating the entire history of Vaishnavism in Bengal during the colonial period.

A decade after the publication of *Vaisnavism in Bengal 1486–1900,* Ramakanta Chakrabarty wrote a book in Bengali titled *Bange Baisnab Dharma: Ekti Aitihasik ebong Samajtatwik Adhyayan* (*Vaisnav Religion in Bengal: A Historical and Sociological Study,* 1996). A question does naturally arise: Is there a difference in the way in which he handles this theme in English, in comparison to Bengali? The former is found to appeal to specialised readers, researchers, and academics; it contains a large number of valuable primary sources that will always help young scholars studying Gaudiya Vaishnavism. The latter, on the other hand, offers a wholesome image of Gaudiya Vaishnavism in a popular style, which explains why it gripped the attention of the general Bengali readers. He explains its ideals and philosophy lucidly in this book, delineating the contours of this religion and reflecting most of its constitutive elements. Thus, the activities of the Vaishnavas and the significance of Gaudiya Vaishnavism in the life and culture of Bengal were discussed for the general readers, who found this book captivating.

Prior to Ramakanta Chakrabarty, there was a trend amongst scholars to explain the Vaishnava sacred texts complete with their philosophical and theological foundations, as is reflected in Sushil Kumar De's pioneering work, *Early History of the Vaishnava: Faith and Movement in Bengal* (De 1961). Among his contemporaries, Hiteshranjan Sanyal's *Bangla Kirtaner Itihas* (*The History of 'Kirtan' in Bengal*, 1989) provided an anthropo-historical study of the social history of Gaudiya Vaishnavism, focusing on how Vaishnava philosophy, and its ideas and ideals were propagated through the *kirtan* (collective devotional singing in praise of Lord Krishna), which became an indispensable part of the practice of the religious rites of Gaudiya Vaishnavas (Sanyal 1989). Joseph T. O'Connell studies the Gaudiya Vaishnava movement from a socio-anthropological approach, analysing the process of 'transformation of the traditionally accommodating character' of this movement during colonial rule through a focus on organisational developments (Dey 2015, 30). On the other hand, Ramakanta Chakrabarty viewed the theme from a sociohistorical perspective and provided a historical narrative of the evolution of this movement from the fifteenth to the nineteenth century, focusing on the sociohistorical context and the impact of the Vaishnava Bhakti movement in Bengal (Chakrabarty 1985). In his Introduction to Hiteshranjan Sanyal's *Trends of Change in the Bhakti Movement in Bengal*, Goutam Bhadra has noted that Chakrabarty 'has underlined the historical role of the Vaishnava heritage in forming various social institutions and cultural traditions in Bengal' (Sanyal 2019, xxii).

Lucian Wong, a well-known scholar in this field, is of the view that Professor Chakrabarty provides an extremely useful overview of some of the key Vaishnava developments and protagonists in Bengal in the nineteenth century (Wong 2015, 305–331).

The trajectory of Vaishnava studies in Bengal has changed and a fair amount of scholarly interest emerged in the decades following the publication of Professor Chakrabarty's work. His legacy has been taken up by younger scholars who have shown an interest in Vaishnavism. Among them are Amiya P. Sen, Varuni Bhatia, Ferdinando Sardella, Lucian Wong, and Santanu Dey, who have worked on Sri Chaitanya's movement and Vaishnavism in Bengal, each with a distinct approach focusing on particular themes in the making of the Vaishnava movement and Gaudiya Vaishnavism.

Thematic Structure and Summary of Content

This collection does not aim to cover all aspects of the sociocultural history of Bengal. Only some select areas where new research is being undertaken or which has evoked debates amongst historians have been chosen. There are a total of thirteen chapters in this volume, which discuss various aspects of Bengali society and culture. Section I is titled 'The Many Worlds of Bengali Culture' while Section II is titled 'Aspects of Bengali Politics, Society, and Economy'. Together, these two sections make up the book's general division. The first deals with intellectual and cultural issues, while the second addresses Bengal's society, economy, and politics. The first section throws light on some new areas of culture, including Vaishnava culture and heritage in colonial Bengal. Vaishnavism in Bengal, or Gaudiya Vaishnavism, has a rich and glorious heritage, and it became a cultural movement that linked the 'life and work of the saint [Chaitanya] to the larger question of formulating a Hindu-Bengali identity'. Ultimately, it became a popular cultural and religious tradition in Bengal in the late nineteenth and early twentieth century (O'Connell and Sen 2020, 118). In this section, the contributors have addressed some important, yet relatively under-researched issues about this culture, such as the role of women in the evolution of Bengali Vaishnava traditions, the role of individuals in the making of Vaishnavism in nineteenth- and twentieth-century Bengal, and so on.

In the second section, the contributors have ventured to explore some new areas of research related to the society, economy, and politics of colonial Bengal.

Chapter One, Santanu Dey's 'Texts and Traditions: Collating the Vaishnava Heritage and Issues of Authenticity in Colonial Bengal', deals with the debate on the authenticity of a text titled *Gobindadaser Kadcha* (*The Tale of Gobindadas*, 1895), which is supposed to have been written by Gobindadas Karmakar, who claimed to be a close associate of Sri Chaitanya. This contains an account of Sri Chaitanya's religious tour of south India during 1510–1512, illustrating Chaitanya not only as a reformer, but also as a man of humility. In the context of the emergent religious and cultural milieu of colonial Bengal, the author investigates the controversy surrounding the genuineness of this document amongst scholars, and the consequences of this debate. While contextualising the cultural process in colonial Bengal, the author traces the exploration of vernacular texts and manuscripts from the late nineteenth century by individual litterateurs, devoted Vaishnava scholars, and institutions, and shows how Bengali literature was influenced by early modern Vaishnava texts. Dey discusses why the *Kadcha* became a matter of public concern, and also why and how it was appreciated by one group of scholars but denounced by others. He shows that while the debate on the *Kadcha* remained inconclusive, it produced certain results, both expected and unexpected. The author concludes that the debate brought Gobindadas into prominence in his supposed birthplace, Kanchannagar, a suburb of Burdwan town, where fellow members of his community, Karmakar, tried to establish him as a historical figure.

Chapter Two, Arun Bandopadhyay's 'Bhaktisiddhanta Saraswati and the Making of Vaishnavism in Modern Bengal', delves into the development of Vaishnavism in Bengal in the late nineteenth and early twentieth century with special reference to the role of Bhaktisiddhanta Saraswati. The chapter begins by situating the sociocultural and religious changes leading to the emergence of a non-dualistic Vedantic philosophy in the nineteenth century—starting from Rammohan and ending with Vivekananda—when Vaishnavism failed to carve a place in intellectual discourse, leading to the subsequent decline of its popular practices. It then goes on to examine, in the light of historical, philosophical, and religious ideas, how Vaishnavism in Bengal received a new orientation in this period, linking the contribution of Bhaktivinoda Kedarnath Datta and his son Bimala Prasad Datta (Bhaktisiddhanta Saraswati) to the revival of Vaishnavism in Bengal. Kedarnath was attracted to the Vaishnava concept of *bhakti* (devotion or piety) in his youth and gradually became involved in the propagation of Vaishnavism. Bhaktisiddhanta Saraswati, a man with a profound knowledge of mathematics, sanskrit, philosophy, religion, and culture, was influenced by his father's vision of Vaishnava society with its cultural implications on the one hand, and the idea of the devotional Vaishnav on the other. The chapter investigates how Bhaktisiddhanta devoted himself to rekindling Vaishnavism in Bengal through his thoughts and actions. It examines, in the light of the arguments raised by prominent scholars of Vaishnavism on the concept of Chaitanya bhakti, how his religious campaign for the development of Chaitanya bhakti in Bengal and the attempt to infuse a new religious idea, that is, pure devotion, to it contributed to the revival of the rich heritage of Vaishnavism in the 1920s and 1930s.

Chapter Three, 'The Fallen Woman and the Saint: The *Baishnabi* in Colonial Bengal' by Varuni Bhatia, cogently portrays the part played by women in the evolution of the Bengali Vaishnava traditions, arguing that through their activities, the women Vaishnava devotees had shaken the patriarchal base of Vaishnavism in Bengal. Raising pertinent questions on the lives and works of some Vaishnava women (who were known as 'Baishnabis'), the chapter throws light on the picture of an ideal Vaishnava devotee and critically examines the life and character of Bengali Baishnabis as depicted in Bengali literature (especially in the works of Bankimchandra Chattopadhyay, Rabindranath Tagore, Abanindranath Tagore, Saratchandra Chattopadhyay, Lal Behari Day, and others) and other sources of the colonial period. In this context, the author has also highlighted the Baishnabis' varied social identities, ranging from devotees to *sevadasis* [female attendants and/or companions or servants associated with a Vaishnava institution or guru] and prostitutes. The author shows that as women gained entry to the arena of Vaishnavism, patriarchal dominance within Bengali Vaishnavism was challenged and threatened by the women who participated in both the religious and secular worlds. This chapter also discusses how the *akhara*, the monastic residence attached to a shrine and a significant Vaishnava institution, influenced the life of the Baishnabis who participated in it as stakeholders. While studying the life story of the Bengali Baishnabis in this historical context, the chapter explores the life and works of a thespian of exceptional calibre, Binodini Dasi, situating her as a devotee and a famous stage performer; unfortunately, despite her talent as an actress, she was left humiliated by accusations of prostitution.

Even though Chapter Four, Kailash Chandra Dash's 'Sri Chaitanya, Jagannatha Das, and Puri: *Jagannatha Charitamrita* Revisited', discusses *Jagannatha Charitamrita, Odia Bhagavata,* and other Odia cultural pieces and so is not technically a part of ethnic Bengal, we decided it best to include it in the first section rather than the second. In actuality, we are discussing Bengal in the more traditional and extensive geocultural sense rather than the more contemporary administrative one under which Odisha and Bihar separated into different provinces. In any case, Vaishnavism brought Bengali and Odia culture together during Chaitanya's period.

The chapter focuses on *Chaitanya Charitamrita* [hagiographical work authored by Krishnadas Kaviraj in the early seventeenth century] vis-à-vis *Jagannatha Charitamrita* in the socioreligious life of Odisha, especially Chaitanya's association with Atibada Jagannatha Das, the author of the *Odia Bhagabata*. The author speaks of Dibakar Das's biographical work on Jagannatha

Das, titled *Jagannatha Charitamrita*, a comprehensive study of seventeenth-century Vaishnavism in Odisha that differed from the Vaishnavism of Sri Chaitanya and his Gaudiya followers. Revisiting this text, Dash explains the nature of the relationship between Gaudiya Vaishnavas and Odia Vaishnavas in the pre-colonial phase in the light of recent controversies surrounding the identity of Jagannatha Das, the author of *Odia Bhagavata*, and Atibada Jagannatha Das. The author argues that of the three editions of *Jagannatha Charitamrita*, the last, published in 1963, is accepted as authentic, and provides an account of Atibada Jagannatha Das's association with Chaitanya. He asserts, in the light of the ongoing debate among scholars—and challenging their assertions—that Atibada Jagannatha Das and Jagannatha Das are one and the same person. Das is believed to have been the founder of the Atibadi sect in Odisha. The chapter also delineates the interesting features of *Jagannatha Charitamrita*, the classical work that reflects on the Jagannatha cult formed on the basis of Chaitanya's ideas, and glorifies Jagannatha Dhama (Puri) as a significant centre of the Krishna cult for Gaudiya Vaishnavas. He also informs us that the Atibadi Sampradaya [community] existed in Bengal in the first quarter of the seventeenth century. Chaitanya spent a large part of his life in Odisha, and Odia Vaishnavism received a new fillip with Chaitanya at the centre.

Chapter Five, 'Wax, Shellac, and Rabindranath Tagore: An Engagement on Record' by Dipannita Dutta and Subhayu Chattopadhyay, focuses on the recording of the voices of Bengal's revered cultural figures, especially Rabindranath Tagore, in the early twentieth century against the backdrop of the history of sound-producing instruments like the phonograph and gramophone, and their commercial prospects that led to the emergence of reputed recording companies. Initially, the lead in the marketing of these luxury goods in colonial Bengal came from foreign enterprises. But alongside them, Bengali entrepreneurs were also brave enough to enter this field. The authors explain how these entrepreneurs demonstrated their business acumen by successfully approaching leading poet-cum-singers such as Tagore and Dwijendralal Ray to record their voices, and thereby fulfilled their business objectives. Dutta and Chattopadhyay examine Tagore's engagement in recording his voice on phonograph and gramophone. In this context, the chapter sheds light on the history of the recording of Tagore's songs and recitations by leading recording companies of Calcutta in the early twentieth century, such as The Talking Machine Hall, The Gramophone Company Ltd, and Hindusthan Record. Finally, the chapter explores Tagore's critical and perfectionist approach to the quality of the tune, rhythm, and musical notes of his recorded songs. All this led to the emergence of a unique trend, known as 'Rabindra-Sangeet'.

Chapter Six, titled 'Bengali Folk Responses to Hegemonic Orthodoxy and Social Hierarchy: *Jari, Baul,* and *Maijbhandari* Songs' by Amit Dey, uses an analytical approach to present a thematic survey of beautiful folk songs such as *jari, baul,* and *maijbhandari,* focusing on their historical development and the way they responded to the emerging scripturalism and orthodoxy in colonial Bengal. The author argues that understanding the folk songs helps develop a perception of the culture of Bengal in the nineteenth and twentieth centuries, and, therefore, contextualises these songs in their historical perspective. Providing a short account of the origins and development of these songs, the chapter examines how the bauls, mendicant singers, speak out against social inequality and religious orthodoxy through their songs, which dealt with mysticism, humanism, and religious harmony. Similarly, he explains how the jari singers shed light on the grievances of rural Muslims against socioeconomic exploitation. More importantly, while discussing the characteristic features of these songs, the author observes that the Vaishnava perception that Radha and Krishna are one and identical influenced the jari and baul singers. The chapter also explains the emergence of maijbhandari singers of east Bengal districts, who demonstrated their liberal attitude towards all religions with their songs that reflected the contemporary socioeconomic conditions of Bengal. Dey asserts that these songs turn our attention to the poverty and misery of the poor and the social divisions among Muslims in Bengal. He concludes that mystical Islam in rural Bengal was portrayed through these songs.

Chapter Seven, 'Bijoy Krishna Goswami and the Reform Movement in Nineteenth-century Bengal', by Sujata Mukherjee, throws light on the contribution of a Brahmo-turned-Vaishnava, Bijoy Krishna Goswami, to the socioreligious life of nineteenth-century Bengal. The author has addressed some significant issues concerning Goswami's association with and dissociation from the Brahmo Samaj, his contribution to Vaishnavism, and his attempt to infuse a liberal and universalistic spirit into religion. The orthodox sections of the society opposed him for questioning the validity of some traditional practices and customs. The chapter contests the ongoing scholarly interpretation that Bijoy Krishna was a leader of Vaishnava revival in nineteenth-century Bengal and that his association with the Brahmo Samaj, as well as his progressive approach in the Brahmo reform movement, was 'incidental' and a mere 'aberration'. In this context, the chapter examines the causes of his leaving the Brahmo Samaj and emphasises that his rationalist and progressive spirit had led him to protest the violation of Brahmo tenets by Keshab Chandra Sen and secede from the Samaj. Examining Bijoy Krishna's role as a Brahmo missionary, the author argues that his liberal and universalistic approach to the Brahmo congregation was denounced by members of the Sadharan Brahmo Samaj, with which he ultimately severed ties. Finally, the chapter argues that Bijoy Krishna viewed Vaishnavism through a liberal and universal outlook, which antagonised orthodox Vaishnavas. He was a believer in religious universalism and considered orthodox Vaishnava practices meaningless. The author dwells on Goswami's achievements and projects him as a modern, rational, and liberal thinker who gave us a new insight into and a better understanding of religion.

History and literature are closely connected, and both deal with human activities. The relationship between the two with special reference to south India and its history, as reflected in modern Bengali literature, is the subject of Chapter Eight, 'The Other Gaze: South India in Select Bengali Historical Narratives' by

Ranjeeta Dutta. The chapter centres on Saradindu Bandopadhyay's historical novel *Tungabhadrar Tire* (*By the Tungabhadra*, 1959), which created a historical consciousness of sorts among Bengali readers. The novel focuses on the Vijayanagara Empire (1336–1646) of south India and represents the complex relationship between history and historical fiction. Dutta unfolds the historical context of the novel, illustrating the long reign of this Empire. She argues that the novelist collected information from historical sources, was aware of the history of Vijayanagara, and that some of the personalities and events described have a historical basis. The novel talks about fifteenth-century political intrigues, contests, and conflicts, as well as romantic liaisons in the Vijayanagara Empire. The narrative attempts to construct distinct trajectories of history and presents south India as an exceptional region. This chapter also underscores the Hindu-Muslim binary contest in the discourse of the novel, which refers to some Muslims as fanatics who gradually overpowered the Hindus, subjugating all of south India except Vijayanagara. However, the author refutes the novelist's sectarian attitude and affirms that contemporary trends of history-writing and the spirit of the time impacted his sense of history, which was reflected in the novel. Dutta concludes that the novel does not provide an accurate history but can be considered an important source of information about south Indian culture.

Rabindranath Tagore's concept of internationalism as well as his universalistic spirit of humanism have been embraced by a cosmopolitan audience. His ideas of liberal humanism are also reflected in his vision of nationalism, and this has been explained in Chapter Nine, 'Rejection of Nationalism and Much More: Reading Tagore's *Nationalism* 100 Years On' by Anuradha Roy. She revisits Rabindranath Tagore's *Nationalism* (1917) and reconstructs the context of and processes that shaped his rejection of nationalism. The chapter analyses some unexamined aspects of the book relating to nationalism, culture, and society (in the modern sense of the terms). The significance of the book lies not only in its rejection of nationalism, but also in its raising certain fundamental questions regarding civilisation, society, and human nature. The author argues that in the post-Swadeshi years, Tagore had a change of heart and consequently, his relationship with the nationalist movement took a new turn, culminating in his turning away from what he considered its radical nature. Tagore disdained the greedy and corrupt nationalism that went against humanism, liberalism, and rationalism. Besides stating that nationalism of the West had originated in the greed for wealth and led to human exploitation, Tagore also pointed to the inhuman elements of Eastern nationalism, and warned the latter not to imitate Western nationalism. Tagore also raised certain fundamental questions about society, human nature, and modern civilisation that shed light on these concepts. The civilisation that he decried had evolved from the cultural ethos of the West, and his critique highlights his aversion to such a society. Finally, the author underscores the limitations of Tagore's ideas and thoughts as reflected in the book, evaluating them rationally and objectively.

Chapter Ten, Rila Mukherjee's 'Seas, Rivers, Estuaries: Three Moments in the Social and Cultural History of Waterborne Circulations in Eastern India', investigates how water is socially, politically, and ritually constituted in the history of mankind, emphasising our relations with water and how it enters the fields of culture and politics. Water is around us in different forms, and occupies a place in our consciousness. The chapter shows how water has been perceived by humankind and sheds light on some transformative moments in human awareness of the seas, rivers, and estuaries at focal points in the history of the people in eastern India. The author explains why and how water is imbued with social and religious significance in different contexts and locations. The places where two or more rivers meet are considered holy places by the Hindus. The confluence of the Ganges with the Bay of Bengal, that is, Gangasagar, is also sacred. The Ganges is highly esteemed by the people of Bengal (and other parts of India) and its water is privileged over that of other rivers. Mukherjee has delineated why the water of the Ganges and not of the Padma is regarded as sacred. This chapter reviews how water becomes a source of danger when the rivers overflow, causing a flood, and studies the transformative role of water in Bengal and eastern India. Finally, the author discusses the various forms of waterscapes (oceans, seas, rivers and estuaries, lakes, etc.), contesting their colonial constructions as bounded by contiguous landmass and river valleys that alter people's waterborne interactions.

Chapters Eleven and Twelve, Rajat Datta's 'Indian Finances and British Rule in Eighteenth-century Bengal' and Bipasha Raha's 'Nitya Gopal Mukherji: An Agricultural Enthusiast in Colonial Bengal', deal with the socioeconomic components of colonial Bengal. Datta unearths the state of finances in Bengal during the early period of the East India Company's administration. While discussing the changing context of business and finances and focusing on the Company's finances, resources, and financial policies, he examines the regional economy of Bengal and its banking system in the early eighteenth century. The author argues that the Company faced a continual shortage of funds and therefore the search for resources became the primary cornerstone of its fiscal policy, leading to a close connection with indigenous finances in the late eighteenth century. The chapter explores how the money market emerged and operated in colonial Bengal, resulting in a bridge between the Company and indigenous bankers, who provided credit to the former. It argues that European finance was largely dependent on the bankers of Bengal and upcountry bankers as well, who came to Bengal from Lucknow, Awadh, and Benaras to fill the vacuum in the money market created by the fall of the Jagat Seths. Thus, money flowed from other parts of India to Bengal. Finally, the chapter discusses the tremendous growth of commercial opportunities, diffusion of marketplaces, and consequently trade and commerce in eighteenth-century Bengal, in which indigenous traders belonging to different castes participated, breaking the traditional caste-oriented professional practices.

[Unfortunately, Professor Rajat Datta (1956–2021) was unable to see this volume in print, as he passed away after the final text had been submitted for publication. We hope that his work and scholarship will live on in memory, serving as an inspiration to budding researchers.]

Bipasha Raha studies the contribution of Nitya Gopal Mukherji, a leading agricultural scientist, towards invigorating Bengal's agriculture. Mukherji demonstrated his profound knowledge in agriculture and agricultural chemistry during his professional career in the Civil Engineering College, Shibpur, in the early twentieth century. Against the backdrop of the emergence of educated youth and their growing interest to make a career in agricultural science in the 1870s, at a time when agriculture, along with the question of cultivators and their means and methods of production, attracted the attention of the Bengali literati, the author unfolds the needs of agriculture, the mainstay of the majority of Indians, by examining Nitya Gopal's two remarkable handbooks—one on agriculture and the other on sericulture—that reiterated the agricultural development of the country. The chapter delves into Nitya Gopal's knowledge about the means and methods of production, their constraints and how to overcome them, and examines the significance of the handbook of agriculture, discussing its salient features and the major issues related to scientific and productive agriculture. Raha observes that Nitya Gopal looked forward to the agricultural improvement of the country, for which he prescribed certain technicalities and scientific methods related to the fertility of the soil, irrigational measures, control of pests, use of agricultural implements, preventing famines, and so on. The chapter also talks about Nitya Gopal's concept of agricultural education and how that could be spread through village schools to foster effective agricultural practices in Bengal. The author states that unlike nationalist leaders, Nitya Gopal offered little criticism of the colonial administration for its neglect of agricultural policies; however, he was undeniably proficient in agricultural science and its utilisation for agricultural advancement.

The last chapter, Achintya Kumar Dutta's 'Prosperity, Dominance, and Social Mobility: Emergence of a Mobile Caste in Colonial Southwest Bengal', concentrates on the emergence of the Ugra Kshatriyas as a dominant caste in southwest Bengal and their attempt to attain a higher status in the regional caste hierarchy, explained through a study of their role in the economy of the region they lived in. In the context of the debate among historians, the chapter states that although agriculture became the mainstay of their livelihood and the main source of their income, it was not their original occupation. They were engaged in military pursuits in the eighteenth century, but changing circumstances had pushed them towards agricultural land. The author shows that Ugra Kshatriyas were a dominant and influential caste in the agrarian and commercial sectors of Burdwan district, noted for their entrepreneurial activities. Prosperity brought them to prominence, and they exerted their influence as big landholders or *jotedars*, grain merchants, moneylenders, and substantial peasants. Dutta throws light on the process of *kshatriya*-isation with reference to the reformation zeal and organisational abilities of the Ugra Kshatriyas, and their attempts to improve their sociocultural practices and elevate the social position of the entire caste. Many members of the community were active in politics and in the literary field as well. The chapter focuses on their sociocultural activities in this region during the colonial period. Their successes in the socioeconomic and cultural fields aided their ascent to a higher standing in the caste system. The control over agricultural land and production facilitated the foundation of their social dominance. Finally, the author explains how they attained a ritual and caste status that was higher than that of their neighbours.

Endnote

1. Ramakanta Chakrabarty, in his work titled *Bismrita Darpan: Nidhubabu, Babu Bangla O Gitratna* (1971), argues how Ramnidhi Gupta ('Nidhubabu'), incorporating the style of Hindi tappa songs in Bengali, introduced a new genre known as *akhdai* song (a form of poetic and musical composition) tuned with the classical *ragas*, which greatly influenced the musical style used in the theatre, *jatra* (a form of dramatic entertainment), and *panchali gan* (a long narrative Bengali song, usually sung in praise of a deity).

SELECT REFERENCES

Bandyopadhyay, Kausik. 2011. *Scoring off the Field: Football Culture in Bengal, 1911–80*. New Delhi & Oxford: Routledge.

Bandyopadhyay, Sekhar (ed.). 2001. *Bengal: Rethinking History Essays in Historiography*. New Delhi: Manohar.

______. 2004. *Caste, Culture and Hegemony: Social Dominance in Colonial Bengal*. New Delhi: Sage Publications.

Banerjee, Milinda. 2018. *The Mortal God: Imagining the Sovereign in Colonial India*. Cambridge, UK: Cambridge University Press.

Banerjee, Tarasankar. 1987. 'A Note On the Changing Pattern of Historical Research on Modern India in West Bengal'. In Tarasankar Banerjee (ed.), *Indian Historical Research since Independence*, 108–113. Calcutta: Naya Prokash.

Basu, Swapan, and Indrajit Chaudhuri (eds). 2003. *Unish Shataker Bangali Jiban O Sanskriti* (*Life and Culture of Bengalis in the Nineteenth Century*). Calcutta: Pustak Bipani.

Bhattacharya, Sabyasachi (ed.). 2020. *A Comprehensive History of Modern Bengal, 1700–1950*, Vols I–III. New Delhi: Primus Books.

Bose, Neilesh. 2014. *Recasting the Region: Language, Culture, and Islam in Colonial Bengal*. New Delhi: Oxford University Press.

Chakrabarty, Ramakanta. 1971. *Bismrita Darpan: Nidhubabu, Babu Bangla O Gitratna* (Forgotten Mirror: Nidhubabu, the Bengal of babus, and *Gitratna*).

______. 1985. *Vaisnavism in Bengal, 1486–1900*. Calcutta: Sanskrita Pustak Bhandar.

______. 1996. *Bange Baisnab Dharma: Ekti Aitihasik ebong Samajtatwik Adhyayan* (*Vaisnav Religion in Bengal: A Historical and Sociological Study*). Calcutta: Ananda Publishers Pvt Ltd.

______. 2002. *Bangalir Dharma, Samaj O Sanskriti* (*Religion, Society and Culture of the Bengali*). Calcutta: Subarnarekha.

______. 2005. *Amar Katha* (*About Myself*). Calcutta: Bangiya Sahitya Parisat Pathak Samaj.

Chaudhuri, S. B. 1955. *Civil Disturbances during British Rule in India, 1765–1857*. Calcutta: World Press.

De, Sushil Kumar. 1961. *Early History of the Vaishnava: Faith and Movement in Bengal*. Kolkata: Firma K. L. M., 2e.

Dey, Santanu. 2015. 'Resuscitating or Restructuring Tradition? Issues and Trends among Gaudiya Vaishnavas in the late Nineteenth and early Twentieth Century Bengal'. Ph.D. dissertation, Jawaharlal Nehru University, New Delhi.

Hatcher, Brian A. 2000 [1996]. *Idioms of Improvement: Vidyasagar and Cultural Encounter in Bengal*. New Delhi: Oxford University Press.

Kosambi, D. D. 1956. *An Introduction to the Study of Indian History*. Bombay: Popular Prakashan.

Majumdar, Rochona. 2009. *Marriage and Modernity: Family Values in Colonial Bengal*. Durham, USA, and London: Duke University Press.

O'Connell, Joseph T., and Amiya P. Sen. 2020. 'Directions for future Research on Vaisnavism in Colonial Bengal: An Unfinished Note by the Late Joseph T. O'Connell, edited and expanded by Amiya P. Sen'. In Ferdinando Sardella and Lucian Wong (eds), *The Legacy of Vaisnavism in Colonial Bengal*, 12–22. Oxford and New York: Routledge.

Palit, Chittabrata. 2006 [1980]. *New Viewpoints on Nineteenth Century Bengal*. Calcutta: Progressive Publishers.

Roy, Tapti. 2018. *Print and Publishing in Colonial Bengal: The Journey of Bidyasundar*. London: Taylor and Francis.

Sanyal, Hiteshranjan. 1989. *Bangla Kirtaner Itihas (The History of 'Kirtan' in Bengal)*. Calcutta: K. P. Bagchi & Co.

______. 2019. *Trends of Change in the Bhakti Movement in Bengal*. New Delhi: Oxford University Press.

Sarkar, Sumit. 1997. *Writing Social History*. New Delhi: Oxford University Press.

Sartori, Andrew. 2008. *Bengal in Global Context History: Culturalism in the Age of Capital*. Chicago and London: University of Chicago Press.

Sen, Amiya P. 1993. *Hindu Revivalism in Bengal, 1872–1905: Some Essays in Interpretation*. Delhi: Oxford University Press.

______. 2010. *Explorations in Modern Bengal c1800–1900: Essays on Religion, History and Culture*. New Delhi: Primus Books.

______. 2019. *Chaitanya: A Life and Legacy*. New Delhi: Oxford University Press.

Sinha, Pradip. 1996 [1967]. 'Social Changes'. In Narendra Krishna Sinha (ed.), *The History of Bengal (1757–1905)*, 384–428. Calcutta: University of Calcutta, 2e.

Wong, Lucian. 2015. 'Gaudiya Vaisnava Studies: Mapping the Field'. *Religions of South Asia* 9 (3), 305–331.

SECTION I

The Many Worlds of Bengali Culture

1

Texts and Traditions*

Collating the Vaishnava Heritage and Issues of Authenticity in Colonial Bengal[1]

Santanu Dey

Literary productions of a community are widely accepted as cultural repositories that enable a community to sustain its identity and facilitate its self-assertion. However, the arduous processes through which such literary heritages are constructed, mediated, and memorialised, especially the role played by literary forgeries, their identification, and indictment, along with the creation of literary norms to expunge them constitute an invisible underbelly that has seldom received academic emphasis. This chapter looks at one such hoax that rocked the Bengali literary world in the late nineteenth and early twentieth century. Literary forgeries have always baffled experts from around the world (Bagnani 1960, 228–244). They are supposed to have a disorienting effect on readers as they tend to loosen their hold on reality, by deforming and falsifying one's understanding of the past. Nevertheless, hoaxes are not to be dismissed simply for being what they are. As Mark Jones states, 'Fakes do far more than that. As keys to understanding the nature of our vision of the past ... as subverters of aesthetic certainties, they deserve our closer attention ... they claim our reluctant admiration' (Jones, et al. 1990, 16).

---

*An earlier version of this chapter was previously published as 'Dinesh Chandra Sen and the Archiving of a Vaishnava Literary Heritage: Search for Bengali identity in Colonial Bengal', in *Bengal: Past and Present (A Journal of Modern Indian and Asian History)* 132. This version reproduced with the kind permission of the journal.

Counterfeit literary texts, both in manuscript and printed form, have been reported from across the globe.[2] Interestingly, it was common practice within pre-colonial Indian literary traditions for anonymous authors to claim legitimacy for their texts by ascribing them to some famous author. Sometimes the art of plagiarising was carried a step further by composing texts and claiming historical value for them. Even within the corpus of Vaishnava literature in early modern eastern India there are several texts which have been considered spurious in nature, but none have been condemned as vociferously as *Gobindadaser Kadcha* (*Notes of Gobindadas*; hereafter referred to as *GDK*), supposedly written by Gobindadas Karmakar, a low-caste disciple and associate of Sri Chaitanya (1486–1533), who pioneered the Bhakti movement in medieval Bengal. The Gaudiya Vaishnava tradition is one which had a very diffuse system of institutionalising its devotional ethos to bind its religious community or communion of devotees. As Joseph T. O'Connell has shown, they passed down the 'charismatic authority' of Chaitanya through a dense repertoire of 'soft' and 'medium' institutions. The former included 'symbolic' means of institutionalisation such as Vaishnava literature and devotional practices, while the latter included the prominent associates of Chaitanya known for their intensity of devotion and asceticism (O'Connell 1999).

By the seventeenth century, the texts recognised as 'legitimate' by most Vaishnavas mainly included the sacred hagiographies (especially the *Chaitanya Charitamrita* by Krishnadas Kaviraj, the *Chaitanya Bhagavat* by Brindavan Das, the *Chaitanya Mangala* by Jayananda, among others) and theological-ritual commentaries written in Sanskrit, in Brajabhasha (western Hindi vernacular of seventeenth-century north-central India), and in Bengali. Such texts were composed by a mixed group of followers ranging from the *Sada Goswamis* or six Goswami theologians (Rupa, Sanatan, Jiva, Gopal Bhatta, Raghunath Bhatta, and Raghunath Dasa), who were deputed by Chaitanya to formulate the essential tenets of Bengali Vaishnavism at Brindaban to Bengali disciples settled in various parts of eastern India. With the passage of time, as the number of texts began to swell and sectarian interpretations became widespread, there was an attempt to weed out non-conforming texts. Scholars of the early nineteenth century such as Biman Bihari Majumdar tried to compare and corroborate information based on various hagiographical works on Chaitanya (Majumdar 1959, 405–489). He has listed a rather large number of purported 'spurious accounts' (see Table 1.1).

TABLE 1.1: List of Bengali Vaishnava Texts*

Name of the Work	Author	Year of Publication	Publisher
Bhaktiratnakar	Narahari Chakravarti	1857	Anandacharan Maitra
Sri Chaitanyadayabali	Pradyumna Mishra	1892–1893	Chaitanyacharan Das
Vamsi Siksha and Murali Vilasa	Anonymous	1892 & 1894	Bhagnapada
Sita Charitra	Lokenath Das	1897	Achyutacharan Chaudhuri
Advaitaprakash	Ishana Nagara	1896–1897	Achyutacharan Chaudhuri
Abhiram Ram Das	Anonymous	1895	Prasanna Kumar Goswami
Prema Vilasa	Nityananda Das	Undated	Ramnarayan Bidyaratna
Advaita Mangal	Haricharan Das	1901	Brajasundar Sanyal
Balyalilasutram	Laudiya Krishnadas	1915–1916	Achyutacharan Chaudhuri
Premavivarta	Jagadananda Pandit	1930	Gaudiya Math
Sitagunakadamba	Anonymous	1936	Amulyacharan Ghosh Vidyabhushan

Note: *Published in colonial times, whose authenticity has been disputed.
Source: Information collated from Majumdar (1959, 405–489).

Pre-modern cultures of literacy did not offer the requisite means, or perhaps adequate access, to everyone to enable them to produce texts. Indeed, approving the notion of sectarian legitimacy, Narottam Das, the author of a Vaishnava work titled *Nabaradhatattwa Nirupan*, instructs: 'Let none but your disciple see this book, hide it away and guard it as preciously as your life' (Bhattacharya 1981, 26). While the existence of an entrenched societal hierarchy meant that Brahmins retained a privileged access to literacy, it was not an entirely closed system. Even among the six Goswami theologians at Brindaban, Raghunath Das was a Kayastha who belonged to a rich zamindari family from Saptagram in the Hooghly district of Bengal. Manuscript writers thus required a high level of authorial competence before their works found acceptance within the tradition. Such competence derived not only from one's literary and linguistic skills and caste orientation, but also from one's aesthetic knowledge and appropriate theological grounding. It was a combination of these qualities that enabled a text to attain legitimate status within the territorially scattered groups of Gaudiya Vaishnavas in early modern times. There were instances when texts written by disciples were rejected by others for their supposed 'incorrect' interpretation.

At another level, Vaishnava scriptural conventions of the medieval period were fortunate in containing a lot of historical data on their authors, their guru lineages, their places of residence, and even the year of completion of the text, either in the introductory or the concluding stanzas. This tendency towards 'biographic encoding' gave Vaishnava texts a high degree of corroborative potential. In the nineteenth century, however, when such manuscripts were printed, there was hardly any textual referencing of the multiple manuscript versions. Proof-checking was by no means a standard practice. Moreover, as the discovery of unknown manuscripts—or new versions of known manuscripts—occurred almost simultaneously with their publication, particular words, stanzas, and even chapters were sometimes unknowingly substituted, edited, or even obliterated in an emergent era of mechanised print production. Such trends within the production, circulation, and consumption of books and knowledge in the Persianate context have also been noted by some scholars of early modern India (Green 2010).

This chapter tries to document one such debatable encounter that this process of unearthing Vaishnava manuscripts led to in colonial Bengal. I try to locate the public life of a religio-literary controversy in colonial Bengal, centring on the *GDK*. I probe the contours, the content, and the context of this debate, and the varied impact that it produced in colonial Bengal. The chapter will not attempt to analyse or verify the 'authenticity' of the *Kadcha* as such, but only try to reconstruct the historical debate over its authenticity as an entry point to probe the boundaries between 'sacred' and 'profane' texts, between the 'authentic' and the 'spurious', and between the identification of the 'original' and 'fake' tradition within the context of Vaishnavism in colonial times.

Bengali Vaishnavism and the Colonial Setting

The pioneering works of Ramakanta Chakrabarty have laid bare the essential features of the Vaishnava movement in Bengal till the nineteenth century. It is important to contextualise the period and identify the almost parallel cultural processes in operation in colonial Bengal, in the hope that this will help us to locate the controversy in its historical setting.

The colonial era saw the transition from a predominantly oral and manuscript-based culture to a print-oriented culture that broadened the circulation of texts. The 'preservative powers' of print led to an increased power of dissemination, promoted the standardisation of printed matter, and provided fixity to written texts. Print is considered to have revolutionised intellectual communication and linked readers of different social cross-sections in an ideological and intellectual space that provided the setting for the creation of a 'public sphere' (Eisenstein 1980; Febvre and Martin 1976). Although it is common practice to consider that the pre-print cultures of literacy in Bengal were circumscribed within the high class/caste segment of pre-colonial society, or that the coming of print cultures in the colonial period created an overnight broadening of the frontiers of readership, determining the exact impact of print in colonial India has been a rather vexed historical issue. The role of print in the emergence of a 'public sphere' in colonial India and in refashioning religious identities, especially by middle-class intellectuals, has long been accepted by different scholars (Basu 2002; Ghosh 2006; Joshi 2010, 202–221).

There was also a growing tendency, almost at the level of an emotional investment, among the educated Bengali intelligentsia of the late nineteenth century towards the collection, documentation, archiving, and publication of local vernacular texts and manuscripts. This was done both at the institutional level (by the Asiatic Society, the Bangiya Sahitya Parisat, and the University of Calcutta) and at the individual level (by noted litterateurs/compilers such as Nagendranath Basu, Dinesh Chandra Sen, and Chittaranjan Das, among others). The noted antiquarian Haraprasad Sastri's (1853–1931) account considers that in 1868, on the suggestion of the then Viceroy of India, Sir John Lawrence (1864–1868), a sum of Rs 24,000 was allocated annually for the preservation of manuscripts in various Indian languages. Out of this, around Rs 3,200 was given to the Bengal government, which in turn forwarded it to the Asiatic Society, first under the charge of Rajendralal Mitra (1822–1891) and then, after his death, to Haraprasad Sastri. Sastri was intimately connected to the programme of manuscript collection when he was placed in charge of the Sanskrit collection of the Asiatic Society in 1891. This collection drive under the auspices of the Asiatic Society with the help of 'travelling pundits' led to the collection of around 11,000 manuscripts in different languages by 1914 (Sastri 1981, 340–341). Devoted Vaishnavas and scholars also began collecting manuscripts from the late nineteenth century onwards, from traditional Vaishnava centres such as Brindaban, Nabadwip, Katwa, Srikhanda, Santipur, Baranagar, and various places in Odisha.

Another influence was the spread of Western education and the university system that spurred the growth of new academic disciplines like History and Literature (Chatterjee 1995, 1–29). Attempts to examine and archive the glory of the Bengali language and literature had begun in earnest in the latter half of the nineteenth century. There was also an added desire to standardise the written form of Bengali by removing excessive Sanskrit influence as well as coarse colloquial words. Thus began a conscious move towards chronicling the evolution of Bengali literary history and a quest for precise dating from the second half of the nineteenth century onwards. Institutions such as the Bangiya Sahitya Parisat were established to standardise and spur research on Bengali language and literature. The growing nationalist impulse in the wake of the anti-Partition (of Bengal)/Swadeshi movement in Bengal in 1905 led to an urge to retrieve and document vernacular manuscripts as a form of expression of 'self-identity' (Bhadra 2011, 3–58). This manuscript 'hunt' not only laid the foundations for a literary history of the Bengali language, such as Dinesh Chandra Sen's *Bangabhasha o Sahitya* (*Bengali Language and Literature*, 1896), but more significantly, it brought to public attention the fact that early modern Vaishnava texts had played a formative role in the evolution of Bengali literature. For instance, Ramgati Nyayaratna (1831–1894), a teacher in Baharampur College, in his *Banglabhasha o Bangla Sahitya Bishayak Prastab* (*Proposal regarding Bengali Language and Literature*, 1874), proposed that the 'Chaitanya phase', which stretched from 1485–1752, took Bengali literature beyond the limited bounds of courtly consumption, transforming it into a vehicle for mass propagation. He opined that:

> Since their religion was open to all, they [Chaitanya's disciples] began to travel across the lands, like the later-day Christian missionaries, in order to attract the imagination of the masses; thus, they began to write their religious tenets not in Sanskrit, which would have made it understandable to the intellectuals alone, but in the vernacular medium of Bengali for easy comprehension by the masses. Thus, it would not be out of place to call this phase the classical era of Bengali textual production ('*Banglagranthapranayaner adikal*'). (Nyayaratna 1874, 55; translation mine)

Similarly, Rameshchandra Datta in his *Literature of Bengal* (1877) emphasised the egalitarian focus and the 'spirit of freedom and individuality' of the Chaitanya era (Datta 1877, 88–100). It was within this context of the expanding boundaries of Bengali literary history that Dinesh Chandra Sen tried to give centre-stage to the folk and Vaishnava literature of the region. He tried to project Bengali as an equal stakeholder among the world of languages. In this way, Sen began to posit a nationalist literary identity for Bengali in the last decade of the nineteenth century. As a result, Vaishnava texts rapidly emerged as sites of scholarly enquiry. As scholars began to research these sectarian texts, they began producing a body of literary knowledge quite independent of the limited sectarian interpretations so far accorded to these texts by the community of Vaishnava believers.

Finally, there was a rapid spread of Vaishnava religious journals, such as *Sajjantoshani, Gauranga Sevak, Bishnupriya Patrika,* etc., and Vaishnava institutions, from the local Hari Sabhas and Haribhaktipradayini Sabhas in the 1870s and 1880s to the Gauranga Samaj (1899), the Sri Krishnachaitanya Tattva Pracharini Sabha (1909), the Gaudiya Vaishnava Sammilani (1911), and the Gaudiya Math (1918), which slowly led towards religious mobilisation and sectarian consolidation among Bengali Vaishnavas. It was within this milieu of religio-cultural developments in colonial Bengal at the transitional cusp of the nineteenth and twentieth century that the *GDK* controversy erupted.

Tracing the Kadcha Debate

Till the early colonial era, Chaitanya was memorialised by his followers in Bengal essentially through a hagiographic lens. He was conceived as a partial or complete incarnation of Krishna, as an androgynous incarnation of both Radha and Krishna, as a great Sanskrit scholar and ascetic, and also as the inspiration behind the growth of numerous popular religious cults in Bengal. But one may locate at least three definite ways in which the Bengali Hindu intelligentsia appropriated Chaitanya at the turn of the twentieth century: as a religious reformist; in their tendency towards historical veracity; and lastly, in their desire to trace in the Chaitanya tradition the marker of Bengali literary genius (Bhatia 2017, 1–10). However, the parallel strands of Vaishnava sectarian resuscitation and academic literary-historical analysis by scholars in colonial Bengal were to come at loggerheads with each other over the authenticity of the *GDK*. No such account was known to exist till its sudden discovery and publication in 1895 by Jaygopal Goswami (1829–1916), the head *pandit* (teacher) of Santipur High School, in the Nadia district of Bengal. He had received some renown as a writer of Vaishnava and other miscellaneous literary works like *Charugatha, Shaibalini, Ratnajugal, Sahityamuktabali, Sitaharan,* and *Basabdatta,* among others (Sengupta and Basu 1976, 166). The *GDK* caught the immediate attention of contemporary Vaishnavas as well as literary scholars, since it claimed to provide an eye-witness account of Chaitanya's travels in south India. This was not readily available in the more standard and accepted Vaishnava biographies such as the *Chaitanya Charitamrita* or the *Chaitanya Bhagabat*. In this scenario, determining the historicity of the *GDK* became almost a public concern, and a range of tracts, booklets, articles, and public speeches were produced. However, the non-availability of the manuscript of the *GDK* soon turned it into a source of vigorous contention, with some castigating it as a 'literary forgery', or a 'Black Forgery' (Dasgupta 1937), while others hailed it as a 'historical' account that provided a rare vision of the real human personality of Chaitanya (Sen 1925).

What were the reasons for this unusual opprobrium? This was expressed best by Bepin Vihari Dasgupta, a little known Vaishnava believer from Dhaka in the 1930s:

> It [the *Kadcha*] has done a world of mischief; for about forty years, this infamous production has deluded historians, misguided scholars, led astray antiquarians.... What is worse, it has deeply wounded the religious susceptibilities of the Vaishnabas [*sic*] of Bengal. The motive that actuated the forger to play this unholy hoax on the unwary public is either love of lucre or a cheap notoriety for a new discovery in the field of Vaishnava literature, or both. We urge our countrymen to

> take concerted action to have this pernicious '*kadcha*' banned ... a book that misrepresents Sree Gouranga, who is the fountain-head of much what is true, good and beautiful in the culture of Bengal. (quoted in Majumdar 1959, 107–108)

The term '*Kadcha*', which literally means 'Diary or Notes' or sketches, was not new within the Vaishnava tradition; see, for instance, the *Kadcha* by Murari Gupta and the *Kadcha* by Swarup Damodar, among others. Written as a single and continuous versified narrative consisting of 2,460 verses without formal internal divisions, the *GDK* purported to be a true account of the approximately twenty-two-month long south Indian pilgrimage of Chaitanya from 7 *Baisakh* of *Saka* 1432 (April 1510) to 3 *Magh* 1434 (January 1512). This account claimed to document Chaitanya's triumphal progress through southern and western India, not so much as a persuasive argumentative reformer but as a man of supreme humility. It begins with a self-portrayal by Gobinda Das Karmakar, the blacksmith writer who hailed from Kanchannagar in Burdwan district, and who became a servant-cum-companion of Chaitanya during his journey across the entire southern half of the Indian subcontinent, from Puri to south India and then up the west coast to Gujarat, and thence across central India by the banks of the Narmada river back to Vidyanagar (modern Rajamahendri), and then onwards to Puri again, covering almost seventy-eight places. It articulated Chaitanya's appeal to the plebian rural masses, as confirmed by the conversion of common lay folk and even of rural brigands. The *Kadcha* thus valorised the personal charisma of the leader over and above the rather stoic image of a reformer.

Let us take a sample of the reactions that the *GDK* elicited from the late 1890s till the 1940s. The movement against this text seems to have gone through two phases. During the first phase there was an uncritical acceptance of its value as a historical document, akin to that of the acclaimed Vaishnava, Sisir Kumar Ghosh, for his multi-volume biography of Chaitanya, titled *Sri Amiya Nimai Charit*. The noted antiquarian Haraprasad Sastri, who wrote two articles on it in the *Calcutta Review* (1898), was not entirely unaware of the criticisms against the document, but chose to support its historicity:

> ...we know that, shortly after Chaitanya's death, the headship of the [Vaishnava] church fell to Nityananda, and the personal followers of Chaitanya were at a discount. The standard works were all composed by the men belonging to the dominant party; and this party was so bold as to ignore the existence of venerable followers of Chaitanya like Narahari Sarkar, the head of the Vaidyas of Srikhanda, in [*sic*] Cutwa, who are still held in great respect by all classes of people. It is, therefore, not strange that they should omit to mention a poor monk like Gobinda. (Sastri 1898a: 79–80)

Sastri praised the *GDK* for its 'simple', 'lucid', and 'expressive' language, in contrast to the 'exaggerated' and unrealistic [*aprakrita*] descriptions of the standard hagiographies, as well as for its lack of sectarianism. It was this line of argument that Dinesh Chandra Sen later supported when he republished the *GDK* in 1926. He applauded the *Kadcha*'s chronological accuracy, which he felt was ample testimony of Gobinda's being 'a man on the spot'. As the foremost literary historian of the times, Sen also took a historicist position:

> As the *kadcha* is free from miraculous tales, abounding in other biographical works, accepted as standard authorities on Chaitanya's life, being ... a simple and unassuming record without much regard for orthodoxy or sectarian conventions, a section of the Vaishnavas have been disposed to think that it is by no means a fitting sketch of the great apostle. (Sen 1925, 567)

He considered the very dissonance of the text vis-à-vis other established hagiographies as a signifier of its authenticity, and began using it for his literary analysis of Chaitanya in his *History of the Bengali Language and Literature* (1911), *Caitanya and his Companions* (1917), *Vaisnava Literature of Bengal* (1917), and *Caitanya and his Age* (1922). These lectures and publications, where Sen enshrined the Chaitanya Vaishnava traditions as the core essence of Bengali literary culture, were delivered to a community of teachers, scholars, and students within a university. Sen's personal reputation as a modern literary scholar and the fact that most of his works were published from the Calcutta University Press provided Vaishnava texts with a hitherto unprecedented intellectual academic anchoring. Sen was adamant in his belief in the *GDK* as an eye-witness account:

> The Charitamrita was written 93 years after the Kadcha. In a country like India one knows full well what monstrous fables grow around a great apostle within a few years of his death.... But in matters in which the Kadcha does not agree with the standard biographies, I for myself, would, even at the risk of incurring the umbrage of a section of the orthodox Vaishnavas, give credit to the Kadcha, as written by a man on the spot in preference to the later works, whatever the sanctity they may carry in popular Vaishnava opinion. (Sen 1925, 572–573)

For Sen, the essentially humanising attributes of emotional felicity in Chaitanya were far more important than his supernatural attributes, as enshrined in conventional Vaishnava hagiographies.

The anti-*Kadcha* agitators were concerned that a literary scholar's approval of the *GDK*, purely in terms of a historical portrayal of Chaitanya that bypassed or obliterated his divine personality, would greatly devalue Chaitanya's image within the Vaishnava community. Thus, they structured their criticism in two forms; first, as a defence of Vaishnava faith and belief—as one writer from Chittagong contended, although there were several fake books doing their rounds in the market, the agitation against the *Kadcha* was especially urgent since 'with this issue is connected the greatest pride of Bengal, the name of Sri Chaitanya'. They exclaimed with horror and apprehension that

> the book which has engendered criticism from the entire Vaishnava community, whose false foundation can be perceived clearly in the light of subtle judgment, is attaining the most exalted position in the world of history due to the efforts of a handful of self-willed persons. (Ghosh 1936, 270)

Moreover, it was also framed as a defence of the Bengali language, since they argued that the ascription of a later writing to an earlier date would inevitably hinder efforts to historicise Bengali literature. They branded Sen's regard for the *GDK* as a blasphemous contamination of the entire educated and civilised world of Bengal. The major critics were sectarian leaders like Madhusudan Goswami Sarbabhauma from Brindaban. In 1929, on behalf of the Vaishnava community, he condemned the *Kadcha* as a 'monstrous' conspiracy by a *Sakta*[3] worshipper who, on realising the absence of any account of Chaitanya's southern India pilgrimage, ventured to fill the lacuna. He satirically concluded,

> We think that Gobinda Das's *Kadcha* is a recent and fictitious account, since it has been 'born' [discovered] 410 years after the birth of Sri Mahaprabhu. Within these years so many litterateurs, poets, historians and scholars have been born but none could extract the *Kadcha* from its incubation. (Goswami Sarbabhauma 1929 [1336 BS], 171–173)

The most vociferous denunciators of the *Kadcha* were the ubiquitous devoted Bengali Vaishnava middle-class intelligentsia, comprising lower officials, journalists, and teachers hailing from the rural districts, who had been participating actively in Vaishnava resuscitation programmes.[4] This group also received the patronage of some influential pious zamindars, such as Ray Bahadur Radhaballabh Chaudhuri of Sherpur in Mymensingh, who presided over one of the *sabhas* denouncing the *GDK*'s validity (Ghosh 1936, 270). Detractors tried to historicise their struggle against the text in terms of a crusade, thus designating it as a 'movement'. Even the noted contemporary historian Sir Jadunath Sarkar (1870–1958) wrote a brief foreword to a book condemning the *Kadcha* as a forgery (Dasgupta 1937, iii). Arguments and counter-arguments against the *GDK* in the public domain often degenerated into acrimonious mutual slandering. The *Amrita Bazaar Patrika* of 1 May 1935 referred to an anti-*Kadcha* resolution drawn up by the Gaudiya Vaishnava Sammilani of Calcutta, where they supposedly 'established' that it was 'inauthentic' and a 'product of false imagination ... opposed to *Sastric* doctrine', which needs to be 'boycotted'. The assembly also urged the faithful community to form a committee 'to find out ways and means to prohibit publications of spurious Vaishnava literature published both from the University and from outside' (Sreemani 1935, Preface). Copies of this resolution were purportedly sent to the Calcutta University authorities. Thus, a form of religious inquisition and literary censorship was sought to be enforced, which bore the marks of religious mobilisation and consolidation along sectarian lines, by the early twentieth century.

In the absence of a verifiable manuscript version of the *GDK*, debates were directed towards an examination of its internal evidence. There were various sub-themes—ranging from historical errors, social impropriety, moral lapses, use of colloquial Bengali, cartographic misrepresentations, and, curiously enough, even Chaitanya's culinary habits—that the public debate over the *GDK* touched upon. One important point of criticism was the alleged sacrilegious portrayal of Chaitanya's character by Gobinda Das. The notable fact is that in the early twentieth century, this sort of evidence constituted a valid method for judging a document's historicity. A parallel example is the use of astrological calculations in the University of Calcutta thesis by Biman Bihari Majumdar in 1939 for ascertaining the chronology of different events in Sri Chaitanya's life (Majumdar 1959, 1–5).

Almost all anti-*Kadcha* writers considered the tract as teeming with 'modern words and expressions'. However, the verbal morphology of the *GDK* was defended by Dinesh Chandra Sen, who argued that since Gobinda Das had very little bookish learning, he did not imbibe the Vaishnava hagiographical style and thus wrote in simple colloquial Bengali. However, Sen also added an Appendix containing a list of words appearing in the *GDK*, claiming 'signs of antiquity' for them; for example, *piba=pan kariba* (I shall drink), *mopane=mor pane* (looking towards me), etc. Some archaic Brajabuli words mentioned in the *GDK* were also listed: for instance, *bat=vakya* (word or sentence), *thora=alpa* (a few), *knaha=kothay* (where), etc. At one point, even Sen unapologetically accepted that the *Kadcha* was not an entirely accurate textual representation. But he defended such textual changes by citing the dilapidated—in his words, the 'worm-eaten'—condition of the manuscript that forced its editor to fill in these voids in order to make it readable—a practice widely adopted by contemporary publishers. Detractors, however, charged Sen with doctoring the text, citing the dissonance between the two editions. As against the 1895 version, the second edition of 1926 carried many irregularities due to the replacement of modern words used by Jaygopal Goswami with their older Sanskritised *sadhubhasha* or chaste literary Bengali equivalents. Sen was also charged with tampering with the text by leaving gaps in exactly those places in the second edition where the text of the first edition had appeared glaringly modern. One author pointed out over sixty separate instances of linguistic discrepancy in the *GDK* (Dasgupta 1937).

The other issue related to locating the exact identity of Gobinda Das, the supposed author of the *GDK*, within the scriptural repertoire. Colonial Bengali encyclopaedists such as Amulyadhan Raybhatta mention almost twenty renowned Vaishnava personalities with the name Gobinda as prefix, including the author of the *GDK* (Raybhatta 1924, 131–141).[5] There is indeed no denying the fact that there is no mention of Gobinda as Chaitanya's companion during the latter's south Indian pilgrimage in any of the authoritative hagiographies. At the same time, these texts do mention the existence of a companion who travelled with Chaitanya as his personal attendant. According to the *Kadcha* of Murari Gupta, he was Vishnudas, while Kavi Karnapura and Krishnadas Kaviraj consider his name to have been Krishnadas Dwija or Kalakrishnadas (Stewart and Dimock 1999, 485). B. B. Majumdar contends that in view of such differences in biographic referencing, it is not altogether improbable that this person's name might well have been Gobinda Das. This does not appear to be altogether fallacious since all three names are synonyms of Krishna. It may well be possible that after Chaitanya's ostracism of Kalakrishnadas as a result of the latter's attraction towards a lady named Bhattamari, who belonged to a south Indian tribe (as mentioned by both Krishnadas Kaviraj and Kavi Karnapura), hagiographers wanted to conceal the real identity of this man and so substituted his name with an alias possessing a similar meaning (Majumdar 1959, 402–403).

Turning to the charge of geographical inconsistencies, Dinesh Chandra Sen considered the sheer diversity of information and geographical detail as a prima facie marker of the *GDK's* validity. Later critiques, however, highlighted several inconsistencies. In 1925, Amritalal Sil pointed to Chaitanya's inhuman feat, claimed in the *Kadcha*, of travelling from the river Ghoga near Ahmedabad to Jafarabad in just three days, even though the distance between these places is 160 miles (Sil 1925, 473). These doubts led others to discuss such anomalies as 'Geographical Blunders'. As a specific instance, it was pointed out that the place Rashalkunda in the *GDK* was a distortion of 'Russel-konda', a military station named after one Mr Russell, in all probability George Edward Russell (1787–1863), who was Commissioner during the Guntur war of 1835–1837, and which is located about 80 miles south of Puri. For Dasgupta, this constituted clinching evidence that the *Kadcha* was surely composed in the nineteenth century (Dasgupta 1937, 82–83). In a similar manner, he exposed the text's adoption of anglicised forms of south Indian place names, such as 'Trivanku' for Travancore instead of the medieval place name 'Tiruvidankodu', and Tanjore instead of Tanjavur. Some took exception to the *GDK*'s mention of Chaitanya receiving '*ata-chuna*' (wheat pulse) as alms from the local villagers, seeing this as an intriguing detail since the entire Coromondal zone was a rice-consuming area (Sil 1925, 473).

Another important point of criticism was the alleged sacrilegious portrayal of Chaitanya's character by Gobinda Das. Apparently they took special offence to the *GDK*'s mention that during some of his divine trances, Chaitanya lost not only his consciousness but also his clothes. One tract writer also lambasts the portrayal of Gobinda Das's gluttony in the *Kadcha*. The redemption of prostitutes or *sevadasis* such as Baramukhi at Ghoga in Gujarat, mentioned in the *GDK*, was vigorously refuted by critics. Dinesh Chandra Sen argued that since Chaitanya was born to redeem the fallen, 'it is wrong to go about erecting boundaries in the flow of the flood of love that was unleashed from heaven to earth' (Sen and Goswami 1926, 53). Thus, public debates over the *Kadcha* opens up to us a variety of analytical strands regarding contemporary Bengali Vaishnava society, their tensions, perceptions, and expectations.

In these circumstances, the agitators raised wild allegations against Dinesh Chandra Sen. They claimed that Sen supported the *Kadcha* so vehemently because he wanted to defame Vaishnavism and reduce it to the 'baser varieties of Vaishnavism'.[6] Nagendra Kumar Ray, one of the numerous little-known tract writers, alleged that:

> From a reading of the writings of Dinesh Chandra Sen it will always seem that he is bent on popularizing Sahajiya views within society; but he is unwilling to bear the responsibilities himself. The aim of propagating the form of Sahajiya love within society through laying the burden on the Vaishnavas is apparent in all his writings. (Ray 1926, 148–149)

He also indicted Sen for pouring 'poison' into the study of Bengali literature, which has 'in the last thirty years diseased society and led to its moral denigration'. This mutual slandering led anti-*Kadcha* protagonists to place the entire oeuvre of Dinesh Chandra Sen under scrutiny and reveal specific instances when he had misrepresented Chaitanya.

Why were his critics so vehement? This shows that the public sphere, especially by the 1920s, was influenced by majoritarian/communitarian voices. Their articles are filled with exhortations to the entire Gaudiya Vaishnava community to rise up collectively against profane representations. Vaishnavas in Bengal had been consolidating their organisational enterprise through the creation of assemblies and Hari Sabhas from the late nineteenth century onwards, which came in handy during this agitation.

Fallouts of the GDK Controversy

In the Gaudiya Vaishnava tradition, which was a highly textualised one, much emphasis was laid on the notion of 'legitimate' canon

(O'Connell 1999, 215–239). In the absence of the original manuscript, the *GDK* represented a spurious text for the lay Vaishnava believers. Although non-Brahmin writers of prominence did exist within the Gaudiya Vaishnava tradition, the discovery of the *Kadcha,* written by a low-caste Karmakar/blacksmith companion of Chaitanya, represented an invasion of the sacred precincts of the hagiographical space. What seems clear is that there can be no inviolate universal standard of fixing the 'authenticity' of a text, especially in the case of a religious tradition. Enquiring into the ways in which new canons are formed, Rakefet Sela-Sheffy argues that the complex process of canon formation tries to strike a balance between orthodoxy and heresy in the canoniser's use of previously existing canons. He contends that

> Depending on their starting position, canonizers either rely on traditional agencies of authority or venture to present themselves as inventers of the wheel. Accordingly, their action is governed by either the tendency to evoke long established canonical repertoires as sources for legitimation and prestige, or by that of rejecting these repertoires in their aspiration to establish their own sources of legitimation. (Sela-Sheffy 2002, 156)

Authenticity, in a literal sense, is always a construction; it is what or how divergent groups view a given notion in any given situation.

However, in the end, both sides in the contest seem to have escaped relatively unscathed, despite the heated debates that the *GDK* generated. The Centenary Issue of the Department of Modern Language and Literature, University of Calcutta, showered posthumous glory on Dinesh Chandra Sen as the initiator of historical research on the Bengali Vaishnava tradition (Singha 1974, 250–254). Sen retained his faith in the *Kadcha* till his death, and even mocked the conservatism of the Vaishnava community in his work *Brihat Banga* (1935):

> The time has arrived when we need to adopt a policy of either accepting or denying the historicity of the sacred biographies of Chaitanya conventionally valued by the conservative

> Vaishnava community. We must not get cowed down by the fear of the Gosains.... Everybody loves one's own home but if someone else points out the garbage it contains that would only help to increase rather than decrease its glory.... The devotion of the devotees is a precious commodity but historians too have their responsibility. (ibid., 681–682)

Sen recalls how a prominent Vaishnava Goswami had bargained with him, stating that if he accepted the supernatural aspects of Chaitanya mentioned in the *Chaitanya Bhagabat* and the *Chaitanya Charitamrita,* then they would give up their struggle against the *Kadcha* (ibid.). Posthumously, Sen retained his share of enthusiasts who admired his sentimental construction of the past (Chakraborty 2004, 672). However, his pro-*Kadcha* stand was later rejected by most literary scholars of the mid-twentieth century. A number of scholars working on Vaishnava history, including Ramakanta Chakrabarty, Tony Stewart, and Rebecca Manring, have considered the text as inauthentic (Manring 2005, 134–135). The orthodox Vaishnava community, on the other hand, never took a sympathetic view of the *Kadcha*. This is symptomatic of the extent to which the religious tradition has been able to hold its sway over the community of believers, despite the controversy.

The public utterances and remonstrations for and against the *GDK* produced some intended and other unintended results. The first important fallout of the debate was the reassertion of the need for a secularised literary history of Bengali, within which the Vaishnava heritage was given primacy. Such debates also promoted an urge towards historicising Vaishnava lives/texts and chronological dating. The simple hagiographic retelling of Vaishnava lives that formed a usual part of sacred discourses till the late nineteenth century began to shift towards a modernist urge to locate them as historical figures within a contextualised frame. The first such text on Vaishnava history, titled *Vaishnava-Itihas,* which carried an account of the lives and works of ancient Vaishnava teachers and poets, Vaishnava festivals, and places of pilgrimage, was written in 1905 (Chattopadhyay 1905). More elaborate was Murarilal Adhikari's *Vaishnava Digdarshini,* which claimed to be 'a thousand year history of Vaishnavism' (Adhikari 1925). Such efforts to historicise the tradition within a positivist mould, despite its shortcomings, represented a method that was eagerly adopted by many contemporary writers. Articles analysing the exact date of composition of Vaishnava texts, particular events, and the organisation of famous *mahotsavs* or festivals, and estimating the life-span of Vaishnava personalities became staple fare in contemporary Vaishnava periodicals.[7] Numerous *padas* or verses written by less-known or unknown Vaishnava poets also began to be documented in contemporary periodicals (Mitra 1924). Thus, a modernist inquisitiveness that led to historicising the Vaishnava tradition brought into the public domain an enormous amount of new data regarding places, figures, verses, and events, which had till then remained hidden in the realms of an amorphous localised sacred culture.

Finally, regardless of whether the *Kadcha* was a clever concoction or a true historical document, it seems to have ultimately served the cause of the Karmakar community to which Gobinda Das belonged.[8] Interestingly, one of the unintended fallouts of the debate was a growing sanctification of the figure of Gobinda Das Karmakar by members of the Bangiya Karmakar Samiti (Society of the Karmakar Caste of Bengal) at his native village of Kanchangram in Bardhaman district. By the mid-twentieth century, they had even gone on to build a temple and lodging house there, which was renamed as Gobindadham (the abode of Gobinda), with week-long public celebrations of anniversaries held every year (see Image 1.1). The choice of the suffix *dham* for Gobinda Das' birthplace at Kanchangram, paralleling Nabadwipdham (Chaitanya's birthplace in Nadia district) at least in name, is interesting for it tries to claim a sort of divine spatial symmetry, even though the connection remains tendentious. Derived from the Sanskrit root *dhaman*, meaning the domain where the earthly/manifest as well as the eternal/unmanifest aspects of divine play (*lila*) occurs, the usage of the word by Gobinda Das' followers in the early twenty-first century seems to be a conscious attempt to inscribe sacred legitimacy onto his personality.

Image 1.1: Marble plaque set up by the Bangiya Karmakar Samiti at Gobinda Das Karmakar's supposed birthplace at Kanchannagar, Bardhaman, West Bengal

Photo credit: Author.

The fate of Gobinda Das Karmakar seems to have undergone a further transformation from the late twentieth century. From a symbol of caste consciousness, Gobinda Das gradually began to be assimilated as a historical figure embodying the sub-regional cultural achievement of Bardhaman district by local historians and district gazetteers. Most authors who have written on the history of the district in the latter half of the twentieth century (for instance, Chattopadhyay 2000; Chaudhuri 1994; Dan 1992; Sen 1966) note Gobinda Das' contribution as a companion of Chaitanya and hail him as a 'son of the soil' alongside other famed writers such as Brindaban Das, Narahari Sarkar, and Krishnadas Kaviraj. The real turnaround for Gobinda's fortunes, however, came in the 1960s and 1970s when migrant refugees from East Bengal, some of whom were Vaishnavas, began to settle on the deserted lands along the banks of the Damodar river adjacent to Kanchannagar. Stone plaques in the temple premises attest to the fact that in the 1980s, some of these men constructed a small temple dedicated to Gobinda Das, which was also facilitated by local political leaders (as learnt during fieldwork in Bardhaman; see Image 1.2).

Image 1.2: Present temple named Gobindadham at Gobinda Das Karmakar's supposed birthplace at Kanchangram/Kanchannagar, Bardhaman district, West Bengal

Photo credit: Author.

The iconographic positioning and representation of the idols inside the temple, with Radha–Krishna in the middle, flanked by Chaitanya and Nityananda on either side and Gobinda Das sitting at the base, magnifies the latter's role as a true disciple of the tradition (see Image 1.3). The Kadcha Kavi Gobinda Das Seva Trust, a committee established in the year 2000, began organising regular festivities, including a ten-day long birth anniversary celebration of Gobinda Das, from the fifth day after Dol Purnima (celebrated as the birthday of Chaitanya). In 2018, they celebrated Gobinda Das' 550th birth anniversary.

Image 1.3: Idols of Radha–Krishna flanked by Nityananda (left) and Chaitanya (right), with Gobinda Das sitting at the base inside Gobindadham temple

Photo credit: Author.

Image 1.4: Kadcha Kavi Gobinda Das Seva Trust

Photo Credit: Author.

Madhusudan Karmakar, the editor of a recent publication of the *Kadcha*, states that, 'Today Gobindadham is a lively new Brindaban' (Karmakar 1997). Thus, over the course of just around 120 years from the last decade of the nineteenth century, the identity of a person named Gobinda Das Karmakar and his supposed literary work, the *GDK*, underwent phases of acceptance and rejection and left its indelible mark across different registers ranging from Vaishnava scriptural heritage, Vaishnava belief, and the Bengali literary corpus.

IMAGE 1.5: Entrance gate of the present Gobindadham at Bardhaman

Photo credit: Author.

ENDNOTES

1. Earlier versions of this chapter were presented in Dhaka in August 2015, at the Oxford Centre for Hindu Studies, Oxford University, in February 2018, and at Calcutta University in March 2018. I am grateful for the inputs received from Tanika Sarkar, Ferdinando Sardella, Lucian Wong, and Amiya Sen.

2. A brief glimpse of textual fabrications across diverse literary cultures reveals its wide prevalence as a category. For instance, in Japan, numerous texts like *Murasaki Shikibu* (a diary of Murasaki Shikibu), *Suma no ki* (a diary written supposedly by Sugawara no Michizane), and *Shiki Monogatari* (a miscellany attributed to Kamo no Chomei) have been challenged as fabrications (Kimbrough 2002, 133–171). Similarly, generations of scholars have queried the genuineness of the twelfth-century Russian 'masterpiece', *Slovo o Polku Igoreve* (*The Lay of the Campaign of Igor*) (Struve 1946: 213–218). Another such case of forgery relates to the Scottish Poems of Ossian, which were supposedly translated from the Gaelic into English by John MacPherson around 1760. The Ossianic controversy, as it has come to be termed, was long drawn-out and lasted for almost fifty years (Murphy 1986, 567–591).

3. Shaktas are a set of believers in Hinduism who conceive and worship the goddess or Devi in varied forms as the supreme, ultimate, eternal reality of all existence. Within Bengali religious traditions as they evolved in the early modern times, the Shaktas and the Vaishnavas sometimes had an antagonistic stance towards each other, and often tried to contest or demean the other.

4. These were men like Yogendramohan Ghosh, Amritalal Sil, Nagendranath Ray, Rasikmohan Vidyabhushan (a Brahmin pandit well-versed in Sanskrit scriptural as well as English learning, and later editor of the two major religious journals, *Bishnupriya Patrika* and *Gauranga Samaj*), Rasamay Mitra (an eminent school administrator of Calcutta who played a significant role in the rejuvenation of Hare School and Hindu School), Sisir Kumar Ghosh and his nephew Mrinal Kanti Ghosh (who received the title '*Bhaktibhushan*' for his efforts towards spreading Vaishnava devotion).

5. Apart from Govinda Karmakar, this list, which I think has several overlaps, included Govinda (a disciple of Shyamananda who went to Brindaban); Govinda Adhikari (a disciple of Krishnadas Punjabi of Multan); Govinda Kaviraj (of the Nityananda lineage); Govinda Kaviraj (also known as Das Govinda or Govinda Das, a renowned *pada* composer and a disciple of Srinivas Acharya); Govinda Gati or Gatigovinda Thakur (the youngest son and disciple of Srinivas Acharya at Jajigram); Govinda Gosain (a disciple of Kasihswar Gosain at Brindaban, mentioned in the Chaitanya Bhagabat as a contemporary of Rupa Goswami); Govinda

Ghosh (a disciple of Chaitanya at Agradwip); Govinda Chakrabarty (a disciple of Srinivas Acharya); Govindananda Chakrabarty (Chaitanya's disciple); Govinda Datta (a kirtaniya from Sukhchar village); Govinda Das (a disciple of Srinivas Acharya, mentioned in the Karnamrita); Govinda Bhakat (a devotee of Chaitanya at Brindaban, contemporary to Rupa Goswami); Govinda Bhritya (a Kayastha servant of Chaitanya and disciple of Iswar Puri); Govindaram (a disciple of Srinivas at Brindaban); Raja Govindaram (a disciple of Narottama Dasa, mentioned in the *Narottam Vilasa*); Govinda Ray (a disciple of Narottama); and Govindananda Thakur (mentioned in Abhiram Das' text *Patparyatan*).

6. There has been a long struggle within Bengali Vaishnavism between the conservative caste-conscious strands and the broader heterogenous and populist guru-centric Sahajiya strands of Vaishnavism from at least the eighteenth century onwards.

7. For instance, Mrinal Kanti Ghosh of the *Anandabazar Patrika* wrote a series of fourteen historical queries about chronologically marking varied episodes of Vaishnava history, such as the date of Srinivasa's arrival in Bishnupur, the date of the Kheturi *mahotsav* (grand festival), among others, in a letter addressed to Achyutacharan Tattwanidhi, the famed Vaishnava scholar of Sylhet in 1923, which were published in the periodical *Birbhumi* [Ghosh 1923].

8. The Karmakar caste in Bengal, synonymous with the Kamar, was distinguished from the Lohars because the former did not confine themselves to working only with iron, but broadened their skills to working any form of metal (Risley 1891, 1, 388–392). This was represented even in the origin myths of the community, when the gods tried to avenge the repeated defeats at the hands of the demon Lohasura, who had gained the gift of immortality through his austerities. Since no godly weapon could kill Lohasura, Indra, with the assistance of Shiva, created a mortal Kamar to defeat him with a blacksmith's 'weapon' (read instruments). This Kamar was able to goad Lohasura into proving his immortality by getting into a furnace, and then worked the bellows so hard that the latter died. It was the dissection of the molten remains of Lohasura into eight parts that is said to have produced the eight sub-castes of the Kamars. Risley suggests that the name Kamar, 'far from indicating a common origin, is merely the functional designation of an extremely heterogeneous group' (Risley 1891, 1, 389).

Select References

Adhikari, Murarilal. 1925. *Vaishnava Digdarshini ba Sahasra Batsarer Sankshipta Baishnab Itihas*. Calcutta: Sri Ram Press.

Bagnani, Gilbert. 1960. 'On Fakes and Forgeries'. *Phoenix* 14 (4), 228–244.

Basu, Shamita. 2002. *Religious Revivalism as Nationalist Discourse: Swami Vivekananda and New Hinduism in Nineteenth Century Bengal*. New Delhi: Oxford University Press.

Basu, Yogendramohan. 1927 [1334 BS]. 'Kadcha Andolaner Sankshipta Itihas'. *Sadhana* 2 (5), 264–288.

Bhadra, Gautam. 2011. *Nyara Battalay Jay Kawbar?* Calcutta: Chhatim Books.

Bhatia, Varuni. 2017. *Unforgetting Chaitanya: Vaishnavism and Cultures of Devotion in Colonial Bengal*. New York: Oxford University Press.

Bhattacharya, Asutosh, and Asit Kumar Bandyopadhyay (eds). 1974. *Subarnalekha: Adhunik Bharatiya Bhashabibhager Subarnajayanti Smarakgrantha*. Calcutta: Calcutta University Press.

Bhattacharya, Jatindramohan. 1981. 'Puthir pare boi'. In Chittaranjan Bandyopadhyay (ed.), *Dui Shataker Bangla Mudran o Prakashan*. Calcutta: Ananda.

Chakraborty, Dipesh. 2004. 'Romantic Archives; Literature and Politics of Identity in Bengal'. *Critical Inquiry* 30 (3), 654–682.

Chakrabarty, Ramakanta. 1985. *Vaisnavism in Bengal, 1486–1900*. Calcutta: Sanskrit Pustak Bhandar.

Chatterjee, Partha. 1995. 'The Disciplines in Colonial Bengal'. In Partha Chatterjee (ed.), *Texts of Power: Emerging Disciplines in Colonial Bengal*, 1–29. Minneapolis: University of Minnesota Press.

Chattopadhyay, Ekkari. 2000. *Bardhaman Jelar Itihas o Loksamskriti*, Vol. I. Kolkata: Radical Publications.

Chattopadhyay, Harilal. 1905. *Vaishnava-Itihas*. Calcutta,

Chaudhuri, Yogeshwar. 1994. *Bardhamaner Itihas o Sanskriti*, Vol. 3. Kolkata: Pustak Bipani.

Dan, Sudhir Chandra. 1992. *Bardhaman Parikrama*. Kolkata: Book Syndicate Private Limited.

Dasgupta, B. V. 1937. *Govinda's Kadcha: A Black Forgery*. Dacca: Harinath Press.

Datta, Rameshchandra. 1877. *The Literature of Bengal Being an Attempt to Trace the Progress of the National Mind in its Various Aspects, As*

Reflected in the Nation's Literature from the Earliest Times to the Present Day; With Copious Extracts from the Best Writers. Calcutta: Stanhope Press.

Eisenstein, Elizabeth. 1980. *The Printing Press as an Agent of Change: Communications and Cultural Transformations in Early Modern Europe*. Cambridge: Cambridge University Press.

Febvre, Lucien, and Jean-Henri Martin. 1976. *The Coming of the Book: The Impact of Printing, 1450–1900*, D. Gerard (trans.). London, New York: Verso.

Fuller, Jason D. 2003. 'Re-membering the Tradition; Bhaktivinoda Thakura's "Sajjantosani" and the Construction of a Middle Class Vaisnava Sampradaya in Nineteenth-century Bengal'. In A. Copley (ed.), *Hinduism in Public and Private: Reform, Hindutva, Gender and Sampradaya*, 173–210. New Delhi: Oxford University Press.

_____. 2005. 'Reading, Writing, and Reclaiming: Bhaktivinoda Thakura and the Modernization of Gaudiya Vaishnavism'. *Journal of Vaishnava Studies* 13 (2), 75–94.

_____. 2009. 'Modern Hinduism and the Middle Class: Beyond *Reform* and *Revival* in the Historiography of Colonial India'. *The Journal of Hindu Studies* 2, 160–178.

Ghosh, Anindita. 2006. *Power in Print: Popular Publishing and the Politics of Language and Culture in a Colonial Society*. New Delhi: Oxford University Press.

Ghosh, Mrinalkanti. 1923. 'Vaishnava Sahityer Kal Nirnay'. In Kuladaprasad Mallick (ed.), *Birbhumi (Nabaparyay)* 6 (8) (1330 BS), 33–39.

_____. 1936. *Govinda Daser Kadcha Rahasya*. Calcutta: Nalini Press.

Jones, P., Mark Craddock, and N. Barker, et al. 1990. *Fake? The Art of Deception*. Berkeley: University of California Press.

Goswami Sarbabhauma, Madhusudan. 1929 [1336 BS]. 'Kadcha'r Kritrimata'. *Sadhana* (Radhagovinda Nath [ed.]) 4 (3), 171–173.

Green, Nile. 2010. 'The Uses of Books in a Late Mughal Takiyya: Persianate Knowledge between Person and Paper', *Modern Asian Studies* 44 (2), 1–25.

Joshi, Sanjay. 2010. 'Re-Publicizing Religiosity: Modernity, Religion, and the Middle Class'. In Sanjay Joshi (ed.), *The Middle Class in Colonial India*, 202–221. New Delhi: Oxford University Press.

Kargupta, Sourav. 2010. 'Dineshchandra Sen's *The Folk Literature of Bengal*: The Canonisation of Folk and the Conception of the Feminine'.

In Hans Harder (ed.), *Literature and Nationalist Ideology: Writing Histories of Modern Indian Languages*, 126–148. New Delhi: Social Science Press.

Karmakar, Madhusudan. 1997. *Mul, Sankshiptasar O Parishishtadi Saha Gobindo Daser Kadcha*. Calcutta: Deys Publishing.

Kimbrough, R. Keller. 2002. 'Apocryphal Texts and Literary Identity: Sei Shonagon and "The Matsushima Diary"'. *Monumenta Nipponica* 57 (2), 133–171.

Majumdar, Biman Bihari. 1959. *Sri Chaitanya Chariter Upadan*. Calcutta: Calcutta University Press, 2e.

Manring, Rebecca J. 2005. *Reconstructing Tradition: Advaita Acarya and Gaudiya Vaisnavism at the Cusp of the Twentieth Century*. New York: Columbia University Press.

Mitra, Sibratan. 1924. 'Aprakashita Prachin Padabali'. *Birbhumi (Nabaparyay)* 6 (12) (1331 BS), 42–44.

Murphy, Peter T. 1986. 'Fool's Gold: The Highland Treasures of MacPherson's Ossian'. *English Literary History* 53 (3), 567–591.

Nyayaratna, Ramgati. 1874. *Banglabhasha o Bangla Sahitya Bishayak Prastab*. Hugli: Budhoday Jantra (Samvat 1930).

O'Connell, Joseph T. 1999. 'Chaitanya Vaishnava Movement: Symbolic Means of Institutionalization'. In Joseph T. O'Connell (ed.), *Organizational and Institutional Aspects of Indian Religious Movements*, 215–239. New Delhi: Manohar.

Ray, Nagendra Kumar. 1926. 'Govinda Daser Kadchas O Ray Bahadur Doctor Dineshchandra Sen'. *Sadhana* 1 (3) (1333 BS), 148–149.

Raybhatta, Amulyadhan. 1924. *Brihat Sri Vaishnava Charit Abhidhan*. Panihati: Manasi Press.

Risley, H. H. 1891. *The Tribes and Castes of Bengal: Ethnological Glossary*, official edition, Vol. I. Calcutta: Bengal Secretariat Press.

Sardella, Ferdinando, 2013. *Modern Hindu Personalism: The History, Life, and Thought of Bhaktisiddhanta Sarasvati*. New York: Oxford University Press.

Sastri, Haraprasad. 1898a. 'The Diary of Govinda Das'. *Calcutta Review* 106, 79–96 and 372–383.

———. 1898b. 'The Topography of Govinda Das's Diary'. *Calcutta Review* 107, 172–184.

———. 1981. 'Bangiya Sahitya Parishader Sabhapatir Abhibhashan; 1321 BS'. In Satyajit Chowdhury (ed.), *Haraprasad Sastri Rachana*

Samagra, Vol. 2, 340–341. Kolkata: Paschim Banga Rajya Pustak Parshad.

Sela-Sheffy, Rakefet. 2002. 'Canon Formation Revisited: Canon and Cultural Production'. *Neohelion* 29 (2), 141–159.

Sen, Anukul, and Narayan Chaudhuri (eds). 1966. *Bardhaman Parichiti*. Kolkata: Book Syndicate Private Limited.

Sen, Dinesh Chandra. 1896. *Bangabhasha o Sahitya*. Comilla: Chaitanya Press.

______. 1911. *History of the Bengali Language and Literature*. Calcutta: Calcutta University Press.

______. 1917. *The Vaishnava Literature of Medieval Bengal*. Calcutta: Calcutta University Press.

______. 1922. *Gharer Katha O Yug Sahitya*. Calcutta: Jigyasa.

______. 1923. *Mymensingha Gitika*. Calcutta: Calcutta University Press.

______. 1925. 'Kadcha by Govinda Das'. *Calcutta Review* (Third Series) 14 (3), 567–573.

______. 1928. *The Descriptive Catalogue of Bengali Manuscripts*. Calcutta: Calcutta University Press.

______. 1935. *Brihat Banga*, Vol. II. Calcutta: Calcutta University Press.

______. 1936. *Asutosh Smritikatha*. Calcutta: Indian Publishing House.

Sen, Dinesh Chandra, and Banowarilal Goswami (eds). 1926. *Govinda Daser Kadcha*. Calcutta: Calcutta University Press.

Sengupta, S., and A. Basu (eds). 1976. *Sansad Bangali Charitabhidhan*. Calcutta: Sahitya Sansad.

Sil, Amritalal. 1925. 'Govinda Daser Kadchar Aitihashikata'. *Prabasi* 25 (4), 470–482.

Singha, Sukdeb. 1974. 'Vaishnava Sashtra o Sahitya Vichare Kolikata Vishwavidyalayer Dan'. In Asutosh Bhattacharya and Asit Kumar Bandyopadhyay (eds), *Subarnalekha*, 250–254. Calcutta: Calcutta University Press.

Struve, Gleb. 1946. 'Slovo o Polku Igoreve: An Eighteenth-Century Fake?' *The Slavonic and the East European Review* 24 (63), 213–218.

Sreemani, Charuchandra. 1935. *Sri Chaitanyadeber Dakshin Bhraman*, Vol. 2. Calcutta: Puran Press.

Stewart, Tony, and E. C. Dimock (eds). 1999. *Chaitanya Charitamrta of Krsnadas Kaviraj; A Translation and Commentary by E. C. Dimock Jr.* Cambridge, MA: Harvard University Press.

Tattwabachaspati, Madhusudan. 1926. *Gaudiya Vaishnava Itihas (Vaishnava Bibriti)*. Hooghly (1333 BS, 2e).

2

Bhaktisiddhanta Saraswati and the Making of Vaishnavism in Modern Bengal

Arun Bandopadhyay

I shall specify the thematic limits of this chapter and its purpose at the very outset. Based largely on a critical reading of Ferdinando Sardella's recent biography of Bhaktisiddhanta Saraswati (Sardella 2013) and developed in response to some of the questions raised by him—some of which were also dear to Professor Ramakanta Chakrabarty, the renowned historian of Vaishnavism in Bengal—the author wishes to highlight and articulate at the very beginning the four-fold limits of its theme and coverage. First of all, the study focuses on the limited biography of Bhaktisiddhanta Saraswati (1874–1937), insofar as his thought and activities concerned Vaishnavism in general, and Bengal in particular. The budding idea of global Vaishnavism that Bhaktisiddhanta floated has not been dwelt on here. This brings us to the second limitation that the use of the word 'making' in the title proposes to cover. Although Vaishnavism in Bengal has a history of over 500 years, much of which was a subject matter of Professor Chakrabarty's own study (Chakrabarty 1985), the chapter covers its formulations only in the late nineteenth and early twentieth century, which is roughly the lifetime of Bhaktisiddhanta himself.

There are other limits of our coverage also. As part of Bhaktisiddhanta's own orientation and projection, Vaishnavism is taken here as Chaitanya bhakti (devotion directed towards Lord Chaitanya) as propagated by the Gaudiya Math (Vaishnava monastery named after and located in the Gaudiya region of Bengal), established by him in 1920. The particular formulation of

Vaishanvism as Chaitanya bhakti, in its historical and philosophical connotations, is an important focus of this chapter. Finally, Bengal provides a specific spatial relevance in the entire discourse, without which the deliberations made here will be largely out of focus, both thematically and historically. These four aspects virtually act as limitations of this contribution, but they also give it a purpose: locating Vaishnavism and its agency in the form of its nodal activity with a specific region, time, and personality.

The argument is structured in three parts. First, the general background of the religious and cultural story of Vaishnavism is sought in the nineteenth century, in the way non-dualism in religious thought received its cultural prominence in the course of the Bengal Renaissance, and probably even thereafter. This was the classic period of interaction between Eastern and Western thought, a continuance of the comparison amongst different religions of the world, and a gradual acceptance of the universal direction of discourses in comparative religion, finally leading to the strength of and support for a non-dualistic Vedantic view in Indian tradition. Vaishnavism, with its long premodern past and a markedly theistic emphasis, gradually receded in importance from the intellectual deliberations of Renaissance Bengal.

The second part contextualises the contribution of Bhaktivinoda Kedarnath Datta (1838–1914) and his son, Bhaktisiddhanta Saraswati (1874–1937), from the point of view of their lifetimes, the latter more than the former for the present purpose. We have analysed the early, middle, and late career of Bhaktisiddhanta mainly in the context of Bengal, and the issues and questions that confronted him prominently through his multifarious activities during those times. His unique re-interpretation of Chaitanya bhakti is critically appreciated here, showing how history and philosophy joined hands to give new meanings to his efforts towards 'making' Vaishnavism of his time.

The final section is devoted to an evaluation of Bhaktisiddhanta's legacy. It provides an assessment of his life's work in Bengal in the context of his contributions to the development of Vaishnavism; however, the section proceeds in two different directions in search of answers to two questions: (*i*) should we consider this legacy merely in the light of what happened later (in the future); and/or (*ii*) should we judge it as part, even a limited part, of a life significant in its own terms, for the time that it covers? This section will also try to evaluate some of the issues he had raised in the broader context of what has been called modern traditionalism.

Religious and Cultural Discourses and Vaishnavism in the Nineteenth Century

Ramakanta Chakrabarty's monumental work (Chakrabarty 1985) dwells on both the pre-modern history of Vaishnavism in Bengal and its nineteenth-century after-effects, covering a long period from 1400–1900. It shows the attraction and potency of the Vaishnava religion at the populist levels and its complex social interactions in the three centuries following the birth and lifetime of Sri Chaitanya (1486–1534), as also its relative disappearance from prominence in the nineteenth century. One prominent factor leading to this disappearance, as argued by Chakrabarty (more in his Bengali work than in English; see Chakrabarty 1996), is the internal abuses of Vaishnavism as perceived by nineteenth-century Bengali society. In this story, what is often forgotten is the phenomenal social and cultural change that occurred in Bengal in the course of the nineteenth century.

As argued by Ferdinand Sardella (Sardella 2013, 14–53), the root of this change can be found in the emergence of what has been called the *bhadralok* (a loosely defined literate group of Bengali gentlemen who had no engagement with rigorous manual work) in the nineteenth century. From the many confusing meanings of the word bhadralok, one that stands out is that of an educated class, a queer mixture of East and West in terms of education, taste, thought, and proclivity. In the religious plane, the most significant manifestation of this change was the emergence of non-dualism or Advaita Vedanta as the predominant intellectual query of the time. This trend was most clearly seen in the religious thought and activities of Rammohan Roy (1772–1833), Keshabchandra Sen (1838–1884), Bankimchandra Chatterjee (1838–1894), Bipin Chandra Pal (1858–1932), and Swami Vivekananda (1863–1902), but its earliest emphatic pronouncement came from an English missionary, William Ward. As early as 1817, Ward suggested that *Brahman*, which he understood as the Divine Spirit, was at the core of the theology of the Hindus, and added, 'The whole system of Hindoo theology is founded upon the doctrine that the Divine Spirit, as the soul of the universe, becomes, in all human beings, united to matter; ... that the human soul is, in other words, God himself' (Ward 1817, Vol. 1, 219).

In contrast, Ward noted many ethical shortcomings among the large number of Vaishnavas in Bengal, 'Nearly one half of the Hindoo population of Bengal are Vaishnavas, composed principally of the lower orders ... the distinguishing vice of this sect is impurity, as might be expected ... from the obscene nature of the festivals held' (Ward 1817, Vol. I, 219).

It is therefore clear that while there was a decline in the importance of Vaishnavas from the standpoint of the bhadraloks, Vedantins came more into prominence during the nineteenth century. It is true, however, that there was a dualist section among the Vedantins, particularly represented by the Ramanuja school in south India. Much later, W. S. Urquhart, who had been the Principal of Scottish Church College and a Professor of Philosophy at the University of Calcutta, noted the relative unimportance of this school:

> ... it has been estimated even by a follower of Ramanuja that out of the total number of Vedantins, 75 per cent are adherents to Sankara, and only 15 per cent of Ramanuja.... And that this popularity is not merely accidental, but is based upon and justified by a considered estimate of the significance of Sankara's teachings... (Urquhart 1928, 64–65)

But the more important point here is to explain the emergence of the emphatically non-dualistic turn taken by religion and philosophy in India in the nineteenth century. One important root was no doubt Rammohan Roy, who brought several seminal points into public discussion: (*i*) propagation of monotheism since 1804, and his later, more polemical reading of Vedantic literature, as evident from the publication of *Vedantasura* in 1815; (*ii*) his rejection of the worship of images and the performance of temple rituals; and (*iii*) his determination to show that Hinduism could be made compatible with modern progressive values. However, what is often ignored is that Ramakanta Roy, the father of Rammohan, was a Vaishnava, and Tarini Devi, his mother, came from a Sakta family. Although Rammohan rebelled against the traditional order, Sardella has found that in 'the end he adopted a Vedantic non-dualistic approach that was blended with theistic notions; but it was mainly upon this *advaitic* framework that the Brahmo Sabha was founded' in 1828 (Sardella 2013, 24). The Brahmo Sabha later became the Brahma Samaj, which was purged of most of its Sankara Vedantic elements by Debendranath Tagore after his joining the Sabha in 1842, and the subsequent formal change of its name. When Keshabchandra Sen came to the forefront of the Brahmo Samaj in the 1870s, he introduced various devotional practices inspired by Chaitanya Vaishnavism, which the staunchly non-dualistic sections of the Samaj roundly disliked (Kopf 1979). However, Keshabchandra was instrumental in creating a new interest in Vaishnavism among the bhadralok of Bengal.

Both Bankimchandra Chatterjee and Bipin Chandra Pal mixed their respective religious thoughts with political ideas in two different ways. Bankim's study of the *Krishna-Charita* (1886) propagated, in contrast to the erstwhile religious, social, and literary interpretations, an ideal Krishna who embodied all the qualities of a national hero sought after through one's imagination (Kaviraj 1995), and pronounced all other accounts as interpolations. Bipin Chandra Pal, on the other hand, was a political leader very active in Bengal in the early twentieth century. In his political thought and activity, he developed a form of theological idealism that regarded the progress of society as an unfolding of God's immanent presence in history (Pal 1973).

The classic expression of non-dualistic Vedanta was found in the voice, thought, and writings of Swami Vivekananda. He made two important suggestions: (*i*) *Advaita* constitutes the central philosophy of Hinduism; and (*ii*) non-dualism represents the 'perennial truth' of all religious traditions and culture, despite their apparent differences. However, unlike Rammohan, he believed that image worship played an indirect role in preparing the mind for the ultimate realisation of Brahman (the Divine Spirit). Most importantly for Vivekananda, there was no other god than the *jiva* or conscious being (hence the relevance of the term *daridra Narayana* [the Supreme Being in the form of the poor], coined by him), an understanding that created a fundamental bridge between his views on religion and society. By one stroke, Advaita and his construction of 'Practical Vedanta' were designated as superior to Bhakti, implying a downplaying, directly or indirectly, of the popular expressions of devotional practice associated with Vaishnavism.

An argument has been developed from the discipline of philosophy as to why and how this preponderance of and emphasis on Advaita Vedanta came into being in the philosophical circles in Bengal in the nineteenth and early twentieth century. As recently postulated by Pradyot Kumar Mukhopadhyay very forcefully in his Bengali book on the outlines of the study of Indian philosophy in the twentieth century, this was surprising as far as Bengal was concerned. Of the six branches of Indian philosophy, Nyaya, including *navya* Nyaya, was most extensively and creatively studied in Bengal; however, it was Vedanta that was given prominence (Mukhopadhyay 2018). Mukhopadhyay located the answer to the puzzle beyond the internal thrust of the discipline: nationalism and universalism, as variously formulated at the time.

As argued by Sardella, the creation of modern Advaita Vedanta was largely the product of the .bhadralok of Bengal, along the lines of the fundamental changes that overtook society, education, religion, and the general worldview (Sardella 2013, 53). The decline in popular practices of Vaishnavism was a natural corollary of this. However, both processes may be more complex than apparently postulated, as well as linked. In this context, we can think of Andrew Nicholson's masterful analysis of how pre-modern India conceptualised and reflected upon the philosophical issues of unity and plurality, and his emphasis that this endeavour was not an artificial product of modernity and revisionist hybridity as asserted by Orientalists, but an authentic autochthonous aspect of theological deliberations long before colonial rule (Nicholson 2010). At the very least, more research is required on both. Non-dualism has a long history in India, and its religious, social, and philosophical ramifications are many. Similarly, the so-called decline of Vaishnavism can be perceived from both the bhadralok and the popular points of view. The effort to understand its 'making' in late nineteenth- and early twentieth-century Bengal is therefore to be launched from a variety of planes—historical, philosophical, and the deeply 'personal'—in the realm of Vaishnava religious ideas.

Bhaktisiddhanta Saraswati and the Making of Vaishnavism

In this section, we shall concern ourselves directly with the 'limited' biography of Bhaktisiddhanta Saraswati as instrumental in the 'making' of Vaishnavism in Bengal in the late nineteenth and early twentieth century. As we have indicated earlier, the words 'limited' and 'making' require further explanation. We are aware of an incipient global role in Bhaktisiddhanta's propagation of Vaishnavism, particularly in the later part of his career, but we are less concerned about it in this chapter. Our predominant concern is Vaishnavism in Bengal, and its rejuvenation due to the efforts of Bhaktisiddhanta in his lifetime. However, this word 'limited' does not exclude a brief understanding of the activities of his illustrious father, Bhaktivinoda. Kedarnath Datta, as Bhaktisiddhanta continued some of Bhaktivinoda's activities as well. The word 'making' here has a direct implication—that of comprehending the multiple features of the transformation that occurred in Bengal with regard to Vaishnavism under the pivotal agency of Bhaktisiddhanta during the end-nineteenth and early twentieth century.

Our narrative begins with a brief reference to Bhaktivinoda Kedarnath Datta, who happened to be the major influence on his son Bhaktisiddhanta's life. Born in a remote village called Ula (also known as Birnagar) in the district of Nadia on 2 September 1838, to the lineage of an influential Kayastha family of Hathkhola in Calcutta, Kedarnath Datta was brought up in hardship in childhood, but his later education took place in the fairly good atmosphere of Calcutta in the company of such people as Satyendranath Tagore and Keshabchandra Sen. After a good Western education, Kedarnath initially became a teacher, but later joined the government service to ensure a more comfortable living. He was first exposed to the rationalism of the Brahmo Samaj, then leaned towards Christianity, but finally began to reflect on theism in the modern world (Bhativinoda 1916). As he had been raised in a Sakta family, his experience of Vaishnava literature was initially limited. He came to be engaged in a period of intense study and prayer, became associated with the popular Vaishnava group of Kartabhajas (a Vaishnava sect of southern Bengal engaged in radical social and cultural practices) in his youth, which then led to the realisation that Vaishnava bhakti was the 'all-encompassing focal point of his life' (Sardella 2013, 61). He was in Jagannath Puri for five years, between 1869 and 1874, on official work when he studied Vaishnava literature intensively in Sanskrit with the help of local pundits. It was here that Bimalaprasad, the sixth of his eleven children, was born in 1874, to be later known as Bhaktisiddhanta Saraswati. It should be remembered that Bhaktivinoda Kedarnath Datta was engaged in a lifelong mission to propagate Vaishnavism in Bengal, both before and after his retirement in 1894, simultaneously bequeathing the onus of extending it further to his illustrious son Bhaktisiddhanta. He passed away in 1914.

Bimalaprasad began his education at an English school in Ranaghat, and was later transferred to Oriental Seminary in Calcutta. Bhaktivinoda initiated his son in *Harinama* (singing the name of Hari) at a fairly early age, and with profound respect for his father, the son responded by developing a strong moral character, self-discipline, and deep commitment to Krishna bhakti. Sardella has divided Bhaktisiddhanta's life into three phases—1874–1900, 1901–1917, and 1918–1937—representing, respectively, his early intellectual upbringing, the middle years of intense spiritualism, and the final years, when his role in the religious movement of his time became pronounced (Sardella 2013, 54–133). Slightly deviating from this characterisation of Bhaktisiddhanta's career, we make two divisions, one for the late nineteenth and early twentieth century, and the other for the 1920s and 1930s. We consider the significant dividing line as March 1918, when Bhaktisiddhanta took full *sannyas* (renunciation), quite unlike the modern tradition of Chaitanya bhakti in Bengal. Our suggested division, we hope, will help us understand the 'limited' biography of Bhaktisddhanta as a causal instrumentality in the 'making' of Vaishnavism in Bengal.

We argue that Bhaktisiddhanta's intellectual and spiritual journeys should be taken together, particularly during the first forty-five years of his life. Fairly early in his childhood, Bimalaprasad accompanied his father on a pilgrimage, and met yogis, gurus, and other religious leaders. When he was just about nine years old, he had memorised the entire Bhagavad Gita, and at eleven, his father entrusted him with the task of proofreading the newly established Vaishnava periodical *Sajjanatoshani*. Around the same time, he had the opportunity to meet the leading Vaishnavas of Bengal, who came to attend the Visva Vaishnava Raja Sabha (Royal World Vaishnava Association) set up by his father in 1885.[1] He studied in Serampore Union School till 1887, and then joined Calcutta Metropolitan Institution. At the age of seventeen, he became a member of the Chira Kumar Sabha (Lifelong Bachelor Association), and he 'remained a celibate throughout his life' (Sardella 2013, 66). He studied Astronomy, Mathematics, and Logic with traditional Sanskrit *pundits* such as Maheshchandra Chudamani and Sundara Lala,[2] who awarded him the title 'Siddhanta Saraswati' in 1889. At Sanskrit College, he continued his study of astronomy, and further began to learn Sanskrit Grammar, Nyaya, and Vedanta. Simultaneously, he carried on with his learning of bhakti literature, such as Narottama Das's *Prarthana* and *Prema-bhakti-chandrika*, and Bilvamangala Thakura's *Krishna Karnamrita*, in Sanskrit.

He also served as a close associate of his father when the latter established the Navadipadhama Pracharani Sabha (Society for the Popularisation of the Sacred Site of Nabadwip) in 1893. At Sanskrit College, Bhaktisiddhanta Saraswati was embroiled in several controversies with renowned professors, in connection with meaningful readings of astronomical texts. Confronted with debates on the matter, he did not forsake his views, instead choosing to leave Sanskrit College.

Around the closing year of the nineteenth century, Bhaktisiddhanta was merely twenty-five years old, but his intellectual and spiritual inclinations were moving in multiple directions. In 1899, he started writing in *Nivedana*, the Calcutta weekly that his father had launched, and which contained both religious and secular news. He also wrote a Bengali booklet titled *Bange Samajikata* (*Social Formation in Bengal*) that same year, where he analysed the relation between religion and society, 'providing not only an historical account based on indigenous categories of knowledge but also a critique of Indology and Western historiography' (Sardella 2013, 74). He particularly questioned the colonial discourse against Hinduism/Vaishnavism, which was three-fold: (*i*) it lacked a sense of history; (*ii*) it was devoid of a moral structure; and (*iii*) it was not based on any rational philosophical system. For him, Hindu society, although unnecessarily divided by the multiplicity of castes, was intrinsically a community united by a common religious and social foundation, and oriented towards principles of devotional service to God and a vision of the spiritual brotherhood of all beings. The booklet contained the seeds of his future polemics against *varnasrama* and for a global society based on bhakti.

On the personal spiritual plane, an important change occurred to Bhaktisiddhanta during this time. He came in contact with Gaura Kishora Dasa Babaji, a highly regarded Vaishnava mystical ascetic who frequented his father's circles, and Bhaktisiddhanta was initiated by him in 1900. As he reminisced later, it happened to be an extraordinary event in his life:

> No education could have prepared me for the good fortune of understanding my master's attitude.... Before I met my master, I have not written anything about real religion. Up to that time, my idea of religion was confined to books and to a strict ethical life but that sort of life was found imperfect unless I came in touch with the practical side of things. (*Sajjanatoshani* 1917, Vol. 19, quoted in Sardella 2013, 75)

From his father, Bhaktisiddhanta inherited a vision of Vaishnava society with its cultural implications, and a sense of societal involvement. Gaura Kishora Dasa Babaji, his guru, introduced him to the intimate practice of *raganuga bhakti*, a form of devotional service pursued by advanced Vaishnavas. Thus Bhaktivinoda and Gaura Kishora represented two versions of Chaitanya bhakti, one for the layman and the other for the ascetic.

After his initiation, Bhaktisiddhanta abandoned the usual living style of the bhadralok and began to dress in a simple white or green cloth. He visited Jagannath Puri and went to south India to explore the customs and teachings of other Vaishnava sects, such as those of Madhava and Ramanuja. He also visited Mayapur, the assumed birthplace of Sri Chaitanya, several times during this period. He lived a life of austerity, sleeping on the floor and eating simple food, and spent time in study, writing, and contemplation. He began to question the authority of the hereditary Brahmins, and started propagating a new concept of Vaishnavas as a higher ideal. He concluded that Vaishnava texts paid respect to both hereditary Brahmins and to those who had achieved that position through initiation, without differentiating between the two. As Sardella has argued, he also made an important distinction between the godly (*daiva*) varnasrama practised by those who wish to please God, and the mundane varnasrama practised by those hostile to God. Indeed, the higher ideal that he subscribed to implied that anyone in the world may attain Krishna bhakti or complete devotion to God. The most learned and the most ignorant are both entitled to embrace it. Consequently, there began a lifelong confrontation between him and Nabadwip's hereditary Brahmins over the social status, spiritual capacities, and priestly rights of the non-Brahmin castes. At one point, the hostility of his opponents increased so much that it was rumoured that his life was in danger.

In June 1914, Bhaktisiddhanta lost his father, and his guru Gaura Kishora also passed away a year later. In June 1920, six years after her husband's death, Bhagavati Devi, Bhaktisiddhanta's mother, also left the world. Meanwhile, in March 1918, Bhaktisiddhanta self-initiated himself into sannyas. It is important to note that although Sankara and the Vaishnavas of south India had long followed this tradition of renouncing the world at certain points in their lives, the Chaitanya tradition in Bengal had no such precedent. It was a unique moment, and its full implications in the making of Vaishnavism are yet to be charted out. A new series of activity and thought associated with it, as roughly evident from the history of the making of Vaishnavism in Bengal in the 1920s and 1930s, happened to be the cardinal feature of the last part of his biography.

Herein lies the relevance of what we have called the second part of Bhaktisiddhanta's 'limited' biography. During this period, he engaged more deeply with two different 'activities': his organisational involvement with the religious movement for the development of Chaitanya bhakti in Bengal, and the cultivation of deeper thoughts and practices akin to a kind of religious personalism on the subject. Already in 1919, Bhaktisiddhanta had tried to revive his father's Visva Vaishnava Raja Sabha, and in this connection had made a series of attempts to establish a forum for discussing various aspects of the Chaitanya movement throughout the 1920s. Partly motivated by the age-old Vrindavan Sabha (*cf.* six Goswamis of Vrindavan as cult figures in the sixteenth and seventeenth centuries) and partly modelled on a non-sectarian Chaitanya as a hero of universal brotherhood and intellectual freedom in the twentieth century, Bhaktisiddhanta propagated the idea of *suddha bhakti* (pure devotion) at a level much deeper than that of his father. For Bhaktisiddhanta, suddha bhakti appeared as free from the mere products of knowledge (*jnana*) or mundane action (*karma*). It was solely directed towards the service to God and devoid of any ulterior motives other than love alone.

Indeed, throughout the 1920s, as he himself later admitted, the periodical *Sajjanatoshani* became 'strictly the organ of the Suddha-bhakti movement' (Bhaktisiddhanta in *Harmonist* 1927, 25 (4), cited in Sardella 2013, 102). After making a survey of various places during his lecture tours in Kashi, Lucknow, Jaipur, and Dwaraka, he established the Gaudiya Math at Bagbazar, Kolkata under the auspices of the Gaudiya Mission in October 1930 as part of the rich cultural heritage of Vaishnavism in Bengal. It was here that Abhay Charan De (later known as A. C. Bhaktivedanta) took formal initiation from him, and much later, in 1966, established a global organisation known as ISKCON (International Society for Krishna Consciousness) with its headquarters in Mayapur, West Bengal.

Two aspects of this second part of Bhaktisiddhanta's life require critical consideration. One was his view of varnasrama as articulated during this period, and the other was his evolving thought on Chaitanya bhakti. As regards the first, Bhaktisiddhanta's intention was not to start a social reform movement, but to raise critical spiritual arguments against it. He considered the contemporary caste system as an inferior social construction, which was inadequate as a tool for Vaishnava bhakti. At one stage, he even went to the extent of making Vaishnava bhakti the essence of a new varnasrama, which would only distinguish people on the basis of whether they had this bhakti or not. In this, he partly agreed with Mahatma Gandhi's ten questions to Shastri Parishad on untouchability as formulated in December 1932, but partly disagreed, in that he opposed it not only from a social perspective, but also through spiritual considerations. For all practical purposes, his advanced view on the caste system by the mid-1930s was conflicted, as evident from his letter dated 6 April 1935 (Sardella 2013, 120). It is probable that he took a cautious position on the matter only for the sake of wider acceptability and viability of his bhakti movement.

Chaitanya bhakti, on the other hand, was a deep-rooted concept in Vaishnavism, which Bhaktisiddhanta had formulated in a particular way in his lifetime. As argued by Dipesh Chakrabarty, confusion about a liminal space in colonial and indigenous society gave birth to a notion of 'homelessness', at the mental and cultural level (Chakrabarty 2002). Extending this concept of homelessness to an esoteric level, Sardella postulates that for Bhaktisiddhanta, this was not just a product of colonial displacement but 'a primary existential condition of humanity, born of the tension between the forces of nature (*prakriti*) and its alleged metaphysical root (*aprikiti*)' (Sardella 2013, 104). Viewed from this perspective, what Bhaktisiddhanta did was merely harmonise the two through the medium of bhakti intrinsic to itself. He rejected the modern Vedantic model of work (*seva*) for the uplift of the masses as an equivalent of divine worship because of its failure to address people's existential problems with regard to bhakti. Through Chaitanya bhakti, he also made clear his opposition to political activism that associated Krishna with the process of nation-building. In this sense, he did not subscribe to the views of Bankimchandra, who was known to his father Bhaktivinoda, nor did he accept Bipin Chandra Pal's belief that God unfolded through the material and social evolution of humanity. Bhaktisiddhanta firmly believed that *jiva* was a metaphysical being, while the body and mind were the products of nature. This distinction makes room for a special place for bhakti at all times, for all human beings together. This pure bhakti could never be motivated by anything other than pure love, which happens to be an end in itself.

Bhaktisiddhanta passed away on 1 January 1937, leaving behind a crisis of succession in his order. He had had a will registered as early as 1923, but controversies arose in its interpretation. He had, however, also left his last instruction—that ten to twelve senior disciples should form a governing committee to run the Chaitanya movement launched by him. Although this instruction was not carried out immediately for various reasons, it was given a new lease of life much after his death, in the third and fourth quarters of the twentieth century, when the global organisation of ISKCON was formed. But that is a different story so far as our narrative is concerned.

Bhaktisiddhanta and Vaishnavism in Bengal: A Hidden and Pronounced Legacy

It is now time to conclude this brief study on the making of Vaishnavism in Bengal in the late nineteenth and early twentieth century, and the evaluation of one of its principal instrumental agency. Our first question is: What is the significance of this 'making'? We agree that this cannot be comprehended without reference to what happened during the Bengal Renaissance of the nineteenth century, and the deep impact it had on the way religious thoughts were reformulated. The unusual importance given to Advaita Vedantic thought was accompanied by the simultaneous degradation of popular Vaishnavism. In this context, we have evaluated the significance of the making of Vaishnavism in the lifetime of Bhaktisiddhanta Saraswati. We have been concerned here only with his efforts to rejuvenate Vaishnavism in its local context, keeping its global dimensions out of the purview of our study for the time being. In this sense, we speak here only to its 'limited' historical significance.

We have also touched upon several religious and philosophical issues. Non-dualism is one of them. We have provided a social, religious, and intellectual account of its development in the nineteenth century, as well as of its many later variants. We have focused on a number of luminaries of modern Bengal, such as Rammohan Roy, Bankimchandra, Vivekananda, and Bhaktisiddhanta. Monotheism and theism were often juxtaposed, and their synthetic balances highlighted. It is in this context that we should take Chaitanya bhakti not only as another religious and philosophical issue, but also as the one that was historically reformulated in the process of social and cultural change in Bengal. Bhaktisiddhanta was the pivotal agent here, although he had many opponents, at the intellectual, social, political, and philosophical levels. Even so, the universal significance of Chaitanya bhakti at the existential level of humankind cannot be denied.

Third, it has also been argued that Bhaktisiddhanta was instrumental in the making of Vaishnavism to such a large extent because of his following of a variety of what has been called modern traditionalism (that is, a reinterpretation of tradition along modern lines) as a methodology. There is no denying the fact that he was himself the product of bhadralok society, with access to both Western and Indian traditional education; but in his intellectual and spiritual journey, he largely deviated from the bhadralok trajectory. Elsewhere, Pradyot Kumar Mukhopadhyay has explained this methodology (of modern traditionalism) as originating mostly in a particular trend of philosophical studies in Bengal in the twentieth century, with particular reference to the work of philosophers such as Krishnachandra Bhattacharya and a number of his followers in the first half of the century (Mukhopadhyay 2018, 48–50); however, its religious aftermath has not been studied. It is well-known that Bhaktisiddhanta made traditional religious thinking more apt and up-to-date with the use of such instruments and artefacts as modern associations, printing press, periodicals, and leaflets, but I believe there must be something more in his venture and his entire philosophising of the Vaishnava bhakti movement in the current context, which is to be explored in future.

Finally, as Sardella has argued, in his making of Vaishnavism in Bengal, Bhaktisiddhanta laid special stress on a kind of Vedantic personalism, an idea which not only came as a clarification of the core of Vaishnava philosophy from one of its most important protagonists in modern Bengal, 'but it was also a reaction to turn toward impersonalism (or non-dualism) in modern Hinduism' (Sardella 2013, 236). Bhaktisiddhanta considered the process of bhakti as transformative for the self, which in its turn shared a social world of 'emotions, relationships and consciousness' that impacted on human beings. In this sense, bhakti had the potential to change the collective values and objectives that formed the basis of human society. It was his belief that by changing the quality of human consciousness, 'it was possible to reach a state where the non-material self could be free from the worldly constraints and realize the true potential of personhood' (ibid., 223). This is in sharp contrast to Ranajit Guha's view of bhakti, as 'an ideology of subordination *par excellence*' in its social, economic, and political connotations (Guha 2005, 259). However, for Bhaktisiddhanta, the role of suddha bhakti is crucial here. There is reason to believe that this idea and practice of religious personalism was perfected only in the second part of Bhaktisiddhanta's life. On the surface, the thought and practice may seem a-historical; yet there is scope for situating it in different times at a deeper level. We have not done this. Such an exercise requires further research on and exploration into modern Vaishnava personalism.

Last but not least, a brief comment on our epithet 'limited' as far as Bhaktisiddhanta's biography is concerned in this narrative of the making of Vaishnavism in Bengal. As we have already indicated, we deliberately avoided all global aspects in this narrative. Such a narrative was given its classic expression when Hinduism, cloaked as culture, was spread from a region such as Bengal to a wider global arena, as it did in the nineteenth and twentieth centuries (Sartori 2008, Ch. 4). Obviously, the global aspects became most pronounced when ISKCON was formed, which led to a renewed emphasis on Krishna consciousness at an international level. But is posterity the only guide of the past (future of the past), or does the past also incorporate rudiments of the future (past leading to the future)? Whatever the answer, we consider the study of Chaitanya bhakti a valid subject for understanding the history of Vaishnavism in modern Bengal, without ignoring the separate significance of its illustrious offshoot, Krishna consciousness, developed at the international level in a later period.

Endnotes

1. When it was founded in Calcutta in that year, noted personalities such as Sisir Kumar Ghose, founder of the *Amrita Bazar Patrika*, and Bipin Bihari Goswami, a caste leader from Bhagnapara, actively supported it by regularly attending its meetings. 'Young Bimala also attended and

through his father met many of the leading Vaishnavas in Bengal as well as the other important members of the *bhadralok*' (Sardella 2013, 65).

2. Both were important traditional Sanskrit scholars in Calcutta in the last quarter of the nineteenth century, but very little is known about them.

Select References

Bhaktivinoda, Kedarnath Datta. 1916. *Svalikhita Jivani* (in Bengali), Lalit Prasad Datta (ed.). Calcutta: Lalit Prasad Datta.

Bimala Prasada Siddhanta Saraswati. 1899. *Bange Samajikata: Varna o Dharmagata Samaja* (in Bengali). Calcutta.

Chakrabarty, Dipesh. 2002. *Habitations of Modernity: Essays in the Wake of Subaltern Studies*. Chicago: Chicago University Press.

Chakrabarty, Ramakanta. 1985. *Vaishnavism in Bengal, 1486–1900*. Calcutta: Sanskrit Pustak Bhandar.

______. 1996. *Bange Vaishnava Dharma: Ekti Aitihasika ebang Samajtattvika Adhyayana* (in Bengali). Kolkata: Ananda Publishers.

Guha, Ranajit. 2005. 'Dominance without Hegemony and its Historiography'. In Ranajit Guha (ed.), *Subaltern Studies 6: Writing on South Asian History and Society*. New Delhi: Oxford University Press.

Kaviraj, Sudipta. 1995. *The Unhappy Consciousness: Bankimchandra Chattopadhyay and the Formation of Discourse in India*, SOAS Studies on South Asia. New Delhi: Oxford University Press.

Kopf, David. 1979. *The Brahmo Samaj and the Shaping of Modern Indian Mind*. Princeton, N.J.: Princeton University Press.

Mukhopadhyay, Pradyot Kumar. 2018. *Bingsha Shatake Bangalir Darshan Charchar Ruprekha* (in Bengali). Kolkata: Sutradhar.

Nicholson, Andrew. 2011 [2010]. *Unifying Hinduism: Philosophy and Identity in Indian Intellectual History*. New York: Columbia University Press, and Ranikhet: Permanent Black.

Pal, Bipin Chandra. 1973. *Memoirs of My Life and Times*. Calcutta: Bipinchandra Pal Institute.

Sardella, Ferdinando. 2013. *Modern Hindu Personalism: The History, Life and Thought of Bhaktisiddhanta Saraswati*. New York: Oxford University Press.

Sartori, Andrew. 2008. *Bengal in Global Concept History: Culturalism in the Age of Capital*. Chicago: Chicago University Press.

Urquhart, W. S. 1928. *The Vedanta and Modern Thought*. London: Humphrey Milford.

Ward, William. 1817. *A View of the History, Literature and Religion of the Hindoos; Including Translations of Their Principal Works*, 2 vols. London: Committee of the Baptist Missionary Society.

Periodicals

Sajjanatoshani, Bengali periodical published monthly by Bhaktivinoda, and edited by Bhaktisiddhanta from 1914.

The Harmonist. Sree Sajjana-toshani, English and Sanskrit monthly published from Calcutta, 1927–1936.

3

The Fallen Woman and the Saint

The *Baishnabi* in Colonial Bengal

Varuni Bhatia

In his singular essay, 'Bangiya Baishnab Dharme Striloker Sthan,' Ramakanta Chakrabarty provides us with a critical appraisal of the role of women in Bengali Vaishnava traditions—both in its doctrinal aspects and in its historical expressions (Chakrabarty 2001, 85–95). The essay is among the first of its kind that elaborates upon the histories of significant women leaders who contributed to the consolidation and spread of Vaishnavism in early modern Bengal. These women appear in Vaishnava hagiographic literature as initiating gurus, community builders, influencers, and exemplars. Most of these women, Chakrabarty notes, happen to be the wives, daughters, and daughters-in-law of the primary disciples of Chaitanya. The lives of older and prominent Vaishnava women, both theologically significant ones such as Radha and the *gopi*s (the milkmaids who adore Krishna in Vaishnava theology), as well as historically crucial ones such as Sita Devi, the wife of Advaita Acharya (Manring 1998, 2004), or Jahnava Devi, the wife of Nityananda (Brzezinski 1996; Chakrabarty 2001), raise an important question for us: How do exemplary and prominent women in Bengali Vaishnavism relate to the ordinary female Vaishnava? The presence of female gurus notwithstanding, how did ordinary Vaishnava women relate to the doctrine and praxis of *raganuga bhakti* (erotic devotion), with its firm foundations in the ideal of the *parakiya* (other man's woman)?

The notion of erotic devotion remains central to the manner in which *bhakti* (devotion) was conceptualised within Vaishnava doctrine in Bengal and Vrindavan. In Vrindavan, erotic devotion emerges through the growth of a systematic devotional praxis of raganuga *sadhana* (bodily practices), wherein the devotee cultivates a highly emotional state of attachment to the divine being, Krishna (Haberman 2001). Chaitanya's close disciple, Nityananda, was closely associated in Bengal with the development of this type of devotion. In colonial Bengal, practitioners of *sahajiya* ('sexo-yogic' practices) were particularly identified as the spiritual descendants of Nityananda. Most sahajiya groups were considered to belong to one or the other Vaishnava 'sect' in colonial Bengal, while some were decried as being 'deviant' sects (Bose 1927, Dasgupta 1995 [1946]). In contemporary times, the Bauls of Bengal and Bangladesh are most closely associated with sahajiya practices and, because of this, the lives of Baul women are often seen as being in a dichotomous relationship to the pietistic lives of the Vaishnava *bhadramahila* (middle-class woman), with her concern for domesticity and everyday ritualistic religiosity (Knight 2011; Sarbadhikary 2015).

The lives of middle-class Vaishnava women such as Rashsundari Devi (1809–1890) and Nagendrabala Mustafi (1878–1906) remind us of a world of domesticity and virtue run by men, where piety and devotion become instruments of agency (Sarkar 2001; Walsh 2004). Both Rashsundari and Nagendrabala were published authors by the late nineteenth century, and both wielded their pens primarily to express devotion. In the process, though, they were successful in inserting themselves into the pages of a history otherwise written by men. Their lives, however, also provide us a glimpse into the incommensurable experiences of a Vaishnava bhadramahila when compared to a Baul or a Jat-Vaishnav (Vaishnava by caste) woman. One such woman, Binodini Dasi (1863–1941), gained immense popularity as an actor and a stage performer in Calcutta during the late nineteenth century. In her autobiography, however, she sees herself merely as a *patita* (a fallen woman) and a sinner, incapable of being anything except the 'other' woman in men's lives.

In the following pages, I will unpack these parakiya or 'other' women in Bengali literature and history to reconceptualise this category through the lens of women's agency. Parakiya here stands not only for its doctrinal significance within Gaudiya Vaishnavism, but also for its social and cultural ramifications. They are the 'other' women due to their marginal position outside of the mainstream social and cultural mores. In doing so, I show that more often than not, Vaishnava women were as much a product of their caste and class status as they were of their religious affiliations. At the same time, the erasure of the devotional element from the lives of these women renders them vacant in a significant manner. Hence, it is important to understand them as simultaneously constituted by their religiosity and by their social status.

Unpacking the 'Fallen Woman': The *Baishnabi* in Literature and History

Aage besye, pare dasye, madhe madhe kutni
Sarba karma parityajyo ekhon bostumi.

I was a prostitute first, a maid-servant later, and
a procuress in between; now at last I am a Vaishnavi.

(Quoted and translated in Chatterjee 1989, 188, fn30)

There is hardly an image as seductive and secretive as the *baishnabi* (a female mendicant Vaishnava) in Bengali literature from the colonial period. At once erotic and ascetic, beautiful yet unattainable, a subaltern woman unchained by domesticity and yet one with access to upper-caste *bhadralok* households and their inner chambers, the baishnabi emerges as a mystified figure in literary accounts from colonial Bengal. And yet, when one searches for the same elusive baishnabi in the archives, she is most often to be found in spaces of litigation, primarily around rent payment and/or collection and tenancy rights.

Who is a baishnabi? If we go by popular perceptions, constituted in no small part through literary stereotypes, a baishnabi is a female Vaishnava who makes a living by singing and begging—the term most often used in colonial records in this context is 'mendicancy'.

In literary texts, ethnographic descriptions, and missionary accounts, the baishnabi is most prominently represented as a vagabond, whose morals are suspect, and who is always ready to sing for money. The novels of Bankim Chandra Chattopadhyay (1838–1894) go a long way to produce this literary stereotype of a lone, mendicant, wandering woman. His famous novel, *Bishabriksha* (*The Poison Tree*, 1873), contains one of the most evocative characterisations of such a figure in modern Bengali literature. Bankim describes the sudden appearance of a baishnabi in the women's inner quarters in the house of a local landed elite in these words:

> At this moment, there appeared amongst them a *Boisnavi* (female mendicant) exclaiming, '*Jai Radhika!*' (Victory to Radhika).... Looking up, all saw in astonishment that the *Boisnavi* was young and of exceeding beauty.... Her trembling lips, well-formed nose, large lotus eyes, pencilled brows, smooth, well-shaped forehead, arms like a lotus-stalk, and complexion like a *champak* flower, were rare among women.... The *sandal* mark on the *Boisnavi's* nose was long and fine, her hair was braided, she wore a *sari* with a coloured border, and carried a small tambourine in her hands. She wore brass bracelets and over them, others made of black glass. (Chattopadhyay 1884, 53–55)

This baishnabi is clearly marked out as a low-caste woman (actually a man in drag, but that is a different story!), whose presence in the inner chambers is a matter of some consternation. Initially, she is told to leave the women's courtyard and return to her correct place, that is, outside the family's shrine, where mendicants from ritually impure castes are fed once every week. However, she is allowed to stay on when she sings *kirtans* (Vaishnava devotional songs) in an incredibly melodious voice, enthralling the women of the landlord's family.

Bankim's descriptions laid down, in an almost formulaic fashion, the manner in which female members of the Vaishnava orders would be described in literature henceforth. For instance, Melville Kennedy, author of an important early twentieth-century book on Bengali Vaishnavism, referred to Bankim's influential portrayal of the baishnabi in his novel *Bishabriksha* when discussing Vaishnava women in colonial Bengal (Kennedy 1993 [1925]). And Abanindranath Tagore (1871–1951) emphatically stated, 'I have personally seen all that you read in Bankimbabu's novels' while describing the inner chambers of the Jorasanko Tagore household during its daily late afternoon coiffure session, when the women listened to the melodious songs sung by a baishnabi while their hair was being dressed and bangles fitted (Tagore 1944, 51). Ironically, Bankim personally harboured an extreme distaste for the baishnabi, considering her little better than a prostitute. In his capacity as Deputy Magistrate, he had written to the Magistrate of Murshidabad, advising against employing literate baishnabis as school teachers because their 'loose morality ... is separated by a very fine line ... from prostitution' (Chatterjee 1993, 172, fn2).

The most striking aspect of Bengali literary depictions of the baishnabi was the excessive eroticisation of her physical appearance. Her bodily comportment received the most attention and was described in great detail, followed by her association with musical instruments and her voice. In the stories of Bankim and, later, Saratchandra Chattopadhyay (1876–1938), the baishnabi almost invariably carried a *khanjani* (a small percussion instrument) and was always ready to entertain with songs, provided she was adequately reimbursed for her labours. Rabindranath Tagore (1861–1941), in his short story 'Boshtumi', while breaking away from the over-identification of the baishnabi with her sexuality, reproduced yet another stereotype—that of a lone, wandering woman seeking deliverance while remaining enveloped within pathos and personal tragedy (Tagore 1951, 658–668). Here, too, the mystification continues in the language itself, whence the ageing boshtumi remained shrouded in the morning fog as she wandered through the lanes of the village, singing plaintively.

The writings of Lal Behari Day (1824–1892) demonstrate latent strains of sexuality and sexual attraction in his description of how a young widow from a rural landed household became a baishnabi (Day 1874, 225–234). The girl in question was Aduri, who accompanied her mother-in-law on a pilgrimage to prominent regional Vaishnava holy places—Puri, via Shantipur and Nabadwip. During a particularly impassioned and vigorous kirtan performance by a *bairagi* (a Vaishnava mendicant), Aduri was asked to become his partner. She accepted initiation (the term used is *bhek*, literally, 'garb') and joined the ranks of the bairagis. Lest we think her life was one of humiliation and begging thereafter, we are told that years later, the same Aduri, now a well-established baishnabi, saved the life of her erstwhile mother-in-law after she had been abandoned on her way to a pilgrimage by her own co-travellers.

While literary accounts and memoirs romanticise the figure of the baishnabi by turning her into a mysterious and seductive beauty on the one hand, or a bundle of pathos and tragedy on the other, she appears in religious tracts, both Christian missionary and Hindu reformist ones, most prominently as the female assistant who abets the sahajiya devotional practices of the male bairagis. In these descriptions runs a deep anxiety concerning the baishnabi as a woman in possession of sexual energies untamed by marriage and domesticity, who was, simultaneously and for that very reason, most vulnerable to the ills of prostitution. Melville Kennedy defines baishnabis as 'maid servants' who, 'as a rule ... are also concubines' (Kennedy 1993 [1925], 170–171). An administrative report on the district of Maldah stated, in a matter of fact fashion, that the bairagis of this district would gather annually at the Ramkeli fair to find themselves a temporary partner, leading to the popular saying that 'the bairagi buys his wife at the Ramkeli *mela* (fair) for Rs. 1–4' (Lambourn 1918, 32–33).

Female Vaishnavas were considered nothing more than an instrument of their male partners' spiritual endeavours—*sevadasis* (female companions and/or servants) who lacked agency. Additionally, the baishnabi was perceived as a common prostitute. These stereotypes circumscribed the baishnabi within the triad of her body, her voice, and her sexuality, and delimited her from the world of productive labour on the one hand, and her own desires and aspirations on the other. Recent ethnographies of the female performers of sahajiya devotion (Knight 2011; Sarbadhikary

2015) across the religious and national identities that run through the Bengali-speaking region of the globe question these notions. Lisa Knight, in her study of Baul women, notes that they do not think of themselves as mere appendages to their male partners' sadhana. And yet, they often struggle with the chasm between the respectability afforded by the tag of 'wife' and being a 'good Baul' (Knight 2011).

In colonial-era sources—from administrative reports to literary works—there is a striking overlap between how a woman ended up as a baishnabi and as an entertainer and sex-worker (*baiji*, *beshya*). The slippage between the figures of the baishnabi and the beshya was not merely a literary trope. It made its way into the accounts of missionaries and administrators as well, who used this information as yet another piece of evidence to discredit the entirety of Bengali Vaishnava traditions (Bhatia 2017). The question of caste, however, remained central to such slippages. Between 1858 and 1875, women belonging to ritually and economically marginalised castes, such as 'barbers, milkmen, malis, jugis, kaibartas, and Haris,' were amongst the largest group of migrants in Calcutta participating in sex-work (Chatterjee 1993, 161). It is also around the same time that women, often from similar backgrounds, were starting to enter the newly emerging world of Bengali theatre for the first time. It is not unlikely that many of these women came from families that practised Vaishnavism—some of them may even have been Jat-Vaishnava, such as Binodini Dasi. William Ward mentions in his writings that '[a]t Calcutta nearly all the women of ill-fame profess the religion of Choitunyu at their death, that they may be entitled to some sort of funeral rights' (Ward 1815, 174). Chatterjee argues that while many baishnabis were not involved in formal sex-work, they were often understood to be prostitutes by colonial officials and by bhadralok reformers equally. Vaishnava *akharas*, a kind of monastic residence attached to a shrine, became 'places of refuge for many destitute women,' which later were considered nothing more than dens of prostitution (Chatterjee 1993, 165).

The akhara was a key Vaishnava institution in eastern India during the early modern period, continuing into the colonial period. The akhara and similar cenobitic institutions allow us to recast the figure of the female ascetic beyond her body, voice, sexuality, and personal tragedies, and within a more nuanced and complex set of relationships that include questions of land, property, tenancy rights, inheritance, and spiritual authority (Kasturi 2009). Vaishnava akharas and *maths* in Bengal and north India were similar to institutions such as the *samgha* (Buddhist monastery) and *khanqah* (Sufi hospice), insofar as they were 'collective residential organisations of novice monks, the ordained, and dedicated lay disciples' (Chatterjee 2013, 36–37). These institutions have historically been spaces that connected vast landscapes into a 'monastic geographicity', which included land grants, patronage, sacred kinship based upon discipleships and guru lineages, as well as a range of conjugal agreements, including but not limited to marriage (Chatterjee 2013, 98–103). It was not unheard of for women to head a monastic institution such as the math or the akhara. This was especially true for women who were involved in kinship relationships with one or more male members of the institution, ranging from sexual partners to gurus and mother(-figures). Such practices, however, would be frowned upon by colonial law, which viewed asceticism through the lens of strict celibacy (Kasturi 2009).

Vaishnava akharas in Bengal, too, allowed women to reside therein, and women were able to assume positions of authority as well. For instance, the Vaishnava journal *Shri Bishnupriya Patrika* carried an article on the *shripat* or 'seat' of Nakul Brahmachari in Ambika (Anonymous 1890, 21–24). The article rued the denigration of the holy spot because it was now in the control of two women, one of whom had been a companion of the last *mahanta* (caretaker-priest) of the shripat. The reformist authors took this opportunity to strongly criticise the presence of women in these monastic residences attached to a temple, and laid down the necessity of maintaining the distinction between householder Vaishnavas and monks, where the latter had to be celibate. The presence of women was deplored as a form of 'pollution' rendered upon the holy space by a couple of 'black sheep' (*kulangar*). Thus, in purging women from any kind of managerial, administrative, or authoritative positions in monastic institutions, colonial law and Hindu reformers often worked in tandem.

After the Permanent Settlement of Bengal in 1793, the range of 'ownership' rights of women associated with monasteries were severely curtailed—especially with the debates around the question of women's inheritance being resolved bearing the upper-caste Hindu wife in mind (Chatterjee 2013). Court cases from the twentieth century concerning women who carried the last name 'Baishnabi' bear out this 'infrastructural power' of the state (Singha 2003), where colonial law worked to define the baishnabi (in all likelihood, Jat-Vaishnava women) as either a small-time cultivator or a prostitute. A 1939 case bears out how one Raj Kumari Baishnabi, daughter of Chandra Nath Pramanik, becomes key in defining who exactly constitutes the 'raiyat' under Act 10 of the Bengal Rent Act of 1859.[1] The act defines 'raiyat' as an 'actual cultivator', where substantial portions of the land were still under cultivation. Raj Kumari Baishnabi, it was alleged by the plaintiff Mirja Shamsuddin, had been using the land not for cultivation, but for residential purposes. Baishnabi, it was noted by lower courts, had been in possession of this piece of land since 1914 and had used it for cultivation until 1918, after which date it had been in use for residential purposes. The lower court had decreed that the use of the land was not for cultivation, and hence the transfer of land to her in 1914 under Act 10 of the Bengal Rent Act did not apply. Baishnabi filed an appeal petition against the ruling of the Deputy Commissioner of Darjeeling to the Calcutta High Court, which upheld her right as a 'raiyat' and granted her occupancy rights on the said land. In another case, involving Kalikumari Baishnabi and Monomohini Baishnabi, the final decision rested heavily on the fact that the plaintiff, Kalikumari, was 'a prostitute, and leased the defendant's [Monomohini] house for subletting it to prostitutes'.[2] Instead of returning the security deposit, Monomohini had handed over a promissory note of Rs 500 to Kalikumari upon the latter vacating the premises. But she was unable to pay and hence Kalikumari took the matter to the court. The Calcutta High Court dismissed Kalikumari's appeal to recover the remainder of the security deposit that was owed to her. In its decision, the Calcutta High Court noted that '[t]he whole contract as evidenced by the promissory note in this suit is the repayment of the balance of the security deposit for the lease of the house taken *for immoral purposes*'. The use of the premises for 'immoral purposes' was cited as the reason for dismissing this appeal.

Hence, in the colonial period, we can see the baishnabi's participation as a stakeholder in Vaishnava monastic geographicity in Bengal being severely curtailed by colonial law as well as bhadralok religious reformers. Simultaneously, the baishnabi was increasingly being defined by her caste and class location—as a small-time peasant, a tenant and sub-tenant, or a sex-worker. The latter would emerge as the most damning, and perhaps the most permanent, of these definitions.

The 'Fallen Woman' on Stage: Acting and Becoming Chaitanya

It is in this broader historical context that one needs to situate the life story of one remarkable woman of Calcutta's nineteenth-century theatre world—Binodini Dasi. Binodini was born in Calcutta into a Jat-Vaishnava family, comprising her mother and grandmother. She had a younger brother who died at a very young age, leaving her mother disconsolate with sorrow. Her grandmother and mother rented out accommodation to poor working-class individuals and families in Calcutta. The descriptions provided by Binodini suggest that some of their tenants were women who earned their living by entertaining patrons through song and dance. Binodini was introduced to the theatre at the tender age of ten—or perhaps even younger—by the patrons of one of the tenants whom Binodini admired a lot (Dasi 1969). The absence of a male figure in the household and the references to tenants who were not couples in a normative, conjugal sense, and who could be heard verbally abusing each other all night, suggest that Binodini spent her early years in a context that William Ward would certainly have described as replete with 'women of ill-fame' and which Bankim (notwithstanding his appreciation of her acting talents) would have called 'loose morality'. Indeed, the charge of prostitution never left Binodini who, on multiple occasions in her memoirs, referred to herself using terms of humiliation and lowliness, including prostitution (Bhattacharya 1998, 37).

Jat-Vaishnavas were a sect of subaltern Vaishnavas who were inspired by Nityananda's raganuga bhakti, and who worshipped Chaitanya as a deity (Das 1960). By the eighteenth century, all those who followed raganuga devotion came to be recognised as a separate community 'who had renounced their *varna*, *gotra*, and caste identities to become Vaishnavas' (Bandyopadhyay 2004, 85). During the colonial period, several householder Jat-Vaishnavas, who were increasingly being recognised as a separate caste, tried to embrace a life of social orthodoxy by practising endogamy and Hindu marriage rituals (Das 1960). Binodini's life, however, was a far cry from the kind of domesticity and respectability that the Jat-Vaishnavas of Bengal were endeavouring towards in this period. She joined the world of Bengali theatre in its infancy, and rose quickly to become a prominent performer on stage. Soon, Binodini was playing the lead character in many popular plays. At the height of her thespian glory, in the early 1880s Binodini performed the role of Chaitanya in Star Theatre's adaptation of *Chaitanya-Leela*, a drama based on Chaitanya's life by the well-known dramatist, Girish Chandra Ghosh (1844–1912).

In her landmark study of Binodini, Rimli Bhattacharya argues that invoking the devotional paradigm to understand Binodini's stage performance as Chaitanya Mahaprabhu undermines the labour that goes into such a task (Bhattacharya 1996, 1998). In this chapter, I ask if it is possible to go beyond the dichotomy between the devotee (looking for salvation) and the worker (whose redemption lies primarily in her labours). I do so by (re)introducing the praxis of Vaishnava sadhana where the individual uses both her mental faculties and her physical senses to develop a perfected inner self. How do Binodini's own writings help us to reconceptualise the particularities of this sadhana? What happens to the almost exclusively male praxis of raganuga sadhana, which borrows in no mean fashion from Sanskrit dramaturgy and takes the practice of imitation very seriously, when a female stage actor attains similar results in the course of playing a role? In short, can the female actor be momentarily transformed into an androgynous saint in the process of imitating and embodying on stage?

In his study of bhakti saints, John Stratton Hawley invites us to consider the exemplary aspects of these iconic figures, where the saintly figure operates as a paradigm for others to follow in the path of devotion (Hawley 1987). In a different but related vein, A. K. Ramanujan argues that the bhakti saints of India display certain tropes of sainthood, primary amongst which is occupying a liminal, in-between space (Ramanujan 2004). This could be between man and woman, god and devotee, or sinner and saint. Hence, an upper-caste saint must eschew his caste privileges, while a lower-caste saint must show evidence of his inner purity in hagiographic accounts. Women saints break the paradigms of domesticity, stability, and that of the 'good wife' to adopt masculine and/or itinerant ways of being. We see all these at work in the image of Chaitanya as a medieval bhakti saint. He is both householder and ascetic, a stickler for Brahmanical norms as well as its greatest opponent, androgynous, and, perhaps most importantly, human and divine simultaneously. Could Chaitanya be an exemplar for other devotees to follow? Gaudiya Vaishnava doctrine does not present him as such. Since he is understood to be divine, he does not make himself available for imitation in the same way that the gopis do. Nonetheless, within sahajiya devotional practices and within non-mainstream forms of Vaishnavism in Bengal, Chaitanya was specifically seen as an exemplary figure who could be, and should be, imitated. And Binodini certainly imitated him in the most avant-garde fashion, that is, on the proscenium stage, in the decade of the 1880s.

Binodini's life, when examined through the lens of religion and gender, shows a specifically gendered subjectivity of the otherwise masculine notion of a 'sinner' pleading for deliverance. It is possible that the notion of the patita, the fallen one, operates as a trope in her memoirs rather than being reflective of an authentic subjectivity. Nonetheless, it allows for a gendered constitution of a term that was even otherwise being invoked within the Vaishnava reformist devotional milieu of the late nineteenth century. She refers to her lord as *patitpavan* (saviour of the fallen ones), and begs on multiple occasions to be 'delivered' from this sinful existence. She reflects a keen awareness of the fact that she shall never be a woman who will experience the respectability of married life, or the satisfaction of rearing children (she gave birth to one daughter, who died at a young age). She also reveals a deeply pained consciousness of the fact that her heart, just like her body, will forever be considered up for sale. In her desire for 'respectability', accompanied by her knowledge of its impossibility, she remembers a little-known figure from Chaitanya's hagiographies—the prostitute who was hired to seduce Haridas in order to lure him away from his chosen path of devotion.

The devotional fervour of her writing catapults her life narrative towards a crucial climax—that of playing the role of Chaitanya on stage. This is the role that she is most remembered for even to this day, primarily as a result of later reproductions of her life. That said, she also spends the most amount of time in her memoir talking about playing this particular role, when compared to any of the other characters she had played. It is possible that in doing so, she participates in the very same 'redemptive' narratives that have already been woven around her—as a 'fallen woman' saved by the men in her life, from Ramkrishna Paramhansa to Sishir and Girish Ghosh (Bhattacharya 1996). But her detailed descriptions of her own state of *mind* and *body* while playing the role remain evocative testimonies to a process that was internally transformative for her—regardless of whether or not it was socially redemptive. This role, moreover, came at the pinnacle of her acting career. Binodini retired from the world of theatre soon after playing the character of Chaitanya successfully for a few years.

In *Amar Katha* (*My Story*), Binodini narrates the strenuous training sessions that she had with Sishir Kumar Ghosh (1838–1911), editor of *Amrita Bazar Patrika* and a prominent Vaishnava of the times. She describes the act of rehearsing and playing the character of Chaitanya on stage as nothing short of a form of sadhana. She writes that as a result of Sishir Ghosh's urging, she started meditating upon the 'lotus-feet' of the Mahaprabhu during these sessions. She would pray to him outside of the sessions as well, calling upon him thus: 'O Gaur Hari, saviour of the fallen! Show compassion to this lowly fallen woman!' (Dasi 1969, 44). She recalls the trepidation she felt at her first performance as Chaitanya, where she tried to calm her nerves by doing every sacred thing that she could do—from taking a dip in the Ganges to purify herself to uttering the names of Durga 108 times (ibid., 45)! Then, as she enacted Chaitanya on stage, Binodini speaks evocatively about her inner transformations. Reading her memoirs, one senses that she is no longer playing the *role* of Chaitanya/Nimai, but is embodying him as an adept devotee would in the process of attaining her inner or 'real' form in the eternal play of Krishna.

In raganuga devotion, the devotee must *act* out the role of the intimate associate of Krishna who has been assigned to her/him as their *siddha-rupa* ('ultimately real body', which is revealed through sadhana) (Haberman 1985, 49–50). An adept devotee, however, eventually takes her siddha-rupa to 'unlimited, unpredictable, and spontaneous' dimensions (ibid., 52). In Binodini's narrative, we see a literal unfolding of the act of acting on stage as Chaitanya leading to a state of transformed and heightened consciousness (lit., *chaitanya*) within herself. She speaks of 'developing an internal vision' (Dasi 1969, 45) and feeling as if someone else was speaking through her. Binodini notes how she was unable to distinguish between the stage and the real world. 'I felt as if someone else was speaking from inside my heart. I am no-one. I lost all sense of selfhood' (ibid.). She uses familiar tropes to connote a state of devotional ecstasy, such as horripilation, trembling, weeping, dancing, and, finally, losing consciousness (ibid., 45–46). These characteristics are mentioned repeatedly in the hagiographical corpus associated with Chaitanya as signs of reaching a heightened or ecstatic state of devotion. And while Radha and the gopis experience all of these bodily signs of devotion in Vaishnava literature (Holderege 2015), it is worth noting that ordinary Vaishnava women in Bengal were rarely depicted as participating in this kind of an embodied devotion. Radha, it must be emphasised, was never the preferred exemplar for Vaishnava *women*. When we think of the religious worlds of the Vaishnava bhadramahila from the same period, we notice a sharp distinction, not only from the raganuga kind of sadhana, but also from any kind of imitation or role-playing whatsoever. Women occupied ritual roles, and were usually delegated the responsibility of preparing the worship of the Vaishnava images consecrated at their homes or family temples. Worship itself would be done by either the male authority or (in case the family was not adequately upper caste, such as Bipin Chandra Pal's) a Brahmin priest would be employed for the same purpose.

In Gaudiya Vaishnavism, Chaitanya is understood as simultaneously divine and devotee, male and female. As the playwright Girish Chandra Ghosh noted in his Foreword to her autobiography, Binodini was able to convincingly represent Chaitanya as a divinity who is 'Krishna within and Radha without' (Bhattacharya 1998, 216). We see here a double displacement of her gendered self—as a woman playing the role of a man who is himself pining for his Lord in the manner of a lovelorn woman. Within Gaudiya Vaishnavism, embodied devotion was reserved primarily for men—not doctrinally, but certainly in practice. Men, in Gaudiya Vaishnava devotional praxis, often imagine themselves as women—the intimate girlfriends of Radha witnessing the love-play between Radha and Krishna. For a woman to reach these states of embodied devotion was simultaneously prescriptive and radical. Prescriptive, because she was practising what was in effect a well-established form of Vaishnava sadhana, and radical because her practice challenged the normative gender roles of a respectable Vaishnava woman in contemporary Bengal. Binodini's lack of respectability thus acts as a buffer against the prescriptions of social norms over devotional praxis and allows her to clasp at sainthood, howsoever fleetingly. She illustrates that a woman saint 'fights not with temptation, but with family, husband, molesters.... Not conversion, but the freedom to pursue her god' (Ramanujan 2004, 289). In many ways, the famous words supposedly uttered to her by Ramakrishna when he came to watch her play this role—'May you possess heightened consciousness, beloved daughter!' (Dasi 1969, 47)—articulate what her own narrative points towards: that she was momentarily transformed into the charismatic devotee-divinity while enacting this role on stage. Ramakrishna, far from being the male authority figure who authenticates her experience of devotion, becomes the conduit through which Binodini expresses her state of being in these moments.

Conclusion

In conclusion, I would like to return to the question I began with: What would a feminist historiography of Bengali Vaishnava traditions look like? Taking the practice of raganuga bhakti with the parakiya or 'other' woman at its centre as a key aspect of Gaudiya Vaishnava devotion, I ask how one may (re)imagine the place of women within its devotional praxis. In doing so, I have tried to go beyond the necessary initial step of recovering the lives and actions of key Vaishnava women in order to appreciate the 'other' marginalised women of Bengali Vaishnavism. I show that the ordinary Vaishnava woman—the baishnabi or boshtumi—is as much a product of her caste and occupational location as she is of her gendered self. However, the baishnabi also operates as a powerful trope in Bengali literary traditions, in male reformist narratives, and in Christian missionary writings. In these pages, the female Vaishnava turns into a series of negatives—the destitute and vulnerable woman, the tragic and tortured mother, the sex-worker, the beautiful but disreputable singer, and the manipulative beggar.

Taking the thespian Binodini Dasi as an illustrative example, I show how women from Jat-Vaishnava backgrounds were being construed by these very stereotypes of the baishnabi as prostitute. Nonetheless, Binodini herself offers us a brilliant example of how this star of the world of late nineteenth-century Calcutta theatre was able to momentarily but radically intervene in and break existing gender stereotypes around the role of Vaishnava women in Bengal. When read against the grain of how prominent male members of the society represented her life, the passages in *Amar Katha* are a constant reminder to us that the 'fallen woman' does not need a saint for redemption—for the fallen woman, due to her marginal status in respectable society, is the most appropriate conduit for intense, ecstatic devotion. Binodini's remarkable success lies in her ability to bring Chaitanya to the forefront in a rare series of proscenium performances that blur the lines between the actor and the role they are playing.

Endnotes

1. *Raj Kumari Baishnabi vs. Mirja Shamsuddin and Others*. A.I.R. (29) 1942 Calcutta 330.
2. *Kali Kumari Baisnabi vs. Mono Mohini Baisnabi*. A.I.R. 1935 Calcutta 748.

Select References

Archival Sources

All India Reporter. 1942 (29). Calcutta, Nagpur: D. V. Chitaley.

All India Reporter. 1935. Calcutta, Nagpur: D. V. Chitaley.

Lambourn, G. E. 1918. *The Bengal Gazetteers: Malda*. Calcutta: The Bengal Secretariat Book Depot.

Secondary Sources

Anonymous. 1890. 'Shri Nakul Brahmacharir Pat'. *Shri Bishnupriya Patrika* 1 (3), 21–24.

Bandyopadhyay, Sekhar. 2004. *Caste, Culture, and Hegemony: Social Domination in Bengal*. New Delhi: Sage.

Banerjee, Sumanta. 1994. 'The Radhas of Medieval Bengal: Fifteenth and Sixteenth Century Women Poets'. *India International Centre Quarterly* 21 (4), 27–40.

Bhatia, Varuni. 2017. *Unforgetting Chaitanya: Vaishnavism and Cultures of Devotion in Colonial Bengal*. New York: Oxford University Press.

Bhattacharya, Rimli. 1996. 'Benediction in Performance: Reverberations of the Chaitanya Lila from 1880s'. *Jadavpur Journal of Comparative Literature* 33, 28–63.

_____ (trans.). 1998. *My Story* and *My Life as an Actress*. New Delhi: Kali for Women.

Bose, Manindramohan. 1927. 'An Introduction to the Post-Chaitanya Sahajiya Cult'. *Journal of the Department of Letters* XVI, 1–167.

Brzezinski, Jan. 1996. 'Women Saints in Gaudiya Vaisnavism'. In Steven J. Rosen (ed.), *Vaisnavi: Women and the Worship of Krishna*, 59–86. New Delhi: Motilal Banarsidass.

Chakrabarty, Ramakanta. 1996. *Bange Baishnab Dharma: Ekti Aitihasik ebong Samajtattvik Adhyayan* (*Vaishnavism in Bengal: A Historical and Sociological Study*). Kolkata: Ananda Publishers.

_____. 2001. *Bangalir Dharma, Samaj o Sanskriti* (*Religion, Society, and Culture of the Bengalis*). Kolkata: Subarnarekha.

Chatterjee, Indrani. 2013. *Forgotten Friends: Monks, Marriages, and Memories of Northeast India*. New Delhi: Oxford University Press.

Chatterjee, Partha. 1989. 'Caste and the Subaltern Consciousness'. In Ranajit Guha (ed.), *Subaltern Studies VI*, 169–209. Delhi: Oxford University Press.

Chatterjee, Ratnabali. 1993. 'Prostitution in Nineteenth Century Bengal'. *Social Scientist* 21 (9/11), 159–172.

Chattopadhyay, Bankim Chandra. 1884. *Bishabriksha* (*The Poison Tree*), Miriam Knight (trans.). London: T. Fischer Unwin.

Das, Ajit. 1960. *Jat Baishnab Katha* (*The Jat-Baishnab Story*). Kolkata: Charubak.

Dasgupta, Shashibhushan. 1995 [1946]. *Obscure Religious Cults*. Calcutta: Firma KLM.

Dasi, Binodini. 1969. *Amar Katha o Anyanya Rachana* (*My Story and Other Writings*), Nirmalya Acharya (ed.). Kolkata: Subarnarekha.

Day, Lal Behari. 1874. *Govinda Samanta or The History of a Bengal Raiyat*. London: Macmillan and Company.

Haberman, David L. 1985. 'Entering the Cosmic Drama: *Lila-smarana* Meditation and the Perfected Body'. *South Asia Research* 5 (1), 49–57.

_____. 2001. *Acting as a Way of Salvation: A Study of Raganuga Bhakti Sadhana*. New Delhi: Motilal Banarsidass.

Hawley, John S. 1987. 'Introduction: Saints and Virtues'. In John S. Hawley (ed.), *Saints and Virtues*, xi–xxiv. Berkeley: University of California Press.

Holderege, Barbara A. 2015. *Bhakti and Embodiment: Fashioning Divine Bodies and Devotional Bodies in Krsna Bhakti*. London: Routledge.

Kasturi, Malavika. 2009. '"Asceticising" Monastic Families: Ascetic Genealogies, Property Feuds and Anglo-Hindu Law in Late Colonial India'. *Modern Asian Studies* 43 (5), 1039–1083.

Kennedy, Melville. 1993 [1925]. *The Chaitanya Movement: A Study of Vaishnavism in Bengal*. New Delhi: Munshiram Manoharlal.

Knight, Lisa. 2011. *Contradictory Lives: Baul Women in India and Bangladesh*. New York: Oxford University Press.

Manring, Rebecca. 1998. 'At Home in the World: The Lives of Sita Devi'. *International Journal of Hindu Studies* 2 (1), 21–42.

_____. 2004. 'Sita Devi: An Early Vaisnava Guru'. In Karen Pechilis (ed.), *The Graceful Guru: Hindu Female Gurus in India and the United States*, 51–64. New York: Oxford University Press.

Pal, Bipin Chandra. 1932. *Memories of my Life and Times*. Calcutta: Modern Book Agency.

Saraswati (Mustophi), Nagendrabala. 1902. *Amiyagatha* (*My Own Story*). Kalikata: Saracchandra Chakrabarti.

_____. 1904. *Garhasthya Dharma ba Naridharmer Parishishta* (*Duties of the Householder or Women's Duties*). Bardhaman: Khagendranath Mustophi.

Pauwels, Heidi. 2012. 'Radha'. In Knut A. Jacobsen, Helene Basu, Angelika Malinar, Vasudha Narayanan (eds), *Brill's Encyclopaedia of Hinduism*. Available at https://brill.com/fileasset/downloads_products/35696_mudras.pdf (accessed April 2023).

Ramanujan, A. K. 2004. 'Men, Women, and Saints'. In Vinay Dharwadkar (ed.), *The Collected Essays of A. K. Ramanujan*, 279–294. New Delhi: Oxford University Press.

Sarbadhikary, Sukanya. 2015. *The Place of Devotion: Siting and Experiencing Divinity in Bengal-Vaishnavism*. Berkeley: University of California Press.

Sarkar, Tanika. 1999. *Words to Win: The Making of Amar Jiban—A Modern Autobiography*. New Delhi: Kali for Women.

———. 2001. *Hindu Wife, Hindu Nation: Community, Religion, and Cultural Nationalism*. New Delhi: Permanent Black.

Singha, Radhika. 2003. 'Colonial Law and Infrastructural Power: Reconstructing Community, Locating the Female Subject'. *Studies in History* 19 (1), 87–126.

Stewart, Tony K. 2010. *The Final Word: The Caitanya Caritamrta and the Grammar of Religious Tradition*. New York: Oxford University Press.

Tagore, Abanindranath. 1944 (1351 BS). *Jorasanker Dhare*. Kalikata: Visva Bharati Granthalaya.

Tagore, Rabindranath. 1951 (1357 BS). 'Boshtumi'. In *Galpaguchha*, 658–668. Kolkata: Visva Bharati.

Valpey, Kenneth R. 2006. *Attending to Krsna's Image: Caitanya-Vaisnava Murti-Seva as Devotional Truth*. London: Routledge.

Walsh, Judith. 2004. *Domesticity in Colonial India: What Women Learned when Men Gave them Advice*. Lanham: Rowman and Littlefield.

Ward, William. 1815. *A View of the History, Religion and Literature of the Hindoos*. Serampore: The Mission Press, 2e.

4

Sri Chaitanya, Jagannatha Das, and Puri

Jagannatha Charitamrita Revisited

Kailash Chandra Dash

Introduction

Chaitanya Charitamrita (a biographical study of Sri Chaitanya) by Krishnadas Kaviraj, composed in the first quarter of the seventeenth century, is an imperishable contribution to the Chaitanya movement in eastern India (Dimock 1999, 29–30). It presented a comprehensive study on the life and activities of Sri Chaitanya, besides providing an account of his link with Purushottama-Puri and his association with many famous Odias during the period of Prataparudra Gajapati. But there was no description of his association with the so-called *Pancha Sakhas* (five associates—Jagannatha, Balarama, Ananta, Achuytananda, and Yasobanta). Prabhat Kumar Mukhopadhyay's insightful article, 'Chaitanya Yuger Udiya Vaishnava Gana' ('Odia Vaishnava Songs in the Age of Chaitanya'), hints at Chaitanya's link with Jagannatha Das.[1] However, *Jagannatha Charitamrita*, a popular treatise of the seventeenth century, mentioned, among other aspects, the association of Atibada Jagannatha Das with Chaitanya.[2] This was a biographical study on Atibada Jagannatha Das and was possibly composed after *Chaitanya Charitamrita* gained popularity in Odisha in the seventeenth century. Although this text followed the *Chaitanya Charitamrita* in form, it had many innovations. *Jagannatha Charitamrita* was the first Odia text to narrate not only Chaitanya's life and activities in Puri till his death, but also present a comprehensive account of Vaishnavism in Odisha, which was different from the Vaishnavism of Sri Chaitanya and his Gaudiya followers. Hence, this chapter proposes to revisit the *Jagannatha Charitamrita*, which was composed with the purpose of establishing cordiality between Gaudiya Vaishnavas and Odia Vaishnavas in the light of recent controversies surrounding the identity of Jagannatha Das, the author of *Odia Bhasa Bhagavata*, and Atibada Jagannatha Das.

Jagannatha Charitamrita, Atibada Jagannatha Das, and *Odia Bhagavata*

To begin with, the *Jagannatha Charitamrita* and its author, Dibakara Das, need a fresh introduction. Jagannatha Das was the founder of the Bada Odia Matha, a Vaishnava monastery in Puri, and was the exponent of the Atibada *sampradaya* of the Vaishnava faith in Odisha. He was given the title Atibada and was active in sixteenth-century Odisha and particularly during the stay of Chaitanya in Puri.[3] Dibakara Das was the sixth-generation disciple of Atibada Jagannatha Das, and wrote the *Jagannatha Charitamrita* towards the second quarter of the seventeenth century (Das 1963, 70–76). Of its three editions, the last one, published in 1963, has been accepted as the correct text, and the association of Sri Chaitanya with Atibada Jagannatha has been comprehensively narrated in the second, third, fourth, sixth, and seventh chapters of this text. The most important aspect of this text concerns the real identity of Jagannatha Das. Most of the writers in Odisha and Bengal from the 1930s have accepted that Jagannatha Das, the author of *Odia Bhagavata*, was identical with Atibada Jagannatha Das.[4] The *Odia Bhagavata* was well-known in Odisha during the time of Chaitanya in the sixteenth century, and Jagannatha Das composed it in appreciation of the interpretation of Sridhara Swamy (a native of Odisha famous for his new interpretation of the Sanskrit *Bhagavata*). The *Odia Bhagavata* gave Jagannatha Das no such epithet like Atibada. Still, Atibada Jagannatha Das has been generally accepted as Jagannatha Das, the author of the *Odia Bhagavata*. In 1985, a famous Odia critic, Satchidananda Mishra, pointed out for the first time that Atibada Jagannatha Das of the *Jagannatha Charitamrita* was different from the Jagannatha Das of the *Odia Bhagavata*.[5] His view was contested by another famous literary critic in Odisha, Natabara Samantaray, who emphatically stated that Jagannatha Das was the same Atibada Jagannatha of *Jagannatha Charitamrita* (Samantaray 1985, 553–566).

The context of the *Odia Bhagavata*, as stated in all three editions of *Jagannatha Charitamrita*, has to be examined to test the identity of the two.[6] The 1913 edition of *Jagannatha Charitamrita* mentioned:

> *Bata Ganeshanka Agrare/*
> *Sri Bhagavata Nirantare//*
> *Padhunathanti Sukhapai/*
> *Ganesha Deuthanti Kahi//*
>
> (He used to read Sri Bhagavata before Bata Ganesha, and Ganesha used to help him.)

The 1963 edition, on the other hand, says:

> *Bata Ganeshanka Agrata/*
> *Rachile Bhasa Bhagavata//*
> *Padhuna Thanti Sukhapai/*
> *Ganesha Deuthantikahi//*
>
> (He composed *Bhasa Bhagavata* before Bata Ganesha. He used to read it with pleasure and Ganesha used to help him.)

Satchidananda Mishra stated that in the 1913 edition, there was no reference to the composition of the *Bhagavata* in Odia by Jagannatha Das, as in the same edition (of *Jagannatha Charitamrita*) there was only a reference to his reading of the *Bhagavata*. Both *Rachile Bhagavata* (the *Bhagavata* that was composed) and *Padhile Bhagavata* (the *Bhagavata* that is recited) are different aspects. He also stated that since the 1963 edition had been prepared by the Bada Odia Math founded by Atibada Jagannatha Das, the *Rachile Bhagavata* (composed Bhagavata) was a later addition, intended to prove that Jagannatha Das, the author of the *Odia Bhagavata,* and Atibada Jagannatha Das were the same person. However, Satchidananda Mishra's argument cannot go unchallenged, as he does not seem to have correctly interpreted the 1913 edition. The lines suggest that Atibada Jagannatha Das used to read the *Sri Bhagavata* before Bata Ganesha, who helped him by clarifying his doubts. This does not indicate that he was reading the Sanskrit Bhagavata; the mention of only *Bhagavata* may suggest that he was reading passages from the *Bhasha Bhagavata* (Bhagavata in Odia) before Bata Ganesha, who helped him by checking his translation from the Sanskrit. So the omission of the *Bhasa Bhagavata* composition in the 1913 edition does not really establish that Jagannatha Das was different from Atibada Jagannatha Das. The former, who composed the *Odia Bhagavata,* could not have been a different person who lived during the lifetime of Atibada Jagannatha Das, whose *Odia Bhagavata*—despite the opposition it faced from the Brahmins—was well-known during the period when Chaitanya was in Puri. How could Chaitanya be ignorant of this Jagannatha, given that he did have contact with another Jagannatha, whom he called Atibada?[7] And how did Atibada Jagannatha Das respond to this *Odia Bhagavata* by another, unknown Jagannatha Das?

Again, appreciating Natabara Samantaray, we may also state that in the 1913 edition as well as in the 1963 edition, there is the statement *Padhunathanti Sukhapai* (reading with pleasure; this was a translation into Odia), which is significant in this context.[8] Sarala Das, the author of the Odia *Mahabharata,* which was composed at least 100 years before Jagannatha Das, stated that Devi Sarala had inspired and blessed him while he was writing the *Mahabharata* in Odia, and not the *Mahabharata* in Sanskrit. This was why he called himself Sarala Dasa (a title indicating his submission to the Goddess). Following this, we may state that Bata Ganesha used to help Jagannatha Das while he was writing the *Odia Bhagavata* by clarifying his doubts on the Sanskrit terms and passages in the *Bhagavata.* According to Dibakar Das, many years after the death of Sri Chaitanya, Atibada Jagannatha Das advised his disciples to read the *Bhagavata:*

> *Sri Bhagavata Bhakti Grantha/*
> *Padhiba Suniba Nirata*
>
> (One should always read and listen to Sri Bhagavata, a devotional text.) (Samantaray 1985, 560)

Here, his *Bhagavata* does not mean the Sanskrit *Bhagavata* but his *Prakrita Bhasa Bhagavata* (his *Odia Bhagavata*). He did not refer to the former, which his disciples found difficult to read and understand. Thus, from this perspective, the identities of Atibada Jagannatha Das and Jagannatha Das, the author of the *Odia Bhagavata*, seem closely connected.

Recently, Professor Gaganendranath Dash, in his brilliant article on the *Odia Bhagavata*, presented many interesting arguments, complete with proper interpretations of the context, regarding this identity.[9] He observed that Dibakara Das, in his *Jagannatha Charitamrita* composed in imitation of the *Chaitanya Charitamrita*, provided a context to the Atibada title and Chaitanya's link with Jagannatha Das (of the *Odia Bhagavata*) in order to neutralise the opposition presented by the Gaudiya Vaishnavas to the *Odia Bhagavata*.[10] In fact, Krishnadas Kaviraj's *Chaitanya Charitamrita* had gained wide popularity in Odisha as an authentic text on the life and times of Chaitanya in the early decades of the seventeenth century. But the author was silent on Jagannatha Das, and the cause of this silence is still shrouded in mystery. Kaviraj had no personal contact with Sri Chaitanya, and so his information on Chaitanya's stay in Puri was derived from his contemporaries. Some important persons of the Gajapati of Odisha were connected with Chaitanya during the latter's stay in Puri. But the famous Jagannatha Das, the author of the *Odia Bhagavata* (Atibada Jagannatha Das), is not mentioned as having been in touch with him. One can argue that Jagannatha Das's *Odia Bhagavata* did not become immediately popular and that Sri Chaitanya therefore had no information about him. Jagannatha Das became famous for his *Odia Bhagavata* in course of time, possibly after the death of Chaitanya. As Gaganendranath Dash stated, the Gaudiya Vaishnavas had no interest in the *Odia Bhagavata*, which did not speak of Radha, instead presenting a new character of a gopi called Brundabati.[11] There was opposition to the *Odia Bhagavata* from many other quarters besides the Gaudiya Vaishnavas, who remained active in Puri in the post-Chaitanya period as well.[12] Therefore, a traditional narrative on Sri Chaitanya's connection with Jagannatha Das was offered after the *Chaitanya Charitamrita* attained popularity in Puri. Dibakara Das was a great Vaishnava and belonged to the same group as Jagannatha Das. He appreciated this traditional narrative linking Sri Chaitanya in Puri with Jagannatha Das, the composer of the *Bhagavata* in Odia, and elaborated on the context in his masterpiece, *Jagannatha Charitamrita*.

What Dibakara presented in his *Charitamrita* (hagiographical study on Jagannatha Das) might have been his own construction, as stated by Gaganendranath Dash, elaborated upon with additions like the title Atibada. This title of Atibada for Jagannatha Das was not, however, used by Bhupati Pandita in his *Premapanchamrita*, which he composed following the advice of Chaitanya Das, a follower of Jagannatha Das.[13] *Radha Manjari* and *Dutibodha* (two texts in Odia), composed by yet another Jagannatha Das, contain information about this title of Atibada bestowed upon Jagannatha Das, according to Satchidananda Mishra (1985, 241–253). However, the Bada Odia Math founded by Jagannatha Das was at no time known to have been called the Atibadi Math. According to Mishra, the Atibadi Sampradaya was known to have existed in Bengal in the first quarter of the seventeenth century (Mishra 2002, 48–49). Rupa Kaviraja, the founder of this Vaishnava sect, was not in harmony with the Gaudiya Vaishnavas (Haberman 2001, 98–100). Mishra pointed out that Rupa Kaviraja became Atibadi after following in the path of Jagannatha Das. Contrary to Mishra's view, we may state that Dibakara Das was the first to mention this title for Jagannatha Das in his hagiographical study in the first quarter of the seventeenth century. In that case, Rupa Kaviraja's group must have been popular before Dibakara Das circulated the news about the Atibada title being bestowed on Jagannatha Das. Rupa Kaviraja was criticised as Ativadhi or Ativaidhi for his new interpretation of the works of Rupa Goswami. Rupa Kaviraja was described as a disciple of Srinivasa Acharya or of his daughter, Hemalata Thakurani, who were both followers of Jiva Goswami (Goswamy Sastry 1949, xliii: Haberman 2001, 104). Dibakara Das wrote his *Jagannatha Charitamrita* much after Rupa Kaviraja, and possibly before the end of the seventeenth century, in which case Dibakara Das had appropriated the context of Ativadhi or Ativaidhi Rupa Kaviraja for his hagiographical study on Jagannatha Das, and, influenced by the idea of Rupa Kaviraja's Ativaidhi title, constructed the Atibada title for Jagannatha Das. 'Atibada' was more appropriate to Odisha while 'Ativadhi' was popular in Bengal. Later, in the nineteenth century, this group was branded as the Kaviraji group in Bengal and Odisha. In course of time Atibadi became prominent in Odisha as well, and continued to be used.

Satchidananda Mishra is also of the view that Chaitanya's friend Jagannatha Das was a somewhat plump person (*prithulakaya*), also echoed in *Jagannatha Charitamrita,* which justifies the title Atibada (which means 'very big' in Odia). He was also the eldest of all the other Jagannatha Dasas (for instance: Jagannatha Das, one of the sixteen disciples of Atibada Jagannatha Das; Jagannatha Das, a disciple of Haridas Thakur; Siddha Jagannatha Das of Siddha Bakula Math, Puri; Jagannatha Das, a disciple of Gadadhar Pandit, a close follower of Sri Chaitanya; and Jagannatha Das of Navadvipa, a follower of Nityananda) (Mishra 2002, 48–49). So he was, according to Mishra, called 'Atibada' by Chaitanya, which means a senior among many others of the same name. This, however, is incorrect as we have no evidence to connect all these Jagannatha Dasas as having been conversant with Sri Chaitanya in Puri. Second, there is no evidence before Dibakara Das's hagiography, *Jagannatha Charitamrita,* showing that this title Atibada had been bestowed on Jagannatha Das on behalf of Sri Chaitanya. Although there is a reference to a contact between Sri Chaitanya and Jagannatha Das in *Vaishnava Lilamrita,* an Odia text composed by Madhava Pattnaik, who is described as a contemporary of Prataparudra Gajapati, we have considered it inauthentic (Dash 2017, 9–28). On the other hand, appreciating the arguments of Gaganendranath Dash in the context of the opposition to the *Odia Bhagavata,* we may state that after Dibakara Das composed the *Jagannatha Charitamrita* in the early seventeenth century, Bhagavatakara (author of the *Odia Bhagavata*) Atibada Jagannatha Das became famous and was declared to have been associated with Chaitanya, firmly establishing both his position and that of his *Odia Bhagavata*.

Sri Chaitanya, Odia Vaishnavas, Gaudiya Vaishnavas, and *Jagannatha Charitamrita*

The *Jagannatha Charitamrita* is a significant text in Odia which provides a new reading of Odia Vaishnavism with Chaitanya at the centre. Although it is a hagiographical study of Atibada Jagannatha Das, the composer of the *Odia Bhagavata*, it provides an interesting perspective on Jagannatha Puri as a significant centre of the Krishna cult of Gaudiya Vaishnavas, who then considered Brindaban the real centre of the worship of Radha-Krishna.

In order to understand the nature of this text, it will be necessary to revisit the immediate context—the post-Chaitanya phase in Bengal till the first quarter of the seventeenth century. The six immediate followers of Sri Krishna Chaitanya, the so-called six Goswamins of Brindaban, were left the task of elaborating and defining the doctrines, creeds, and practices of Bengal Vaishnavism in the post-Chaitanya period (De 1986 [1961], 166–167). Rupa Goswamin first systematised the supreme religious emotion of *bhakti* in his *Bhakti-Rasamrita Sindhu* and its supplement, the *Ujjala-Nilamani* (ibid.). His *Bhakti Rasa Sastra* was a rhetoric of bhakti appreciated as a standard text of amorous sentiment for the medieval Vaishnavas of Bengal in the post-Chaitanya phase. Krishnadas Kaviraj's *Chaitanya Charitamrita* (Madhya Lila) was a summary of both these works. Kaviraj also emphasised on the Madhura Rasa in terms of Vaishnava emotionalism, the Sringara or erotic sentiment of Krishna as the real hero. Jiva Goswamin, in his *Priti Sandarbha*, further refined this accepted theory of the origin and development of Rasa. In the post-Chaitanya phase, Bengal

Vaishnavism presented itself as a deliberate historical religion promulgated by a definite founder, but in the practical workings of the system by the Vaishnava Goswamins, the teachings of Chaitanya (the master) barely found a place. Except for the visual obeisance and homage to Chaitanya and general passages testifying to his identification with the supreme deity, almost nowhere in the extensive works of Sanatana, Rupa, and Jiva can one find any direct reference to his personal views and teachings. Instead, they were concerned with the godhead of Krishna and his *lila*. Thus, the revival of Vaishnavism on an enduring scale in the post-Chaitanya phase in eastern India centred on the attractive personality of Chaitanya, with the enthusiasm and support of the people who served him and his cause in various ways (Sen 2019, 89–90.).

The theology found in the works of Nabadwipa followers was concerned more with simple and direct faith and a depiction of the passionately devotional life of Chaitanya, rather than those of the Brindaban Goswamins. They emphasised *Gaura-Pramaya Vada* (a theory that conferred on Chaitanya a status comparable with that of Krishna himself), which was absent in the teachings of the Brindaban Goswamins. They also focused on the Radha-bhava (the friendly mood of Radha) of Chaitanya, that is, they regarded Chaitanya as encapsulating both Krishna and Radha in one personality (Sen 2019, 229). Sanatana's *Brihat Bhagavatamrita* and its supplement *Laghu Bhagavatamrita* (which was written by his brother Rupa and followed by their nephew Jiva) was an important part of Bengal Vaishnavism. Dibakara Das had well understood the whole object behind the works of the Brindaban Goswamins, who only projected Brindaban as the centre of the Vaishnavas of eastern India, intending their reinterpretation and considerable revision to forge an intimate link between Bengal Vaishnavism and Utkala Vaishnavism. A fresh movement initiated by Rupa Kaviraja and his so-called Ativadhi/Ativaidhi group in Bengal Vaishnavism in the first quarter of the seventeenth century influenced Dibakara to present a new reading of Vaishnavism in eastern India, with Sri Chaitanya and Jagannatha Puri—instead of Vrajaloka or Brindaban—at the centre of his theory.

According to Dibakara Das, Jagannatha Dhama (the centre of Jagannatha Puri) is superior to Brajapura or Brindaban, Ayodhya, Dvaraka, Badrika, Kasi, and many other important centres of pilgrimage in India. Here is the land of *Adimula* (the creator at the very beginning), who is far superior to the ten incarnations of Vishnu, Brahma, Shankaras, Dibakara, and other gods. Dibakara considers Jagannatha the *Sarvatma* (all-pervading spirit). Jagannatha Puri comprises the *Pancha Tirtha*—the Markandeya Sara, Indradyumna Sara, Jagannatha, Baladeva, and the Ocean. It is the seat of two gods—Jagannatha and Baladeva. The *Jagannatha Charitamrita* describes the iconography of Jagannatha with an emphasis on bhakti by citing a discussion between Nityananda and Sri Chaitanya in Puri. In *Jagannatha Charitamrita,* Lord Jagannatha is identified with Sri Krishna, who grants *bhakti* and *mukti* (devotion and deliverance) to the devotees. Dibakara Das imaginatively constructed a discussion between Chaitanya and his companions—the *sad Gosain* (six followers), and others like Jagannatha Das, Sarvabhauma, Odia Kasi Mishra, Jagadananda Chakravarty, Mukunda Datta, Damodar Chakravarty, Haridasa, Srinivasa, Gadadhara, Acharya Gopinatha, and Murari Gupta—in Jagamohana of the Jagannatha temple. He also narrated the meaning of the *Harinama Tattva* (significance of the theory of Hari or Krishna) by citing evidence from the scriptures. There is emphasis on the cult of Radhakrishna and on the *Nirguna Tattva* (theory of formlessness) as well, as he considers the Jagannatha Trinity a symbol for *Nirguna Tattva*. There is also a description of *Raganuga bhakti* (a Vaishnava theory on devotion) in the *Jagannatha Charitamrita*.

Dibakara Das had used Sanskrit lines from *Brahma Samhita* in many places (Samantaray 1981, 45–47). In some of these lines we can detect an explanation for the Jagannatha cult in the *Purushottama Kshetra* (the centre of Jagannatha in Puri) in the dialogues between Nityananda and Sri Chaitanya. This spiritual typology is also evident in the *Chaitanya Charitamrita*. Natabara Samantaray holds that the explanation of the Jagannatha cult in *Jagannatha Charitamrita* was purely a reflection of the ideas of Sri

Chaitanya, as seen clearly in the sixth chapter (Das 1963, 77–87). He further stated that the religious ideas in *Jagannatha Charitamrita* were purely based upon Chaitanya's spiritual philosophy (Samantaray 1981, 44–53). On the other hand, Dibakara constructed the Jagannatha cult in his *Jagannatha Charitamrita* on the basis of the ideas of Chaitanya as narrated in the *Chaitanya Charitamrita* of Krishnadas. Although the Gaudiya Vaishnava philosophy as narrated in *Chaitanya Charitamrita* was based on *Brahma Samhita*, it was actually not related to the Jagannatha cult; however, despite that, Dibakara Das based the cult of Jagannatha on the Radhakrishna cult of *Chaitanya Charitamrita*. His attempt seems to have been to combine Gaudiya Vaishnavism (the Bengal Vaishnavism) with Odia Vaishnavism, with greater emphasis laid on Purushottama Kshetra, the seat of Purushottama or Jagannatha in *Jagannatha Charitamrita*. Within this, the *Radhakrishna Prema Darshana* found a new orientation and brilliant articulation.

The *Jagannatha Charitamrita* became a key source for a comprehensive survey of medieval Odia Vaishnavism for the later writers of both Gaudiya Vaishnavism and Odia Vaishnavism. While in *Chaitanya Charitamrita* Chaitanya was held up as an incarnation of Brajendra Kumar Srikrishna, in *Jagannatha Charitamrita* Jagannatha became the incarnation of Krishna. As stated by Samantaray, Dibakara Das must have reacted sharply to the extraordinary popularity of Sri Chaitanya in Purushottama Kshetra, and the attempt of the Gaudiya Vaishnavas to establish the Prema Darshan of Radha–Krishna before countless believers of Jagannatha (Samantaray 1981, 44–53). In *Jagannatha Charitamrita*, a hagiographical study of Atibada Jagannatha was not the only objective; there were two other objectives besides (ibid., 70–71). The first was to establish and articulate the greatness and significance of Jagannatha, the presiding deity of Puri whom even Chaitanya, the incarnation of Krishna, adored the most, before both Gaudiya Vaishnavas and Odia Vaishnavas. The second objective was to describe the system of worship of this deity and the inner significance of the cult of Jagannatha.

Chaitanya Charitamrita, *Jagannatha Charitamrita*, and the Cult of Jagannatha

As discussed above, *Jagannatha Charitamrita* was singularly important in the seventeenth and eighteenth centuries not only because it was a hagiography of Jagannatha Das, a popular figure in pre-colonial Odisha, but also because it was composed as an articulation of the inner significance of the cult of Jagannatha of Puri for the Vaishnavas of Bengal and Odisha. Dibakara Das appropriated the context of *Chaitanya Charitamrita* because he wanted to describe the cult of Jagannatha through Chaitanya, who had visited and stayed in this area for many years till his death. While Chaitanya, a devotee of Radha–Krishna, found in Jagannatha his only happiness till he vanished into the body of Jagannatha (as cited in *Jagannatha Charitamrita*), Dibakara wanted to establish Puri as the greatest centre of religion before all Vaishnavas. He thereby ignored Brindaban, the seat of the Gaudiya Vaishnavas, which they appreciated as the only centre of Radha–Krishna. The association of Chaitanya with Atibada Jagannatha Das, author of the *Odia Bhagavata*, and Matta Balarama Das during his stay in Puri, as narrated in *Jagannatha Charitamrita*, became the basis for the construction of the so-called *Pancha Sakha* (five disciples) tradition in pre-colonial Odisha, with Sri Chaitanya given the central place. Although Kaviraj's *Chaitanya Charitamrita* provided no description of the association of Balarama, Jagannatha, Achyutananda, Yasobanta, and Ananta (the five disciples), this was stated in *Sunya Samhita* of Achyutananda. Well-known Odia critics like Natabara Samantaray and Satchidananda Mishra have evaluated the *Sunya Samhita* as an eighteenth-century text on the basis of several internal factors (Mishra 2002, 90–148; Samantaray 1981, 1–43, 81–112). Possibly *Jagannatha Charitamrita*, by associating Balarama and Jagannatha with Chaitanya, paved the way for the construction of the *Pancha Sakha* group in association with Chaitanya. While the *Pancha Sakha* tradition was built around the eighteenth century, it was accepted as originally belonging to the sixteenth century because the five disciples were believed to have been the companions of Chaitanya during his stay in Puri. From this point of view, we may regard the *Jagannatha Charitamrita* as a significant text for the study of medieval Vaishnavism in eastern India.

Conceptually, in *Jagannatha Charitamrita* Dibakara Das made a considerable advancement in studies on Chaitanya and his movement in eastern India through a brilliant construction of the idea of Chaitanya in association with Jagannatha Das, and by shifting the sacred centre of the Gaudiya Vaishnavas from Brindaban to Jagannatha Puri. Although considerable emphasis has been given to *Chaitanya Charitamrita* as an important text in the historiography of the Chaitanya movement in eastern India, *Jagannatha Charitamrita*, composed in the mid-seventeenth century, was hardly appreciated. This text not only intended to highlight the *Odia Bhagavata* of Jagannatha Das in eastern India, but it also wanted to combine the Gaudiya Vaishnavas and Odia Vaishnavas in one sacred centre—Jagannatha Puri—despite their different views on Radha (Krishna's divine consort) and Brajalok-Brindaban, the sacred seat of Radha–Krishna. He interestingly combined the ideas of the Radha–Krishna cult of the *sad Goswamis* in the post-Chaitanya phase with those of the Rupa Kaviraja group in his text and created a new theory—a Radha–Krishna cult in the land of the wooden god Jagannatha.

The *Jagannatha Charitamrita* achieved extraordinary popularity in eastern India in the eighteenth and nineteenth centuries, because of which the Atibadi group was included in the religious sects of the Hindus. This sect also came to be well-appreciated by the followers of Chaitanya in Bengal and Odisha (Dutta 1884, 224). From a historiographical standpoint, Dibakara Das's *Jagannatha Charitamrita* was extremely significant as it highlighted for the first time a parallel Vaishnava preacher in Jagannatha Das and his centre, Jagannatha Puri, against Chaitanya and his six followers and their centre, Brajalok-Brindaban, which were presented in the *Chaitanya Charitamrita* of Krishnadas Kaviraj.

Endnotes

1. *Chaitanya Charitamrita* is entirely silent on the association of the *Pancha Sakhas* of Odisha with Sri Chaitanya. However, in his learned article, Prabhat Kumar Mukhopadhyay discussed the association of Jagannatha with Sri Chaitanya. He even quoted from the *Vaishnava Bandana* of Debaki Nandan Das, although this text seems to be unreliable. He found in *Chaitanya Charitamrita* a term called 'Mahasoyar' which he believed related to Jagannatha Das; this, however, is incorrect (Mukhopadhyay 1931, 881–888).

2. Dibakara Das, the author of *Jagannatha Charitamrita*, lived during the mid-seventeenth century (Mahapatra 1969, 87–88). The earliest reference to *Jagannatha Charitamrita* was made by Man Mohan Chakravarty in 1898 (Chakravarty 1898, 340–342). So far, we have three printed versions of *Jagannatha Charitamrita*: one by Sudarsana Nanda Sharma, published in 1913; the second, enlarged version revised by Pandit Janardana Kar was published under the title *Jagannathamrita Gita* or *Sri Jagannatha Charitamrita* in 1927 in Cuttack; and the third and full version was published by the Bada Odia Matha, Puri in 1963.

3. Jagannatha Das was a contemporary of Sri Chaitanya in Puri in the first quarter of the sixteenth century (for details, see Mishra 2002, 58–64; Pattnaik 1935, 585–594; Samantaray 1981, 444–480). According to the *Jagannatha Charitamrita*, Sri Chaitanya conferred the title 'Atibada' (which means 'the best') to Jagannatha Das for his interpretation of the *Bhagavata*.

4. For an example in this context, see Majumdar (1959); Pattnaik (1935); Samantray (1981). The most important article that seeks to establish the identity of Atibada Jagannatha Das and Jagannatha Das, the author of the *Odia Bhagavata*, was written by Professor Gaganendranath Dash and included in the collection *Studies in the Bhagavata*, published by the Institute of Orissan Studies in Bhubaneswar in 1988. (Dash 1988: 149–64). Professor Gaganendranatha Dash has recently enlarged this version with more arguments which he gave me to read. I read and used his arguments with considerable interest (Dash n.d.). I am grateful to Professor Dash for this enlarged version.

5. For the first time in 1985, Satchidananda Mishra, a well-known critic of medieval Odia literature, rejected this conflation of Atibada Jagannatha Das with Jagannatha Das, the author of *Odia Bhagavata*

(Mishra 1985, 241–253). In 1987 the famous Odia literary critic Professor Dasarathi Das stated in an article that Jagannatha Das was different from Atibada Jagannatha Das. He also admitted that Dibakara Das, who composed the *Jagannatha Charitamrita* in the *Nabakshyari* style, concentrated on the founder of the Atibada Odia Matha in Puri, as well as on the significance of the Jagannatha cult. Jagannatha Das had always been conscious of his caste (Brahmin), while Atibada paid no heed to it at all. However, if Jagannatha Das was conscious of the significance of his Brahmin caste, how could he undertake the translation of the Sanskrit *Bhagavata* into Odia, given that Brahmins in his time were not in favour of such translations? Dasarathi Das also stated that Jagannatha Das had composed the *Odia Bhagavata* because he had been instructed to do so in a dream by *Murari* (Jagannatha, Krishna); but in *Jagannatha Charitamrita,* Dibakara Das was silent about this fact. Rather, he stated that Atibada had read and interpreted the *Bhagavata* with the help of Ganesha. This does not provide a strong argument for contesting the identity of Jagannatha Das, because the reference to Murari is found only in the tenth *skanda* of the *Odia Bhgavata.* Had Lord Murari or Krishna appeared to him in a dream, this should have been mentioned in the very first *skanda,* and not at the end.

Thus, the Jagannatha Das who composed *Odia Bhagavata* actually had no such pro-Brahmanical attitude, and therefore was identical with Atibada Jagannatha Das. An important question is: How could Dibakara Das use the Nabakshari style in his *Jagannatha Charitamrita,* which had for the first time been adopted by Jagannatha Das, instead of the style used in *Chaitanya Charitamrita,* which he actually imitated in his work? The text of *Jagannatha Charitamrita* also seems to have been constructed by Dibakara Das to justify the legitimacy of the *Odia Bhagavata* before all opposing groups. So the position of the *Odia Bhagavata* was the central problem before Dibakara Das, for which he seems to have undertaken the task of composing the *Jagannatha Charitamrita.* There were therefore not two Jagannathas but only one Jagannatha Das, who was both Atibada and the author of *Odia Bhagavata* (Das 1987, 147–158).

6. In all printed editions of *Jagannatha Charitamrita,* there is an unmistakable reference to the *Bhagavata* in Odia.

7. The content of the *Odia Bhagavata* indicates that he was a contemporary of Gajapati Prataparudra, and hence Jagannatha Das was a contemporary of Chaitanya. When Dibakara Das wrote about the title

of 'Atibada', which was conferred on Jagannatha Das by Sri Chaitanya, he was referring to Jagannatha Das, the author of *Odia Bhagavata*.

8. In *Jagannathamrita Gita* or *Sri Jagannatha Charitamrita* published in 1927, the lines are:

Bata Ganesanka Agare/
Sri Bhagavata Nirantare/
Bakunathanti Sukhapai/
Ganesa Deuthanti Kahi

(He used to read Bhagavata before the god Bata Ganesha, and the latter helped him, in translation and interpretation). (*Sri Jagannatha Charitamrita* 1927, 6)

In these editions, although different terms such as *Padhunathanti* and *Bakunathanti* were used in the context of the *Bhagavata*, it cannot be identified with the Sanskrit *Bhagavata*. These terms were meant for the *Odia Bhagavata*, which was a literal translation of the Sanskrit *Bhagavata* by Jagannatha Das. Much before the publication of the Bada Odia Math *Jagannatha Charitamrita*, Ratnakara Kara, on the basis of the existing manuscripts in 1932, published his text, which could state that Atibada Jagannatha Das had translated the Odia Bhasa *Bhagavata* (*Odia Bhagavata*) from the Sanskrit *Bhagavata* near Bata Ganesh of Puri, and that people could gather there to listen to it (Kara 1932, 7). Considering this, we may state that there was only one Jagannatha Das during the time Sri Chaitanya spent in Puri, who prepared an Odia version of the *Bhagavata* from Sanskrit, which he used to read in front of Bata Ganesha for revisions, changes, as well as popularity. Hence Natabara Samantaray, who identified Jagannatha Das, the author of *Odia Bhagavata*, with Atibada Jagannatha Das on this basis, is absolutely correct (Samantaray 1985, 559–560).

9. See the reference to Gaganendranatha Dash's article in note 4 above.

10. Dash expanded his theory on the opposition to the *Odia Bhagavata* mounted from several quarters during Sri Chaitanya's stay in Puri and after his death in his recent article, 'Odia Bhagavata by Jagannatha Dasa: Controversies, Conflicts, Schisms—Attempts at Resolution' (Dash n.d.). I am grateful to him for sharing the first draft with me. According to Gaganendranath Dash, another important aspect of the identity of the Odia *Bhagavatakara* (author of the *Odia Bhagavata*) Jagannatha Das and that of Atibada Jagannatha Das was the Nabakshyari style of writing. As discussed earlier, the *Odia Bhagavata* used this style while the *Chaitanya*

Charitamrita did not; the latter followed the *Chaturdasakshyari* (fourteen words) style in most cases. Dibakara Das, who followed the *Chaitanya Charitamrita* style in his *Jagannatha Charitamrita*, appreciated the *Odia Bhagavata* style of writing, which indicated his regard for *Bhagavatakara* Jagannatha Das.

11. See the reference to Gaganendranatha Dash's article in note 4 above.

12. After the death of Sri Chaitanya, the Gaudiya Vaishnavas visited Puri where Chaitanya disappeared into the body of Jagannatha. The *Odia Bhagavata* does not include Radha but introduced Brindabati instead, which the Gaudiya Vaishnavas did not appreciate. So there was opposition to the *Odia Bhagavata* which needed to be neutralised, and Dibakara Das sought to resolve it in his *Jagannatha Charitamrita*, in which he accepted that Jagannatha Das had been born from the laughter (*hasya*) of Radha. This step was no doubt necessary to satisfy the Gaudiya Vaishnavas, for whom Radha was the central element of their philosophy. For a more elaborate context, see the article of Gaganendranath Dash in note 4.

13. *Prema Panchamrita* by Bhupati Pandita, edited by Lakshmikanta Chaudhury. Attempts were made to neutralise the opposition to *Odia Bhagavata* by Dibakara Das in his *Jagannatha Charitamrita*, and later by Bhupati Pandita in his *Prema Panchamrita* (*Five Nectars of Love*), which played a key role in inventing a strategy for reconciliation.

Select References

Chakravarty, Man Mohan. 1898. 'Notes on the Language and Literature of Orissa'. *Journal of the Asiatic Society of Bengal* 67 (3–4), 340–342.

Chaudhury, Lakshmikanta (ed.). n.d. *Prema Panchamrita*. Cuttack: Prachi Samity.

Das, Dibakara. 1963. *Jagannatha Charitamrita*. Puri: Bada Odia Math.

Das, Dasarathi. 1987. 'Dibakara Dasanka Jagannatha Das'. In K. C. Mishra (ed.), *Bhagavata Parichaya*, 147–158. Bhubaneswar: Institute of Orissan Culture.

Dash, Gaganendranath. n.d. 'Odia Bhagavata by Jagannatha Das: Controversies, Conflicts, Schisms—Attempts at Resolution'. Unpublished paper received from Gaganendranath Dash.

Dash, Gaganendranath. 1988. 'Odia Bhagavata by Jagannatha Das and Oppositions to It'. In K. C. Mishra (ed.), *Studies in the Bhagavata*, 149–164. Bhubaneswar: Institute of Orissan Studies.

Dash, Kailash Chandra. 2017. 'Vaishnava Lilamrita Revisited'. *Utkal Historical Research Journal* 30, 9–28.

De, Sushil Kumar. 1986 [1961]. *Early History of Vaishnava Faith and Movement in Bengal*. Kolkata: Firma KLM Private Limited.

Dimock, Edward C. 1999. *Chaitanya Charitamrita of Krishnadas Kaviraj: A Translation and Commentary*. Boston, MA: Harvard University Press.

Dutta, Akshay Kumar. 1884. *The Religious Sects of the Hindus*. Calcutta: New Sanskrit Press.

Goswamy Sastry, Krishna Gopal. (ed.). 1949. *Sara Sangrahah, A Work in Gaudiya Vaishnavism*. Calcutta: University of Calcutta.

Haberman, David L. 2001. *Acting as a Way of Salvation: A Study of Raganuga Bhakti Sadhana*. New Delhi: Motilal Banarsidass.

Sri Jagannatha Charitamrita. 1927. Cuttack: Arunodaya Press.

Kara, Ratnakara. 1932. *Atibada Jagannatha Das*. Cuttack: Saraswata Press.

Mahapatra, Kedarnath. 1969. *Khurudha Itihasa* (*History of Khurda in Odia*). Bhubaneswar: Sarada Press.

Majumdar, Biman Bihari. 1959. *Chaitanya Chariter Upadan*. Calcutta: Calcutta University.

Mishra, Satchidananda. 1985. 'Aneka Jagannatha Das' (Many Jagannatha Das). *Jhankara* 37 (3), 241–253.

———. 2002. *Atitara Varnabodha: Prachina Odia Sahitya Charcha* (*Writings of the Past: Ancient Odia Literature*). Cuttack: Arya Prakashani.

Mukhopadhyay, Prabhat Kumar. 1931. 'Chaitanya Yuger Udiya Vaishnava Gana' (Odia Vaishnava Songs in the Age of Chaitanya). *Prabasi* 31 (1), 881–888.

Pattnaik, Sitaram. 1935. 'Bhaktakavi Jagannatha O Odia Bhagavata' (Bhaktakavi Jagannatha and Odia Bhagavata). *Sahakara* 16 (7–8), 585–594, 681–692.

Samantaray, Natabara. 1981. *Odishara Dharmadharare Panchasakha Parikalpana* (*Construction of Panchasakha in the Religious Tradition of Odisha*). Bhubaneswar: Granthalaya.

———. 1985. 'Bhagavatakara Hi Atibada Jagannatha Das' (Atibada Jagannatha Das is the Composer of Bhagavata). *Jhankara* 37 (7), 553–566.

Sen, Amiya P. 2019. *Chaitanya: A Life and Legacy*. New Delhi: Oxford University Press.

5

Wax, Shellac, and Rabindranath Tagore

An Engagement on Record

Dipannita Dutta and Subhayu Chattopadhyay

Please do remember, when you were busy in your play—
I sang a song at times when withered leaves fall away.
Rabindranath Tagore

Thomas Alva Edison's invention of the 'phonograph', the first recording machine in history, in 1877 paved the way to a new world where sound could be recorded and reproduced at the will of the person/s concerned. It was one of the first technological innovations in the world that could preserve a part of the living self of a human being even beyond their lifetime. Within slightly more than a decade, in 1888, Emile Berliner from Hanover, Germany invented the 'Gramophone', a recording machine that actually passed the test of time in the long run. Initially, nobody could really visualise the machine's enormous potential as far as its entertainment or commercial usages were concerned. It is with the foundation of the Gramophone Company as a syndicate in April 1898 in London that the commercial prospects of the gramophone could be seen as an actual reality in the years to come, in the near future. Therefore, it was initially a tussle between the phonograph and the gramophone, as far as the recording equipment was concerned. The phonograph was a cylinder made of wax, whereas the gramophone was shaped like a disc, and made of shellac. Although the phonograph finally lagged behind the gramophone in the race, mainly because of the difficulty of making several copies from the master record, the former had an edge over the latter in terms of the quality of sound they produced. However, the commercial prospects of both devices did not go unnoticed from the very beginning, and necessary steps were taken in that direction by entrepreneurs to ensure that this technological marvel should travel to different parts of the world, especially from the Occident to the Orient.

Indian Chapter of Sound Recording

By the turn of the twentieth century, both cylinder records and flat disc records had become known artefacts in Indian society. In 1901, the Gramophone Company first opened their branch office in Calcutta, the then capital of the British Indian Empire. However, by that time the cylinder record, that is, the phonograph, produced and distributed worldwide by the French company Pathephone, was already known in this part of the world[1] (De 1990, 3–4). The first public demonstration of Edison's phonograph took place in the USA, which was first reported by the Bengali periodical *Samachar Chandrika* on 9 January 1878 for the knowledge of the Indians. The first public demonstration of the phonograph in India took place in Calcutta, which was reported by *Sambad Prabhakar* on 21 December 1878 (Sharma 2012, 39). The phonographs were commercially introduced in India only after the establishment of the office of the Mutoscope and Biograph Company in Calcutta on 7 July 1901 by J. Watson (Joshi 1988, 147). It is also known that the same company acted as the agent in the sale of gramophone records and equipment in India as well. In this context, it should be pointed out that during the initial years of the twentieth century, the phonograph and the gramophone became symbols of status, and possession of these worthy showpieces was considered an elite affair in this part of the world as only the affluent section of society could afford them. Edison had a clear idea of the Indian milieu and filed a declaration in December 1878 for the grant of patent through his agent, William James Simmons, to market his phonographs in British India (Sharma 2012, 29). India, with its incredibly wealthy Maharajas and Nawabs, was still an alluring destination for novelties and luxury commodities, and this attracted the recording experts of foreign companies keen to further their business interests.

It is interesting to note that during this period, Hemendra Mohan Bose (1864–1916) was the first Indian to venture into this field to make recordings of his own. Bose was a known entrepreneur in contemporary Bengali society, and his entry into the field of sound recording added a new dimension to the ever-expanding sector (Ghosh 1988, 226). With time, competition among recording companies gradually started to become intense, as many of them could understand that in order to ensure their commercial prospects, they had to take into account the cultural tradition, social practices, and contemporary political mood of this country. From a commercial perspective, each company was in dire need of an Indian talent who could represent them; and Rabindranath Tagore, the poet, singer, and composer (who was to be India's first Nobel Laureate later in 1913), was the first and foremost choice for every recording company as the best representative of the spirit of the era and the place. This chapter has been divided into four sections: Tagore's early interaction with the phonograph for commercial purposes, Tagore's recordings for the gramophone, his recordings for Hindusthan Record, and finally, Tagore's recorded speeches and recitations.

Tagore and the Phonograph

It was a common practice of all recording companies all over the world during the initial period to record and reproduce the voices of famous public figures; and their operations in South Asia in general and the Indian subcontinent in particular followed much the same path. It gave them a legitimacy of sorts in the eyes of prospective buyers, which ultimately ensured their commercial interests. For example, the inventor, Thomas Alva Edison, himself recorded a rhyme on 29 November 1877, to be followed later by his recorded speeches such as 'Future of Electricity' (1908) and 'We Should Not Forget' (condemning World War I in 1919), among others (Ghosh 1999, 48–49). The other famous people whose voices were recorded during the early recording era included Theodore Roosevelt, Leo Tolstoy, William Gladstone, Queen Victoria, the poet Alfred Lord Tennyson, and even Florence Nightingale.

However, in India, the much-tested formula underwent a slightly different experience. First, the phonograph or cylinder records made an early appearance here in comparison to the gramophone, if only to establish itself as the newest technological wonder of the West; and the Indian response was one of hesitant acceptance, if not reverence. Second, while in other countries the recordings of leading public figures from the highest level of administration could feature as obvious choices, in India, a British colony, the same recordings of Queen Victoria or Prime Minister Gladstone were considered to have an even greater impact on the common people. Third, considering the commercial prospect of the huge Indian market, the recording companies, using both the phonograph and the gramophone, concentrated on securing the voices of widely accepted figures in India in general and Bengal in particular; and Rabindranath Tagore was the obvious choice on both counts. Finally, it should be mentioned that in Indian recordings, unlike other parts of the world, songs with lyrics and melody were more welcome than speeches and rhymes.

During the late nineteenth century, a few enlightened families of Calcutta kept actively abreast of the latest knowledge as well as inventions/discoveries of the Western world, through different means such as scientific journals, philanthropic patronage to the budding scientific talents of the region, the popularising of scientific and technological thought in the vernacular, or collecting the latest technological tools. The Tagores of Jorasanko was one such family, whose members had realised that the promotion of science and technology was one of the prime needs of the time. Their home in

Jorasanko was in proud possession of a phonograph machine even before the turn of the twentieth century. A private literary club, called the Kham Kheyali Sabha, was established in 1896 at the Tagore home, and listed on the agenda of its first meet was '*Phonograph Jantro Shrobon*' ('Listening to the Phonograph Machine') ('Khamkheyali Sabhar Karjo Bibaroni'). The meeting was hosted by Gaganendranath, Balendranath, and Rabindranath Tagore. Many years later, Rathindranath Tagore, while discussing the proceedings of that Kham Kheyali Sabha in his *Pitrismriti* (*Reminiscences of My Father*), referred for the first time to Hemendra Mohan Bose, better known as H. Bose, and the quality of his recordings (Tagore 1980, 21–22). However, Rabindranath Tagore had been introduced to the recording machine even prior to that, when Jagadish Chandra Bose, the famous scientist, bought a phonograph as his personal possession. Debendra Mohan Bose, the renowned physicist, refers to the phonograph machine owned by J. C. Bose and to recordings of some of the members of the Brahma Samaj (Brahma Society), including Tagore (Bose 1891–1892). Jagadish Chandra was very impressed with Hemendra Mohan Bose's recording technique, and it was he who took the initiative to record Rabindranath's songs on H. Bose's wax-cylinder phonograph records (Home 1958). H. Bose recorded Rabindranath's voice on phonograph cylinders for the first time between 1900 and 1905. Initially, Bose restricted those Tagore records for private circulation only. By the beginning of 1906, he had established his concern, 'The Talking Machine Hall', in Dhurrumtollah Street, Calcutta (present-day Dharmatala Street in Kolkata), and one of his first advertisements in *The Bengalee* was for publicly available copies of cylinder recordings of Rabindranath Tagore, Dwijendralal Roy, a famous poet, playwright, and musician of the time, and a contemporary singer named Satya Bhushan Gupta (*The Bengalee* 1906, 2; see Image 5.1). It seems that what Bose began as part of his personal passion for music had turned into another example of his entrepreneurial venture. He chose the best talents of contemporary Bengal in the field of music and used them to ensure the commercial success of this venture.

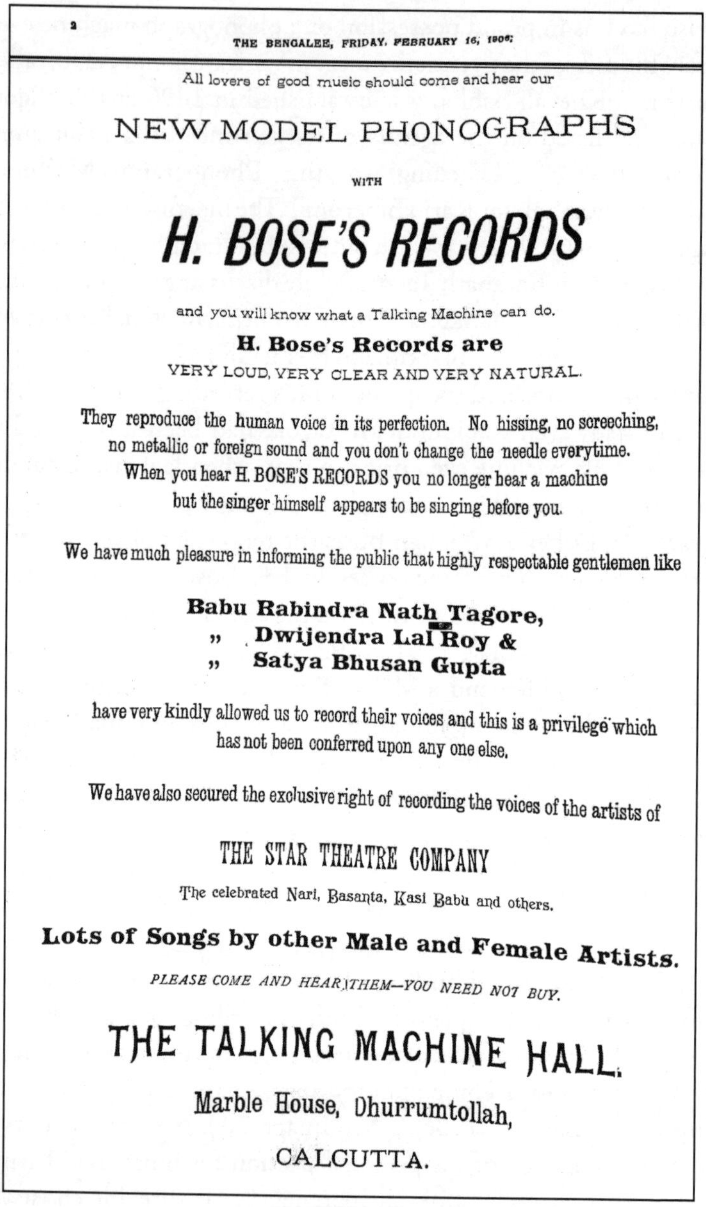

2 THE BENGALEE, FRIDAY, FEBRUARY 16, 1906.

All lovers of good music should come and hear our

NEW MODEL PHONOGRAPHS

WITH

H. BOSE'S RECORDS

and you will know what a Talking Machine can do.

H. Bose's Records are

VERY LOUD, VERY CLEAR AND VERY NATURAL.

They reproduce the human voice in its perfection. No hissing, no screeching, no metallic or foreign sound and you don't change the needle everytime. When you hear H. BOSE'S RECORDS you no longer hear a machine but the singer himself appears to be singing before you.

We have much pleasure in informing the public that highly respectable gentlemen like

Babu Rabindra Nath Tagore,
" Dwijendra Lal Roy &
" Satya Bhusan Gupta

have very kindly allowed us to record their voices and this is a privilege which has not been conferred upon any one else.

We have also secured the exclusive right of recording the voices of the artists of

THE STAR THEATRE COMPANY

The celebrated Nari, Basanta, Kasi Babu and others.

Lots of Songs by other Male and Female Artists.

PLEASE COME AND HEAR THEM—YOU NEED NOT BUY.

THE TALKING MACHINE HALL.

Marble House, Dhurrumtollah,

CALCUTTA.

IMAGE 5.1: Advertisement of H. Bose's Records, in *The Bengalee*, 16 February 1906

Photo credit: Dipannita Dutta.

There is no reference to recordings of Rabindranath Tagore's voice being commercially released before the Partition of Bengal (in 1905). Although H. Bose had had the privilege of recording Tagore's voice on phonograph before 1905, it was the contemporary politico-social and cultural waves splashing through Bengal following the announcement of the plan for Partition by Lord Curzon that surely encouraged him to cash in on the potential presented by the commercial release of Tagore's patriotic songs on records. His business acumen, possibly coupled with his *swadeshi* (nationalist) spirit, led him to approach Tagore (who mostly recorded swadeshi songs, both written and composed by himself) for the 'Talking Machine Hall'. Of those swadeshi songs, special mention may be made of *Bande Mataram, Oi Bhubana Mohini, Sarthak Janam Mago, Jodi Tor Dak Shune Keu Na Ashe*, etc. Tagore also recorded a single recitation of *Sonar Tari* during the same time (Ghosh 1988, 227). The Talking Machine Hall published a two-volume catalogue titled 'H. Bose's Record' from Marble House, Calcutta in March 1906. This catalogue mentioned the titles and numbers of the records containing Tagore's songs for Bose's Phonograph, split into record numbers and the corresponding songs in Bengali (see Table 5.1).

The poet was then around forty-five or forty-six years of age, with a powerful and melodious voice. It is to be remembered in this context that at that time, no electrical method had yet been discovered to either record a voice or regulate volume. The clarity of a recorded voice was solely dependent on its rich and forceful texture. Different accounts of the period in question bear evidence of Rabindranath's melodious and bold voice. In his reminiscences, Rathindranath Tagore has narrated that as a young man, his father was endowed with such a strong and beautiful voice that people would be mesmerised when he sang[2] (Tagore 1980, 21). It should also be mentioned, however, that later generations took the view that Rabindranath's recorded voice was of poor quality and did not match his persona; to the contrary, it sounded somewhat effeminate. But in her reminiscences, Pratima Debi quoted Rabindranath, who himself endorsed the rich quality of his voice[3] (Debi 1962, 56).

Table 5.1: Catalogue of Records of Tagore's Songs

Sl. No.	Record No.	Title
1.	350 *Vande Mataram*	*Vande Mataram*
2.	351 *Sarthok Janom*	*(Sarthok janom amar jonmechhi ei deshe)*
3.	352 *Pather Gaan*	*(Amra pathe pathe jabo sore sore)*
4.	353 *Desher Mati*	*(O amar desher mati…)*
5.	354 *Dwidha*	*(Buk bendhe tui danra dekhi…)*
6.	355 *Hobei Hobe*	*(Nishidin vorsha rakhis, ore mon hobei hobe)*
7.	356 *Baan*	*(Ebar tor mora gaange baan esechhe)*
8.	357 *Eka*	*(Jodi tor daak shune keo na aase)*
9.	358 *Matrimurti*	*(Aji bangla desher hridoy hote kakhon aponi)*
10.	359 *Baul*	*(Je tomay chhare chharuk)*
11.	360 *Baul*	*(Je tore pagol bole)*
12.	361 *Baul*	*(Jodi tor vabna thake phire ja na)*
13.	362 *Baul*	*(Apni abosh holi tobe bol dibi tui kare)*
14.	363 *Prayas*	*(Tor aponjone chharbe tore)*
15.	364 *Baul*	*(Ghore mukh molin dekhe golis ne, ore bhai)*

Source: De 1993, 25–26.

Rathindranath also mentioned that the available records of his father's voice belonged to a much later period, when the poet was older and his voice had lost much of its strength; moreover, even those recordings of the ageing Rabindranath might not have been preserved with adequate care for posterity[4] (Tagore 1980, 22). Therefore, it is clear that the impression about the poor quality of Rabindranath's voice among later generations of people is indeed a misconception. Krishna Kripalani, the famous Tagore scholar, wrote in this context that:

> … the physical voice in which the poems were recited and the songs sung by Tagore in his lifetime has a historical and human interest of its own. It is a pity that when his voice was rich and sonorous there were no facilities for recording

> it. When the facilities were available the voice had lost much of its quality and even what quality was there could not be adequately reproduced as the studios in those days were technically ill-equipped judged by modern standards. This limitation needs to be kept in mind by the listener. (Roy 1971, Foreword)

The above references are proof of the lasting influence of Rabindranath's voice over his audience. However, it is said that a severe throat infection had damaged his tonal quality to a great extent, from which he never recovered fully for the rest of his life (ibid., 4). His address at Manchester University in 1913 bears testimony to the fact that his voice had become distorted, as reported by Shahid Suhrawardy, a student at the university[5] (Ghosh 1988, 226).

Rabindranath and the Gramophone

In 1902, when the recording engineer of the Gramophone Company, Fred Gaisberg (1873–1951), visited India on a recording tour, records of *Brahma-Sangeet* (songs of high philosophical value, indicating the human oneness with the Creator/Almighty) composed by Tagore were already in circulation. The Gramophone Company first opened their branch office at 6/1 Chowringhee, Calcutta in October 1901 and then at 8/2 Dalhousie Square, Calcutta by May 1902 (Sharma 2012, 44). It is evident from the letter of J. Watson Hawd, a representative of the Gramophone Company in India who possessed a shrewd business acumen, that the Gramophone Company was from the beginning in need of records of 'native' songs by 'native' people, because they had realised that only English records would never take them far in this part of the world (De 1990, 6). The poet, his attractive timbre coupled with his creative genius, became an obvious choice to the sound experts of the Gramophone Company. In 1907, when the first record factory was opened at 139, Beliaghata Main Road, Calcutta, the Gramophone Company's foremost choice was *Brahma-Sangeet* in Tagore's voice (Sen 1961).

Prior to the Nobel Prize for Literature being awarded, many songs written/composed by Tagore had started to feature in others' voices on the gramophone records. However, as there was as yet no custom of mentioning the name of the lyricist or composer on the record, Rabindranath Tagore's name as the music composer/song writer cannot be found in these records either. It was in attempt to streamline the prevalent practice and ensure a composer's due that the solicitor Khagendranath Chattopadhyay, on behalf of Tagore, sent a notice to the Gramophone Company on 10 March 1915, asking them to pay his client the royalty due to him for the songs he had composed, and which had been sung by others on records already in circulation in the market (De 1993, 29). Thus ensued a long correspondence spanning almost a decade between Morgan and Company, the firm of solicitors acting on behalf of The Gramophone Company, and Chattopadhyay. Sometime around March 1924, Rabindranath Tagore consented to having his voice recorded by Robert Edward Beckett, the recording operator of The Gramophone Company Limited (Inreco 1977, 21). However, these recordings were not released until February 1927 (ibid.). The reason behind such a delay was probably Tagore's reluctance to authorise the release of the records to the public. Morgan and Company dealt with the royalty issue and an agreement was finally signed between The Gramophone Company Limited ('the company') and Doctor Rabindranath Tagore, D.L. ('the composer'), on 5 October 1926. The agreement decided that,

> The Company shall pay to the Composer or his nominee royalty of eight *annas* for each double sided record of any of the Composer's said songs or recitations manufactured or to be manufactured by the Company PROVIDED ALWAYS that the Company shall at all times be at liberty to determine the selling price for all records the subject of this Agreement. (De 1993, 29)

Image 5.2 provides the first and last pages of the four-page 'Agreement'.

COPY OF THE AGREEMENT BETWEEN GRAMOPHONE COMPANY AND DR. RABINDRANATH TAGORE.

AN AGREEMENT made the fifth day of October One thousand nine hundred and twenty-six BETWEEN THE GRAMOPHONE COMPANY LIMITED a Company incorporated under the English Companies Acts and having its Registered Office at Hayes in the County of Middlesex in England and carrying on business at amongst other places 139, Belliaghatta Road in the suburbs of Calcutta (hereinafter called "the Company") of the one part and DOCTOR RABINDRA NATH TAGORE D.L. of No. 6, Dwarka Nath Tagore Lane in the town of Calcutta aforesaid (hereinafter called "the Composer") of the other part WHEREBY IT IS AGREED as follows :-

1. The Company shall for the consideration hereinafter stated have the exclusive right for ever to manufacture, multiply, publish and sell all records for use on Talking Machines already made by the Composer of the songs and recitations mentioned in the Schedule hereunder and shall for a period of five years from the date hereof have such exclusive right to manufacture, multiply, publish and sell all further records which may hereafter be made by the Composer of the said songs and recitations.

2. The Company shall have the exclusive property in and the sole right for ever to manufacture and multiply all records so made or to be made by the Composer of the said songs and recitations and the Composer shall not during the continuance of this Agreement talk or sing or carry out any performance for the purpose of making talking machine records of the said songs and recitations.

3. The Company shall pay to the Composer or his nominee a royalty of eight annas for each double sided record of any of the Composer's said songs or recitations manufactured or to be manufactured by the Company PROVIDED ALWAYS that the Company shall at all times be at liberty to determine the selling price for all records the subject of this Agreement.

Image 5.2a: First page of Agreement signed between Tagore and The Gramophone Company

Source: Inreco 1977, 29, 30. [This was a compilation of essays as a tribute to Tagore, released on the poet's birthday that year.]

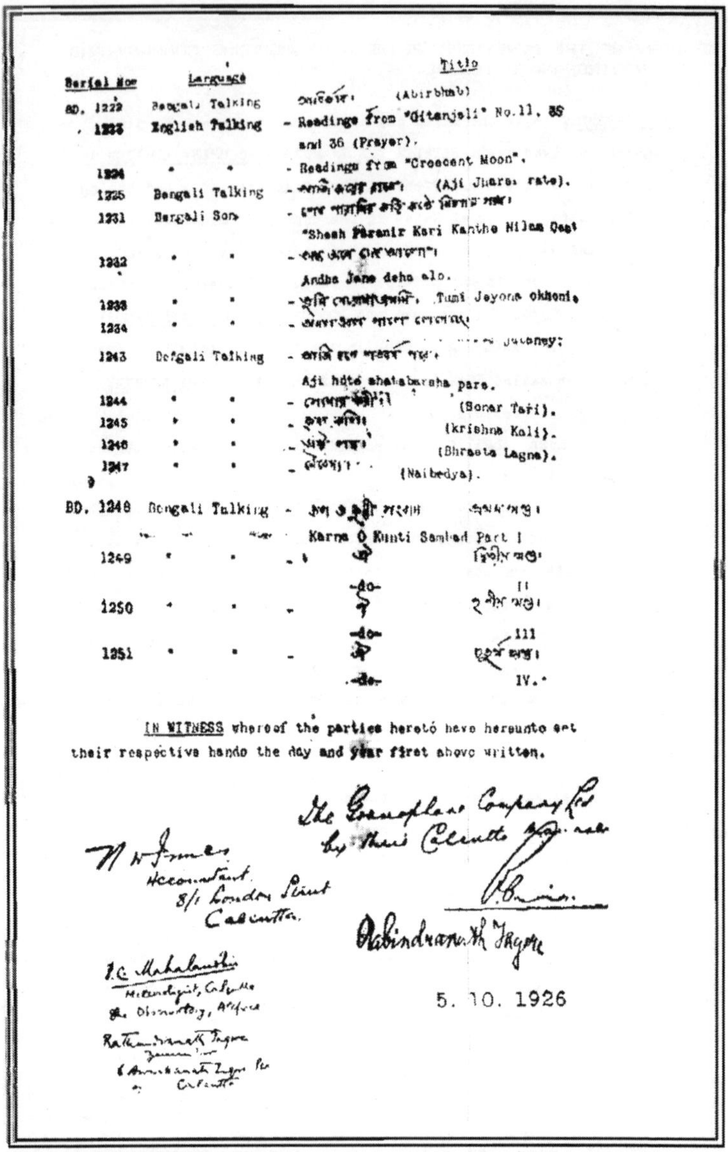

Serial No.	Language	Title
BD. 1222	Bengali Talking	[illegible] (Abirbhab)
1223	English Talking	- Readings from "Gitanjali" No. 11, 35 and 36 (Prayer).
1224	" "	- Readings from "Crescent Moon".
1225	Bengali Talking	- [illegible] (Aji Jharer rate).
1231	Bengali Song	- [illegible] "Shesh Paranir Kari Kanthe Nilam Gest
1232	" "	- [illegible] Andha Jane deho alo.
1233	" "	- [illegible], Tumi Jeyona okhoni,
1234	" "	- [illegible] ... journey;
1243	Bengali Talking	- [illegible] Aji hote shatabarsha pare.
1244	" "	- [illegible] (Sonar Tari).
1245	" "	- [illegible] (krishna Kali).
1246	" "	- [illegible] (Bhrasta Lagna).
1247	" "	- [illegible] (Naibedya).
BD. 1248	Bengali Talking	- [illegible] Karna O Kunti Sambad Part I
1249	" "	- -do- [illegible] II
1250	" "	- -do- [illegible] III
1251	" "	- -do- [illegible] IV.

IN WITNESS whereof the parties hereto have hereunto set their respective hands the day and year first above written.

5. 10. 1926

Image 5.2b: The last page of Agreement signed between Tagore and The Gramophone Company

Source: Inreco 1977, 29, 30. [This was a compilation of essays as a tribute to Tagore, released on the poet's birthday that year.]

It is difficult to state what prompted the poet to take this step. It might have been because of the huge amount of money he needed at the time for the infrastructural development of the *ashrama* at Santiniketan. Or was he unhappy with the taken-for-granted attitude of The Gramophone Company? Although the answer is not very clear to us, the signing of the agreement is evidence in itself of the very just and professional attitude of the poet, who had been deprived of his rightful dues by a giant foreign recording company like The Gramophone Company for over a decade.

After the agreement was signed, The Gramophone Company first released the poet's recording in February 1927. In the meantime, since 1921, the Company had already begun releasing their records under a new label, called 'HIS MASTER'S VOICE' or HMV. Further releases were made from The Gramophone Company Limited recording sessions in September 1927 and in May 1928. All of these releases were made under HMV with red labels, which usually sold for Rs 4 each, Re 1 higher than the regular black label series. It is noted that the playing speed of the record is mentioned on these discs—some were to be played at 78 rpm (rotation per minute), while some others were played at 80 rpm. The real purpose of this indication was possibly only to enrich the voice quality (Inreco 1977, 22). The Gramophone Company's advertisement of Tagore's records on the occasion of their release is presented in Table 5.2. The elaborate advertisement, which mentioned Tagore's recitation from the *Gitanjali*, the Nobel Prize-winning work of the poet, apart from other numbers, no doubt points to The Gramophone Company's big achievement of getting Tagore's voice on their records.

In 1926, The Gramophone Company introduced the electrical method in its recording technique. The Company decided to inaugurate this new venture with a recitation by Tagore. He obliged, and recited *Karna-Kunti Sambad* for this occasion (De 1993, 30). Around this time the poet also recorded a good many other records for The Gramophone Company, which featured recitations in his voice as well. A detailed account (excluding the copies of the original records that the company made later on) of all the recordings that Tagore did for The Gramophone Company under the HMV label from 1927 onwards is given in Table 5.2.

Table 5.2: Complete List of All of Tagore's Recordings under HMV, 1927 Onwards

Matrix No.	Item	Record No.	Date/Category
BD1222	Abirbhab	P 8366	Talking (Bengali), Feburary 1927
BD1223	Readings from *Gitanjali*	P 8368	Talking (English), February 1927
BD1224	Readings from 'Crescent Moon'	P 8368	Talking (English), February 1927
BD1225	Aji Jharer Rate	NA	Talking (Bengali), n.d.
BD1231	Sesh Paranir Kari	P 9132	Song (Bengali), September 1927
BD1232	Andha Jane Deha Alo	P 8367	Song (Bengali), February 1927
BD1233	Tumi Jeo Na Ekhoni	NA	Song (Bengali), n.d.
BD1234	Amala Dhabala Pale Legeche	NA	Song (Bengali), n.d.
BD1235	Amare Ke Nibi Bhai	P 9132	Song (Bengali), September 1927
BD1236	Kakhan Je Basanta Galo	NA	Song (Bengali), n.d.
BD1237	Ami Sansare Mana Diachhinu	P 8367	Song (Bengali), February 1927
BD1238	Nai Ba Elay Jadi Samay Nai	NA	Song (Bengali), n.d.
BD1239	Ganer Surer Asan Khani	NA	Song (Bengali), n.d.
BD1240	Anek Diechha Nath	NA	Song (Bengali), n.d.
BD1241	Bela Galo Tomar Path Chaye	NA	Song (Bengali), n.d.
BD1242	Bhalobesha Sakhi Nibhrite Jataney	NA	Song (Bengali), n.d.
BD1243	Aji Hote Shatabarsha Pare	P 8366	Talking (Bengali), February 1927

(Contd)

Table 5.2 (Contd)

Matrix No.	Item	Record No.	Date/Category
BD1244	Sonar Tari	NA	n.d.
BD1245	Krishna Kali	P 9133	Recitation (Bengali), September 1927
BD 1246	Bhrashta Lagna	P 9133	Recitation (Bengali), September 1927
BD 1247	Naibedya	NA	Recitation (Bengali), n.d.
BD1248	Karna O Kunti Sambad – Part I	P 9915	Recitation (Bengali), May 1928
BD1249	Karna O Kunti Sambad – Part II	P 9915	Recitation (Bengali), May 1928
BD1250	Karna O Kunti Sambad – Part III	P 9916	Recitation (Bengali), May 1928
BD1251	Karna O Kunti Sambad – Part IV	P 9916	Recitation (Bengali), May 1928

Source: Inreco 1977, 39–40.

Although the agreement signed between Tagore and The Gramophone Company pertained chiefly to the question of royalties, the Company was also forbidden to release any of Tagore's recorded songs without the poet's consent. Rabindranath was extremely critical of the quality of the records he had made for The Gramophone Company, and for a long time, Tagore would grant or reject the sample records after listening to them personally. He was not prepared to compromise on the timbre, rhythm, or musical notes of his songs, which compelled him to check the recording sample several times before giving his final authorisation. The Gramophone Company had by then emerged as the largest company to control the sound recording industry; yet they agreed to Tagore's perfectionist approach without any further discussion on the matter. However, the agreement signed between The Gramophone Company and the poet was to have many far-reaching consequences, such as the slow but steady growth of the unique genre of 'Rabindra-Sangeet', the establishment of the Visva-Bharati Music Board, the strict guidelines that governed the singing of 'Rabindra-Sangeet', the need to obtain permission from the Music Board before releasing records of 'Rabindra-Sangeet', and so on.

Tagore and Hindusthan Records

In a letter written to Basanti Devi, the wife of Deshbandhu Chittaranjan Das, in 1932, Tagore referred to a certain Chandi Charan Saha who had returned from Europe with an advanced knowledge of sound recording (De 1993, 32) and had established the Hindusthan Musical Products and Varieties Limited. The legacy of Hindusthan Records was originally started in around 1895 at 23/5 Dharmatalla Street, Calcutta by Moni Lal Saha, the father of Chandi Charan Saha (ibid., 22), who founded M. L. Shaw Ltd and soon became one of the leading talking machine dealers in Calcutta by the beginning of the twentieth century. By 1905, M. L. Shaw Ltd had been appointed the agent for Nicole Record Co. Ltd., and their booming business in talking machines and disc records continued till the 1920s, when Chandi Charan Saha took over the business and started steering it in a new direction. In 1931, Chandi Charan Saha (who later became widely known as C. C. Saha) allied with J. N. Ghosh (the founder of Megaphone Co.) and B. B. Sen (founder of N. B. Sen & Bros) to establish the Hindusthan Musical Products and Varieties Syndicate Ltd (Inreco 1977, 22). At a time when C. C. Saha was looking forward to further advancements in his business, The Gramophone Company was keen to retain its recording monopoly in the Indian market. George Cooper, Managing Director of The Gramophone Company, having anticipated the plans of C. C. Saha and his allies, became desperate to prevent them from entering the world of disc record production, which would naturally challenge The Gramophone Company's monopoly. Cooper approached Saha and tried to persuade him to not set up a disc record pressing factory, offering him instead the opportunity to press records for The Gramophone Co. Ltd, under the label of Hindusthan Records. Meanwhile, the Neumann recording machine that Saha had used to record voices for his recording company had not proved successful. He made a few recordings of Rabindranath Tagore, but the recording quality of the Neumann machine was unsatisfactory. Understanding the need of the hour, Saha therefore agreed to the proposal offered by The Gramophone Company, and started working in collaboration with them.

However, in 1932 at the age of seventy-one, Tagore gave his consent to Saha's request to record for Hindusthan Records, and recorded a number of recitations. Tagore's first recording under the Hindusthan Records label, with two recitations of 'Ami Jakhon Babar Moto Habo' and 'Tobu Mone Rekho', was released in August 1932 (De 1993, 33). Between 1932 and 1940, Rabindranath Tagore made a small number of other recordings, of just four titles per session, for the Hindusthan Musical Products and Varieties Syndicate Ltd, with Nirad Baran Bannerjee as the recording engineer. These are, in all probability, the last 'studio' recordings that Tagore made. A detailed account of all the recordings that Tagore made for the Hindusthan Company is given in Table 5.3.

TABLE 5.3: Tagore's Complete Recordings for the Hindusthan Company

Matrix No.	Item	Series No.	Date/Category
MLS16	Amar Parana Loyey Ki Khela	H 49	Song (Bengali), July 1933
MLS17	Hriday Amar Nacherey	H 49	Recitation (Bengali), July 1933
MLS18	Tabu Maney Rekho	H 1	Kirton (Bengali), August 1932
MLS19	Tumi Eso Hey	H 1700	Song (Bengali), n.d.

(Contd)

Table 5.3 (Contd)

Matrix No.	Item	Series No.	Date/Category
MLS20	Kangal Amarey	H 1700	Song (Bengali), n.d.
MLS21	Not Traced	NA	n.d.
MLS24	Ami Jakhan Babar Mato	H 1	Recitation (Bengali), August 1932
MLS?	Tomar Surer Dhara (Duet with Rama Devi)	NA	Song (Bengali), n.d.
HSB918	Mone Koro Jano	H 342	Recitation (Bengali), n.d.
HSB919	Lookochuri	H 342	Recitation (Bengali), n.d.
HSB2357(1)	Jhulan	NA	Recitation (Bengali), n.d.
HSB2357(2)	Jhulan	H 812	Recitation (Bengali), n.d.
HSB2358	Aasha	H 812	Recitation (Bengali), n.d.
HSB2359	The Vision	H 872	Recitation (English), January 1940
HSB2360	The Trumpet	H 782	Recitation (English), January 1940
HSB3200	Duh Somey	H 990	Recitation (Bengali), n.d.
HSB3201	Sonar Tari	H 990	Recitation (Bengali), n.d.
HSB3202	Authorship	H 991	Recitation (English), n.d.
HSB3203	The Hero	H 991	Recitation (English), n.d.

Source: Inreco 1977, 43, 45.

It may be pointed out here that Tagore had a special affinity towards Hindusthan Records. He had sent his blessings to the Hindusthan Company and wished it all success for the future. It goes without saying that the poet did not share such a relationship with The Gramophone Company, for whom he actually recorded far more than he did for Hindusthan Records.

Other Records of Rabindranath: India and Abroad

There is yet another type of record on which Tagore's recitations and speeches at home and abroad have been preserved. The collection of those preserved at the West German Film and Radio Library may be classified into following heads:

i) Frankfurt, 1921: Recorded a poem titled 'Is it then True?'
ii) Frankfurt, 1921: Recorded an English speech (duration: 3 minutes 15 seconds).
iii) Personal recording, Germany, 1921: Sanskrit hymn.
iv) Prussian Library, 1921: Recorded a speech (titled 'The Message of the Forest') and a song ('Mor bina othe kon sure baaji').
v) Germany, 1930: Recorded a speech on 'Principles of Art'.
vi) Sweden, 1930: Recorded the poem 'Jhulan'. (De 1993, 35)

Tagore's recorded speech preserved in the Prussian Library, 'The Message of the Forest', was damaged during World War II. However, it was later retrieved and was finally sent to Santiniketan. We quote a few lines from this speech: 'India's grand achievement which is still stored deep within her heart is waiting to unite within itself, Hindu, Moslem, Buddhist and Christian, not by force, not by apathy of resignation but in the harmony of active co-operation' (ibid., 36–37).

In India, other than the recording companies, All India Radio (AIR) was the only concern to record Tagore's voice on a number of occasions. A detailed list of AIR recordings is given below; all the items were either speeches or recitations of his own poems (Roy 1971, 19–23).

i) 'Jadio Takhankar Ingrezi': Two extracts from the Convocation Address delivered at the University of Calcutta, February 1937.
ii) 'I Know that the Day': Recitation from *Gitanjali*, recorded in Puri, May 1939.

iii) 'I Have Got my Leave': Recitation from *Gitanjali*, 1939.
iv) 'In Salutation to Thee': Recitation from *Gitanjali*, 1939.
v) 'Rabi Pradakshin Pathe': Recitation from *Parisesh*, 1939.
vi) 'Aye Tirtha Devatar': Recitation from *Gitali*, 1939.
vii) 'Hey Mor Sandhya': Recitation from *Gitali*, May 1939.
viii) 'Hey Mor Chitta': Recitation, 1939.
ix) 'Viswa Jure Kshudha Itihasey': Recitation, n.d.; broadcast from Ottawa Radio Station on 29 May 1939.
x) 'Jedin Chaitanya Mor': Recitation, May 1939.
xi) 'When my Mind was Released': Recitation, n.d.
xii) 'Ajana Sey Desh': Recitation; broadcast from the newly inaugurated Dacca Radio Station in 1939.
xiii) 'Sorrow's Flood-Tide': Recitation, 1940.
xiv) Sanskrit verses delivered at the end of the dance drama *Chitrangada* at Santiniketan, early 1940.
xv) 'Those who Struck Him Once': Recitation, 1940.
xvi) 'Bhagaban Tumi Jugey Jugey': Recitation, early 1940.
xvii) 'Age after Age, Time and Again': Recitation, n.d.

In September 1946, Columbia Gramophone Co. Ltd, Calcutta (an associate company of The Gramophone Co. Ltd.) released two discs containing copies of Tagore's recordings on acetate discs made by AIR, which were broadcast later on.

Conclusion

This discussion, with its special focus on Tagore's interaction with sound-recording devices, leads us to some plausible conclusions. First, it has been proved beyond doubt that the recordings of Tagore's voice available today do not bear his original voice, but a different and/or a distorted version of it. Second, it is evident that Tagore was genuinely enthusiastic about H. Bose's cylinder records of Pathephone and Chandi Charan Saha's Hindusthan Records, most probably because of their 'swadeshi' nature. In between, he consented to have only one foreign company record his voice, that is, The Gramophone Company, with whom he shared a very professional relationship. One is not sure whether his relationship with The Gramophone Company was out of compulsion, because of the legal angle, or whether it was the poet's conscious decision to choose this giant Company in order to convey his creations to a larger audience, keeping in mind their worldwide distribution network. Third, Tagore's initial spontaneous recordings for H. Bose's cylinder records point to the influence of the contemporary swadeshi mood. One is well aware of the persuasive power of the print medium during the swadeshi days, but there is hardly any in-depth study of the influence that the swadeshi songs recorded and played during that time might have had on the people's spontaneity to come together for a common cause. The songs and recitals recorded and reproduced through the recording machines could be shared by a larger audience, including that section for whom the print media was out of reach, thereby creating the possibility of a commonly shared and ever-growing sentiment among a wider section for the cause of swadeshi. Fourth, Tagore again rose to the demands of the time when, on the eve of World War II, he criticised the greedy imperialist nations of the world and recorded for AIR his speech on the theme 'Viswa Jure Kshudha Itihasey' in 1939. In a logical culmination of this theme, Tagore, in the last public address of his life titled 'Sabhyatar Sankat' ('Crisis of Civilisation'), delivered in 1941, elaborated on the greedy materialist culture of the contemporary West and hoped for the arrival of the Great Man (*Oi Mahamanab Aase*) who would save human civilisation. Finally, it is to be mentioned that true to his poet's consciousness, Tagore, in his recorded 'The Message of the Forest', emphasised the need for harmony amongst the citizens of the world, which has unfortunately remained ever elusive.

However, even today, as soon as the needle on the gramophone moves along the grooves, it is with Tagore's convincing voice, talking of a future world based on fraternity and solidarity among human beings, that one is once again ignited with hope and enthusiasm.

Endnotes

1. Here are a few examples that indicate the possession of phonograph machines and records by Indians even before the twentieth century:

i) In 1894, when Swami Vivekananda went to the USA to attend the Parliament of World Religions in Chicago, he wrote a letter dated 5 September to his friend, Sri Manmatha Nath Bhattacharyya, then a high official of the Finance Department of the Government of India, mentioning that he was sending a 'Phonograph' to the ruler of Khetri in India.

ii) Maharaja Lal & Sons, the oldest HMV dealer in Delhi, narrated in the Annual Report of the Company in its eighty-second year that in 1895, they had started dealing in cylindrical rolls, popularly known in India as '*Churi*' (as they resembled bangles), and the phonograph ('*Churi-ka-baja*', or bangle music).

iii) In 1898, Hemendra Mohan Bose (better known as H. Bose, perfumer, in the business circles of Calcutta) imported a cylindrical phonograph (Serial No. C. 6616) from Thomas Alva Edison and started his own business, Bose's Record. His showroom was situated at 61, Bowbazar Street, Calcutta. [list ends]

2. Rathindranath wrote: '*Jouban bayose baba ki mishti athocho joralo golay gaan gaite parten, loke taar gaan shonbar jonyo kirakom pagol hoye jeto, jara na shunechhe tara kalpona korte parbe na*' ('Father used to sing in such a bold yet melodious voice in his youth that people would be crazy to listen to his renditions. Those who have not listened to that voice cannot even imagine what it was like!' Translation by the authors).

3. '*Amar alpo bayosher se-gola aar nai. Tomader ekhon aar ki shonabo? Peyechhilam bote ekta golar mato gola. Kintu bhagoban diye kere niyechhen, ekhon ki aar gaite ecche kore? Sei shesh geyechhiloom Tarak babur barite Congress Committee-er adhibeshane. Sedin bolte ki, nijer desh ebong jatir upor dhikkare raag korei, sei sabha tei sur bosiye gola chhere diyechhiloom— "Amay bolo na gahite bolo na!/ Eki shudhu hasi-khela, promoder mela/ shudhu michhe katha chhalona". Golar mato gola sarbosadharon ke sei shesh shuniyechhi. Takhon modhyome dhore chhere ditoom sur, pakhir mato se ure cholto surer dhape dhape porday porday*' ('I don't have the voice now that I

had in my youth. What can I sing for you now? I had indeed been given an ideal voice. But the Almighty has taken back whatever He had given earlier. Therefore, I do not wish to sing again. The last time I sang in the residence of Tarakbabu, on the occasion of a meeting of the Congress Committee, it was out of disgust and anger towards my country and its people that I suddenly started to sing impromptu, putting melody to the words. That was the last time I sang out to the people with an ideal voice texture.'] (Debi 1962 [1369 BS]; translation by the authors).

4. '*Gramophone takhon abishkar hoy ni, taar golar record koyekti matro ache, kintu tao bridhho bayoshe neoa, takhon gola pore gechhe. Takhonkar dine phonograph name machine chhilo, momer cylinder-er upor record uthto. Tar nakol neoa jeto na. "Kuntaleen"- er H. Bose ei machine edeshe amdani koren. Tini babar golar bistor record niyechhilen. Koyek bachhor purbe taar chhele Nitin ke ei record gulir khonj nite boli. Dukkher bishoy, bohu anushandhaner por koyekti matro cylinder paoa gelo—segulio takhon nashto hoye gechhe*'

('Gramophone was not invented yet, recordings of his voice were few in number, and that too in his old age; the charm of his voice had been eroded by that time. In those days, there was a machine called the *Phonograph*, where recordings were done on a cylinder made of wax. Only one copy could be made from the master record. Mr. H. Bose, of *Kuntaleen* fame, first imported this machine to this country. He had taken several records of father's voice. A few years ago, I asked his son Nitin to search for those records. But unfortunately, in spite of a thorough search, only a couple of cylinders could be recovered, and even those had been ruined.'] (Tagore 1367 BS; translation by the authors).

5. Suhrawardy said,

> One thing I noticed that afternoon in the vast hall of Manchester College, cramful [*sic*] with a brilliant and awe-inspired crowd of Professors, Deans and Undergraduates that the Poet's voice was ill-suited to large audiences. Even in private conversation when he first spoke to me, I was struck by a certain discrepancy between his appearance on which nature had showered her most exquisite gift of beauty and dignity, and his voice which did not seem to belong to his magnificent exterior. In itself the voice was melodious and expressive but it might have belonged to anyone else. It possessed a fine timbre but lack in tonality. (Ghosh, 1988, 226)

Select References

The Bengalee. 16 February and March 1906.

Bose, Debendramohan. 1891–1892 (1298 BS). *Paricharika*, a Bengali monthly.

De, Santosh Kumar. 1990. *Gramophone in India: A Brief History*. Calcutta: Uttisthata Press.

_____. 1993 (1400 BS). *Kobi Kantho O Koler Gaan* (*Voice of the Poet and the Recorded Songs*). Santiniketan: Visva-Bharati.

Debi, Pratima. 1962 (1369 BS). 'Rabindranath'. *Masik Basumati* Baishakh.

Ghosh, Amitabha. 1999. 'Pre-Commercial Era of Sound Recording in India'. *Indian Journal of History of Science* 34 (1).

Ghosh, Siddhartha. 1988. *Karigari Kalpana O Bangali Udyog* (*Imagining Technology with Bengali Entrepreneurs*). Kolkata: Deys' Publishing House.

Home, Amal. 1958 (1365 BS). 'Rabindra Sangeet Smritikatha', *Desh* Jaishtha.

Inreco (The Indian Record Manufacturing Company Limited). 1977 (1384 BS). *Rabi Pranam*. Calcutta.

Joshi, G. N. 1988. 'A Concise History of the Phonograph Industry in India'. *Popular Music* 7 (2).

Khamkheyali Shabhar Karjo Bibaroni, File No. 152. Santiniketan: Rabindra-Bhavana.

Roy, Kshitis. 1971. *Voice of Rabindranath: A Chronicle of Recordings*. Santiniketan: Visva-Bharati.

Sen, Premendra Kumar. 1961. 'His Master's Voice'. *Rabindra Shato-Barshiki* (Special Issue on the Occasion of the Birth Centenary of Rabindranath Tagore). Calcutta: The Gramophone Company Ltd.

Sharma, A. N. 2012. *Bajanama: A Study of Early Indian Gramophone Records*. Lucknow, Mumbai: Kathachitra Prakashan.

Tagore, Rathindranath. 1960 [1367 BS]. *Pitrismriti* (*Reminiscences of My Father*). Kolikata: Jijnasa.

6

Bengali Folk Responses to Hegemonic Orthodoxy and Social Hierarchy

Jari, *Baul*, and *Maijbhandari* Songs

Amit Dey

Introduction

Jari is a kind of dirge that was hugely popular in pre-Independence eastern and northern Bengal. The term originated from the Persian word '*zaridan*', meaning lamentation. In the Urdu-speaking world, it is called '*marsiya*'. The genre commemorates the martyrdom of Hussain, the beloved grandson of the Prophet Muhammad, in the tragic battle of Karbala. However, it is not sung exclusively during Muharram; in some places, it is treated as a seasonal song and not necessarily as a religious song. Although it glorifies and glamourises the members of the Prophet's family (this practice of glorification of individuals is not encouraged by the hegemonic orthodoxy) who sacrificed themselves during the Battle of Karbala, contemporary sociopolitical and economic issues can often be incorporated in Jari. It recognises India's composite culture and played a significant role against the divisive impact of colonial rule. Jari also poses a challenge to hegemonic orthodoxy and social oppression. Since Jari and *Baul* songs are not composed by theoreticians, politicians, or economists but by folk poets, we notice in this genre the identification of the immediate oppressors of the peasant community, such as the zamindars or moneylenders, rather than the State itself. At times, they seem unable to differentiate between the colonial State and the proselytising Christian missionaries, regarding the latter as representatives of hegemonic orthodoxy.

For purposes of self-defence, they brought into play cosmogonical theories which added a new dimension to the exquisitely beautiful Bengali folk songs.

This chapter aims to contextualise Jari and Baul songs in a historical perspective. Unlike the folklorists or linguists, we are not necessarily interested in the literary merit of this genre. Rather, using these as non-archival sources, we have aspired to read between the lines. Such an exercise is particularly significant in the understanding of the Bengal countryside during the nineteenth and twentieth centuries. Since ours is a pioneering effort, our journey is characterised by a paucity of secondary or historiographical literature.

Baul Songs

The Bauls of Bengal belonged to a community of mendicant singers known for their liberal attitude towards all religions. There is much controversy amongst scholars concerning the origin of the word '*baul*'. According to one view, it originated from the Sanskrit word '*vatula*', meaning mad or crazy. Another view suggests that the word 'baul' has its origins in the word '*vyakula*', meaning impatiently eager. A third view states that the word is a possible derivative of the Arabic word '*auliya*', which means holy men, saints, or companions; partly due to Sufi influence, many Arabic and Persian words (such as 'auliya') had been incorporated into the Bengali language. The Bauls were influenced by both Sufism and Vaishnavism, although they are identified neither as Hindu nor as Muslim, and were opposed to the caste system as well. The Baul cult perhaps existed in Bengal as a definable religious group as early as the early sixteenth century. However, it is the nineteenth century that can be regarded as the heyday of the Bauls, as that is when the famous exponents of Baul songs, such as Faqir Lalan Shah (d. 1891), Panju Shah (b. 1851), and Lalan's disciple Duddu Shah flourished.

The Bauls are mostly seen in Kushtia, Khulna, Pabna, Rajshahi, Faridpur, Dhaka, and Birbhum districts. They generally wear a kind of odd white *jobba* (long flowing garment) and play a single-stringed musical instrument called *ektara,* made out of the hollowed and dried cavity of a gourd, while singing. The interpretation of symbols is very important in sociocultural history. Here, historians have the opportunity to collaborate with folklorists and anthropologists, particularly in the context of the increasing importance of the multidisciplinary approach in the social sciences. Unlike the Ashrafs (aristocratic Muslims), the Bauls, who were mendicant singers, lacked the resources to procure expensive musical instruments. The indigenously manufactured ektara was cheap but useful, and became integral to the process of identity formation of the agrarian population. The Ashraf preferred to settle in urban pockets and traced their genealogy to Central or West Asia. The folk poets were rural and gladly identified themselves with local religio-cultural symbols. The ektara symbolised musical performances, and music itself offers a challenge to hegemonic orthodoxy. It is an established fact that both Gandhi and Tagore anticipated this potential of music to reach the masses and also symbolically challenge the forces of hegemonic orthodoxy (the latter, especially, is often hostile to the performing arts). It is not surprising that Rabindranath's celebrated novel *Gora* begins with a famous Baul song. Thus the ektara, which is inseparable from the Bauls, posed a challenge to social hierarchy and religious orthodoxy (Karim 1980, 168).

During the Mughal period, there was a great number of Hindu and Muslim zamindars in Bengal. But by the eighteenth and nineteenth centuries, nearly all the great Muslim families had lost their zamindaris to the Hindus. First, the laws of inheritance prevalent among the Muslims led to minute subdivision among heirs. Second, the operation of Sale Laws in the aftermath of the Permanent Settlement (1793) under British rule also contributed to the decline of Muslim zamindars. In theory, this affected both the Hindu and Muslim zamindars; however, in effect it contributed to the dispossession of Muslim zamindars, as those who supplanted the old zamindars (both Hindu and Muslim) were almost always Hindus.

The Resumption (after 1828), which involved the takeover of *lakhiraj* lands by the State, also deprived many Muslim families of their livelihood. The Bengali novel *Abdullah* by Qazi Imdadul Huq showed how the Muslim landed aristocrats, who had been indifferent to the management of their landed properties, were losing the estates to their shrewd Hindu employees. The novel also talked about how those erstwhile Muslim landed aristocrats took shelter in Islam, which became their last fortress, and organised *milad*[1] to preserve their declining influence in Muslim society. This also paved the way for the growth and sustenance of a Prophet-centred piety.

Another factor that contributed to the impoverishment of rural Bengal was the destruction of craft industries. It is important to bear in mind that, once British paramountcy had been established in India by the first two decades of the nineteenth century, the economy of Bengal became increasingly dependent on the Western industrialised economy. Instead of exporting its high-quality cloth, Bengal's economy became almost wholly agricultural, relying heavily on the export of primary goods such as indigo and jute. The Muslim cotton-weavers of Bengal, who were called *jolahas*, could no longer compete with the comparatively cheaper cotton goods from the cotton mills of the United Kingdom.

As a result of their impoverishment from the beginning of the nineteenth century, many Muslims joined the ranks of the mendicant singers to sing in honour of the Prophet, their mystical leader, who would guide them to safety in that period of turmoil. Mysticism, humanism, and syncretism are the basic ingredients of Baul songs, which also reflect various aspects of the social and economic conditions affecting people in the Bengal countryside. A mystic outlook, coupled with social inequality, gave birth to many minor religious sects and religions. The Bauls and Jari singers, who represented the Bengal countryside, had first-hand experience of the social and economic inequality which reduced men to insignificance. The Bauls were not religious reformers, but they did fight against social inequality, hatred, and corruption through their songs (Karim 1980, 173).

Jari Songs

Jari, as stated earlier, is a kind of dirge, which owes its origins to the tragic events of Medina and Karbala that led to the deaths of Hazrat Imam Hassan and Hussain. The Shia community of South Asia commemorates the events of Karbala in the month of Muharram by singing *marsiyas* or dirges on the deaths of Hussain and his followers. Marsiyas are usually sung in Urdu, while Jari is its Bengali counterpart, sung generally during Muharram in Bangladesh and parts of West Bengal in India. Both valour and pathos characterise Jari, which depicts the unparalleled heroism of Hussain and his followers on the battlefield of Karbala and the tragic scene connected with their deaths. According to one scholar, Jari originated in the sixteenth century at a time when Sufism and Vaishnavism appear to have had a substantial influence on each other (Eaton 1996, 227–288). Jari has maintained its popularity among both Hindus and Muslims in the Bengal countryside. In the district of Mymensingh (in Bangladesh), the Shia community performs Jari to commemorate the events of Karbala in the month of Muharram, but in districts like Jessore and Khulna (also in Bangladesh), Jari is not treated as a religious song; rather, it is a seasonal song and is not necessarily performed in the month of Muharram either. In the era of social, economic, and political decay that followed the Battle of Plassey (1757) against the British, a battle symbolically regarded as the Karbala of Bengal with Siraj-ud-daula resembling Hussain the martyr, the Muslims of Bengal turned to their Prophet and other members of his family for spiritual and moral guidance.

Like the Baul songs, Jari too reflects the grievances of the rural population against the prevalent social and economic disparities. Nineteenth-century Bengal witnessed several peasant uprisings against the colonial rulers, which inspired the Jari singers who emphasised the harmony of Bengali religious communities in the face of the divisive impact of colonial rule. If we keep in mind this historical background of Jari, it will be easier for us to understand why it became so popular during the Non-cooperation and Khilafat movements. This category of songs is to be sung in a group, or to be more precise, between two contesting groups, which can create a dramatic atmosphere during village performances. Jari songs are sung to the accompaniment of dancing, and musical instruments such as the *dhol* (cylindrical drum beaten on two ends), *shehnai* (musical instrument resembling an oboe), cymbal, harmonium, and *tabla* (a pair of small drums) are used during the performance. The entire group of singers and musicians follow the instruction of a group leader called *bayati*, who conducts the performance. A bayati generally wears a white *panjabi* (loose shirt), pajamas, or *lungi* (cloth wrapped round the hips), with a white cloth around the shoulder. He also wears a pair of *nupurs* (ankle bells, which create a jingling sound) round his ankles and carries a *khanjari* (small tambourine) in his hand.

Maijbhandari Songs

Maijbhandar was a famous centre of *marifati* (esoteric) songs in Chittagong. Marifati songs of this area were known as maijbhandari songs after their place of origin, and their singers were called maijbhandari singers or simply, maijbhandaris (Alam 1985, 18–39). The establishment, growth, and sustenance of centres are significant in both scriptural and mystical Islam, so much so that sometimes the place-names are mentioned alongside the names of charismatic saints or *ulama*, such as Abdul Huq Dehlawi or Keramat Ali Jaunpuri. Delhi, Badaun, and Ajmer are well-known places of Islamic or mystical learning. Compared to them, Maijbhandar is the least publicised, and neither is the maijbhandari tradition considered a mainstream mystical tradition. The emergence of Maijbhandar as a mystical centre through the transmission of Bengali mystical songs can be interpreted as the assertion of regional or folk Islam, or as the provincialisation of Islam. A comprehensive understanding of this process is necessary in order to understand the nature of identity formation so far as the local Muslim community is concerned. Of course the custodians of scriptural or mainstream (?)[2] Islam often derecognise such regional variations, and have a proclivity to homogenise Islam. These divergent approaches can often help us differentiate between a historian and a theologian. The latter can overcome such constraints by embracing a multidisciplinary approach.

However, it should be mentioned that the maijbhandari singers were not merely confined to Chittagong, but became popular throughout Bangladesh. The maijbhandari singers used to have a *murshid* or spiritual guide, and functioned to a large extent like a Sufi sect (Alam 1985, 33). This focus on the murshid is significant as he often competes with the mullah as a source of authority within the village community. This is not unnatural because Chittagong has a rich tradition of Islamic mysticism, and is also known as the land of the twelve auliya (Sufis). The maijbhandaris did not follow any institutionalised religion and demonstrated a liberal attitude towards other religions. They were even popular among a section of the liberal-minded educated population. A maijbhandari singer required a *dholak* (drum) for his performance and a harmonium was often played in tune with his song. However, maijbhandari tunes lacked variety. Maijbhandaris also had long hair and were fond of smoking the hookah (ibid., 89, 91); these aspects posed a symbolic challenge to the Sharia-centred mullahs or custodians of scriptural religion. Contemporary social and economic conditions were reflected in the maijbhandari songs, and among their religious themes, cosmogony featured prominently.

Now that we have introduced the Baul, Jari, and maijbhandari songs, we shall provide a thematic presentation of these genres.

Nur-i-Muhammadi or the Light of Muhammad

One of the central themes of mystical prophetology is that of the *Nur-i-Muhammadi* (the Light of Muhammad). According to Muslim rationalists, theologians, and metaphysicians, the first thing that the Creator called into existence was intellect, an excellent and perfect substance in which the form of all things was contained and from which other beings emerged in a phased manner. The Sufi notion of creation owes its origin to the philosophical ideas of al-Farabi and Ibn Sina, who tried to establish a connection between the divine light (*nur*) and the intellect, the former being communicated to the latter at the first instance by the prime cause, the Creator. The nur is the light of the sun, around which everything revolves. And around this nuclear concept of nur, the Sufis developed the doctrine of *Nur-i-Muhammadi,* which is believed to have been created before all things (Roy 1983, 114–115, 121; Schimmel 1985, 123–144).

Now this very emphasis on the philosophical dimensions in which the likes of al Farabi or Ibn Sina were involved could be regarded as an explicit challenge to hegemonic orthodoxy and polity, since the latter remains sceptical about such aspects; in fact, this tension is visible even today. The authoritarian State often viewed intellectuals and philosophers as a potential threat to its authority. In Bengal, philosophical ideas popularised by both philosophers and Sufis have featured widely in popular Islam, from the medieval period to the present century. The Christian missionaries intensified their activities in the countryside of nineteenth-century Bengal, giving rise to a period of religious competition (Dutta 1992). It is important to remember in this context that in the same period, the Bauls of Bengal were also singing songs around the concept of *Nur-i-Muhammadi,* presenting the Prophet Muhammad and his mediation of creation as a source of authority (Rushd 1964, 10–13). In doing so, the Bauls were probably subconsciously responding to the missionary enterprise, which aimed to enhance the status of Jesus Christ and Christianity as compared to Islam and its Prophet. It may also be mentioned here that the north Indian Muslim religious group called the Barelwis, who also had a rural base, responded to the missionary challenge in a similar fashion by focussing on the Sufi doctrine of *Nur-i-Muhammadi* as a source of authority (Metcalf 1982, 296–301).

The image of the Prophet as a source of authority is expressed in a well-known song of Lalan Shah's:

> My Prophet is the Pilot of the other World. All meditation is useless if the Prophet is not remembered, he is the beginning and he is the end and he changes shape and form according to his own pleasure. The sky, the earth, and the wind together with water are all born of his luminous spirit ... God assumed the shape of the Prophet.
>
> The slave Lalan says, 'Seraj became a dervish because of the quality of his Master'. (Rushd 1964, 13)

The last two lines are significant since they point to the importance of depending on a spiritual guide to attain the status of a Sufi saint. The guide who could trace the line of his spiritual ancestry back to Muhammad himself was regarded as a perfect spiritual guide (Talib 1968, Introduction). Another point worth remembering here is that unlike in urban Bengal, intercessory and ecstatic Sufism continued to play an important role in the countryside. Literacy rates were comparatively higher in urban Bengal, and so people had access to printed *sirats* (biography of the Prophet) and other forms of religious literature. Under such circumstances, the role of the middleman in religious matters became less and less important, and the newly emerging educated urban Muslim middle class started to play an active role in religious matters. But in the semi-literate or illiterate world of the Bengal countryside, people had limited or no access to printed sirats. The Sufis thus played the role of mediators between God and rural Muslims, and along with ecstatic and intercessory Sufism, they were greatly accepted in the Bengal countryside. This acceptance, however, was regarded as a threat by the ulama or the self-appointed custodians of scriptural Islam or hegemonic orthodoxy. The vernacularisation process, in which the Sufis were involved, was posing a challenge to the process of Arabisation (the scripture was available in the Arabic), much to the consternation of the ulama. Interestingly enough, many of those writing on Islam in the Bengali language in the late nineteenth century had to seek the sanction of the ulama to legitimise their endeavours. In Bengal, the legitimacy of the Bengali language as a vehicle to convey the message of Islam continued to be debated till the end of the nineteenth century (Dey 2006, 130). It will be intriguing to focus now upon a maijbhandari song.

A song in the maijbhandari form, apparently composed in the late nineteenth century, is of exquisite beauty and expresses the *Nur-i-Muhammadi* concept with great clarity. However, the song is unfortunately deprived of its musical qualities in the translated version.

> I cannot recognise the 'light' (nur) which was responsible for the creation of this universe. [When the Arabic letter '*mim*' is placed in the middle of the word '*Ahad*' (one).]
>
> I see the spiritual birth of Ahmad [another name of Muhammad]. The Supreme Lord is playing with divine light (nur) and the mystery of that game is not known to me, so I desire to go into hiding. Seeing the ripples in the ocean of love, I forget the separation between God and man. The divine light is a reflection of divine majesty (*Jalal*) and divine beauty (*Jamal*), since it represents God and Muhammad at the same time. However, I cannot see the reality of God. (Alam 1985, 29–30; translation mine)

The use of words such as *Jalal* and *Jamal* indicates the enduring influence of Persian poetry, in particular the *natiya* (poetry in honour of the Prophet Muhammad) of Shaikh Sadi Shirazi (d. 1292) on the mystic poets of Bengal. Actually, the Islamisation process in nineteenth- and twentieth-century Bengal has to be understood in the context of a subtle tension between the cosmopolitan Perso-Islamic heterogenisation and Arabisation or homogenisation. In pre-colonial or even in pre-Mughal South Asia, the major Sufi texts were produced in the official language, which was Persian. Persian was the language of culture and 'secular' transactions in the subcontinent, Afghanistan, Central Asia, and of course the Safavid Empire.[3] Indeed, it became an experience of 'culture without borders', with a focus on a liberal, spiritual, human, and rational outlook.[4] It is useful to note that folk tradition is not necessarily an antithesis to Islamic high tradition or the Perso-Islamic tradition. In the pre-colonial period, royal or aristocratic patronage largely sustained the Sufi efforts at producing manuscripts in the Persian language (Dey 2020, 45–56). Such manuscripts, which were produced in the Sufi lodges, transmitted the essence of Perso-Islamic traditions among a section of the literate who read Persian. It goes without saying that the literacy rate was higher in urban pockets. This urban dimension has to be kept in mind when we talk about the circulation of the Perso-Islamic mystical tradition. But during the colonial period, Sufism was deprived of any royal or aristocratic patronage. Moreover, in the 1830s, Persian was replaced by English as the official language. Persian faced a threat not only from English, but the colonial era also saw the emergence of various vernacular or regional languages, such as Sindhi, Punjabi, Marathi, Urdu, Bengali, and others. Apart from such linguistic changes, Sufism as an institution faced transformation from within, which reduced the Sufi lodges to insignificance. Under such circumstances, the number of Persian mystical manuscripts would be drastically reduced. But remnants of the Perso-Islamic mystical tradition would survive among the non-Persian-knowing commoners in the Bengal countryside through the circulation of vernacular folk songs which we can define as oral texts, considering their oral mode of transmission. So the presence of mystically symbolic classical terms such as *Jalal*, *Jamal*, *Ahad*, or *Ahmad* in Bengali folk songs is not surprising, but it is certainly interesting. By emphasising such terms, mystical Islam tried to reassert itself in rural Bengal. So the multiple shifts within Islam, that is, from urban to rural, elite to non-elite, and from classical to vernacular, confirm the fact that Islam is not an unchanging religion (Dey 2019, 3–32).

Socioeconomic Issues in Folk Songs

The prevalence of social divisions among the Muslims in Bengal was also reflected in an interesting Jari titled 'Kulsumer Mejbani', or 'The Hospitality of Kulsum', which the poet Jasimudin discovered from a folk singer in the 1950s. As the entire song could not be traced in its complete form, it is not possible to say anything about its composer or the time of composition. But a close analysis of the characters and the socioeconomic issues the song talks about leads us to believe that it was composed sometime in the nineteenth century. The Jari is too long, so for our convenience we shall offer its substance in a translated form.

The Jari is about the two daughters of the Prophet Muhammad—Bibi Kulsum and Bibi Fatima. Kulsum was the wife of Hazrat Usman, who was known for his affluence, while Fatima was the wife of poor Hazrat Ali.

> Once Muhammad visited Kulsum's house and noticed that she had accumulated a vast amount of wealth. Muhammad advised her to distribute that wealth among the poor and needy people of the country to secure an easy access to heaven.
>
> However, this advice had no impact on Kulsum. A little later, Muhammad met Usman, who readily appreciated Muhammad's advice and soon succeeded in convincing his wife of the importance of following Muhammad's advice. Kulsum agreed to arrange for a huge feast at her residence where all the inhabitants of Mecca and Medina would be invited, excepting Fatima. Kulsum said, '*Kebol matra bad robe Fatima Johra, tar kache patra keho na nibe tomra*' ['Only Fatima Johra will be excluded from that party, and I order you (servants) not to send any invitation letter to her']. Although Usman was very annoyed by Kulsum's attitude, the latter remained unmoved and said, '*Barkat* (or Fatima) *sat dare ek kantha pore asbe amar bari, saharer loke lajja amay dibe ghori ghori*' ['Barkat (Fatima) will visit my home in her shabby wrapper, and I shall feel ashamed before my refined urban guests').
>
> At last, on the day of that feast, the entire population of Mecca and Medina, including Muhammad, assembled at Kulsum's residence. Muhammad asked Kulsum why he could not find Fatima and her two sons, Hassan and Hussain, among the guests. The Prophet reminded Kulsum that by excluding them, she had done them a gross injustice. Kulsum arrogantly replied that being a Prophet, he should have been reasonable enough to realise that the presence of Fatima wearing her shabby wrapper would have damaged

> Kulsum's prestige among the refined urban guests. In the meantime, all the food stored in Kulsum's house disappeared in a supernatural event.
>
> Kulsum then tried to purchase foodstuff for her guests by selling her precious necklace, but that too turned into iron. Muhammad then said, '*Khana banayeechbo tumi Barkater ninda kore, gajab korechbe Allah tomar upore*' ('You have tried to feed your guests by criticising Fatima, so God has punished you'). Kulsum asked Muhammad why Allah should be angry when Fatima is criticised. Muhammad replied that Fatima and Allah are inseparable, just like the red and blue colours that belong to the same *kunji* (a type of seed).[5]

The impact of the Vaishnava concept of the identity of Radha and Krishna is very clear in these lines. One of the most complex perceptions of the Vaishnavas is that Radha and Krishna, in their true and basic form (*svarupa*), are eternally one. But they were divided into two separate and individual forms (*rupa*) in order to savour, in a more comprehensive way, the sweetness of each other. This Vaishnava perception influenced both the Jari and the Baul singers. According to Baul philosophy, the Prophet Muhammad, Krishna, and Chaitanya have become both man and superman because of His sudden touch. In other words, the Bauls regard Muhammad, Krishna, and Chaitanya as God incarnate. As Radha is inseparable from Krishna (the incarnation of God), so Fatima too is inseparable from Allah, being the beloved daughter of Muhammad, who is also the incarnation of God. Unlike the *saguna* Bhakti saints, the Sufis do not believe in the theory of incarnation. Both Radha and Fatima enjoy a loftier position in the mystical tradition of Bengal. Both are also women, and it is not surprising that the Bauls pose as women, since they believe that true love can only be experienced by transforming oneself into a woman. From this concept stemmed their notion of *Shain* or the Man of the Heart, who is also the Eternal Beloved in the Sufi tradition. In the imagination of the Muslim mystic poet, Radha (the beloved of Lord Krishna) appears as Fatima and Krishna as Allah.

The remaining part of the Jari states,

> Muhammad then told Kulsum that if she wanted to save her prestige by feeding her numerous guests properly, she must invite Fatima to please Allah. Kulsum accordingly appeared before Fatima and begged to be forgiven. Upon the request of Muhammad, Fatima forgave her sister, but said that as per God's desire, she (Fatima) would be in charge of the food and Ganga (the river Ganges) in charge of distributing drinking water. So Ganga should accompany them in order to make the feast a success. Fatima then asked her son Madar [*Pir* Madar was famous in Eastern Bengal] to secure the companionship of the river Ganges.
>
> Fatima's order was obeyed by Madar. Finally Muhammad, Hassan, Hussain, Fatima, and Ali, who were collectively venerated by the faqirs as *Pak Panjatan* or the five holy persons, began their journey towards Kulsum's house. Upon the request of Fatima, Allah sent Gabriel with food which could be distributed among the numerous guests of Kulsum. (Jasimuddin 1968, 44)

This Jari can be regarded as an important document on the social and economic history of nineteenth-century Bengal. However, it did not lose its relevance in the twentieth century either, since we have shown that the song mentioned above was collected from a Jari singer in the 1950s. We see in the song that annoyed by Kulsum's accumulation of wealth, Muhammad advised her to spend it on the poor and hungry people of the country. Through Kulsum's defiance of her father's advice, the folk poet probably tried to expose how affluent Muslims in rural Bengal had deviated from the path of Muhammad. Allah has said through Muhammad, 'Practice regular charity (*zakat*), whereas Kulsum, who represented the affluent Muslims, was showing indifference to the practice of *zakat*' (Jasimuddin 1968, 44–45). Kulsum's antagonism towards her poverty-stricken sister Fatima actually represents the antagonism that opulent Muslims display towards their poor brethren. However, in the fertile imagination of the folk poet, Fatima, the representative of the have-nots, emerged victorious over Kulsum, who represents the opulent, oppressive feudal lords. This is why we see all the food stored in Kulsum's godown disappear in a supernatural event. Bengal had been struck by famines during the colonial period, and hoarding of this sort had increased the suffering of the people. That experience probably prompted the folk poet to remind the opulent Muslims about Muhammad's advice to Kulsum regarding her religious duty, which involved the proper distribution of her wealth amongst the poor and hungry. It goes without saying that this conversation between Muhammad and his daughter is not supported by historical evidence.

When Muhammad asks Kulsum to appear before Fatima in a repentant mood, we understand that the poet is indirectly asking the affluent Muslims of Bengal to apologise to their less fortunate brethren who were reeling under poverty, largely due to their own indifference towards the latter. Muhammad used to say, '*Al faqr fakhri*' or 'Poverty (meditation in God) is all my pride'. And according to the *faqiri* tradition, poverty and power are juxtaposed in Fatima. The impact of the faqiri tradition is clear in this Jari, proved by the poet's tendency to emphasise on the *telesmati* (supernatural power) of Fatima, so much so that he is even prepared to relegate Muhammad to the background.[6] By depicting Pir Madar as the son of Fatima, the poet has done scant justice to history, but has confirmed his adherence to the *faqiri tattva* (Sufi concept). By seeking the companionship of the holy river Ganges, Fatima actually strengthens the composite culture of South Asia, much to the consternation of the custodians of hegemonic orthodoxy.

Let us now approach an intriguing Baul song. It is interesting to note that the intercessory role of Jesus Christ figures prominently in the New Testament, which has given a higher position to Jesus than to Moses as a mediator between God and men (Swete 1911, 88). So it is not difficult to understand that in an age of religious competition, folk Islam will place greater emphasis on the intercessory role of Muhammad to establish him as a source of authority. Jaher Ali, a relatively unknown Baul of the late nineteenth century, sings in tune with this spirit:

> The worried and pensive Jaher says that the
> Day of Judgement will be troublesome. If you
> want to cross the sirat bridge safely then
> look for an advocate now. (Qasimpuri 1973, 435)

This advocate is none other than the Prophet Muhammad himself, who is expected to plead for the believers on the Day of Judgement (Ali 1938, 782; Qasimpuri 1973, 435; Swete 1911, 88).[7]

The exploitation of the Muslim peasantry by moneylenders was reflected in one Lalan song:

> There's no one in this world so rich
> That I may go to him and fall at his feet
> and tell him my tale of woe.
> The priests...
> cheat you...
> your debt
> no one will be able to pay....
> If the Prophet is entreated
> he will, says Lalan, graciously agree
> to take the entire burden of our debt. (Rushd 1964, 10)

The message is quite clear. Lalan, who came from an agrarian background, was shocked to see the peasantry reeling under the perpetual debt trap created by the *mahajans* (moneylenders). The ulama were not prepared to come to their rescue. Under such circumstances, Lalan advised the rural folk to pray in the name of Muhammad, who would take on the entire burden of their debt (Rushd 1964, 10; Sarkar 1987, 38–43).[8] The underlying meaning is that in the real world, the possibility of paying the debt is remote. But consolation lies in the world beyond, where everyone is deeply indebted to Allah. Only Muhammad is capable of taking on the entire burden of that eternal debt. In this way, the Baul songs could provide solace and self-confidence to the peasantry in rural Bengal, even in the midst of poverty and hunger.

ENDNOTES

1. *Milad* is the birth anniversary of the Prophet Muhammad. *Milad* literature is partly composed in poetry and partly in prose, and can be recited. At times, Urdu couplets are inserted to enhance its religious value.

2. This is a deliberate insertion because to some, folk Islam or popular Islam is the mainstream Islam, and not the scriptural one.

3. The term 'secular' has been used in the medieval context only for the sake of convenience.

4. In fact, myself and my collaborators at Max Weber Kolleg, University of Erfurt, Germany, argue that if modernity implies a broad liberal or eclectic attitude based on the spirit of celebrating multiculturalism, this also emerged beyond the frontiers of the Western world. It can be explored in various Oriental civilisations such as the Perso-Islamic traditions and can be termed as 'alternative modernity', which may not be directly associated with the Industrial Revolution, massive growth of capitalism, or scientific explorations that the West has experienced. The rapid radicalisation of religion since the beginning of the nineteenth century threatened the broad liberal, spiritual, human, and rational outlook associated with Perso-Islamic traditions in general and Perso-Islamic mystical traditions in particular. Radicalisation can be defined as homogenisation or Arabisation, which is not necessarily reduced to linguistic implications. For example, one aspect of this homogenisation process emphasises the narrow concept of 'one country, one language, one religion', which is incompatible with the notions of modernity.

5. I have translated the song from Bengali into English.

6. Rahman 1986; also see Jasimuddin 1968. For an analytical perspective, see Dey 2006, Ch. 4.

7. According to the belief of devout Muslims, there is a bridge over Hell, called the *sirat* bridge, over which all must pass to their final destiny. In Bengali literature, this bridge is popularly called *pulsirat*. It is believed that the feet of unrepentant sinners and hypocrites will slide on this bridge on the Day of Judgement. However, the bridge is not mentioned in the Quran (*vide* Ali 1938, 782; Qasimpuri 1973, 435). Information about Jaher Ali is available in Qasimpuri (1973). He lived in the village of Pabiajor of Netrokona subdivision in Eastern Bengal. He became an expert in music and dance at an early age, and used to compose songs and

lived as a Sufi saint during the last years of his life. Interestingly, Jesus has also been depicted as an advocate in the New Testament (Swete 1911, 88).

8. See Rushd (1964, 10). The majority of peasants in Bengal were Muslims, while most of the mahajans and *zamindars* were Hindu (Sarkar 1987, 38–43).

Select References

Alam, Wahidul. 1985. *Chattagramer Lok Sahitya*. Dhaka.

Ali, Abdullah Yusuf. 1938. *The Holy Quran: Text Translation and Commentary*. Jeddah.

Athar, Ali (ed.). 2020. *Exploring Medieval India through Persian Sources*. New Delhi: National Mission for Manuscripts.

Dey, Amit. 2006. *The Image of the Prophet in Bengali Muslim Piety: 1850–1947*. Kolkata: Readers Service.

———. 2019. 'Sufism and Society in Medieval India'. In Suparna Gooptu (ed.), *Themes and Individuals in History*, 3–32. Kolkata: K. P. Bagchi.

———. 2020. 'Reconstructing the Past through Malfuzat Literature: The Case of Fawaidul Fuad'. In Ali Athar (ed.), *Exploring Medieval India through Persian Sources*, 45–56. New Delhi: National Mission for Manuscripts.

Dutta, Abhijit. 1992. *Nineteenth Century Bengal Society and the Christian Missionaries*. Calcutta: Minerva.

Eaton, Richard Maxwell. 1996. *The Rise of Islam and the Bengal Frontier 1204–1760*. Berkeley: University of California Press.

Gooptu, Suparna (ed.). 2019. *Themes and Individuals in History*. Kolkata: K. P. Bagchi.

Jasimuddin. 1968. *Jari Gan*. Dhaka.

Karim, Anwarul. 1980. *The Bauls of Bangladesh*. Kushtia: Lalan Academy.

Metcalf, Barbara Daly. 1982. *Islamic Revival in British India: Deoband, 1860–1900*. Surrey: Princeton University Press.

Pannenberg, Wolfhart. 1968. *Jesus, God and Man*, first English translation. London.

Qasimpuri, Sirajuddin (ed.). 1973. *Bangladesher Loksangit Parichiti* (*Introducing the Folksongs of Bangladesh*). Dhaka.

Rahman, S. M. Lutfar. 1986. *Bangladesher Jari Gan (Jari Songs of Bangladesh)*. Dhaka.

Roy, Asim. 1983. *Islamic Syncretistic Tradition in Bengal*. Surrey: Princeton University Press.

Rushd, Abu. 1964. *Songs of Lalan Shah*. Dhaka: Bangla Academy.

Sarkar, Tanika. 1987. *Bengal 1928–1934: The Politics of Protest*. Delhi: Oxford University Press.

Schimmel, Annemarie. 1985. *And Muhammad is His Messenger: The Veneration of the Prophet in Islamic Piety*. Chapel Hill: The University of North Carolina Press.

Swete, Henry Barclay. 1911. *The Ascended Christ: A Study in the Early Modern Christian Teaching*. London: Macmillan and Co. Limited.

Talib, Muhammad Abu. 1968. *Lalan Shah O Lalan Gitika (Lalan Shah and Lalan Songs)*, Vol. 1. Dacca.

7

Bijoy Krishna Goswami and the Reform Movement in Nineteenth-century Bengal*

Sujata Mukherjee

Thirty-eight years after its inception, the Brahmo Samaj, the pioneering (socio)religious reform organisation of the Bengali Hindus established by Rammohun Roy (1772–1833) in Calcutta in 1828 (then known as the Brahmo Sabha), was split into two groups (Damen 1983; Jones 1991; Kopf 1978; Sastri 1911). The followers of Debendranath Tagore came to be known as the Adi Brahmo Samaj, while those who followed Keshab Chandra Sen (1838–1884) formed the Indian Brahmo Samaj.

In course of time, there developed a conflict of ideas which led to a further division within the Brahmo Samaj of India, and a split between the followers of Keshab Sen and their opponents that formally took place in 1878. The latter group then came to be known as the Sadharan Brahmo Samaj, and the supporters of Keshab organised the Nava Vidhan or New Dispensation. Another important but less discussed event took place in September 1886 when Bijoy Krishna Goswami (1841–1899), a legendary Brahmo missionary and reformer who played a leading role in both schisms and in the spread of the Brahmo movement in different regions, resigned from the post of missionary of the Sadharan Brahmo Samaj. Goswami, the least Westernised among the Brahmo leaders

---

*An earlier version of this chapter was published as 'Profile of a Reformer: Bijoy Krishna Goswami and "his" Brahmo Message', in Ranjit Ray (ed.), *Retrieving Bengal's Past: Society and Culture in the Nineteenth and Twentieth Century*. Calcutta: Progressive Publishers, 1995. Permission to publish this version received from Rabindra Bharati University.

and hailed as the 'best-loved and most effective Brahmo missionary in Bengal during the nineteenth century' (Kopf 1978, 218), emphasised that he had believed and acted according to the basic tenets of Brahmoism. The Executive Committee of the Sadharan Brahmo Samaj accepted his resignation after much debate and discussion. This incident sparked off a great controversy between the two groups. Bijoy Krishna Goswami's followers demanded that his new methods and views be openly discussed, in order to see whether the basis of the Brahmo Samaj could be broadened to accommodate new experiments (Datta 1293 BS, 272; Roy 1295 BS, 54).

The opposing group of critics pointed out that Bijoy Krishna's characteristic weakness of will, highly impulsive nature, and instability of mind had paved the way for the acceptance of mystic ideas and other beliefs and practices of popular Hinduism, which went against the rational spirit of the Brahmo Samaj (Mitra 1288 BS, 154; Roy 1293 BS, 36). This adverse criticism was echoed in 1899 after Bijoy Krishna's demise at Puri, and again even later (*Dharmatattva* 1306 BS, 221). It was pointed out that he had swung between a rationalism that was entirely antagonistic to his nature and back again to the old Hindu fold. In modern historiography, too, an echo of this view can sometimes be found.

His association of more than a quarter-century with the Brahmo movement has been interpreted as a mere 'aberration'; his pro-radical stance and association with the progressive element as 'incidental', only to be sidelined when the latent pro-Vaishnava revivalistic aspect of his character asserted itself as an intrinsic reflection of his Vaishnava background. Alexander Lipski has portrayed Bijoy Krishna as predominantly a leader of the Vaishnava revival in nineteenth-century Bengal (Lipski 1974).

According to another historian, 'Bijoy Krishna Goswami's life had been a circular pilgrimage from his orthodox Vaishnavism through the Brahmo Samajees of Tagore, Sen, and the Sadharanis, returning finally to the devotional Vaishnavism of Chaitanya' (Jones 1991, 39). At the other end of the scale lies the opinion of Bipin Chandra Pal, a nationalist leader and disciple of Bijoy Krishna, whom the latter initiated in 1895. He described Bijoy Krishna as a modernist who tried to infuse a rationalist spirit into Vaishnavism. He pointed out that Bijoy Krishna's secession from the Brahmo Samaj gladdened those who opposed the progressive propaganda of the Samaj, and who had gathered in increasing numbers until they almost overwhelmed his personality and his teachings in their determined and designed attempt to present him to the people as a great Hindu, saint, and seer of the medieval type. This, in Bipin Chandra Pal's opinion, ultimately blurred the vision of the great and fundamental truths for which he stood (Pal 1964, 8).

This chapter seeks to analyse the nature of Bijoy Krishna Goswami's activities and the role he played in the context of socioreligious changes in nineteenth-century Bengal. It aims to understand his contributions through an analysis of the evolution of different aspects of his ideas and activities. Was he 'predominantly' a leader of Vaishnava revival? Was his association with the Brahmo Samaj only 'incidental' and a mere 'aberration'? Or was he a modernist trying to infuse a non-dogmatic, rationalist spirit into religion? This chapter will address these questions through a scrutiny of the available source materials on Bijoy Krishna.

Early Life

Bijoy Krishna was born on 2 August 1841 in his maternal grandfather's home at Dahakul near Sikarpur in Nadia district. As pointed out by a researcher, the circumstances of Bijoy Krishna's birth, early development, and education indicated that 'Bijoy Krishna Goswami was, among all the Brahmos ... the least Westernized' (Kopf 1978, 219). Another author has reasonably argued that 'The religious career of Bijoy Krishna illustrates the interaction between pre-British culture and the new world of the colonial milieu' (Jones 1991, 39).

He was the tenth descendant of Advaita Acharya, the renowned companion of the sixteenth-century Vaishnava cult figure and leader of the reform movement of Bengal, Sri Chaitanyadev.

His father, Anandokishore Goswami, a devout Vaishnava priest, died when Bijoy Krishna was only two years old. His mother, Swarnomoyee Devi, was not only an intensely religious woman, but also an exceptionally courageous lady who dared to flout orthodox social norms to serve the poor, irrespective of their caste or creed (Bhattacharya 1344 BS, 3–4). Apart from Vaishnava piety, Bijoy Krishna also inherited his mother's philanthropic concern, which was perhaps the genesis of his commitment towards the poor and socially downtrodden.

His life began in the semi-medieval town of Santipur, his ancestral home. Santipur was well-known for three classes of people: the Goswamis (devotional teachers or gurus from the Gaudiya Vaishnava tradition), weavers, and tailors. In early nineteenth-century Bengal, the Goswamis constituted a socially powerful group, patronised by local landlords. From the late eighteenth century onwards, the new rich class of Bengal had become the champions of Gaudiya Vaishnavism. As early as 1811, William Ward pointed out that two persons in ten among the entire Hindu population in Bengal were supposed to be followers of Chaitanya. Although initially Vaishnavism promoted a liberal outlook among Bengali Hindus and furthered the cause of literacy and social consciousness among women, it degenerated over time and eventually failed to spread ethical values (Chakrabarty 1985, 132). The local zamindars of Santipur were patrons of the Krishna cult, and about one-third of the population of Santipur town were Vaishnavas. Santipur was also a noted centre of Sakto worship. However, the religious practices of different sects had degenerated, promoting immoral sexual acts and excessive alcoholism. Apparently, in the atmosphere of generally low moral standards as prevailed in Santipur at the time, social evils were also rampant.

History books record that as a child, Bijoy Krishna shared the religiosity of his traditional orthodox family. 'He was devoted to the idol of Krishna and would fall into ecstatic trances' (Jones 1991, 39). What is not often mentioned is how Bijoy Krishna also had an enthusiasm for reform; he had organised a team of young boys of Santipur, inspiring them to take up social welfare activities. They helped the poor and protected the womenfolk against various social abuses. Thus the local boys, led by Bijoy Krishna, set an example of high moral standards in a traditional society facing moral decay and regressive social norms. Bijoy Krishna's honesty and sincerity even spurred a clash with the local zamindar when he protested against the inhuman treatment being meted out to a poor tenant. His social activities during his boyhood days in Santipur appear almost as a blueprint of the Brahmo reform agenda of later days. Later in his life, Bijoy Krishna joined the liberal reform movements launched by the Sangat Sabha (1860) and Keshab Chandra Sen's Indian Reform Association (1870).

Bijoy Krishna and the Brahmo Samaj

After completing his studies in the traditional Sanskrit curriculum at '*tols*' and '*chatuspathis*' (both centres of Sanskrit education) in Santipur (which had no English-medium school in those days), Bijoy Krishna, along with his friend Aghorenath Gupta, came to Calcutta (Bhattacharya 1344 BS, 19), and took admission in the Sanskrit College in 1859. The marriage of 18-year-old Bijoy Krishna with Yogamaya, the 6-year-old daughter of Ramchandra Bhaduri and Muktakesi Devi, took place around this time. Yogamaya proved to be a loyal and understanding companion in every phase of Bijoy Krishna's life. Bijoy Krishna tried his best to educate his wife and inculcate a liberal Brahmo spirit in her, attempts to which Yogamaya proved extremely receptive. Most of his fellow students at Sanskrit College were atheists, who took pleasure in ignoring social customs. Bijoy Krishna came under tremendous pressure from his peers, who unsuccessfully tried to 'civilise' him by introducing him to Western food and alcohol (Lipski 1974, 212). Until then, Bijoy Krishna had pursued his hereditary profession of '*kulaguru*' (family's religious preceptor), and visited disciples in different parts of Bengal. The study of Vedanta, however, led him to question popular Hindu rituals and customary beliefs. It is also recorded that in Rangpur, an elderly lady had touched his feet and appealed to him to save her from worldly sins (Bhattacharya 1344 BS, 49). It struck Bijoy Krishna that it would be a travesty of truth to act as the saviour of others while remaining ignorant about the correct path to salvation. He immediately abandoned the profession, despite the knowledge that this would lead to tremendous financial hardships.

Assailed by religious doubts, Bijoy Krishna attended Debendranath Tagore's sermons. Debendranath's discourse on 'The suffering of sinners and God's mercy' left an indelible impression on him (Goswami 1950, 5). Around 1861, Bijoy Krishna left Sanskrit College and enrolled as a student in the vernacular section of Calcutta Medical College.

Bijoy Krishna was troubled by the custom of wearing the sacred thread and also about eating meat and fish. He had asked his respected preceptor whether it was a sin to wear the sacred thread and whether it was necessary to eat fish and meat. Debendranath's reply—that the sacred thread was essential and that it was also necessary to eat meat and fish for the sake of one's health—failed to convince Bijoy Krishna, and led to intense mental agony. The 'sacred thread literally stung him like a scorpion' (Pal 1964, 26). He ultimately abandoned the sacred thread, becoming the second Brahmin in Bengal (after Ramtanu Lahiri) to take this bold step. Needless to say, this incident caused a great commotion at Santipur. Bijoy Krishna's mother submitted to his strong will and determination, but he was excommunicated by the orthodox section of Hindu society, since

> [T]he Brahmin who gives up his sacred thread becomes by that one act, immediately, a Sudra or even worse, a Chandala, for not even non-Brahmins like, for instance, the Kayasthas and Vaidyas of Bengal, would touch him or take water from his hands, not to mention cooked food. (Pal 1932, 158)

For three years, Bijoy Krishna studied at the Calcutta Medical College. In his final year, before his examinations, he became involved in a controversy. The Principal of the College wrongly accused a student of theft. In protest, Bijoy Krishna organised a students' strike. This is the first recorded incident of a students' agitation in Bengal. At that time, Bijoy Krishna was a spirited youth of twenty-two years, who made fiery speeches to inspire the student community to fight for a just cause. The issue was ultimately settled when the college authority withdrew the charges. Bijoy Krishna, however, left his studies to throw himself wholeheartedly into the organisation and activities of the Brahmo Samaj. He had already joined the Sangat Sabha, an association of progressive young Keshabites. It was here that Bijoy Krishna came into close contact with Keshab Chandra Sen, who influenced him deeply. After listening to discussions at the Sangat regarding the propagation of Brahmoism in mofussil towns, Bijoy Krishna volunteered to take up missionary work.

Debendranath Tagore instructed Bijoy Krishna to go about preaching at places recommended by Tagore himself. But Bijoy disagreed, and asserted that he would take up missionary work only according to the dictates of his own conscience (Damen 1983, 63). According to modern historians like David Kopf (1978), this was the beginning of the disagreement within the Brahmo Samaj. Bijoy Krishna also opposed Debendranath's proposal to introduce a fixed monthly allowance for Brahmo missionaries. This proves that he had a distinctive character, which he refused to surrender even before his preceptor. His very first missionary venture was undertaken at Baganchra in Jessore, which became the model of a reformed Brahmo village. Bijoy Krishna's work was infused with a vigorous social commitment. At Baganchra, he combined missionary work with teaching and nursing the sick, and he also established a Brahmo 'mandir' and an English school. He worked hard to ensure the spread of women's education.

He was also instrumental in arranging a widow remarriage at Baganchra. Within nine days, he had initiated twenty-three families into the Brahmo Samaj. Bijoy Krishna took up the task of reforming the Pirali community of Baganchra in real earnest. Returning to Calcutta, he continued with his reformist zeal and, supported by the progressive section of the Samaj, questioned the custom of allowing only thread-bearing Brahmins to act as *upacharyas* (assistant ministers) of the Brahmo Samaj. Debendranath had to bow down to pressure and on 21 August 1864, two junior members of Brahmo Samaj, Bijoy Krishna Goswami and Annada Prasad Chatterjee, and one other member of the Brahmo Samaj were ordained as upacharyas. This act was the first in a chain of events that ultimately produced the first schism in the Brahmo Samaj in 1866. The younger generation were in favour of internal reforms in the Brahmo Samaj and the abolition of caste rules, as well as the promotion of social reforms. Thus, they were keen to carry out two types of reforms (Mahalanabish 1941, 67–68). In a letter written in August 1865, Keshab Chandra pointed out that unless the Brahmo Samaj 'keeps pace in the progressive spirit of the age, and is modified so as to suit the new ideas and new wants of society, it will suffer in estrangement, from the sympathy of progressive men and fail to accomplish its higher objectives' (Sophia Dobson Collet Collection 1865a).

Debendranath, on the other hand, advised toleration for the older generation of Brahmos. He pointed out that if the younger generation could take them along as they move forward, 'there shall be greater progress' (Sophia Dobson Collet Collection 1865b). Sivanath Sastri, a follower of Keshub Chandra Sen, declared that the reforms favoured by the younger Brahmos 'would violate the long cherished dream of Debendranath's to preach Brahmoism in a national and acceptable form' (Sastri 1881, 9). According to famous German Orientalist Max Muller, Debendranath and his supporters 'pleaded for toleration of Hindu usages and customs which appeared to them innocent' (Muller 1884, 61).

At a general meeting in November 1866, the founding of the Brahmo Samaj of India was formally announced by the progressive Keshabites. The resolution moved by Bijoy Krishna underlined the importance of the vital issue of nationalism and universalism between the two camps. It was proposed that: 'Men and women of every nation and caste who believe in the fundamental doctrines of Brahmo Dharma, shall be eligible as members of the Brahmo Samaj of India' (Kopf 1978, 135).

Bijoy Krishna also called for a compilation of texts based on all the scriptures of the world. The *Sloka Sangraha* (Collection of Hymns) was prepared, to be used in the Brahmo service. The opening of the Keshabite mandir on 22 August 1869, along with the declaration of Keshab Sen, underlined the universalism of the Brahmo Samaj of India. It was declared:

> Divine Service shall be conducted here in such a spirit and manner as may enable men and women, irrespective of distinctions of caste, colour, and condition, to unite in one family, eschew all manner of error and sin, and advance in wisdom, faith, and righteousness. (Mazoomdar 1887, 206–208)

In October 1865, Bijoy Krishna, Aghorenath Gupta, and Keshab Chandra Sen went to Dacca, Faridpur, and Mymensingh. In Dacca, where they stayed for a month, Keshab Sen conducted services in the local Samaj. By the end of December 1866, Keshab Sen had embarked on an extensive tour, which lasted for about four months, to the North-Western Provinces and the Punjab. Another group led by Bijoy Krishna began touring the towns of East Bengal from December 1866.

Sivanath Sastri pointed out,

> Wherever Bijoy Krishna Goswami and Aghorenath Gupta went, new converts were made and their preaching caused wide-spread ferment. There was no railway then and no steamer service in most of the places they visited. They had to perform most of their journeys in country boats and sometimes on foot. During their tour they often fell amongst people hostile to the reform movement and had to put up with great difficulties. But no difficulties discouraged them. (Sastri 1911, 135)

Historians have pointed out that after 1866, Bijoy Krishna's influence on Keshab Sen became apparent. Bijoy Krishna put forward the idea of composing 'Vaishnava-type songs with Brahmo messages' (Kopf 1978, 223). Apparently, Keshab Sen had been highly impressed when he heard Bijoy Krishna's brother, Brajodulal, sing Sankirtanas (Bhattacharya 1344 BS, 13).

Bijoy Krishna, however, was opposed to any irrational attitude or display of religious emotion. He did not hesitate to attack Keshab

Sen during the 'Monghyr incident'. In June 1868, Keshab Sen had spoken and acted as Chaitanya at the weekly congregation held at Monghyr. People came to regard Keshab Sen as the incarnation of God, and were often moved to 'tears and sobs and ejaculations that were well-nigh hysterical' (Mazoomdar 1887, 193).

Sivanath Sastri wrote, 'People prostrated themselves at the feet of Mr. Sen and prayers were offered to him for intercession on behalf of sinners' (Sastri 1911, 227). In a letter to the Editor of *Som Prokash*, Bijoy Krishna observed:

> It is against the principles of the Brahmos to call Keshab Babu the Saviour, to pray to him for 'salvation', to kiss his feet, and to compose sacred songs in his name. It is the duty of Brahmos to revere Keshab as a human being. Brahmoism recognizes only God as the saviour. We request Keshab Babu to dissuade other Brahmos from this dangerous course. (Goswami 1868)

Despite this ideological clash, however, there was no personal enmity or bitterness between the two men. After Keshab Sen returned from England in 1870, he established the Indian Reform Association. Bijoy Krishna was placed in charge of the charity section and also participated in women's education programmes. During an outbreak of a severe malaria epidemic in Behala in the late nineteenth century, Bijoy Krishna and his team worked hard to provide relief among the malaria-stricken population (Kar 1317 BS, 155). Bijoy Krishna also continued his missionary tours in East Bengal, where 'chiefly through his endeavour, the Bengal renaissance, which had been restricted for the most part to urbanized Calcutta, now spread to the municipal settlements of East Bengal' (Kopf 1978, 226).

Within the Brahmo Samaj of India, there gradually developed an ideological difference between two groups around the broad questions of democracy and social reform. The Brahmo Samaj had, after prolonged struggle, been successful in compelling the British government to pass the Civil Marriage Act in 1872, which fixed the minimum age of marriage of the bridegroom at eighteen and of the bride at fourteen. Keshab Sen himself acted in contravention of this Act when he arranged the marriage of his 13-year-old daughter to the 15-year-old son of the Maharaja of Cooch Behar. More than the declaration of the marriage, it was Keshab Sen's undemocratic attitude which alienated the radical group and precipitated a crisis. When the marriage took place, the progressive faction or constitutionalists attacked Keshab Sen for having ignored the wishes of fifty Samajes. Although they belonged to different regions, they had condemned the marriage in one unequivocal voice as being inconsistent with the recognised and accepted principles of the Brahmo Samaj.

On 9 May 1878, Bijoy Krishna called for the organisation of a new Samaj, to be conducted on a 'constitutional basis'. He also formulated a set of guiding principles for the proposed Samaj, which included an acceptance of the electoral principle for executive officers, and representative principles by which only 'anusthanic' or practising Brahmos would have the right to decide a policy. This finally led to the creation of the Sadharan Brahmo Samaj on 15 May 1878 at a meeting in the Town Hall of Calcutta.

Bijoy Krishna's association with radical and progressive Brahmos and his assumption of the leadership have been interpreted as 'incidental', and even 'incongruous' (Lipski 1974, 222). However, as mentioned earlier, it is evident that Bijoy Krishna assumed the leadership and actively organised the movement against Keshab Sen at this critical juncture quite consciously, acting according to his own rational judgement. His was a deeply idealistic stance, and he could not but react instantly to any deviation from the basic principles on which the strength of the Samaj had been built. In 1878, Bijoy Krishna once again embarked on his mission to reach the grassroots level of society and spread the message of the newly founded Sadharan Brahmo Samaj. In June 1878, he went to Dacca to work as the acharya of the East Bengal Brahmo Samaj. His speeches and prayers at Dacca, Faridpur, and Barisal revitalised the movement and enabled new converts. Based on his wide range of experience, Bijoy Krishna drew up a plan of action to be followed by the *Sadharanis* (members of the Sadharan Brahmo

Samaj). He suggested that married male Brahmos who were not yet engaged in missionary work should start involving themselves in such activity. At places where the Brahmo Samaj was not yet established, missionaries were to travel and popularise the Brahmo faith. Bijoy Krishna pointed out that the present condition of the Brahmo Samaj had aroused misgivings in the minds of people. Therefore, it was the urgent duty of the missionaries to restore the Brahmo faith to its original position of respect. He held that while it was absolutely necessary to struggle for the truth, the missionary should be above factionalism. Liberalism and honesty were to be promoted. Every missionary should practice humility and reject pride, but not at the cost of their character. He also believed that doing one's assigned task with devotion was on par with prayer. Bijoy Krishna was convinced that these simple principles would help to popularise Brahmoism among the educated bhadralok class, as well as the common people.

According to Bijoy Krishna, many had misunderstood Brahmoism to be a religion practised by ascetics and mendicants. Therefore, it was the duty of the Sadharan Brahmo Samaj to dispel that misconception and popularise the essence of Brahmoism. As the expansion of the Samaj would facilitate the entry of the poor and downtrodden within its fold, Bijoy Krishna suggested that every Brahmo should contribute to building up a fund to help the poor. Between 1878 and 1880, for nearly two-and-a-half years, he acted as acharya of the East Bengal Brahmo Samaj and also went on missionary tours to different places. His devotional prayers, lectures on the interpretation of Hindu scriptures, and mythological stories attracted a large audience. Through Bijoy Krishna's tours, the Brahmo Samaj was revitalised and the demoralising effects of the schisms and factionalism were overcome. In his speech as acharya, Bijoy Krishna emphasised that the abandonment of the worship of Brahma, as originally practised by the Aryans, was really responsible for the deterioration of the country. Therefore, it was necessary to revive it to bring about religious improvement, which was the key to the country's well-being. In 1880, Bijoy Krishna established a Brahmo Samaj at Gaya.

ALIENATION FROM THE BRAHMO SAMAJ

Despite Bijoy Krishna's involvement in missionary activities, it seemed that 'religious transformation during that period (1878 to 1886) alienated him more and more from the leadership in the Sadharan Brahmo Samaj' (Lipski 1974, 222). There existed factional feuds within the Brahmo Samaj, which possibly disturbed him. His spiritual quest and longings led him to explore the beliefs of many non-conformist sects that existed on the fringes of Hindu society. This search had actually begun before the Cooch-Behar marriage, while he was at Baganchra, when he had gone to the Kartabhajas, Bauls, Sahajiyas, Muslim fakirs, etc. He also repeatedly visited Ramakrishna Paramhansa, the great sage at Dakshineswar. At last, in July 1883, he probably found what he was looking for. As Bijoy said, 'Finally at Gaya a mahatma of the path of Nanak had mercy on me and instructed me in Yoga' (De Sarkar 1402 BS, 161). Bijoy Krishna's Guru, Brahmananda Paramhamsa, was a Punjabi Brahmin living near Manasarovar, whom he met in the Akash Ganga Hill region in Gaya. It is significant to note that he was a follower of Guru Nanak, for Nanak's teachings was one of the components that had shaped Bijoy Krishna's eclecticism. The Brahmo congregations led by Bijoy Krishna increasingly became meeting places for all sects and communities, including Brahmos, Hindus, and Christians. After 1883, he began initiating people in 'yoga' as well.

This new path could be embraced by all—there was to be no discrimination between rich and poor, educated and uneducated, low or high caste, male or female, as explained by Bijoy Krishna himself (Goswami 1357 BS, 9–10). All this created a great ferment and generated criticism among Brahmos. Bijoy Krishna asserted that he was a believer in Brahmo monotheism. According to him, the fundamental truth of religion could be found in all sects and communities, as true religion could never allow differences among people. He expressed these views in a letter issued from the missionary's residence in Calcutta in May 1886. At the same time, Bijoy Krishna sent his letter of resignation from the Sadharan Brahmo Samaj, which was accepted by the Executive Committee. Sivanath Sastri wrote:

> The cause of his [Bijoy Krishna's] separation was an unhappy difference that had sprung up between himself and the members of the Samaj about some later developments of faith and practice that marked his conduct during the previous three or four years. During that period he had begun to associate with orthodox Hindu mendicants from whom he imbibed certain mystic ideas, which were not in keeping with the reformed principles of the Brahmo Samaj. (Sastri 1911, 311)

Bijoy Krishna's resignation, as noted earlier, created a commotion, and led to protests and counter-protests. His only known reaction had been to state; 'If the Brahmos did not protest I would have thought that the Brahmo Samaj had died a rotten death' (ibid., 285). Bijoy Krishna's resignation undoubtedly affected the Sadharan Brahmo Samaj adversely, contributing to its decline. Sivanath Sastri's account clearly shows that in the post-Bijoy Krishna phase, the activity of the Samaj was confined to social and constitutional issues. According to him, the absence of a charismatic personality and the loss of missionary drive contributed to the decline of the Samaj.

After leaving the Sadharan Brahmo Samaj, Bijoy Krishna founded an ashram at Gendaria (Dacca) in 1888, which became a meeting place for Hindus, Brahmos, as well as Muslim fakirs. His rejection of caste and community discrimination and emphasis on religious harmony were apparent in the fact that he initiated Christians like Mr Kembel and Muslims like Sheikh Kashimuddin (Chaudhuri 1973, 40). His visit to the Kumbha Mela in Allahabad in 1894 has been regarded as a high point in the revival of the Chaitanya cult (Lipski 1974, 229). Here, Bijoy Krishna was opposed by the orthodox section of the Vaishnavas. The same happened in Brindaban, where he wore a mark on his forehead that combined Hindu, Muslim, and Sikh symbols, instead of the traditional *tilak* (a mark on the forehead, made usually from sandalwood paste). Bipin Chandra Pal cited instances of Bijoy Krishna's non-acceptance of traditional Hindu social customs; he consumed bread prepared by Muslim bakers, for instance, and did not hesitate to invite Shaukat Ali, a Mohammedan peon of the Sadharan Brahmo Samaj, to sit on a mat on which a *shalgramsheela* (a sacred stone) had been placed (Pal 1964, 82). Pal furnished numerous other examples of Bijoy Krishna's liberalism and interpreted his Vaishnavism as a modern creed, infused with universalism and rationalism. Religion, to him, basically meant a code of conduct, which involved honesty, non-violence, simplicity, rejection of all sectarian and community bias, etc. Neither the observance of religious customs and rituals nor emotional outbursts during kirtan seemed meaningful to Bijoy Krishna (Chaudhuri 1973, 281). It was love for his fellow human beings, particularly the deprived and downtrodden, irrespective of faith, creed, and caste, that really mattered. A grassroots-level missionary at heart, Bijoy Krishna interpreted the Brahmo messages of universalism and rationalism in his own way to overcome the barriers imposed by caste and community. In Puri, he spent more than Rs 1 lakh in charity and often exposed the acts of the greedy *pandas* (priests at the Jagannath temple, Puri) who cheated the common people (ibid., 519–537). It was in Puri that Bijoy Krishna breathed his last in May 1899.

Reflections

Assessments of Bijoy Krishna are contradictory, and often assume the form of virulent character assassination. He has been painted as a morphine addict who failed to act rationally (Upadhyay 1938, 192–194); at the same time, he is also accused of hatching plans to sever his association with the Brahmo Samaj in order to return to the Hindu fold in self-interest. His mother-in-law and son-in-law are blamed for propagating his supernatural powers in order to attract devotees, and extract money and gifts from them (Prabhudas Krittibas 1991, 194). On the other hand, some of his lifelong companions, like Jogendranath Vidyabhushan (Vidyabhushan 1306 BS, 537), as well as later-day disciples have hailed his anti-idolatrous beliefs, his simplicity, and non-attachment to worldly comforts (Chakraborty 1337 BS, 188).

It would be unjust to describe Bijoy Krishna as merely a revivalist leader of Vaishnavism. He tried to infuse modernist and rationalist values into age-old, traditional religious practices. Throughout his life, Bijoy Krishna's mission was to break the barriers of elitism (unlike many of his Westernised counterparts) and reach the masses. The goal was to bridge the gulf between different sects and communities. Far from being a weak character who reacted impulsively, Bijoy Krishna happened to be a strong-willed personality who never compromised with what was untrue or hypocritical. He displayed independent judgement and the talent of an organiser. He initiated movements of dissent in the face of any discrepancy between belief and action. Throughout his life—including his Brahmo and non-Brahmo phases, when he was supposedly acting as a Vaishnava 'guru'—Bijoy Krishna provoked the wrath of the conservative sections of society for his rejection of orthodoxy and dogmatism. It has been pointed out that 'through reevaluation and synthesis, Bijoy Krishna's saintly ideal represents a modified form of asceticism' (Kopf 1978, 219). It would not be an exaggeration to state that Bijoy Krishna's life represents an untiring exercise in understanding the principles of rationalism, universalism, and liberalism within an indigenous frame of reference, beyond the limits set by Westernised social reformers who failed to break through the barriers of elitism.

Select References

Bagchi, Nabakumar. 1922. *Sri Sri Vijay Kathamrita*. Calcutta.

Bhattacharya, Kalikrishna. 1344 BS. 'Mahatma Bijoykrishna Goswami'. *Santipur Parichay* I. Kolkata: Published by the author.

Brahmachari, Kuladananda. 1336 BS. *Sri Sri Sadgurusanga*. Puri: Published by Sri Sankarnath Bandyopadhyay.

Chakrabarty, Ramakanta. 1985. *Vaisnavism in Bengal (1486–1900)*. Calcutta: Sanskrit Pustak Bhandar.

Chakraborty, Monomohan. 1337 BS. 'Barisale Paitallish Batsar'. *Brahmobadi* Aghran–Pous.

Chaudhuri, Tarinicharan. 1973. *Sadguru Sri Sri Vijaykrishna*. Calcutta: Jijnasa.

Damen, Frans L. 1983. *Crisis and Religious Renewal in the Brahmo Samaj (1860–1884): A Documentary Study of the Emergence of the 'New Dispensation' under Keshab Chandra Sen*. Leuven: Katholieke Universiteit.

Datta, Kalinath. 1293 BS. 'Letter'. *Tattakaumudi* Chaitra.

De Sarkar, Maheschandra. 1402 BS. *Sri Sri Bijoy Bhagabat*. Bishnupur: Sri Sri Bijoy Yogashram.

Dharmatattva. 1306 BS. 'Editorial', Asarh.

Goswami, Bijaykrishna. 1950. *Brahmo Samajer Bartaman Abastha: Amar Jibane Brahmo Samajer Parikshita Bisay O Kayekti Upadesa* (in Bengali). Calcutta, 3e.

_____. 1357 BS. *Ashabatir Upakhyan*. Ramchandrapur.

_____. 1868. 'Letter to the Editor'. *Som Prokash*.

Jones, Kenneth W. 1991. *Socio-Religious Reform Movements in British India*. Cambridge: Cambridge University Press.

Kar, Bankabihari. 1317 BS. *Mahatma Bijaykrishna Goswamir Jiban Brittanta* (in Bengali). Dacca: Bharat Mahila Press.

Kopf, David. 1978. *The Brahmo Samaj and the Shaping of the Modern Indian Mind*. Princeton: Princeton University Press.

Lipski, Alexander. 1974. 'Vijay Krishna Goswami: Reformer and Traditionalist'. *Journal of Indian History* 52 (I), April.

Mahalanabish, Gurucharan. 1974. *Atmakatha*. Kolkata.

Mahalanabish, M. (compiled). 1941. *Brahmananda Sri Keshub Chandrer Patrabali* (Correspondence of Keshub Chandra Sen). Calcutta: Bharatvarshiya Brahmo Mandir.

Mazoomdar, P. C. 1887. *The Life and Teachings of Keshub Chunder Sen*. Calcutta: Baptist Mission Press.

Mitra, Nagendrachandra. 1288 BS. 'Letter'. *Dharmatattva* Sraban, 154.

Muller, F. M. 1884. *Biographical Essays*. New York: Charles Scribner's Sons.

Pal, Bipin Chandra. 1932. *Memories of My Life and Times*, 2 vols. Calcutta: Modern Book Agency.

Pal, Bipin Chandra. 1964. *Saint Bijoy Krishna Goswami*. Calcutta: Bipin Chandra Pal Institute.

Prabhudas Krittibas. 1991. *Sri Sri Bijoykrishna: Prem-Projna o Ninda-oboggnaraloke* (in Bengali). Calcutta: Debmon.

Roy, Anathbandhu. 1295 BS. 'Letter'. *Tattakaumudi* Asarh.

Roy, Banga Chandra. 1293 BS. 'The Movement of Respected Bijoybabu'. *Bangabandhu* Asarh.

Roy, Sitanath, n.d. *1270 Saler Katha* (in Bengali).

Sastri, Sivanath. 1881. *The New Dispensation and the Sadharan Brahmo Samaj*. Madras: Viyavharatharunjinee Press.

_____. 1911. *History of the Brahmo Samaj*, 2 vols. Calcutta: R. Chatterjee.

Sen, Prasanta Kumar. 1933. *Biography of a New Faith*, 2 vols. Calcutta: Thacker, Spink, & Co.; Vol. 2, 8–13.

Tattakaumudi. 1293 BS.

Sophia Dobson Collet Collection. 1865a. 'Letter from K. C. Sen to D. Tagore', 1 August. Calcutta: Sadharan Brahmo Samaj Library.

_____. 1865b. 'Letter from D. Tagore to K. C. Sen', 9 August. Calcutta: Sadharan Brahmo Samaj Library.

The World and the New Dispensation. 1899. 'The Late Babu Bejoy Krishna Goswami', 11 June.

Upadhyay, Sri Gourgovinda. 1938. *Acharya Keshabchandra*, Vol. II, Centenary edition. Calcutta.

Vidyabhushan, Jogendranath. 1306 BS. 'Beerpuja'. *Nabyabharat* Magh.

Section II

Aspects of Bengali Politics, Society, and Economy

8

The Other Gaze

South India in Select Bengali Historical Narrative

Ranjeeta Dutta

> *The historical background to this novel has been compiled from Robert Sewell's* A Forgotten Empire, *along with contemporary manuscripts. Sewell's book is sixty-five years old. Hence I have corrected some of the information in it on the basis of my reading of* The Delhi Sultanate, *edited by Romesh Chandra Mazumdar. Despite the presence of historical characters in my novel, the story is original; it is set in approximately 1430* AD. *The end of the Vijayanagara empire was still a hundred years away.*
>
> *...I would like to state that my story is not* fictionalized history—*it is* historical fiction.
>
> (Saradindu Bandopadhyay, as cited in Sinha 2010b; emphasis mine)

Writing in 1965, the famous Bengali author, Saradindu Bandopadhyay (1899–1970), made a sagacious statement about the relationship between history and historical fiction. By refusing to categorise his novel *Tungabhadrar Tire* (*By the Tungabhadra*) as *fictionalised history*, Bandopadhyay clearly validated the idea of historical fiction, which the academic discipline of history usually considers the ramblings of a fanciful imagination and disregards as a legitimate form of retelling the past. *Tungabhadrar Tire* is one amongst five historical novels written by Saradindu Bandopadhyay. The other four were: *Kaler Mondira* (*The Chime of Time*, 1951),

Gaur Malhar (*Bengal's Music*, 1954), *Tumi Sandhyar Megh* (*You are the Evening Cloud*, 1958), and *Kumarsambhaber Kobi* (*The Poet of Kumarasambhaba*, 1963). Composed within the frame of mystery novels, a genre which the writer is famously identified with, *Tungabhadrar Tire* is a fifteenth-century tale of love and political intrigues, set in the Vijayanagara Empire of south India. The Vijayanagara Empire (1336–1672 CE) was established in the fourteenth century CE against the backdrop of invasions of the Delhi Sultanate under Muhammad bin Tughlaq (1324–1351 CE) and the decline of Hoysala power (1022–1342 CE) in Karnataka and that of the Kakatiyas (1000–1326 CE) in the Telangana-Andhra region. The empire comprised four ruling dynasties, viz., the Sangamas (1336–1486 CE), Saluvas (1486–1491 CE), Tuluvas (1505–1576 CE), and the Aravidus (1542–1672 CE) (Asher and Talbot 2008, 53–63; Stein 1989, 1–30). The first of these, the Sangamas, established and built the capital of the empire near a village called Hampi, along the river Tungabhadra in the Deccan. The narrative is situated on and around the river Tungabhadra and the city of Vijayanagara during the reign of king Devaraya II (1425–1446 CE) of the Sangama dynasty.

My interest in analysing historical fiction for its representations of culture and regions grew during the course of my research on Shrivaishnavism in southern India in the medieval and early modern period.[1] Professor Ramakanta Chakrabarty's scholarly works on Vaishnavism in Bengal helped me to develop a broad latitudinal perspective on the history of religion (Chakrabarty 1985, 1996). Various scholars and friends with whom I discussed Professor Chakrabarty's works often advised me to read Saradindu Bandhopadhyay's *Tungabhadrar Tire*, which according to them offered a window to the city of Vijayanagara and the geography of southern India through its descriptions of the landscape and of the river Tungabhadra, and of the politics of the region as written by a Bengali. Although it is a historical novel, it was recommended to me as a work of history.

Situated within a particular time and space, *Tungabhadrar Tire* created distinct trajectories of history that reflected the general historical and historiographical milieu that the author had inherited and was a part of. In the *Author's Note* at the beginning of the novel, Bandopadhyay admitted that his sources of information and inspiration were the British administrator Robert Sewell's well-known work, *A Forgotten Empire: Vijayanagar* (Sewell 1962 [1900]), and the famous historian R. C. Majumdar's edited volume, *The Delhi Sultanate* (Majumdar 1960).[2] These two works avowedly influenced his perspective and established the historicity of the narrative. The narrative tropes, undoubtedly historical, constructed a specific perception of the region situated in the south of the Vindhyas. Amongst Bengali readers, this novel was considered a significant source of information on the history of south India, and consequently shaped the Bengali view of the south.

Attempting to transcend the binaries of history and fiction, reality and imagination, authentic and inauthentic, this chapter aims to analyse the ways in which modern Bengali literature delineated and represented regions outside Bengal, and the histories associated with them (Saxton 2020; White 2005). As part of the genre of historical novel, *Tungabhadrar Tire* undoubtedly attempted to create a certain kind of historical consciousness (White 2005, 152). However, written in the 1950s and 1960s, these historical novels in general and *Tungabhadrar Tire* in particular also reflected the author's political vision, especially his ideas of nation, pride, and loyalty, and the associated ethics of duty. This chapter is divided into two parts. Part one will outline the significant themes in the novel and present the narrative. Part two will discuss the representations of southern India through the prism of Vijayanagara, as well as the complex relationship between history and historical fiction, the notions of 'truth' and 'imagination', and the construction of the past.

Tungabhadrar Tire: Historical Context, Narratives, and the Novel

Although established in the mid-fourteenth century, the state of Vijayanagara with its subsequent political conquests south of the river Tungabhadra emerged as a consolidated ruling power only in the fifteenth century with the integration of the regions of Tamil Nadu, Andhra, and Karnataka. The credit for strengthening the kingdom, both territorially and militarily, goes to Devaraya II (1425–1446 CE). He established control over the coastal regions of both east and west Deccan and overwhelmed the two rival powers—the Bahamani Sultanate in the Deccan and the Gajapati rulers of Orissa—who challenged his sovereignty and attacked the Vijayanagara state (Asher and Talbot 2008, 53). Both rival states remained prominent adversaries of the Vijayanagara Empire till the sixteenth century. Devaraya II contributed significantly towards upgrading the Vijayanagara army: he increased the imports of war horses, introduced new warfare technology, and recruited several capable Muslim military personnel employed previously in the Bahamani army. These changes were responsible for the several losses suffered by the Bahamanis. Devaraya II was finally successful in expanding the state frontiers to the north (ibid., 54–56; Karashima 1994, 188–194).

In the 1430s, the Gajapatis established their state in southern Orissa and the northeast Andhra region. Devaraya II fought three important battles against the Gajapatis, weakening their power considerably. However, in the fifteenth century the Gajapatis were able to conquer several territories under the Bahamanis and the Vijayanagara state, and advanced as far as the Kaveri in the south. They were finally defeated and almost annihilated by the Tuluva dynasty, especially during the rule of Krishnadevaraya (1509–1529 CE)(Asher and Talbot 2008, 56–59; Stein 1989, 28–30).

The historical context outlined above formed the backdrop to the novel, with the Bahamanis, Gajapatis, Devaraya II, and their political rivalries presented as literary characters and tropes. The author was clearly aware of the history, as evident from the *Author's Note*, in which he clearly acknowledges Robert Sewell and R. C. Majumdar, the two important historians of the Vijayanagara Empire in the early and mid-twentieth century. Devaraya II, his brother Kampana, the Gajapati ruler, and the Bahamani Sultan are indeed historical personalities; the city of Vijayanagara is a genuine historical location; and some of the events associated with them, which the novel describes, do have a historical basis. The river Tungabhadra, the descriptions of its banks, the granite rocky outcrops and hills of the Deccan, Hemkuntha Hill and surrounding caves and forests are undoubtedly actual landscape features. In fact, these historical details scaffold the narratives of romance, loyalty, war, and intrigues in the novels.

As the title suggests, the trope of the river dominates the entire novel. The river is not only the lifeline of the narrative, linking the entire region and space of Vijayanagara city and its surroundings with Bengal and Kalinga, but it also provides continuity for the narrative as well as an arena where different characters are, at various points in time, introduced and incorporated. The story begins with a physical description of the river Tungabhadra, its origins, and its confluence with the river Krishna. The account then, much like a river, flows into metaphorical ruminations and reflections. Nostalgia and the invocation of a time past dominates the tone, constructing a somewhat autobiographical testimony of the river, which, according to Bandopadhyay, formed the basis of history:

> On some silent evening, at a time when the sun has set, but the stars have not risen, stand on the triangular tract of land at the confluence of the Krishna and the Tungabhadra ... you shall hear the Tungabhadra whispering to the Krishna .... so many different names—Harihara, Bukka, Kampana, Devaraya, Mallikarjuna .... accounts of intrigue, of valour, of treachery, of betrayal, of love, of hatred, of laughter, of curiosity, of births, of deaths. This murmur of the Tungabhadra's waves is not history. It is a memoir. But there is always a memoir upon which history is built. (Sinha 2010a, 2–3)

The story, with its various plots and sub-plots, follows. We are introduced to almost all the characters directly in the first person, or in the course of the narration. The two Kalinga princesses, Bidyunmala and Manikankana, are travelling with their royal retinue along the Tungabhadra to the capital city of Vijayanagara. As a part of the political agreement accepting the Vijayanagara ruler

Devaraya's suzerainty, the Kalinga king Bhanudeva had entered into a matrimonial alliance, promising his daughter Bidyunmala in marriage to Devaraya. There is a description of the royal entourage, which comprised the ornate ships, princesses and other members of the royal family, officers, servants, and soldiers. We are informed about Bidyunmala's reluctance and anxiety at this prospective marital alliance and, as a contrast, we are made familiar with the sunny temperament of her sister, Manikankana. Somewhere along the journey, the male protagonist, Arjunvarma, is introduced. His background is kept anonymous, introducing an element of mystery, accentuated by showing him as coming from nowhere, floating unconscious on the river current and subsequently saved by the soldiers on the ship. The author establishes a connection with his readers through the interactions of the various characters on the royal vessels.

As the ships reach the banks of the city of Vijayanagara where a grand welcome awaits them, a fierce river storm blows everything away, separating the Kalinga royal entourage. The author removes the scheming uncle of the princesses and their maid from the scene by marooning them on a distant island, where they remain stranded, never to be found again. An exclusive, isolated, and undisturbed interaction between Bidyunmala and Arjunvarma on the sandy banks presages the forthcoming romance. Thereafter, the narrative focuses on the city of Vijayanagara, the king, the palace, and the court. The Vijayanagara soldiers ultimately rescue Bidyunmala, Arjunvarma, Manikankana, and Balarama, the deft blacksmith from Kalinga. King Devaraya arranges for their stay, allotting accommodation according to their status, with Bidyunmala and Manikankana residing in the royal harem in the palace complex and Arjunvarma and Balarama in a well-furnished cave dwelling outside the city.

The royal wedding is, however, postponed by three months as the Vijayanagara royal priest advises Bidyunmala to undergo purificatory rituals, since she had spent time together with Arjunvarma, a male stranger, after the shipwreck. This interlude provides the backdrop to the romance developing between

Bidyunmala and Arjunvarma. The author finally rescues Arjunvarma from anonymity, attributing to him a high-caste Kshatriya pedigree. He had been forced to flee his home in Gulbarga (in the Bahamani kingdom) in order to save himself from the atrocities of the Muslim rulers in the Deccan. The storyline further builds up Arjunvarma's character as a valiant hero, whose extraordinary skills, commitment to his duty, and unflinching loyalty towards the city and kingdom of Vijayanagara wins over Devaraya. Balarama is simultaneously depicted as a loyal friend and gifted blacksmith who possesses the rare skill of making light and portable canons, which impresses the emperor. However, Arjunvarma falls from grace and is banished from Vijayanagara along with Balarama when Devaraya discovers his clandestine meetings with Bidyunmala. Arjunvarma's chivalry and alacrity wins him an opportunity to re-enter the city when Balarama and he save the kingdom from an impending attack of the Bahamanis, which they accidentally come to know of during their exile. An impressed Devaraya relents and finally accepts the relationship between Bidyunmala and Arjunvarma. The narrative ends with three sets of marriages: between Bidyunmala and Arjunvarma; between Devaraya and Manikankana (who was already in love with the king); and between Balarama and his beloved, the palace maid Manjira.

The account is peppered with political details. Readers are informed about the establishment of the Vijayanagara state by Harihara and Bukka in the fourteenth century, the fraught relations with the neighbouring kingdom of the Bahamanis, and internal dissensions, depicted in the text through the treachery of Devaraya's brother, Kampana. The narrative recounts exciting details about how Kampana hatched a plot to assassinate Devaraya, his attempts being foiled by the timely intervention of Arjunvarma, who was returning from a clandestine meeting with Bidyunmala. Perhaps the most spectacular part of the narrative is the description of the city of Vijayanagara, brought alive through the skillful use of language, metaphors, and allegories. The picturesque depiction of the city and its surroundings clearly attest to Saradindu Bandopadhyay's knowledge of various travellers' accounts, like those of Abdur Razzak from Morocco and Nicolo Conti from Italy, who visited Vijayanagara during Devaraya's reign. It should be noted that Sewell's *A Forgotten Empire* carried a translation of the accounts of Portuguese travellers Domingo Paes and Fernao Nuniz, who visited the city in the sixteenth century during the reigns of Krishnadevaraya (1509–1529 CE) and Achyutadevaraya (1529–1542 CE), respectively (Sewell 1962 [1900], 235–398).

Finally, the literary framework of mystery, intrigues, and secrecy, for which Bandopadhyay is renowned, envelops the entire novel. The appearance of the ghosts of Harihara and Bukka as foreboding an unforeseen catastrophe is one of the thrilling points in the novel (Sinha 2010a, 165–166, 181). The description of caves and hills surrounding the city, and the vague yet intriguing astrological prediction concerning the tumultuous future of Arjunvarma and Balarama keeps the reader glued to the novel (ibid., 134–135).

Imaginaries of the South: History, Landscapes, and Representations

In many ways, Bandopadhyay's *Tungabhadrar Tire* can be considered a certain kind of history-writing that blended 'historical facts' based on evidence with 'imaginations' that ostensibly lacked evidence. However, facts and imagination were both subjective as the Bengali readers, as mentioned earlier, read this novel as a history of south India (which is how it was strongly recommended to me as well). The famous historian R. C. Majumdar is said to have remarked to Saradindu Bandopadhyay: 'You have brought the greatness of ancient Vijayanagara through your splendid novel—we historians are deeply grateful—for people do not read history, but they will read your story' (Sinha 2010b). Majumdar's comment is significant in two respects. First, Majumdar was a professional historian and Bandopadhyay drew information from his work for the novel. Second, the statement indirectly raises questions about 'truth', 'reality', and 'imagination' and their relationship with readers situated in their own specific contexts. Hayden White rightly remarked,

> Because historical discourse wages everything on the true, while fictional discourse is interested in the real.... A simply true account ... based on what the documentary record permits ... can provide knowledge of only a very small portion of what 'reality' consists of. However, the rest of the real, after we have said what we can assert to be true about it, would not be everything and anything we could imagine about it. The real would consist of everything that can be truthfully said about its actuality plus everything that can be truthfully said about what it could possibly be. (White 2005, 147)

In fact, Saradindu's novel reflected an interaction between two kinds of histories: the 'cloistered' history as an academic discipline and the 'public', layman version circulating in informal spheres, which often influenced the academic discipline to reorient itself (Chakrabarty 2015, 6–17, 33–37). Thus, historical fiction has in many ways been the 'nefarious "other" of history' (Saxton 2020, 2).[3] It also represents the past, and the relation between history, truth, and fiction is complex (Nagy 2014, 7–17; Saxton 2020, 1–18; Sliwka 2008, 61–66; Slotkin 2005, 231–236; White 2005, 147–157). It becomes imperative, then, to understand the specific contexts in which particular histories, whether 'cloistered'/ academic or 'public'/fiction, are written.

Tungabhadrar Tire represents the south and its history in certain exceptional and specific ways. The title of Sewell's book, *A Forgotten Empire*, spoke to the fact that the medieval history of southern India had been a neglected area of study. Published in 1900, Sewell's narrative of the history of the Vijayanagara Empire brought to the forefront the idea of a strong centralised state in tandem with the larger and all-encompassing history of medieval India. The significant revelation in this work was the description of the capital city of Vijayanagara, whose splendour and magnificence were presented as unparalleled in the world during the fourteenth century. This was further supported by the otherwise less-known translated accounts of Domingo Paes and Fernao Nuniz. Thus, for the first time, the medieval history of southern India occupied centre-stage, on par with the general history of India with the historiography now attributing to southern India 'strong', 'centralised' empires and kingdoms with institutions of local self-governance and cultures, which were projected as being older than those in the 'North' and, in many ways, superior to them. Further, the history of southern India, in tandem with the history of India as a whole, became synonymous with two distinct cultural types, the first influenced by Sanskrit, Hinduism, and temples with its focus on the Vijayanagara Empire, and the second influenced by Islam, Persian, and northern culture, presented as always hostile and in contradiction to the former. These trends dominated the historiography of southern India till the 1980s.[4]

Interestingly, K. A. Nilakanta Sastri's seminal work, *A History of South India: From Prehistoric Times to the Fall of Vijayanagar* (1955), despite being a part of such historiography, seems to have been overlooked by Bandopadhyay. Similarly, the works of scholars like N. Venkataramanyya and B. A. Saletore, published in the 1930s and 1940s, were also seemingly ignored.[5] Both Venkataramanyya and Saletore were influenced by linguistic identities, and argued, respectively, that the Telugu and Kannada regions and cultures were responsible for the origin and character of the Vijayanagara Empire and the city of Vijayanagara, thus challenging the idea of a homogeneous south (Stein 1989, 4–9). R. C. Majumdar's 1960 work influenced the author, indicating a somewhat selective approach on his part. Such an approach highlighted Bandopadhyay's location as an outsider, whose perspective of the region was characterised by elements of the unknown, the mysterious and exotic, and therefore exceptional. This is evident in the wistful tone of the narrative, which provides a testimony of the lonely river Tungabhadra and speaks of a supposedly lost civilisation waiting to be re-discovered and recovered:

> Nothing memorable has happened in the life of Tungabhadra. No temples, pilgrimages or monasteries have been constructed on her banks ... for only two hundred years, did the

> Tungabhadra live through halcyon days. A wall-enclosed fortress-city had grown around the statues of Birupaksha on her southern bank. The name of that city was Vijayanagar.... Vijayanagar had established its supremacy over all of southern India.... Everyone has forgotten the amazing history interred in the spread-out ruins of Vijayanagar on the southern bank of the Tungabhadra. The Tungabhadra alone has not forgotten. (Sinha 2010a, 2)

Since the river has a topographical eternity and defines the space, to it is attributed the quality of an authentic testament to a long-forgotten historical time, which had witnessed the glory of the Indian naval system in general and the city of Vijayanagara in particular. The description of the city dominates the narrative in the novel. Vijayanagara the city is the arena of action, and is depicted as a land of incomparable riches and opportunities. Everybody, foreigners as well as residents, can find a place for themselves here, and work hard together to contribute to its prosperity. It should be remembered that neither Arjunvarma nor Balarama was an original inhabitant, having come from Bengal and Orissa, respectively.

The prosperity of the city begins from its riverbanks, where the settlement 'was a serpentine, bejeweled girdle. Studded with diamonds, pearls and precious stones of rows of monuments, gardens, jetties and temples' (Sinha 2010a, 51). The urban layout is described in detail with its seven concentric walls that protected the city, fields, rivers, canals, orchards, lavish mansions, bustling markets, grand temples and palaces, music, processions, and so on (ibid., 52–56, 73–75). The throbbing city life is cosmopolitan, comprising a heterogeneous population; especially notable was the presence of Turkish soldiers. That foreigners visited the city is made clear in the novel by reference to the presence of the famous Moroccan traveller, Abdur Razzak (ibid., 96). This cosmopolitanism complemented the rich and ornate palaces (ibid., 76–81, 121–123, 128), mansions, politics, and court proceedings (ibid., 124–16, 128–130). In general, readers are treated to a glamorous city of the past that possessed an elegance characteristic of the present, exemplified in fashionable names like 'Betelnut Avenue'.

The delineation of the city is not restricted merely to its precincts. We are provided with an equally elaborate portrayal of the flora, fauna, geography, old structures, ruins, rich cultural life, and temples located outside Vijayanagara, yet connected to it (ibid., 112–116). The Hemkuntha hill, which had a constant fire burning at its peak symbolising the eternal nature of the city, is located here. Clearly, the glory of the city was linked to the greatness of the Empire, its army, and most significantly, the power of king Devaraya, his outstanding demeanour, temperament, work ethic, and bravery. In a nutshell, the city of Vijayanagara represented the Vijayanagara Empire and the history of south India.

Relations with the Muslim kingdoms of the Deccan underscored the historical discourse as well as the narrative in the novel. Often referred to as the Yavanas, the Muslims were clearly the 'other', allegedly imbued with fanatic enthusiasm for indiscriminate warfare and bloodshed against their opponents, and the exploitation of their own subjects in their kingdoms. In contrast, the Hindus and Devaraya were compassionate, embodying justice and ethical governance. This clash of civilisations clearly placed Vijayanagara on a high moral ground, which made it a haven for everyone. There is a constant lament in the novel about how the Muslims are overwhelming the Hindus, who have been reduced to total subjugation—with the exception of the Vijayanagara Empire. We are informed that Arjunvarma migrated to Vijayanagara to escape the alleged tyranny of the Yavanas who ruled his hometown Gulbarga (Sinha 2010a, 63–65). The wars with the Bahamanis are shown as a crucial turning point in the novel, when historically, it was the wars with the Gajapatis that had far-reaching consequences. The author, however, depicts the Gajapatis as a part of the Hindu confederation, which Devaraya was instrumental in forming in order to counter the Muslim invasions. The turning point in the novel is the Bahamani Sultanate's secret plan to attack Vijayanagara. Arjunvarma and Balarama thwarted the plan—a patriotic act that exonerated them of their alleged betrayal in Devaraya's eyes and earned them prestigious positions in the city. As stated earlier, Devaraya had banished them after discovering Arjunvarma and

Bidyunmala's amorous relationship; this was condemned as treachery and a dereliction of moral duty since Bidyunmala was to marry Devaraya according to the terms of the political agreement made with her father, the king of Kalinga (ibid., 216–245).

Can Saradindu Bandopadhyay be considered a victim of a certain religious worldview? Arunava Sinha, who translated *Tungabhadrar Tire*, is of the opinion—while distancing himself from Saradindu's sectarian worldview—that Bankimchandra Chatterjee's historical novels and 'the new robust Hinduism', the 1947 riots in Kolkata, and the author's own life experiences had all exerted an influence on him (Sinha 2010b). However, it is difficult to bracket Bandopadhyay's ideas within polarised binaries. The trends in history-writing during this period clearly influenced his sense of history, and he was always aware that as a writer of historical fiction, he should be representing the spirit of the times. Therefore, it is Saradindu's commitment to his craft that manifested in a particularistic depiction of politics in his novel. In fact, his fidelity and dedication to historical detail is noteworthy for he does not hesitate to mention the Islamic influence on the palace architecture or the employment of Hindu soldiers in the Bahamani/'Yavana' army (Sinha 2010a, 84, 131).

Thus, despite suffering an ignominious defeat at the hands of a confederacy of five Deccani sultanates of Bijapur, Golkonda, Ahmadnagar, Bidar, and Berar in 1565 CE, followed by the abandonment of the capital, which was thereafter condemned to anonymity, the kingdom of Vijayanagara remained historically significant, and this is clearly emphasised in the novel (Sinopoli and Morrison 1995, 85). This is further articulated in the portrayal of Devaraya as an ideal king, embodying the virtues of chivalry, justice, and righteousness, underscoring the nostalgia of a past kingship as an archetype of modern twentieth-century sovereignty. Although monarchical, such sovereignty is depicted as relevant for crafting the principles of democratic governance as practised by the postcolonial nation-State in which the author was himself situated (Banerjee 2018, 1–50, 108–288, 351–398). In fact, the author did not evoke the metaphors of Vijayanagara and Devaraya 'to resurrect (or exorcise) royal spectres, but to actually construct new political bodies … that of the production of royal nationhood, through entanglements between kingships and nationalist imaginaries … to think about the unity and sovereignty of a nation, crystallised around a singular apex' in a newly independent India still struggling against the hegemonies of British colonialism (ibid., 4–5). Further, such a sovereignty was imbued with 'divine' and 'messianic kingship' and 'the sacralisation of state and polity' (ibid., 8–9). Thus, the city of Vijayanagara, depicted as sacred and idyllic, was analogous to a nascent modern nation sacred to its people, and Devaraya was prototypical of a benevolent leader of that nation-State, one who possessed a personalised political outreach. Such ideas of nationhood and a messianic leader were articulated in several writings in modern Bengal. Saradindu's *Tungabhadrar Tire* reflected such a literary trend, which used reserves from history to develop ideas of a righteous nationalist kingship imbricated with the sacralisation and nationalistic ideas of State through a discursive narrative.

On the one hand, the novel attempted to relate the idea of a single nation through the emotive feelings of patriotism and unflinching loyalty to one's motherland, which is to be protected even at the cost of one's life. On the other hand, it also constructed a category of exceptionalism (Nair 2006, 323–347). Certain themes related to space, region, manners, and customs that delineated the history of 'south India' in a unique manner were highlighted. As an indirect corollary to this, an equally exceptional category called 'north India' also emerged, which became the reference point to further exceptionalise the 'south'. For instance, at the beginning of the narrative, the waters of Tungabhadra is compared to that of the river Ganga (Sinha 2010a, 1). Similarly, the kinship system based on cross-cousin and uncle-niece marriages, which projected the south as an exception, merited a special mention in the form of the secret desire of Bidyunmala's maternal uncle to marry her (ibid., 32).

The Aryan–Dravidian divide, replete with stereotypes of appearance, customs, and cultures, abound in the text. The author highlights the fact that Bidyunmala has a fair complexion as her mother was Aryan, while her sister Manikankana has a 'subdued' complexion as her mother was not Aryan (ibid., 9). This racial dichotomy further acquires political overtones of domination and subjugation in the novel:

> When they arrived in southern India, the Aryans started the splendid custom of taking a non-Aryan woman as wife at the same time as they took an Aryan one. Undoubtedly, it was with a view to increasing the number of one's progeny, but the tradition had persisted precisely because it was an attractive one. The Aryan wife had a higher standing, but the non-Aryan wife was held in high esteem as well. (ibid.)

This exceptionalism reflected a type of history-writing that highlighted a composite geographical space called 'south India,' with its own distinct homogeneous political and cultural identity. Such a distinct form in historiography is related to the ways in which a space was imagined in modern history-writing, where the geographical and the cultural were taken as synonymous and commensurable with one another. Thus, a specific construct of a region was produced in historical epistemology that overlooked any variations.

The adventurous tenor of the novel makes it read somewhat like a travelogue, as it journeys to a new land and unravels its mysteries. Arjunvarma represents a traveller and through his gaze, which is analogous to an ethnographic gaze, the city is described. The story moves forward in a linear manner, through various 'moments of crossing' of different spaces (Chaudhuri 2019, 166). The author uses the river to symbolise the onward journey, thus producing a cohesive narrative through a vivid description of lives, settlements, and activities along the riverbanks. The different spaces in the novel, such as the hills, cities, palaces, forests, and villages, are all connected through the river. In fact, the rivers Godavari, Tunga, and Bhadra provided the significant seamless connection between the eastern, western, and southern regions, and thus represented the unity of landscape so crucial to the idea of the nation. Thus the title, *Tungabhadrar Tire* (*By the Tungabhadra*), is a metaphor representing the eternity of a nation that outlives everything, including the mighty Vijayanagara Empire that once flourished on the banks of the river Tungabhadra.

Conclusion

A question that has always plagued scholars is: Can historical fiction be considered an 'accurate' and 'authentic' representation of the past? (Saxton 2020, 1–4) Moving beyond these categories, novels like *Tungabhadrar Tire* undoubtedly make use of historical evidence. Authors like Saradindu Bandopadhyay were conscious of being engaged in a form of history-writing, and used the historical events that focused on the Kalinga war, the Vijayanagara Empire, king Devaraya, his brother Kampana, the city and its surroundings, the Vijayanagara–Bahamani conflict, and so on as a context for his narratives. It should be noted that Bandopadhyay,

> by using the kinds of literary devices employed by writers of fiction—including topoi, tropes and figures, schemata of thought, characterization, personification, emplotment, and so on ... demonstrated to his readers the difference between a merely truthful account of an event, of the kind provided by most survivor-witnesses, and an artistic treatment of a real event in his past which transcends the truth–reality distinction. (White 2005, 149)

Acknowledgements

This chapter is the beginning of a long-awaited project planned several years ago on historical fiction in Indian literature, mainly Bengali, Hindi, and Tamil literature. I wish to thank my M.Phil student, Arkadeb Bhattacharya, at the Centre for Historical Studies, JNU for helping me with some of the writings of Saradindu Bandopadhyay.

Endnotes

1. Shrivaishnavism is a religious tradition in south India, practised in the present-day states of Tamil Nadu, southern Andhra Pradesh, and southern Karnataka. This tradition considers Vishnu as the supreme god and Ramanuja, a medieval theologian (1017–1137 CE) who systematised the philosophy of Vishishtadvaita, as their important leader. The Shrivaishnava community is divided into two sects—the Vadakalai, the northerners, and the Tengalai, the southerners. The Vadakalais regard Vedanta Desika (1268–1369 CE) as their leader, and Kanchipuram in Tamil Nadu as their sacred centre. The Tengalais regard Manavalamamuni (1370–1443 CE) as their leader and Shrirangam in Tamil Nadu as their sacred centre.

2. There are nineteen chapters in this volume. Six chapters and parts of four other chapters were written by R. C. Majumdar. The rest were contributed by famous historians of that time.

3. Saxton is quoting from White's *The Practical Past* (2014). In his 2005 essay, White also cited Michel de Certeau in a similar context: 'In a well-known essay on history and fiction, Michel de Certeau maintained that "fiction is the repressed other of historical discourse"' (White 2005, 147).

4. With the publication of Burton Stein's work in 1980, the perspectives in the history of south India shifted from a centralised state-centric approach to a complex approach that focused on localities and involved a social and economic analysis. For details, see Stein (1980).

5. For further details, see Saletore (1934); Venkataramanayya (1929, 1935).

Select References

Asher, Catherine, and Cynthia Talbot. 2008. *India Before Europe*. New Delhi: Cambridge University Press (South Asian Edition).

Bandopadhyay, Saradindu. 1366 BS (1959). *Tunghabhadrar Tire (By the Banks of Tungabhadra)*. Calcutta: Bookland Private Limited.

______. 1998. *Oitihashik Kahini Samagra (Historical Fictions)*. Calcutta: Ananda Publishers Private Limited.

Banerjee, Milinda. 2018. *The Mortal God: Imagining the Sovereign in Colonial India*. New Delhi: Cambridge University Press.

Banerjee, Sandeep, and Shubho Basu. 2015. 'Secularizing the Sacred, Imagining the Nation-Space: The Himalaya in Bengali Travelogues, 1856–1901'. *Modern Asian Studies* 49 (3), 609–649.

Chakrabarty, Ramakanta. 1985. *Vaishnavism in Bengal, 1486–1900*. Calcutta: Sanskrit Pustak Bhandar.

———. 1996. *Bonge Vaishnav Dharma: Ekti Oitihasik Ebom Samajtattwik Odhyayon*. Calcutta: Ananda Publishers Pvt. Ltd.

Chakrabarty, Dipesh. 2015. *The Calling of History: Sir Jadunath Sarkar and His Empire of Truth*. Ranikhet: Permanent Black.

Chartier, Roger. 2011. 'History, Time, and Space'. *Republics of Letters: A Journal for the Study of Knowledge, Politics, and the Arts* 2 (2), 1 June, 1–13.

Chaudhuri, Supriya. 2019. 'Indian Travel Writing'. In Nandini Das and Tim Youngs (eds), *The Cambridge History of Travel Writing*, 159–174. Cambridge: Cambridge University Press.

Gooptu, Sarvani. 2015. 'Asia in the Eyes of 20th Century Travellers: Gleanings From Popular Vernacular Journals of Bengal'. *Proceedings of the Indian History Congress* 76, 397–407.

Karashima, Noboru. 1994. *Towards a New Formation: South Indian Society under Vijayanagar Rule*. New Delhi: Oxford University Press.

Majumdar, R. C. 1960. *The History and Culture of the Indian People: Volume 6: The Delhi Sultanate*. Bombay: Bharatiya Vidya Bhavan.

Mazumder, Rajashree. 2019. 'In Search of Mammon's Treasure Trove: Hemendrakumar Roy's Use of Travel in Children's Adventure Literature'. *Studies in History* 35 (2), 250–279.

Murmu, Maroona. 2009–2010. 'Prasanmayee Devi: Imagining and Imaging Aryavarta'. *Journal of History* 27, 33–66.

Nagy, Ladislav. 2014. 'Historical Fiction as a Mixture of History and Romance: Towards the Genre Definition of the Historical Novel'. *Prague Journal of English Studies* 3 (1), 7–17.

Nair, Janaki. 2006. 'Beyond Exceptionalism: South India and the Modern Historical Imagination'. *Indian Economic and Social History Review* 43 (3), 323–347.

Rethinking History. The Journal of Theory and Practice 9 (2–3), June–September 2005.

Rodwell, Grant. 2013. *Whose History? Engaging History Students through Historical Fictions*. Adelaide: University of Adelaide Press.

Saletore, B. A. 1934. *Social and Political Life in the Vijayanagar Empire: A.D. 1346–1646*, 2 vols. Madras: B. G. Paul.

Sastri, K. A. Nilakanta. 1955. *A History of South India: From Prehistoric Times to the Fall of Vijayanagar*. Madras: Oxford University Press.

Saxton, Laura. 2020. 'A True Story: Defining Accuracy and Authenticity in Historical Fiction'. *Rethinking History. The Journal of Theory and Practice*. Available at https://doi.org/10.1080/13642529.2020.1727189 (accessed May 2023).

Sinopoli, C. M., and Kathleen Morrison. 1995. 'Dimensions of Imperial Control: The Vijayanagara Capital'. *American Anthropologist* 97 (1), 83–96.

Sewell, Robert. 1962 [1900]. *A Forgotten Empire: Vijayanagar. A Contribution to the History of India*. Delhi: Publications Division, Ministry of Information and Broadcasting.

Sinha, Arunava (trans.). 2010a. *By the Tungabhadra: Saradindu Bandopadhyay*. New Delhi: Harper Perennial.

———. 2010b. 'A Note on the Translation'. In *By the Tungabhadra: Saradindu Bandopadhyay*, Arunava Sinha (trans.). New Delhi: Harper Perennial.

———. 2010c. 'The Man, the Novel: The Life and Literature of Saradindu Bandopadhyay'. In *By the Tungabhadra: Saradindu Bandopadhyay*, Arunava Sinha (trans.). New Delhi: Harper Perennial.

Sliwka, Carol. 2008. 'Connecting to History through Historical Fiction'. *Language Arts Journal of Michigan* 23 (2), 61–66.

Slotkin, Richard. 2005. 'Fiction for the Purposes of History'. *Rethinking History. The Journal of Theory and Practice* 9 (2–3), June–September, 221–236.

Stein, Burton. 1980. *Peasant State and Society in Early Medieval South India*. New Delhi: Oxford University Press.

———. 1989. *Vijayanagara: The New Cambridge History of India, 1.2*. Cambridge: Cambridge University Press.

Venkataramanyya, N. 1929. *Kampili and Vijayanagara*. Madras: Christian Literature Society's Press.

———. 1935. *Studies in the History of the Third Dynasty of Vijayanagara*. Madras: Madras University Press.

Wagoner, Philip B. 1996. '"Sultan Among the Hindu Kings": Dress, Titles and Islamicization of Hindu Culture at Vijayanagar'. *The Journal of Asian Studies* 55 (4), 851–880.

Wagoner, Philip B. 2000. 'Harihara, Bukka and the Sultan: The Delhi Sultanate in the Political Imagination of Vijayanagar'. In David Gilmartin and Bruce B. Lawrence (eds), *Beyond Turk and Hindu: Rethinking Religious Identities in Islamicate South Asia,* 300–326. Florida: Gainesville.

White, Hayden. 2005. 'Introduction: Historical Fiction, Fictional History and Historical Reality'. *Rethinking History. The Journal of Theory and Practice* 9 (2–3), June–September, 147–157.

———. 2014. *The Practical Past.* Illinois: Northwestern University Press.

9

Rejection of Nationalism and Much More

Reading Tagore's *Nationalism* 100 Years On

Anuradha Roy

Rabindranath Tagore's book *Nationalism* (2007 [1917]), where he completely rejected the ideology of nationalism, is often cited these days to counter the highly authoritarian and coercive variety of nationalism that we can see all around us. This is a nationalism that is seeking to recast Indian national identity along a religious majoritarian and monocultural line. Rereading the book a century after its writing, however, I realised that its value consists of much more than its bold rejection of nationalism. It raises certain questions regarding society and civilisation which are worth heeding today, regardless of the attempt by any particular variety of nationalism, or any ideology for that matter, to aggressively dominate the people.[1] Indeed, the ideas that informed his critique of nationalism in this book were to develop further and constitute a constructive proposal for a kind of humanistic civil religion in a later book, *The Religion of Man* (2005 [1930]), where he moved beyond the question of nationalism in his quest for justice and peace in human order, and also for the complete self-realisation of individual human beings.

This chapter is divided into three parts. The first part, 'Prelude to the Book *Nationalism*', will show how Tagore, who had been deeply involved in the national movement of his country right from his childhood, eventually turned against nationalism. In the second part, 'Reading *Nationalism*', we will read the book itself to see what Tagore says here that goes beyond his condemnation of nationalism while being related to it; how he raises some very fundamental questions regarding society, civilisation, and more importantly, human nature, in this book, with rare insight and wisdom. While the book's rejection of nationalism is indeed important, its engagement with these questions seems to me to be even more profound, and hence more significant. And I think this should place Tagore on the same pedestal as some of the greatest thinkers of the world.[2] In the third part, I will point out the limitations of some of Tagore's views expressed in the book and attempt an overall assessment.

Prelude to the Book *Nationalism*

These days, Tagore is often hailed (or scorned) for his 'anti-nationalism'. But we must remember that he did take quite some time to develop this anti-nationalistic stand. Anyway, whether Tagore was ever a nationalist or not seems to me to be a moot question. More importantly, Tagore's nationalism, had any such thing at all existed, was based on some fundamental human values, which are important even if we take them away from their nationalist moorings. And it is these values that ultimately pushed him away from nationalism and these same values were given exposition in *Nationalism,* making it much more than an 'anti-national' exhortation.

Apparently, Tagore was very much a part of the Indian national movement and any cultural history of this movement cannot but feature him prominently. His love for and reflections on his country evidently germinated in the context of the emergent nationalist movement in the second half of the nineteenth century, particularly because his own family was deeply involved in it. As this movement continued to expand its agenda, adjusting its current programme and future goals, he not only kept pace, but also voiced its most forward and progressive thoughts. Thus, he represented Indian nationalism at its best. And then came a time when he went beyond that, thanks to the remarkable originality of his mind. It is well-known that in the post-Swadeshi years, his relationship with the mainstream nationalist movement of India altered decisively and permanently, culminating in his global and complete denunciation of nationalism itself in the book *Nationalism*. But even after this, he continued to lend support to whatever humane, dynamic, freedom-loving, and courageous elements he found in different streams of the Indian nationalist movement[3] (Roy 2017).

So long as and so far as the nation was a symbol of wider selfhood to him, a symbol of mutuality and living together that is innate to human nature, Tagore lent his support to the nationalist ideology. But his faith in nationalism appeared shaky from at least the late nineteenth century. Even in his Swadeshi days in the first decade of the twentieth century, that is, his most intense nationalist phase, Tagore expressed clear reservations about nationalism. Actually, he had problems with certain modules of nationalism that he saw at home and abroad, because he found them too selfish, aggressive, and coercive. Another problem for him was the close association between the State and the nation; he had a deep-seated distrust of the mechanical and authoritarian character of the State. But had Tagore known that he had the liberty to fashion his own nation rather than cling to any particular modular form, that is, had he thought of nationalism in terms of imagination and creativity—as we do today, thanks to Benedict Anderson's seminal book (Anderson 1983)—and had he been able to dissociate the nation from the State, he would not perhaps have been so impatient with nationalism. Indeed, as Partha Chatterjee has perceptively said, Tagore's *swadesh* (one's own country), a word that occurred frequently in his writings, was not very different from what we know as the nation today (Chatterjee 2005). Tagore had started thinking of the country in terms of imagination and creativity since his Swadeshi days. Much later, he wrote in an essay included in the book *Kalantar* (*Transition of Age*):

> In 1905 I called on the Bengalis to tell them this—create your country inwardly with the help of *atmashakti* (self-prowess), because it is through creation that the truth is realized. Viswakarma finds himself in his own creation. To find one's country means to feel one's own soul on a broader basis. When we create our country with our own thoughts,

> deeds and love, we truly see our own soul in our country. Man's country is the creation of man's mind.[4] (*Rabindra Rachanabali* 1970, 24)

Atmashakti (self-prowess), that is, a concept of inner strength that flowered in a distinguished form in Tagore's collections of poems *Naibedya* (*Rabindra Rachanabali* 1967) and *Utsarga* (*Rabindra Rachanabali* 1971, 10), as well as in his book of essays titled *Atmashakti*[5] (*Rabindra Rachanabali* 1969a, 3) at the turn of the century, meant building of the character and uplift of the soul of every countryman. He wanted his countrymen to counter the West's 'endless vanity', 'crude bragging', and 'pompous luxury at the price of the poor' with the programme of atmashakti, and thus to reject the war-mongering Western civilisation. The myth of the superiority of Western civilisation, both epistemic and moral, had so long acted as a major prop to the nationalists' allegiance to British rule. Tagore now challenged this myth powerfully, thus paving the way for the nationalists' first plunge into an anti-British agitation, which was soon to be occasioned by the Partition of Bengal that took place in 1905.

Atmashakti seeks empowerment by making one feel one's soul on a broader basis and thus necessarily tends to expand the scale of human existence beyond all narrow confines. In fact, it tends to merge patriotism with a very liberal and loving universalism that reaches out to the entire world. We may recall the very popular song composed by Tagore during the anti-Partition/Swadeshi Movement: '*O amar desher mati, tomar pare thekai matha / Tomate bishwamayer, tomate bishwamayer anchal pata*' ('O soil of my country, I bow down to you / Over you Mother Earth has spread the border of her sari)'[6] (*Geetabitan* 1968). This, together with his discovery of the real, the ordinary, and the everyday nation in the countryside, where he also launched a practical project of rural reform, proved to be a decisive factor in his swadesh-related thinking. The Swadeshi Movement was the ultra-nationalist phase of his life. And at the same time, quite paradoxically, he was moving away from nationalism (at least from the way it was manifest around him).

A correlate of atmashakti and another essential component of Tagore's nationalism at this stage was his concept of *manush-bandha* (binding human beings). In an essay titled 'Bharatbarshiya Samaj' ('The Indian Society', 1901), Tagore asserted that the greatness of civilisation (*sabhyata*) lies in its constructive capacity to unify the diverse—'whether you call it "national" or by any other name does not really matter, *the point is to bind human beings* (*manush-bandha*; emphasis mine)'[7] (*Rabindra Rachanabali* 1969a, 3). And in the interests of 'manush-bandha', Tagore privileged society over the nation, which he found unsuitable for the huge, multilayered, and multicultural subcontinent of India. In his essay titled 'Swadeshi Samaj' ('The Indigenous Society'), written a few months later,[8] he upheld '*manusher sange manusher atmiya sambandha sthapan*' ('binding humans as relatives, rather than mechanically') as having been the principal effort of India from time immemorial, although the social mode he had in his mind in this connection was the Hindu caste society, the innate inequality of which he chose to ignore. In any case, the premium on society was also clearly pushing him away from the idea of 'nation', in the European sense of the term.

So atmashakti and manush-bandha are the two pivotal values of Tagore's swadesh-related thinking, and these values are supposed to make *mukti* possible. Mukti is more than freedom or liberty (*swadhinata*), which sounds comparatively mundane. Mukti is the realisation of the human essence. However, unless one is free from external bondages in the world, one cannot attain mukti inwardly. These three underlying values—atmashakti, manush-bandha, and mukti—provided Tagore's nationalism, and later even his anti-nationalism, with a thread of consistency through all shifts and ambiguities.

His Swadeshi phase was the most intensely nationalist phase of his life, and this meant deep involvement in a nationalist movement which was generally Hindu in character. Nevertheless, when one strives for atmashakti, Hindu-ness or any other narrow and restrictive ideology is bound to be de-emphasised. It is well-known that Tagore soon became disillusioned with the Swadeshi Movement, particularly its Hindu character, and sharply repudiated it. The book *Gora* was the first major step in this critique[9] (*Rabindra Rachanabali* 1969b, 6). The caste system, which Tagore had admired in the essay 'Swadeshi Samaj' for its tolerance and all-embracing character, was depicted in *Gora* as an instrument in the hands of the neo-orthodox for the purpose of social oppression, leading to social fragmentation. Ultimately, *Gora*'s patriotism transcended Hinduism to take on a liberal humanitarian colour.

Now began a new phase in his life, one in which he felt compelled to address the question: If India is not Hindu, how do we ensure a singular Indian-ness? This propelled an anguished search on his part for a multicultural and yet singular Indian society. The search seemed fraught with great difficulties, though. In the poem 'Bharat Tirtha' ("The Place of Pilgrimage that is India')[10] (*Geetabitan* 1968), composed in 1910, Tagore presented India as a microcosm of humankind that had already evolved a culture of diversity and synthesis; yet his was not just a static historical picture of synthesis to be conveniently evoked from the past, but a dynamic vision of constant cultural recharging, informed by the ideal of atmashakti. His newly found India, representing a composite culture at the popular level, was to be continuously created in the people's everyday life. When Tagore had advocated atmashakti some years ago, he had had such a hunch, but now he realised it more clearly.

However, the Bharat of 'Bharat Tirtha' was still sanctified as a *tirtha* or a place of pilgrimage. It is something sacred, based on a singular historical principle. Moreover, perhaps unconsciously the poet used some Hindu symbols like *mangalghat* (a consecrated pitcher used for winning divine favour) and *omkardhwani* (the mystic sound denoting the Hindu Trinity) in this song. Perhaps the composite culture of India as perceived by him was still centred on a Hindu core. We must remember that even after this, Tagore admired the Hindu social system for its spirit of tolerance and inclusion in the essay 'Atmaparichay', published in 1912[11] (*Rabindra Rachanabali* 1966, 18), although of course this was a very liberal Hindu-ness, in keeping with his temperament. He was still in two minds about the Hindu-ness of the nation.

Soon, however, Tagore realised that any stress on the composite nature of Indian culture, a singular Indian culture, would willy-nilly privilege Hindu-ness, which would not be quite desirable. Hence, in 1913, he wrote the song 'Janaganamana'[12] (*Geetabitan* 1968), where the country is evoked as an entity made up of many peoples, many landscapes, many histories, and many cultures. In this song, we do not have a composite nation, but a federal one. National unity is ensured by dedicating the land to a god who is called 'Bharat-bhagya bidhata' ('the god who decides India's destiny'), but who is evidently above all nations. Perhaps, for such a huge and multicultural land as India, he saw this as the only practical and healthy solution.

Evidently, Tagore was becoming increasingly uncomfortable about how to ensure a singular Indian-ness. In 'Bharat Tirtha', the pluralities of India are somewhat synthesised, but in 'Janaganamana' they harmonise. In the book *Ghare-Baire*, written in 1915, they are evidently contentious[13] (*Rabindra Rachanabali* 1967, 8). Here, Tagore demonstrated the predicament of a nation goaded on by extremist politics with its violent rhetoric and its encouragement of terrorism among young people. He also showed its distance from the rural masses, particularly how its cultural and political symbolism led to alienation amongst Muslims. The self-aggrandising, corrupt, and rhetorical nationalism espoused by Sandip is juxtaposed against the humane and rational nationalism of Nikhilesh in this book. The novelist himself is evidently sympathetic to Nikhilesh, whose nation is based on the everyday life of its people and their relationships. But this counterpoint character remains ineffectual, and his failure is constantly underlined in the book. Perhaps at that moment Tagore saw the difficulty in the choices, and found himself utterly helpless in negotiating the extremely fractured political reality.

The very next year, he delivered a series of lectures during his tours in Japan and the US, and from these lectures emerged the book *Nationalism*. It carried forward the ideas he had been exploring hitherto and represented their logical maturation. The book contains three chapters: 'Nationalism in the West',

'Nationalism in Japan', and 'Nationalism in India'.[14] That the background to all three was constituted by the ongoing global war is quite evident. To summarise it briefly, he contended that nationalism had sprung from the greedy and unbridled pursuit of wealth that defined the industrial culture of the West. He not only criticised Western nationalism, which had thrived long upon the mutilation of humanity and led to destructive wars, but also expressed his fear of the nationalism of the East. He congratulated Japan for claiming all the gifts of the modern West despite being a child of the ancient East, but warned her to not lose her soul by emulating the West to the extent of imbibing its nationalist spirit (*Nationalism* 2007 [1917], 96).[15] And while talking about India, he targeted the nationalist political parties—he dismissed the Congress for its policy of mendicancy and the extremists (whom he criticised in *Ghare Baire* as well) for relying blindly on the authority of traditions and being socially irresponsible (ibid.).[16] His overall view on nationalism in the book was all too clear: 'The temptation which is fatal for the strong, is still more so for the weak, and I do not welcome it in our Indian life' (ibid., 153). Tagore's demystification of the nation was now complete. He candidly stated that even though he had been taught from his childhood that the idolatry of the nation was almost better than the veneration of God and humanity, he had outgrown that teaching (ibid., 127). Let us now read the book *Nationalism* briefly.

Reading *Nationalism*

In this book, Tagore equates the nation with the State, which he posits against society. Society is natural and spontaneous; it may have a political side, but it thrives on living bonds and seeks harmony. The nation is a machinery of power and wealth, politics and commerce. It is an 'organized self-interest of a whole people' (ibid., 26). It is without soul, driven by greed and jealousy; it fosters ambition and hatred, and dissolves 'personal humanity' (ibid., 22). It has given rise to an inhuman 'political civilization' in place of a civilisation of human relationships. Thus, where cooperation is natural, competition has intruded. But humans are not a pack of hungry wolves,[17] they have their responsibilities to the higher faculties of their nature (ibid., 13–14). Tagore considers Western civilisation abnormal in this respect. He uses the following analogy to describe a society that has transformed into a nation: when a father becomes a gambler and his duty towards his family seems secondary to him; or when he is no longer a man, but an automaton motivated only by greed (ibid., 23). In Tagore's view, this is what the nation turns individuals into. Citizens then become 'the political and commercial man, the man of the limited purpose,' 'not the moral man, the complete man' (ibid., 27). Yet people accept this mental slavery cheerfully and proudly because of their nervous desire to turn themselves into 'a machine of power,[18] called the nation' (ibid., 39). 'Individuals willingly allow the nation to take donkey rides upon his back' (ibid., 56).[19] But this is actually a denial of their true human essence; a process of dehumanisation, so to say. He uses another analogy to make this point—turning a tree into a log, which will burn for men, but will never bear living flowers and fruit (ibid., 51).

Apart from condemning its dehumanising aspect, Tagore mentions the more glaring dangers of nationalism, from both within and outside the nation. Not only does nationalism make some nations victimise some other nations as their colonies, but it also makes them fear each other, 'like the prowling wild beasts of the night time' (*Nationalism* 2007 [1917], 103), and engage in deadly conflicts between themselves out of greed, while its brotherhood is the 'brotherhood of hooliganism' (ibid., 39). He fundamentally questions modern civilisation with its conflict between individual and the State, labour and capital, men and women; between avarice and spiritual inclinations, between 'the organized selfishness of nations and the higher ideals of humanity' (ibid., 72).[20] And he addresses the West thus:

> You say, these machines will come into an agreement, for their mutual protection, based upon a conspiracy of fear.

> But will this federation of steam-boilers supply you with a soul?... What is going to happen to that larger part of the world, where fear will have no hand in restraining you.... But you say, 'That does not matter, the unfit must go to the wall—they shall die and this is science'. (ibid., 45)

In saying so, Tagore stridently criticises Social Darwinism, an influential ideology of the time. It is also to be noted that for Tagore, the idea of harmony amongst men goes hand-in-hand with the harmony of man with nature. So he also critiques nationalism for endangering humanity by dominating nature from the outside, rather than 'making her your own in love's delight'[21] (ibid., 89), which seems to portend today's environmental concerns.

The book has a moral core. Here, Tagore is primarily a moral philosopher who stresses on the human essence. He wants the human essence to realise its freedom. He does not call it mukti, nor does he mention atmashakti or manush-bandha; however, these ideals are evidently present in his mind as attributes of true human beings, in a collective sense as well as at an individual level. He considers mukti, atmashakti, and manush-bandha essential for the unfolding of human capacities, for bridging alienation and moving towards humanism. It may be mentioned in passing that these ideas were to find a more mature philosophical exposition in another series of lectures that he delivered at Oxford in 1930 and published under the title, *The Religion of Man*.[22] In the latter, too, he does not mention atmashakti, manush-bandha, or mukti, but he does talk about man's urge to 'create himself' (the creativity that is the basis of *atmashakti*), to 'develop in his mind an image of his truth according to an ideal which he believes to be universal' (the sense of universality that facilitates manush-bandha), and thus to attain freedom through self-realisation (which is mukti) (*Religion of Man* 2005 [1930], 43).

What I find particularly interesting about *Nationalism* and what takes it a step further from his earlier thoughts is the way Tagore rises above mere sermonising and resolves the dichotomy between the real and the moral, that is, between 'what is' and 'what ought to be', by asserting, in a rather Hegelian manner, that morality is immanent in reality. Tagore sometimes calls reality, with its innate moral quality, the 'truth', which means a higher reality. But sometimes he simply uses the term 'reality'. Indeed, he uses the words 'truth' and 'reality' interchangeably. Let us see how his ingenuity in establishing the moral character of the reality and equating it with the truth fits Tagore into a highly acclaimed philosophical tradition.

All great philosophers striving to change the trajectory of human civilisation for the better had been troubled by the dichotomy between 'is' and 'ought', that is, how to implement in reality what they considered morally desirable. We can try to understand this with reference to Hegel and Marx. Hegel had transcended the opposition between 'is' and 'ought' by stressing that the ideal was immanent in the real, that idealism was not based on man's moral imagination, but was instead a truth. This was because, according to Hegel, there is a rational order of the real. Reason, a unique endowment of the human mind,[23] would journey through the necessary conflicts of thoughts, and their resolution would lead to human progress towards freedom. It is well-known that Marx, faced with the same opposition between 'is' and 'ought', adopted Hegel's dialectic, based on the idea of an 'embedded rationality'. But he turned Hegel on his head; instead of indulging in Hegel's philosophical abstraction, he ascribed absolutism to the material world instead of to the rational spirit of man. His materialistic conception of history—his stress on political economy, social relations of production, the capital-labour nexus, etc.—was not, however, meant to negate consciousness. In fact, it seems that Marx attempted to go beyond the spirit-matter chasm in a reverse manner. Despite his stress on materialism as the driving force of history, the question of morality gradually became a distinct discourse within Marxism, thanks to Marx's notion of 'species being' or 'human essence' (Roy 2014).[24]

Tagore's efforts to converge 'is' and 'ought' with a view to achieving the human good places him on the same pedestal as philosophers like Hegel and Marx, although his position differs from both. Tagore understands that human nature has both good and bad aspects, that both the spirit of morality and mutuality and the spirit of selfishness are innate to it. He also knows that all through, human history has been a history of conflict between good and bad. From the beginning of history, men have had to choose between fighting one another and cooperation, between serving their self-interest and the common interest of all (*Nationalism* 2007 [1917], 120). He, however, asserts that the human world has to be a moral world, not because one could blindly believe in it, but because it was so 'in *truth* which would be dangerous for us to ignore' (ibid., 45–46; emphasis mine). Sometimes, Tagore simply calls it 'reality' instead of 'truth':

> Reality is the harmony which gives to the component parts of a thing the equilibrium of the whole. You break it and have in your hands the nomadic atoms fighting against one another, therefore unmeaning.... The progress of power attains more and more rapidity of pace. And for the reason that it is a detached part of man, it soon outruns the complete humanity. The moral man remains behind. (ibid., 48)

This is a very special view of 'reality', a humanist rather than a naturalist one, and one is tempted to compare this with Marxist theorist Lukacs' call for a totalising outlook on reality (albeit in a different context and as an aesthetic theory). Lukacs contends that our everyday consciousness is fetishistic and fragmented, and so the dialectic within our everyday life produces a need for totality, which is a kind of realism that does not exactly correspond with reality; rather, it stands in opposition to the apparent reality. He stressed on the 'totalizing perspective of reality', on going beyond the 'surface appearance' of a fragmented and distorted reality and totalising its essence as the source of its capacity to defetishise vis-à-vis the false reflection of reality in everyday thought. It is in this way that human beings can experience a release of their latent species consciousness, leading to a convergence of individual and universal levels of experience (Johnson 1984). And this, Lukacs (as well as some later Marxist theorists) claims, is the most radical human need: the need for a human transcendence of the alienation of social life (Heller 1976).[25]

Indeed, it is not just the philosophers but a number of scientists who are also telling us precisely this today, and this establishes the reasoning related to the convergence of 'is' and 'ought' all the more firmly. Science is now telling us that the sense of what 'should be done' lies embedded within human beings themselves, in the evolution of the human mind and body that has been continuing for millions of years. If we go against this process, it will be to our peril. And this is not just an environmental concern; scientists are also worried about the neural health of humans. They are worried that the ecology of human nature embedded in a human's brain-body chemistry is rapidly changing for the worse in the pursuit of psychotropic satisfaction. An individual's desire to be in union with the universal human essence also seems more than an ethical wish today, with science propagating the same as a theory of human dynamics in reality. Science identifies cooperation and mutuality as a major mode of survival, a factor that has so far enabled human life to flourish to its fullest potential in the history of evolution. A cutting-edge area of history called 'deep history', which is neuro-history in methodological terms (and which derives its methodology from the neurosciences), tells us this, too (Smail 2008). However, unlike Hegel or Marx, science does not believe in 'teleology'. Science is not saying that one particular way is the only path to be trodden or pursued. Science gives us the freedom to choose our future.

Tagore was neither a neuroscientist nor an evolutionary theorist, and yet he unerringly used the paradigm of human nature and dealt with the issue of survival and progress of the human species in his analysis. While his emphasis on 'human essence' and the 'true realization of the unity of man' (*Nationalism* 2007 [1917], 16) reminds us of Marx's philosophy concerning human alienation,[26] his prescription, unlike that of Marx (or Hegel, for that matter), seems to lie not so much in human history as in human beings themselves. Tagore analyses human nature in the true manner of a modern scientist to arrive at this solution.[27]

This is how Tagore addressed human nature in *Nationalism*. He drew a parallel between nationalism's rapaciousness and the cruelty in the Hindu cultural code that forces a widow to go without food and water on a particular day every fortnight. He then adds that although men are not so cruel by nature, since piety is a more unreal abstraction, it numbs the morality of the individual, just as a man who would not hurt an animal unnecessarily would cause awful suffering to a large number of innocent creatures 'when he *drugs* his feeling with the abstract idea of "sport"' (*Nationalism* 2007 [1917], 56–57; emphasis mine).[28]

A drug is, of course, the epitome of psychotropic devices, and to him, nationalism seems like a drug. Tagore uses a brilliant analogy to drive home its consequences:

> Man with his mental and material power far outgrowing his moral strength, is like an exaggerated giraffe whose head has suddenly shot up miles away from the rest of him, making normal communication difficult to establish. This greedy head, with its huge dental organization, has been munching all the topmost foliage of the world, but the nourishment is too late in reaching his digestive organs, and his heart is suffering from want of blood. (ibid., 49)

He adds that the West seems to have been blissfully unconscious of this present disharmony in human nature. What worries him is not just that the foliage of the world is being exhausted rapidly, thus endangering the environment in which humans live, but also the no less worrisome question of humanity's organic health, the disintegration of the wholeness of humanity, of dehumanisation.

Tagore addresses the West, trying to bring it to its senses: 'Has not this truth already come home to you now, when this cruel war has driven its claws into the vitals of Europe?' (*Nationalism* 2007 [1917], 49). He, however, sought to end the book on an optimistic note. He believed that the ongoing war signalled the end of the tyranny of the nation, because the veil had been lifted, and in the frightful ongoing war, the West has been forced to confront her own creation (ibid., 59). He expected a strong resistance from the West's own children, who will break themselves free from illusion and refuse to be the 'bond-slaves of machinery' (ibid., 60). Perhaps he also thought that the global war had, in spite of itself, turned the entire world into a neighbourhood, stressing the irrelevance of nationalism all the more. Looking at the worldwide decay, he wrote elsewhere, 'This war has sent out an invitation to man to attend an international *jajna* (meaning sacrificial ceremony)', and he noticed how the young men who had left home in response to this invitation, were moving towards a destination where 'the new sun of the new age is rising amid death and decay' (*Rabindra Rachanabali* 1960, 12).[29] Of course, he was proven wrong. He lived to see another global war fought between nations within two decades. And many years down the line, nationalist insolence has returned with a vengeance in our time. But after all, Tagore was basically a philosopher poet, not a scientist. He had to rely on faith and optimism.

Some Concluding Remarks

There were indeed limitations to Tagore's thinking, as reflected in *Nationalism*. First, attributing every evil of civilisation, even of modern civilisation, to nationalism is somewhat unhistorical. He was eliding the entire project of modernity into nationalism. Instead of treating nationalism as a symptom, he was treating it as a cause of the evil of modernity.

Second, some amount of self-deception is evident in the book, in some respects. Despite a strong condemnation of traditionalism that makes the mind lazy and imprisons it behind fortifications of habits, we do find a sort of historicism in the book. He meant to say that man's earlier history, certainly India's history, had not been so bad. For him, 'political civilisation' is a product of modern nations. India had had other governments before, but the difference between those and the government of the nation is like the difference between the handloom and the powerloom: 'In the products of the handloom the magic of man's living fingers finds its expression ... but the power loom is relentlessly lifeless and accurate and monotonous in its production' (*Nationalism* 2007 [1917], 29). Needless to say, the history of the old States and empires of the world, including those of the subcontinent, would not quite corroborate this. Oppression, domination, tyranny, etc., have been present throughout the history of human civilisation. Tagore also argues that there was a time when all of Eastern Asia, from Burma to Japan, was united with India in the closest ties of friendship, and it was all peace and goodwill, with no pride, no insolence (ibid., 75–76). Again quite unhistorical, we would have to admit.

Evidently, Tagore could not escape the stereotypical binary of material West–spiritual East while writing *Nationalism*—a binary that had been very popular with Indian nationalists since the nineteenth century. Moreover, he equated the material West with the modern and the spiritual East with the ancient. He takes pride in the fact that for a long time, 'the East held the torches of civilization', and that the spiritual ideal of man is still a living thing in Japan, China, and India (ibid., 66). He asserts that the East is like a full-grown tree that has no definite movement but is making inward progress, and compares it with the railway carriage of the West that hurtles towards the terminus station (ibid., 80). The East is a social civilisation, not a political one. However, it has now been overtaken by the outside world propagating a nationalism that has driven its tentacles deep into the Eastern soil, so the time has come for India to make the world problem her own; India must bring the spirit of her civilisation into harmony with the history of all the nations of the world (ibid., 85). He also asks Japan to infuse the spirit of a fuller humanity into the heart of the modern civilisation (ibid., 86).

At times, *Nationalism* sounds like the sermon of a wise old sage from the East, like an Eastern mystic trying to save Western people in the throes of a deep spiritual and cultural crisis. Of course, Tagore dissociates his criticism of the West from any downright denigration of Western culture and people. He acknowledges the greatness of Europe, particularly its literature and art, its noble minds fighting for the cause of humanity and freedom. He seems to have a weakness, and a great respect, for the British in particular (*Nationalism* 2007 [1917], 28), and also seems to believe that the British nation that governs India is one of the best. He particularly praises the law and order of British rule and the peace it has ensured in India, while saying at the same time, 'peace is good, but not more so than life which is God's own great boon' (ibid., 35). He actually desires a complementarity between the East and the West, instead of a one-sided dominance, believing that the two have much to learn from each other. He asserts that while the 'West is necessary to the East' (ibid., 26), someone must convince the West that the East, too, has her own contributions to make in the history of civilisation (ibid., 130). He was in favour of a healthy balance between the ancient spiritual wisdom of the East and the modern material progress of the West.[30]

One of the book's strengths lies in the fact that while Tagore privileges society over politics, his view of society is not uncritical. In the context of India, he dwells especially on her social inadequacies, and on the caste system in particular. He argues that India has tried to manage her diversity through this system, unlike America, Australia, or Europe, which are more favourably situated in terms of a homogeneity of races and so simply sought to exterminate the people they considered aliens (for example, the Native Americans and the African-Americans). He evidently felt some residual admiration for the caste system, arguing that in its origins, the system symbolised India's tolerance, which had evolved a social unity within which different kinds of people could be accommodated and could enjoy freedom within their own boundaries. But now, as different races have come close together, the boundaries seem stifling and the system has become an anachronism. In her attempt at social adjustment, India has set up very rigid boundary walls, thus crippling her children's minds and insulting humanity (*Nationalism* 2007 [1917], 15).[31] He urges that instead of politics, India should pay heed to this serious social problem (here, he particularly criticised the extremists and their pride in the traditional social system). Mere political freedom will not make India free; rather, her social weakness will become a danger in politics. This shows his farsightedness in a way, but was inadequate to meet the needs of the time. He was possibly unaware that about the same time, a young man named B. R. Ambedkar, who was pursuing his Ph.D. on the topic of caste at Columbia University, had written a paper titled 'Castes in India', in which the caste system stood historically condemned as a conspiracy of the upper castes[32] (Ambedkar n.d.), and that very soon, political formations of the Untouchables would lead to an autonomous and radical Untouchable politics that would go against the grain of history.

Nor could Tagore engage at that moment with a new kind of transnationalist political project launched by the Bolshevik Revolution that same year (1917), with a new socioeconomic message of egalitarianism and the full and free development of every individual, which was to arouse great hopes and aspirations in a large part of the world, including India. Later, though, Tagore expressed his admiration for the Soviet experiment, albeit not without some reservations, the grounds of which were proved by history to be highly valid.[33]

Tagore's affinity with Gandhi seems more profound. Gandhi, who had returned from South Africa just a couple of years before Tagore wrote *Nationalism*, promised a new turn to the Indian nationalist movement, and Tagore could not but extend him a warm welcome. Basically both of them wanted the Indian national movement to be much more than a political exercise; they wanted it to have a strong moral basis. But then Tagore became uncomfortable about the way it turned the Gandhian principle into a stratagem and strengthened bigotry and inertia all around, and saw the Gandhian Movement facing the same historical and ideological impasse as the Swadeshi Movement.

Finally, I will only say that even though Tagore's thoughts cannot forge or guide a big political project in today's world, they can perhaps rectify some of the wrongs that are likely to befall any political project. We would naturally invoke him to counter the viciously coercive nationalism flourishing today, the very ideology of which is fascist and aims at a mutilation of humanity. The fact that it also espouses a Hindu nationalism, which was anathema to Tagore, makes his thought an even more robust weapon. But Tagore also cautions us against other political projects, which are seemingly good and vow to promote human welfare and freedom. We would do well to remember that it is the failure of these other projects that facilitates the rise of fascist and tyrannical politics. More importantly, he urges us to turn our attention to society, that is, to ourselves, and restore the human essence in our collective and individual existence. His moral values, civilisational insights, and philosophical wisdom address us in a powerful voice today, trying to show us the right path. It is for us to decide whether to listen to it or not.

The problem with our reception of Tagore (not just of his *Nationalism,* but in general) is that he is like a great river, ever-flowing. So on the one hand, we take from it as much water as can be accommodated in our small bowl. On the other hand, in our religious reverence for the river, we tend to overlook the waste floating in it, which the river cannot help. It seems that we need to be more open in our reception of Tagore, while at the same time be more critical as well.

ENDNOTES

1. As showing the processuality of Rabindranath's thought is a big concern in this chapter, (particularly in its first part), I have to provide the original dates (and other publication details) of all his works that I have cited, which I have done mostly in the notes. But for the actual citations, I have relied heavily on the *Rabindra-Rachanabali* (*Collected Writings of Rabindranath Tagore*), For his songs, I have relied on *Geetabitan* (1968) (*Collection of Songs*). The book *Nationalism,* my most important source, is cited as *Nationalism* 2007 [1917]. I have provided a separate reference list for Tagore's works, with full bibliographic information on RR (the various volumes), *Geetabitan* (1968), and *Nationalism.* All translations in this chapter are mine.

2. Of course, the book can be read from other perspectives as well. However, we will only highlight certain key points Tagore made and ignore a number of other themes he dealt with while making these points. For example, we will not engage with his views on different countries like the US, China, Russia, or Persia, mentioned in the book. Even Japan,

to whom he dedicates a whole chapter, will remain marginal in our discussion. Nor are we especially concerned with the metaphors used in this book, although this could be an interesting subject from a literary point of view.

3. I dealt with this more elaborately in Roy (2017). The first section of this chapter largely derives from this work.

4. The essay '*Satyer Ahvan*' ('The Call of the Truth'), was written in the Bengali year 1328 (*ca* 1921). It was later included in the book of essays titled *Kalantar* (1344/1937).

5. *Naibedya* was published in 1308/1901. *Utsarga* was published much later, but most of its poems had been included in Mohitchandra Sen (ed.), *Kabyagrantha* (1310/1903). *Atmashakti* was published in 1312/1905, and contained '*Nation Ki?*' (What is a Nation?), '*Bharatvarshiya Samaj*', '*Swadeshi Samaj*', and other essays.

6. The song '*O Amar Desher Mati*' was composed amidst the Swadeshi Movement. It is included in the section 'Swadesh' in *Geetabitan*.

7. 'Bharatvarshiya Samaj' was included in the book of essays titled *Atmashakti* (1312/1905).

8. 'Swadeshi Samaj' was included in *Atmashakti* and first published in the journal *Bangadarshan* (Bhadra 1311/1904).

9. *Gora* was published serially in *Prabasi* during 1907–1908.

10. 'Bharat Tirtha' was written on 18 Asharh 1317/1910. It is included in the section 'Swadesh' of *Geetabitan*.

11. The essay 'Atmaparichay' was published in the journal *Tattbabodhini*, Baisakh 1319/1912. It was included in the book of essays *Parichay* (*Identity*; 1323/1916).

12. 'Janaganamana' was written in 1911 and sung for the first time at the Calcutta session of the Indian National Congress on 27 December of that year. It is included in the section 'Swadesh' in *Geetabitan*.

13. *Ghare-Baire* was published serially in the journal *Sabuj Patra* during 1915.

14. *Nationalism*, with three chapters—'Nationalism in the West', 'Nationalism in Japan', and 'Nationalism in India'—and a poem, 'The Sunset of the Century' as an epilogue of sorts, was published in 1917. It has been digitised by the Internet Archive in 2007, from the University of California Libraries, San Francisco (MDCCCCXVII). It is this digitised version that I have used. The page numbers indicated in all references to the book are from this version.

The book is thus described in the 'Preface':

> 'Nationalism in the West' is one of a series of lectures delivered in the United States during the winter of 1916–17. 'Nationalism in Japan' is based upon two lectures delivered in Japan before the Imperial University and the Keio Gujuku University in June and July 1916. 'Nationalism in India', written in the United States late in 1916, is the poet's reflection upon the state of his own country, and gives a completeness to his discussion of Nationalism. The Poem at the conclusion of the book, 'The Sunset of the Century', was written on the last day of the nineteenth century.

This confirms that *Nationalism* represented the maturation of a process of thought that had germinated in his mind from the late nineteenth century.

15. 'What is dangerous for Japan is not the imitation of the outer features of the West, but the acceptance of the motive force of Western nationalism as her own'.

16. The chapter titled 'Nationalism in India'.

17. The metaphor of 'wolves', or more generally, 'predatory creatures' (*Nationalism* 2007 [1917], 33), is used repeatedly in the book.

18. He perhaps means a cog in the machine.

19. Elsewhere he says that the idea of the Nation is one of the most powerful anaesthetics that man has invented (ibid., 57).

20. He says this by way of a caution for Japan: that the high expectations she has generated by accepting opportunities and responsibilities from the hands of modern times will be belied if she merely imitates the modern civilisation of the West and does not address these issues.

21. He says that this is a work of true genius and praises Japan for demonstrating that genius, which she has got 'not by acquirements, but by creations'. He addresses Japan thus: 'The idea of "maitri" (friendship) is at the bottom of your culture—"maitri" with man and "maitri" with nature' (ibid., 92).

22. Hibbert Lectures, delivered in Oxford in 1930, later published in book form. I have used the 2005 edition.

23. Which he also calls the self-consciousness of the Absolute Spirit.

24. I discussed Marx's philosophy and its debt to Hegel in Roy (2014),

25. The theory of 'radical need' in everyday life created by the capitalist order, which is commensurable with man's dissatisfaction with that order and a major motive behind revolutionary struggles, gradually became very important within Western Marxism. I have discussed this elaborately

in Roy (2014), largely drawing insights from Pauline Johnson and Agnes Heller.

26. And, of course, his mention of 'labour and capital' (as cited above) cannot but remind us of Marx.

27. It is true that Tagore sometimes expressed reservations about science. In *The Religion of Man*, he said, 'But men of science tell us that truth, unlike beauty and goodness, is independent of our consciousness.... But may not the explanation be this, that ideal truth does not depend upon the individual mind of man, but on the universal mind that comprehends the individual?' (p. 7). In this book, he also said that science was concerned only with the objective reality, for example, with the biological existence of humankind to the exclusion of his inner nature and his inner urges, which are 'absolutely superfluous for biological existence' (p. 43). But actually, Tagore's stand was close to that of modern science. Indeed, he ultimately showed a concern for biological existence in *The Religion of Man* when he defended this 'truth', that is, the 'spiritual kinship of man which is universal', precisely in terms of man's biological existence. He observed that human races had 'developed in their individual isolation a mentality that is obnoxiously selfish' (p. 140) and cautioned,

> We may come to acquire a strong love for our own colourful race speciality; but if that gives us fitness only for a very narrow world, then, at the slightest variation in our outward circumstances, we may have to pay for this love with our life itself. In the animal world there are numerous instances of complete race suicide. (p. 142)

Tagore did bring to his concern for human beings the aid of scientific knowledge and reasoning, along with philosophy and spiritual inquiry. His interest in and engagement with science is a well-known subject, addressed by a number of scholars. It has been shown how Tagore's sense of belonging to a great interconnectedness, his belief in the spiritual unity of man and in one world was actually more than a mere belief or idealism; how his ideas found an echo in the thoughts of biologist Rachel Carson and the world's first computer programmer, Ada Lovelace, and also how it has motivated the physicist Alan Lightman's poetic ode to science (Popova n.d.).

On the other hand, his ideas have inspired the philosopher (and professor of law and ethics) Martha C Nussbaum's discourse on 'the way to reconcile the individual's pursuit of personal utility with general good', her upholding of cosmopolitanism, that is, the idea of a 'community of human beings in the entire world', instead of mere nationalism or patriotism, as well as her advocacy of Tagore's 'reflections about motivating sympathy and limiting self-interest' as vital for sustaining democracy (Nussbaum 1994, 2012). If Tagore did not invoke science much for understanding human nature (and its implications for the future of humanity), it was perhaps because the science of human nature was not much developed at the time. It was not possible for him, unlike us, to be aware of the recent advances in neurology.

28. When we think of *Jallikattu*, we realise how true this observation is! Jallikattu is traditionally practised in Tamil Nadu. It is an event in which a bull is released into a crowd of people and a number of human participants attempt to grab the hump on the bull's back with both arms and hang on to it while the bull attempts to escape, thus traumatising the animal and also causing injury and death to humans.

29. 'Granthaparichay', *Balaka* (a book of poems, which were mostly written during World War I). *Balaka* is included in *Rabindra Rachanabali*, Vol. 12.

30. By the time Tagore wrote *Nationalism*, his belief in 'one world' had become very strong. This one world comprised both the East and the West (his Santiniketan experiment was a major effort towards this end). In 1921, he wrote to his friend Charles Freer Andrews,

> In you the apparent conflict of the East and the West has unveiled the great beauty of its inner reconciliation. We who are clamouring for vengeance, only conscious of the separateness, and therefore expecting absolute separation, has not read the great purpose of our history right. (Letter dated 6 May 1921, cited in Dasgupta (2018, xx)

But perhaps Tagore had a bias towards the East in his ascribing to her a major role in ensuring this reconciliation. This was also perhaps in view of World War I, which gravely undermined the West's claim to represent what he considered the highest goals of humanity. Sometimes Tagore wanted his own country to take up this task, despite her weakness in material terms. He wrote to his friend Andrews that to judge the measure of man's greatness by his material resources was a 'gigantic illusion' and an 'insult to man'. He argued in the letter, 'It lies in the power of the materially weak to save the world from this illusion' (letter dated 13 March 1921, cited ibid., lix).

31. Elsewhere in *Nationalism*, he says that in order to avoid collisions, India set up boundaries of immovable walls, thus giving to her multitude

of races 'the negative benefit of peace and order but not the positive opportunity of expansion and movement' (p. 138).

32. 'Castes in India: Their Mechanism, Genesis and Development' was a paper read by B. R. Ambedkar at an anthropological seminar in New York on 9 May 1916. It was later published in Vol. XLI of *Indian Antiquary* in May 1917, and was published in book form by a number of publishers later. It is available online as well.

33. In 1923, Tagore sent his blessings to *Samhati* (*Integration*), one of the first journals for workers in Bengal, welcoming workers' growing consciousness of their own power after serving for thousands of years as the vehicles of a civilisation based on their slavery. But at the same time, he expressed doubt about this new development, commenting: 'Power works its tooth and claw from above, but it does not become "Vaishnava" even after climbing down' (*Samhati*, Jyaistha, 1330 by). The same doubt, combined with admiration, can be seen in his *Russiar Chithi* (Letters from Russia, 1931) as well. I discussed Tagore's love-hate relationship with the communists and their movement in Roy (2014).

Select References

Ambedkar, B. R. n.d. *Castes in India: Their Mechanism, Genesis and Development*. Jullundur: Patrika Publications.

Anderson, Benedict. 1983. *Imagined Communities: Reflections on the Origin and Spread of Nationalism*. London: Verso.

Chatterjee, Partha. 2005. *Praja o Tantra*. Kolkata: Anushtup.

Dasgupta, Uma (ed. and introduced). 2018. *Friendships of 'Largeness and Freedom': Andrews, Tagore, and Gandhi: An Epistolary Account 1912–1940*. New Delhi: Oxford University Press.

Heller, Agnes. 1976. *The Theory of Need in Marx*. London: Allison and Busby.

Johnson, Pauline. 1984. *Marxist Aesthetics: The Foundation within Everyday Life for an Emancipated Consciousness*. UK: Routledge and Kegan Paul.

Nussbaum, Martha C. 1994. 'Patriotism and Cosmopolitanism'. *Boston Review* 19 (5).

_____. 2012. 'Rabindranath Tagore: Subversive Songs for a Transcultural "Religion of Humanity"'. *Acta Musicologica* 84 (2), 147–159.

Popova, Maria. n.d. 'The Great Indian Poet and Philosopher Tagore on Truth, Human Nature, and the Interdependence of Existence'. *Brain Pickings*, an online journal. Available at https://www.themarginalian.org/2017/03/07/tagore-mans-universe/ (accessed August 2023).

Roy, Anuradha. 2014. *Bengal Marxism: Early Discourses and Debates*. Calcutta: Samya.

______. 2017. 'The Best of Nationalism and Beyond: Rabindranath's Swadesh'. In Shubhra Chakrabarti and Utsa Patnaik (eds), *Agrarian and Other Histories: Essays for Binay Bhushan Chaudhuri*. New Delhi: Tulika.

Smail, Daniel Lord. 2008. *On Deep History and the Brain*. Berkeley and London: University of California Press.

Tagore, Rabindranath:

Rabindra Rachanabali, Vol. 3. 1969a. Kolkata: Visva-Bharati.

Rabindra Rachanabali, Vol. 6. 1969b. Kolkata: Visva-Bharati.

Rabindra Rachanabali, Vol. 8. 1967. Kolkata: Visva-Bharati.

Rabindra Rachanabali, Vol. 10. 1971. Kolkata: Visva-Bharati.

Rabindra Rachanabali, Vol. 12. 1960. Kolkata: Visva-Bharati.

Rabindra Rachanabali, Vol. 18. 1966. Kolkata: Visva-Bharati.

Rabindra Rachanabali, Vol. 24. 1970. Kolkata: Visva-Bharati.

______. 1968. *Geetabitan*. Kolkata: Visva-Bharati.

______. 2005 [1930]. *The Religion of Man*. New Delhi: Rupa Publications.

______. 2007 [1917]. *Nationalism*. San Francisco: University of California Libraries.

10

Seas, Rivers, Estuaries

Three Moments in the Social and Cultural History of Water-borne Circulations in Eastern India

Rila Mukherjee

Introduction

This chapter aims to understand the historical role of waterscapes in eastern India by showcasing transformative moments in peoples' perception, wherein the sea, the river, and the estuary became focal at different moments in human history.

While water has been vital to human material life throughout history, how humans interact with water has not received due attention. Unconsciously taking their cue from Ptolemy, who saw regions as enclosed by mountains and rivers, historians usually specialise in waterscapes bounded and defined by contiguous landmasses, river valleys, and estuaries. These conceptual water-scapes artificially restrict or distort peoples' waterborne interactions by viewing these as discrete entities, separate from peoples' circulations on land. In such a view, waterscapes are only 'spaces in between' that just need to be 'crossed over'. Colonial history and historiography accentuated this continental perspective by dividing water worlds into discrete, restricted, and controlled spaces, unified by the language of the coloniser. Such perceived spaces imposed order, control, and mastery on marine environments, which human communities and independent sailing peoples, who have always dwelt beyond the power of the State or existed on its margins, have resisted. Colonial perceptions therefore represent waterscapes of desire by the powerful rather than reflections of reality, and nationalist perceptions have followed this continental perspective in India. It follows that attempts to map and narrate the range and vision of marine peoples before their domination and marginalisation by land-based, numerically or militarily superior people offer a way to decolonise their history. Part of this decolonising process involves a form of subaltern history whereby the centrality of water, forever present in the worldview of marine peoples, is restored to its rightful place (D'Arcy 2013).

Circulations by water are not confined just to seas and oceans, but also reference rivers, lakes, and lagoons. Water represents the commons, nourishment, connectivity, and paradoxically, danger as well. In every cultural and historical context water is integral to people's experiences of the landscape and their cosmological understanding of it. Rivers and seas 'bring' and 'carry away'. Rivers in particular epitomise continuity, belonging, desire, memory, and history. They create cultural landscapes through long-term archaeological traces of material relations between water and people. Water bestows emotion and affect, permeating everyday experiences with the dampness of rain, the chill of fog, the relief of a chilled drink in the summer heat, the buoyancy and weightlessness of immersion. We like the shimmer of water surfaces, the vigour of waterfalls, the calming rhythm of waves, the vagaries of the weather; in short, the movement of water through the material world (Strang 2014, 136).

Forms of Water

Understanding the sociocultural implications of waterborne circulations necessitates a study of water in its various forms. Research on the multiple meanings of water offers some rapprochement between cross-cultural themes and cultural specificities. While highlighting the diversity of human-water relations, it provides abundant ethnographic and historical evidence demonstrating major spatio-temporal continuities in societies' engagements with water, and in the metaphors associated with it.

Water is socially, politically, and ritually constituted, but it also has an existence outside the human domain (Edgeworth 2014, 157). Although present around us as liquid, semi-solid, solid, and gas, water occupies the fringes of our consciousness. Flowing between and connecting the human and non-human on multiple systemic scales, a study of water offers local and global perspectives on material relations. It is essential to all ecosystemic processes on local, regional, continental, or planetary scales. We literally think with water as it enables the neurons via which thought is carried, and metaphorically by employing its properties to conceptualise notions of flow. As material that regularly shifts between fluid and solid states, as liquid, steam, ice, drizzle, fog, etc., water highlights the conceptual opposition between movement and stasis. In the process of being ingested, water is incorporated, becoming, at 67 per cent, a major part of the body, demonstrating both the contingent stability of the body and the permeability of the person as an 'assemblage' of both internal and external matter. This helps to underline a reality: that matter is neither ontologically nor literally distinct; all things—and living beings—are dynamically composed of flows of condensed matter (Strang 2014, 135).

Water is regarded as both sacred and profane. Key places, like the sources of the Tigris or the Nile, enabled the construction of mythic-poetic landscapes in ancient Assyria and Egypt. Hymns and odes have been composed to the Ganges and Kaveri rivers. The majority of the world's population, whether Hindu, Christian, or Muslim, believe in the curative and redemptive powers of holy water in its various forms. Confluences are particularly sacred to Hinduism. The term '*sagara*' denotes the junction of the river and the sea, as can be seen in the terms 'Ganga-sagara' and 'Sindhu-sagara', the confluence of the Ganges with the Bay of Bengal and that of the Indus with the Arabian Sea, respectively. There are inland confluences as well. The sacred forty-two-day Hindu festival, the Maha Kumbh, is held every twelve years in Allahabad at the confluence of the Ganges, the Yamuna, and the mythical, subterranean Saraswati River. In 2001, an estimated fifty to seventy million people came to this sacred confluence; in 2013, more than 100 million arrived, sharing a single aim: to erase their sins by bathing in the holy water. In its nature, holy water is the same water in the hydrological cycle as any other, but its significance is fundamentally different: it works because it is holy. Being culture, religion, and nature at the same time, holy water has agency (Oestigaard 2014, 163–164; Strang 2014, 136).

Water is thus an important natural element in Hindu religion and mythology. In the Rig Veda, any mass of water of more than a drop could be an ocean or *samudra*—water in a jar, a small pool, a reservoir, or the ocean itself. Most sacred sites in South Asia, even those situated far inland, contain water in the form of tanks called 'samudra' or 'sagara'. These tanks, built by the ruling classes, represent inland lakes—the Rig Veda defines the Kashmir and Kurukshetra lowlands as inland oceans (samudra), as does the Hebrew Bible, wherein the Sea of Galilee and the Dead Sea are lakes or inland seas.

The reasons for water's religious significance are many. Water precedes creation and reabsorbs it, and is thus associated with both evolution and dissolution. It symbolises fertility because, formless itself, it is nevertheless a reservoir of all possibilities of existence. Bathing in the waters always brings about a regeneration, since immersion implies a temporary regression into the undifferentiated mode of existence and immersion is symbolic of the creation of form. Rites of purification at sacred sites involve bathing in the river or the tank within the temple complex. Many temples are situated along the banks of rivers. Others have water bodies in the form of lakes, ponds, and built tanks for ritual purposes. The association of pilgrimage centres with water can be clearly seen in the number of sacred spots that lie on river banks, at confluences, or on the sea coast. In their female forms, the Ganges and Yamuna rivers are auspicious symbols, appearing in niches within temple precincts. One of the essential objects of worship in the daily ritual of a Hindu householder is a pitcher brimming with water, representing the seat of god. The presence of water in birth, death, and purificatory rituals is common to many religions, but its elaborate use in

Hinduism makes it a very significant element in worship (Sinha 1995, 4–5).

In Bengal, the waters of the Ganges are privileged over the Padma. The Bhagirathi is associated with many sacred Hindu sites, including the significant Sagar (Ocean) Island, where the river finally 'melts' into the sea and where, every *makar sankranti* (an annual Hindu festival held on the day of the winter solstice), hundreds of thousands of pilgrims celebrate. By contrast, there are no venerated sites along the Padma.

Chapman and Rudra write:

> [T]here were two major branches of the Ganga: one ... the Bhagirathi, the other either the Padma or a proto-Padma.... The geological evidence ... suggests that the eastward shift of the Ganga started at least 3000 BP. Ptolemy's Mappa Mundi [in Renaissance reconstructions, reportedly from his original data *circa* 150 AD] illustrates the two arms of the Ganga delta. But it is not possible to derive relative sizes from this information.... Although ... the Bhagirathi ... was never the major distributary of the Ganga, its significance as an historical route is beyond dispute. (Chapman and Rudra 2015, 22)

Culture, Politics, Agency

Water is also a cultural force. The river, the crossing, and the far shore have formed an important symbolic complex in the Indian imagining of transition and transcendence (Eck 1981). Regarding the holy but highly polluted Jordan River, the Vicar General of Latin Patriarchate explained in 2013 the distinction between the physical and the sacred states of water. According to him, it does not matter from a religious perspective whether the water is dense or light, clear or cloudy, polluted or un-polluted, as this does not touch upon the aspect of faith. Water transcends Western concepts, being universal and particular, always in flux and always culture (or religion) and nature at the same time, but in different forms and shapes at various points in history and in specific contexts (Oestigaard 2014, 164–165). Water is useful in dissolving the theoretical divides between 'textual' analyses of material culture and the more abstract processual views of how 'human beings and other organisms are bound in webs of life' (Strang 2014, 136, 138).

Rivers are an essential part of the political geography of a region. Physical features such as mountains and rivers were used in all cultures to mark frontiers. But rivers were also seen as alien forces. The Mauryas saw water routes as inaccessible, full of dangers and indefensible. The *Arthasastra* prescribed that 'ferries shall cross waterways only at fixed points, in order to prevent traitors to the King crossing [into the country]', and 'among water routes, a coastal route is better than one on the high sea because there are a large number of ports [along any coast]. A river route is also good because it poses less serious dangers and is more constantly in use' (Rangarajan 1992, 344, 623; see 2.28.14, 18.24.27, and 7.12.17–28). Later rulers used water to channelise production, demarcate boundaries, and delineate regions (Ghosh 2016; Seshan 2016). However, rivers are also carriers of alien cultures. The *Mymensingh Ballads* reference the horrors of *magh* and *bombete* (bombardier) riverine incursions into estuarine Bengal through *harmads* (armadas). A cause for regional tensions, the Kaveri river waters are disputed every summer by the states of Karnataka and Tamil Nadu in India. Water is a tool of international diplomacy, as is seen in discussions over Teesta water-sharing between India and Bangladesh.

Nowhere in India is the presence of water as pervasive as in Bengal. In almost every village of Bengal, carved and moulded baked-clay panels, made by humble folk artists, adorn brickwork temples, depicting scenes from the Ramayana and the Mahabharata, and offer glimpses into daily rural life. In these terracotta reliefs, which represent processions of warriors, lines of elephants, camels, and horses, or local zamindars and female entertainers travelling in palanquins, a particular theme is journey by boat, depicting leisure, raiding, and warfare (Deloche 1991, 2).

On the other hand, Gaudiya Vaishnavism's peripatetic nature saw land-based travels through the forests of Vrindavan in north India, creating a pilgrimage path through the woods, bowers, and ponds along the banks of the Yamuna that culminated at Bishnupur. The superimposition of a Gaudiya Vaishnava *mandala* there was achieved by naming and giving new significance to the region's geographical features. Its Damodar (another name for the Krishna) and the smaller Kangsabati (Radha) rivers are perceived as male and female lovers in eternal union in the region's lore (Ghosh 2002a, 111; 2002b, 209).

Despite the fluidity of this interactive situation, water is thus dialectical in nature and the human relationship with water is sometimes uneasy. It is marked by a sort of 'push and pull' or 'action and counteraction' nature, yet human-water interactions cannot be solely categorised as a battle between oppositional forces, for people work with flow as well as against it. Even when not in destructive mode, flowing water actively and physically challenges human projects such as dams and barrages. Friction and turbulence, as well as fluidity and consistency, can result. In looking at the archaeological evidence of human-river interactions in the past, a typical scenario that emerges is that people make a material intervention in rivers, but this leads to an unexpected river response (floods, for example), which in turn requires some human reaction (for example, building embankments or canals, or undertaking river-linking), which results in further unexpected river responses, and so on. Both human and non-human participants are drawn into a dynamic entanglement with each other—almost a kind of tussle (Edgeworth 2014, 158–159; Strang 2014, 136). In the analysis of relationships between the human and the non-human, we need to add the sheer power of water; this goes beyond just material resistance to human agency. This is a power that, at its most destructive and dangerous, can ravage, inundate, overcome, and submerge cultural forms. As a negative force (changing river courses, floods, disease, and tsunamis are cases in point), water is also seen as calamitous throughout history.

WRITING THE SPACES OF WATER

Although not immediately apparent, water encircles our lives, covering almost 70 per cent of the earth's surface. Islands and continents make up the rest. Seas and oceans challenge the history of bounded spaces since connectivities forged by water destabilise national narratives—coastal shrines, churches, mosques, and temples across the Indian Ocean rim are sites for praying *across* the water, not just on land.

Water can reach landlocked places. Much like Odisha, Bengal, and upland Sylhet, parts of Central Asia, including Yunnan, used a marine product, *kauri* shells (*cypria moneta*), as currency for almost two millennia, despite having gold and silver. Places located far inland are defined by water: Hyderabad is called the Pearl City, evoking Golconda's maritime link through Masulipatnam port. This gives new meaning to the phrase 'land divides, water unites'.

Pre-modern people, ideas, and objects travelled by water, as do commodities at present. Dependence on sea-lanes has intensified in the twenty-first century, reverting to a maritime orientation:

> [U]nlike the train, plane or automobile, ships and the sea occupy the edges of our consciousness; they are largely invisible and seemingly irrelevant in our everyday lives. But look around the room you are sitting in. It is likely that many of the items surrounding you would have travelled at one stage or another of their life in a ship, across the oceans. (Peters 2010, 1260)

Waterscapes are varied—oceans and seas, rivers and estuaries, and even lakes and lagoons. While in spaces like the Mediterranean, sea-river interactions are included in economic models, in other regions traditional upstream-downstream models, such as Bronson's model for Southeast Asia, which links coast and interior by way of dual-way flows, disregard the unique environmental and human conditions of each areas. Many other areas of the world remain yet un-described from the perspective of their waterways. Such a shift in perception makes a case for a decolonising of regional history by defining it through waterscapes rather than land borders, leading to a maritime space as embracing not just its physical surrounds, nor as a mere cognitive category, but as a *sense of place* (Andaya and Andaya 2014). This 'larger' sea encompasses not only a specific waterscape but also rivers, streams, estuaries, deltas, uplands, and sometimes even remote mountain passes, generating a new regional perspective and an innovative history.

The Sea

For poet Derek Walcott, the 'gray vault' of the sea *is* History (Walcott 1979). The sea is not a uniform space and consists of two regions. The coastal zone is like land, in that it can be claimed, controlled, regulated, and managed by individual State-actors (Steinberg 2001, 115). In the deep sea, the only necessary (or even permissible) regulation is ensuring that all ships are able to travel freely across its vast surface. The sea is a space apart from the travails of everyday life. Filipino islanders view the land as chaotic and the sea as peaceful. Their Olympu, deep-sea site of mysterious happenings and dangerous spirits, is similar to *Kalidaha* in Bengal's *Mangal* texts, denoting a point of passage, a crossroads, a state of transition between the known and the unknown, and the turmoil encountered in the deep sea (Magos 1994, 321, 349, 353; Mukherjee 2011, 125).

The long history of Indian Ocean interactions with the Mediterranean and the Indo-Pacific rim compels us to go beyond the strict geographical and cartographical limits of the Indian Ocean by recognising the differences between the geographical and the historical Indian Ocean (Chakravarti 2019, 29). Persian and Arab traders sailed directly to India and China from the ninth century, distinguishing seas through physical characteristics and not always in terms of their geographical extent. Al-Ya'qubi (d. 897), following oral tradition, said about the spatial and cognitive realms in the ocean that 'whoever wants to go to China must cross seven seas, each one with its own color and wind and fish and breeze, completely unlike the sea that lies beside it' (Lunde 2005). The first of these was the Sea of Fars, which men sailed after setting out from Siraf. It ended at Ra's al-Jumha—a strait where pearls were fished. The second sea, called Larwi, began at Ra's al-Jumha. For al-Ya'qubi, it was a big sea, containing the island of Waqwaq and others that belonged to the Zanj. These islands had kings. One could only sail this sea by the stars. It contained huge fish, and in it were many wonders and things that defied description. The third sea was called Harkand, and in it lay the island of Sarandib [Sri Lanka], with precious stones and rubies. Al-Ya'qubi noted that there were islands with kings, 'but there is one king over them. In the islands of this sea grow bamboo and rattan.' The fourth sea was called Kalah-bar, a shallow sea filled with huge serpents which rode the wind and smashed ships. Here were islands where the camphor tree grew. The fifth sea, according to al-Ya'qubi, was called Salahit and was 'very large and filled with wonders'. The sixth was a rainy sea called Kardanj. The seventh was called the Sea of Sanji, also known as Kanjli. It was the sea of China; one was driven by the south wind until one reached a freshwater bay along which were fortified places and cities, until one reached Khanfu or Canton.

The use of this sea route produced a number of Southern Arabian fables, which then spread along the shores of the Indian Ocean. The best-known fables are the seven sea-borne travels of Sinbad the sailor. He is rich as opposed to his *alter ego*, the poor, land-based porter Sinbad. The sea is thus a metaphor for wealth, while land represents poverty and changelessness.

Along the Indian Ocean rim, peoples' perception of the sea as an intrinsic part of land and its use as commons prevails, despite attempts at State regulation. Marine deities and spirits such as China's Mazu, India's Velankanni, Java's Nyayi Lara Kidul, Africa's Mami Wata, Gujarat's Darya Pir, and Persia's Khwaja Khidr traverse this vast space, protecting fishermen and sailors at sea. Shore temples stretching in an arc from Somanatha, through Mahabalipuram to the temples of Tanah Lot and Uluwatu in Bali are navigation markers in a spiritual waterscape. The Sufi and Badr Maqam shrines from Chittagong to Mergui are examples of the faiths that dot the northern Bay of Bengal littoral. Such shrines ensure fortune, well-being, and safe travel, the eastern Indian Ocean being more subject to typhoons and cyclones than its western counterpart.

Rivers

Rivers—connecting sea to land and signifying memory and history—are crucial components in this pelagic scheme. South Asian writers have pointed to the crucial conceptual terrains embedded in the many religious traditions of Bengal, suggesting that the term 'river' is a misnomer. The modern Western 'river' is specific, with a length, depth, and width. Dissociated from its social context and flowing on the surface of the landscape, it has a particular morphology and flow-regime that can be calculated, managed, controlled, and used. Our perception of rivers remains outside this Eurocentric structure (Sen and Palash 2016, 97).

Rivers signify local time, defining the land and determining the 'landscape' and scope of water-spaces. The Karatoya and Lakhiya rivers (now in Bangladesh) symbolise local time in a country defined by its rivers rather than by the sea, by privileging the river as the chief force that 'creates' the land. The homage *Karatoya Mahatmyan*, composed sometime prior to the second half of the twelfth century, states that the men of Pundravarddhana-pura (identified with Mahasthan in Bogra district) were wise and pure, and the land was elevated and fertile, being filled with tanks, wells, gold (a metaphor for wealth), dancing, and enjoyment (Sen 1929, 20–21, 25–28). Washed by the river, this sacred land was deemed twice blessed.

Bradley-Birt's description of the Lakhiya as memory highlights the centrality of rivers to life itself: 'memories still cling thick around these lower reaches of the Lakhiya, close by where the great rivers meet' (Bradley-Birt 1906, 319). Contrast this statement with Joseph Conrad's description of the Congo River flowing into the southern Atlantic Ocean in his novel, *Heart of Darkness* (2007 [1899]). While Asian rivers were signifiers of civilisation, his description of the Congo River evokes its precedent—a state of nature—and sometimes its opposite—barbarity. Conrad's protagonist Marlow saw it as primordial memory in the novel:

> Going up that river was like traveling back to the earliest beginnings of the world, when vegetation rioted on the earth and the big trees were kings. An empty stream, a great silence, an impenetrable forest.... There were moments when one's past came back to one ... but it came in the shape of an unrestful and noisy dream, remembered with wonder amongst the overwhelming realities of this strange world of plants, and water, and silence. And this stillness of life did not in the least resemble a peace. It was the stillness of an implacable force brooding over an inscrutable intention. It looked at you with a vengeful aspect. (ibid., 85–86)

The river—more than the sea—is an allegory of Time past and present, as opposed to the sea of infinite time. The great Triveni at Prayag is mirrored by the little Triveni in Bengal near Satgaon. The Baul poet Phatik Chand sang: 'Whoever can surmount the vortex of Triveni, where three rivers meet, will float forever on the waves of time' (Darian 1978, 148). This sense of an inexorable time is also found in a twentieth-century description of eastern Bengal's rivers:

> Just below, the Megna, the Ganges, the Brahmaputra, the Dullasery, and the Ishamutty, all unite, and this meeting-place of the giant watercourses is the most historic spot in all Eastern Bengal. The many tides that have ebbed and flowed this way have seen strange scenes.... It has seen great principalities and kingdoms rise and fall, the fleeting glories of a fickle world. On its broad bosom it has borne brave fleets and armies to victory and defeat.... Only the great river ... flows onwards.... (Bradley-Birt 1906, 325)

For Conrad's Marlow, the narrator in *Heart of Darkness*, time on the river is akin to the sea of death: 'The brown current ran swiftly out of the heart of darkness, bearing us down towards the sea with twice the speed of our upward progress; and Kurtz's life was running swiftly too, ebbing, ebbing out of his heart into the sea of inexorable time' (Conrad 2007 [1899], 178).

But in Uttarkashi and Varanasi, and in countless riverine towns of the subcontinent, the *sandhya arati* of the evening puja ceremony reinforces ancient memory, venerating the life-giving force of the Ganges, celebrating its healing properties, as well as its involvement with peoples' lives on its journey to the sea. A good example is the Ganga Sagar (*sagar*, Sanskrit, referencing the Bay of Bengal) pilgrimage in Bengal. The notion of the river-sea continues to influence peoples' lives along the northern Bay of Bengal. From the earliest recorded history, people have called the Brahmaputra River 'Lauhitya Sagar' (*lit.*, the river-sea), Lohit being another name for the Brahmaputra. The harmony of river and sea resonates in other cultures. The people of the Amazon call the river 'rio-mar'—River Sea—similar to Egyptian and Graeco-Roman visions, wherein a flowing stream—the Ocean River (the Nile)—coursed around the Afro-Eurasian landmass (Lewis 1999, 190; Raffles 2007, 315).

It is in the regenerative and transformative potential of waterscapes that a social and cultural history of waterborne circulations achieves importance. English cartographer James Rennell saw an immense riverine world:

> The Ganges and Burrampooter Rivers, together with their numerous branches and adjuncts, intersect the country of Bengal in such a variety of directions, as to form the most compleat [*sic*] and easy inland navigation that can be conceived.... It is supposed, that this inland navigation gives constant employment to 30,000 boatmen. Nor will it be wondered at, when, it is known, that all the salt, and a large proportion of the food consumed by ten millions of people are conveyed by water within the kingdom of Bengal and its dependencies. To these must be added the transport of the commercial exports and imports, probably to the amount of two millions sterling per annum; the interchange of manufactures and products throughout the whole country; the fisheries; and the article of traveling. (Rennell and Banks 1781, 87–88)

Popular perceptions of rivers as *place* differ significantly from the notion of sea/ocean as *empty space*. There is a saying in rural Bengal:

'*Gangey gangey dekha hoy, boney boney dekha hoy na*' ('While rivers meet each other [in the ocean], sisters can never come together on earth' [because they are often married into families who live far away, making it difficult for them to meet]). The *nodi* or river in Bengal is imagined in a wide range of metaphors: *maya nodi*—river of bonds; *bhawbo nodi*—river of life; *bhaaber nodi*—river of love; *kaam nodi*—river of lust. The most generic are songs of yearning and warning referencing rivers, evoking the love-fear relation that humans have with rivers (Sengupta and Chakravarty 2016). Rivers and riverine passages are evoked in Rabindranath Tagore's poem *Sonar Tori* (1894), Adwaitya Mallabarman's *Titash Ekti Nodir Nam* (filmed by Ritwik Ghatak in 1973), Manik Bandyopadhyay's *Padma Nodir Majhi*, Achyut Goswami's *Matsyakanya*, and Samaresh Basu's *Ganga*. The water of the holy Ganges has ritual significance in everyday worship and at transformative moments such as birth, marriage, and death.

While rivers are associated with death, they are also part of life and their lively names resonate. The *Adi Ganga* running through Kolkata is the original rivulet from the Ganges. *Ichhamoti* means a river with '*ichha*' or desire, depending on '*moti*', or its mood. Its 'ichha' was disregarded when British administrator Sir Cyril John Radcliffe partitioned Bengal in 1947 and the river separated the Bengali-speaking people living on its banks into two separate nation-States: India and East Pakistan (later Bangladesh). *Dhaleshwari* (expressing the sense of an overflowing love or emotion) is derived from the Bengali term '*dhal*', used to describe the flood-spate of a river. *Matla*, evoking a drunkard's unpredictable course, is derived from the Bengali word *matal* (Banerjee 2016, 82).

Estuaries

We now move to the crucial role played by estuaries, maritime spaces *par excellence* that serve as the meeting-points of river and sea (Pearson 2011). It is hardly surprising that estuaries receive the most attention in Bengal's historical records. Numerous creeks converge on the Ganges–Brahmaputra–Meghna (GBM) basin where many rivers meet. With over 130 million inhabitants, this delta has a density of more than 200 people per km, making it one of the most densely populated regions in the world. Upwards of 300 million people are supported by it, and approximately 400 million people live in the Ganges River Basin. The total population of Bangladesh is 160 million (73 per cent of which is rural), of whom 122 million inhabitants live inside the GBM river basin. The total territory of India has a population estimated at 1,181 million inhabitants (71 per cent rural), of whom 476 million live inside this river basin (FAO/AQUASTAT 2011, 3). Creeks, some suitable for year-round navigation by large boats, enclose densely-populated low-lying lands, planted with paddy and cotton, full of timber but menaced by tigers. Many were deserted (La Touche 1910).

Rennell saw:

> That part of the Delta bordering on the sea, is composed of a labyrinth of rivers and creeks, all of which are salt, except those that immediately communicate with the principal arm of the Ganges.... Its numerous canals are so disposed as to form a compleat [*sic*] inland navigation throughout and across the lower part of the Delta, without either the delay of going round the head of it, or the hazard of putting to sea. (Rennell and Banks 1781, 92)

Sailing around Dhaka, he wrote:

> January 1st. 1765, at 3 PM arrived at Backergunge, which lies on a very small Creek about 14 miles below the four Creeks. It lies in Latitude 22°-36'...North, about 16 miles from the Great Ganges, 74 from Dacca & 116 from Calcutta. The Inhabitants report that the Sea is about 20 miles to the SSE. (La Touche 1910, 32)

Another example of navigating an estuarine world comes from East India Company official Robert Lindsay in September 1772. En route to Dhaka and Sylhet, he:

> left Calcutta on my way to Dacca by water; we embarked at Balaghaut on the salt-water lake three miles to the eastward, and in a few hours found ourselves in the Sunderbunds,

> completely secluded from the world in a wilderness of wood and water. This navigation is part of the Delta of the Ganges, extending more than two hundred miles along the coast, through thick forests, inhabited only by tigers, alligators, and wild animals peculiar to a tropical climate; the human population is very scanty, the country being overflowed every spring-tide by salt water. It is a dreary waste of great extent, but beautiful in the extreme, the lofty trees growing down to the water's edge with little or no brush or under wood. The innumerable rivers and creeks which intersect this country in every direction form a passage so intricate as to require the assistance of a pilot; its windings are like the mazes of a labyrinth, in which a stranger would find himself immediately bewildered. In twelve days I found myself domiciled at Dacca.... (Lindsay 1840, 16–17)

Lindsay's ship *Augusta,* built in Sylhet, sailed to Macau via Kolkata in 1783. He delineated the gradual transition from estuary to sea:

> [T]hrough a most intricate and hitherto unexplored navigation, to the vicinity of the sea. On the passage down, the ship frequently grounded, but, being furnished with good anchor boats, we hove her off without difficulty. My troubles I thought now at an end, having anchored at a place called Luckypore, near to the confluence of the Ganges and Brahmaputra, two of the largest rivers in the world ... Next morning, (we) embarked in a good sailing boat, and crossed and recrossed this great river, at this place full twenty miles broad, and, after sounding the channel with every attention, nowhere could we find more than fourteen feet water, the Augusta with her water and stores, drawing full seventeen! I leave you, my friends, to judge, in what an awkward situation I was placed,—my ship and cargo, value at the least £40,000, hermetically sealed up in fresh water, without the prospect of ever reaching the ocean. The ridicule I had to encounter for a few hours vexed me—but the question now was, how to get out of the scrape. Two row-boats well manned were now ordered; Captain Thomas embarked in the one, and I took charge of the other. Our object was to abandon the

> large rivers as impracticable, and to search for a passage to sea through the narrow channels, or creeks, with which this wide delta abounds; and we succeeded in finding deeper water in the river called Harringotta, a smaller branch of the Ganges.... The ship was destined to the Straits of Malacca, with a valuable cargo of opium, and eventually to stop at Macao in China; .... It was now the beginning of December, and the most favourable season for getting clear of this dismal and dangerous navigation, the water as smooth as a mill-pond,—and well it so happened, for we had still to cross a bar of ten leagues extent, on which there was not more than six inches more water than the vessel drew; but, as I had previously sounded, and the wind was fair, I recommended the captain to hoist every sail he could set, and thus we forced the ship through black mud till the captain pronounced us in perfect safety. (Lindsay 1840: 82–84)

Perceiving Water

This chapter studied three sets of perceptions in circulation regarding seas, rivers, and estuaries, uncovering in the process the ways in which both outsiders and insiders have interacted with water in Bengal. The notion of 'friction' is useful in this regard, describing a 'generative sea' in which people, processes, and things collide, abrade, and affect each other, shaping and being shaped in the process. This is particularly visible in the case of the Augusta's journey, described in the previous section.

This notion of a generative sea is appealing, resonating with the view of the Actor Network Theory that agency emerges neither from people nor from things, but from a combination of both. Here, the varied waterscapes become actors. But we should also note that the properties of things and persons are not random, but reflect instead long-term evolutionary adaptations and co-development, and consistent patterns of engagement over time. Water is categorised as a resource at various stages in its movements through persons and landscapes. This is critical because it demonstrates very clearly multiple impositions of human agency and control. As notions of 'resources' have become increasingly reductive, reframing things as purely economic 'assets' or 'services', contests for the ownership and control of water have increased in number and intensity. Water is quintessential in its 'resourcefulness'—it has the fluid potential to effect transformations in every sphere of human endeavour, and in this sense constitutes 'über-potential' in material form. In archaeological representations, for example, elements retain an ontological status (Strang 2014, 139–140, 142).

Europeans saw seas as spaces to be crossed; the popular perception in Bengal saw seas of knowledge but also seas of suffering; but early Perso-Arabic literature, imbuing seas with specific characteristics, saw these as fluid spaces to be engaged with instead. In the process, they understood not just physical spaces, but created cognitive ones as well. The Indic-Buddhist worldview saw seas as self-contained and disengaged spaces within which discrete continents, isolated like islands, floated; surprisingly, however, this sequestered perception did not inhibit maritime voyages in ancient India (Sircar 1990).

Rivers were mobile spaces. As the connective thread between past and present, they became allegories of memory and time. They connected places through crucial upstream-downstream links. Riverine sites were nodes in a waterborne network, housing places of pilgrimage and worship. Landing-stages (*ghats*) on rivers structurally expressed the different kinds of connectivity; as points of resource and tax collection, they also introduced an economic element into the landscape.

Estuaries, connective nodes on this river-sea network, were shallow, creek-ridden, and circuitous on the river's journey to the sea. Humid, swampy, and brackish, they were neither littoral nor coastal, with a distinctive character and a peculiar dual nature. Dense in human perception, dotted with minor shrines, they hindered navigation, producing a 'generative sea' space.

Conclusion

Water and waterways have been key factors in the development of societies, from prehistoric times to the present, particularly due to their role as vectors for cultural interactions, material exchange, and the transmission of knowledge. This chapter therefore studied the social and cultural geographies of waterscapes, and not just their economic geography as per the current practice, wherein ports, people, ships, shipping lanes, and commodities are highlighted. In doing so, this chapter also highlighted a regional geography, where a hierarchy of central places emerges, of seas, rivers, and estuaries. The fluidity of these highways of transport and communications is tightly linked to the presence of transit points: spaces with unique geographical characteristics that act as nodal points between different communities, such as estuaries. In some instances, the location might be obscured by the lack of remains, but the impact of those interactions is visible in other ways, such as through language exchanges. Transit points are thus defined as places of intense social contacts, putting objects of physical geography into the domain of the social sciences and humanities. Ideas about cultural landscapes are helpful in considering how things become 'resources,' with all the values and assumptions about their utility—and the primacy of human agency—that this term implies. The core meanings of water as a life-generating, life-connecting source; as the basis of wealth, health, and power; as a transformative medium; and as a metaphorical base for concepts of movement and flow recur so reliably in different cultural and historical contexts that there is little choice but to conclude that its material properties are relationally formative, affecting sociocultural perceptions (Strang 2014, 140, 142).

Select References

Andaya, Barbara Watson, and Leonard Y. Andaya. 2014. 'The "Sea of Malayu": An Ocean Perspective of Malay History.' In David Jones and

Michele Marion (eds), *Discovery and Praxis: Essays in Asian Studies*, 207–220. Albany: SUNY Press.

Banerjee, Sumanta. 2016. 'Riverine Waterscape and Cultural Landscape in Bengali Folklore and Literature'. In Rila Mukherjee (ed.), *Living With Water: Peoples, Lives, and Livelihoods in Asia and Beyond*, 81–89. New Delhi: Primus Books.

Bradley-Birt, F. B. 1906. *The Romance of an Eastern Capital*. London: Smith, Elder and Co.

Chakravarti, Ranabir. 2019. 'A Subcontinent in Enduring Ties with an Enclosed Ocean (c. 1000–1500 C.E.): South Asia's Maritime Profile "Before European Hegemony"'. *Journal of Medieval Worlds* 1 (2), 27–56.

Chapman, Graham P., and Kalyan Rudra. 2015. 'Time Streams: History and Rivers in Bengal'. Occasional Paper, Centre for Archaeological Studies & Training, Eastern India, 1–45.

Conrad, Joseph. 2007 [1899]. *Heart of Darkness*, first serialised in Blackwood's Edinburgh Magazine in three parts. Page numbers correspond to the reprint by The Coyote Canyon Press, Claremont, California, 2007.

D'Arcy, Paul. 2013. 'Sea Worlds: Pacific and South-East Asian History Centered on the Philippines'. In Rila Mukherjee (ed.), *Oceans Connect: Reflections on Waterworlds Across Time and Space*, 23–38. New Delhi: Primus Books.

Darian, Steven G. 1978. *The Ganges in Myth and History*. Honolulu: The University Press of Hawaii.

Deloche, Jean. 1991. 'Boats and Ships in Bengal Terracotta Arts'. *Bulletin de l'Ecole française d'Extrême-Orient* 78, 1–49.

Eck, Diana L. 1981. 'India's "Tīrthas": "Crossings" in Sacred Geography'. *History of Religions* 20 (4), 323–344.

Edgeworth, Matt. 2014. 'On the Agency of Rivers'. *Archaeological Dialogues* 21 (2), 157–159.

FAO/AQUASTAT Survey. 2011. *Ganges-Brahmaputra-Meghna River Basin*. Available at https://www.fao.org/3/CA2138EN/ca2138en.pdf (accessed August 2023).

Ghosh, Pika. 2002a. 'Sojourns of a Peripatetic Deity'. *RES: Anthropology and Aesthetics* 41, 104–126.

_____. 2002b. 'Tales, Tanks, and Temples: The Creation of a Sacred Center in Seventeenth-Century Bengal'. *Asian Folklore Studies* 61, 193–222.

Ghosh, Suchandra. 2016. 'Water, Water Bodies, and Waterscapes in Early Medieval South-Eastern Bengal and Assam: A View from Epigraphs'. In Rila Mukherjee (ed.), *Living With Water: Peoples, Lives, and Livelihoods in Asia and Beyond*, 66–78. New Delhi: Primus Books.

La Touche, T. H. D. (ed.). 1910. *The Journals of Major James Rennell, First Surveyor-General of India, Written for the information of the Governors of Bengal during his Surveys of the Ganges and Brahmaputra rivers 1764 to 1767*. Geological Survey of India, Calcutta: Baptist Mission Press/ The Asiatic Society.

Lewis, Martin. 1999. 'Dividing the Ocean Sea'. *Geographical Review* 89 (2), 188–214.

Lindsay, Hon. Robert. 1840. 'Anecdotes of an Indian Life'. In *Lives Of The Lindsays*, Vol. IV. Wigan: C. S. Simms.

Lunde, Paul. 2005. 'The Seas of Sindbad'. *Saudi Aramco World* 56 (4), July–August, 20–29. Available at https://archive.aramcoworld.com/issue/200504/the.seas.of.sindbad.htm (accessed July 2023).

Magos, Alicia P. 1994. 'The Concept of Mari-it in Panaynon Maritime Worldview'. In Iwao Ushijima and Cynthia Neri Zayas (eds), *Fishers of the Visayas*, Visayas Maritime Anthropological Studies I, 305–355. Quezon City: CSSP Publications.

Mukherjee, Rila. 2011. 'Introduction: Bengal and the Northern Bay of Bengal'. In Rila Mukherjee (ed.), *Pelagic Passageways: The Northern Bay of Bengal Before Colonialism*, 1–260. New Delhi: Primus Books.

Oestigaard, Terje. 2014. 'Holy Water: The Universal and the Particular'. *Archaeological Dialogues* 21 (2), 162–165.

Pearson, Michael. 2011. 'History of the Indian Ocean: A Review Essay'. *Wasafiri* 26 (2), 78–99.

Peters, Kimberley. 2010. 'Future Promises for Contemporary Social and Cultural Geographies of the Sea'. *Geography Compass* 4 (9), 1260–1272.

Raffles, Hugh. 2007. 'Fluvial Intimacies'. In Amita Baviskar (ed.), *Waterscapes: The Cultural Politics of a Natural Resource*, 314–339. Ranikhet: Permanent Black.

Rangarajan, L. N. 1992. *The Arthasastra*. New Delhi: Penguin Books India.

Rennell, James, and Joseph Banks. 1781. 'An Account of the Ganges and Burrampooter Rivers. By James Rennell, Esq. F. R. S.; Communicated by Joseph Banks, Esq. P. R. S.'. *Philosophical Transactions of the Royal Society of London* 71, 87–114.

Sircar, D. C. 1990. *Studies in the Geography of Ancient and Medieval India*. New Delhi: Motilal Banarsidass.

Steinberg, Philip E. 2001. *The Social Construction of the Ocean*. New York: Cambridge University Press.

Sen, Prabhas Chandra. 1929. *Mahasthan and its Environs*. Rajshahi, Bengal: Varendra Research Society, Monograph 2.

Sen, Swadhin, and Wahid Palash. 2016. '"Oh My River with Deep Water, I am Floating on Your Water, Ever Since my Birth": Non-western Perspectives on Reconfigurations of the Embodiments of Water and Landscape with Special Reference to Contemporary Archaeological Discourses'. In Rila Mukherjee (ed.), *Living With Water: Peoples, Lives, and Livelihoods in Asia and Beyond*, 96–114. New Delhi: Primus Books.

Sengupta, Rimli, and Soumya Chakravarty. 2016. 'The River: Yearnings and Warnings'. In Rila Mukherjee (ed.), *Living With Water: Peoples, Lives, and Livelihoods in Asia and Beyond*, 90–95. New Delhi: Primus Books.

Seshan, Radhika. 2016. 'Imagining and Managing Water in Peninsular India'. In Rila Mukherjee (ed.), *Living With Water: Peoples, Lives, and Livelihoods in Asia and Beyond*, 117–124. New Delhi: Primus Books.

Sinha, Amita. 1995. 'Nature in Hindu Art, Architecture and Landscape'. *Landscape Research* 20 (1), 3–10.

Strang, Veronica. 2014. 'Fluid Consistencies: Material Relationality in Human Engagements with Water'. *Archaeological Dialogues* 21 (2), 133–150.

Walcott, Derek. 1979. 'The Sea is History'. In Derek Walcott, *Star Apple Kingdom*. New York: Farrar, Straus and Giroux.

11

Indian Finances and British Rule in Eighteenth-century Bengal

Rajat Datta

Although British rule in Bengal was heralded by a victory of its forces in a small one-sided skirmish (euphemistically called a battle) in a mango grove located at Palashi, it was guided by a different kind of political economy. This was already visible in the run-up to that skirmish when a coterie of landed-mercantile interests came together in support of the English East India Company[1] in what is called a 'conspiracy' against Nawab Siraj-ud Daula. Whether or not it was a conspiracy is a moot point, but what is clear is that their actions were not motivated by personal animosity alone. In their assessment, the Company's potential to cause harm to their interests far outweighed their dissatisfaction with the Nawab. However, their assessments of the business opportunities opened by the Company also attracted these moneyed and commercial sections of Bengal. Theirs was therefore a straightforward pragmatic consideration, but one which had a longer history.

The Changing Context of Business and Finance in Early British Bengal

One significant feature of the eighteenth century was the changing nature of the relationship between bankers and the fiscal system. In the classic Mughal fiscal system, bankers and moneylenders had functioned within the interstices of the revenue flows as creditors, securities (*mal zamin*), and money changers (*sarrafs*). Their roles were important but indirect, and there is very little evidence to support an argument which has tried to link the financial crisis of the Mughal empire in the late seventeenth century with the withdrawal of support of the bankers and the shift towards regional formations (Leonard 1979, critiqued by Richards 1981). Regional economies have their own large banking houses; for instance, Bengal had the Jagat Seths, interspersed with a myriad of small bankers and *mahajans* dealing with capital and credit. But unlike the Mughals, the regional states had fewer resource-producing hinterlands for revenues, and thus had to depend much more than their imperial predecessor on local finances. Thus, there developed a closer relationship between regional kingdoms and regionally-based banking firms (Barnett 1980; Chatterjee 1996; Subramanian 2012). The great firm of the Jagat Seths was located in Murshidabad and Kasimbazar, and thus became an indispensable part of the Nizamat. The responsibility of the revenue flows within and outside Bengal on behalf of the regional state had by the 1720s become the virtual monopoly of this firm (Little 1967, vi–xiv).

In an earlier overview of the colonial transition, I had argued that the regime of the Company was characterised by a new political economy which had three components: (*i*) the utilisation of territorial revenue for commercial purposes, euphemistically called 'investments'; (*ii*) fiscal-militarism; and (*iii*) hunt for resources (Datta 2003). Underlying these was a commercial reach that straddled the Atlantic and Indian Oceans; however, these had their costs. In Bengal, this regime unfolded amidst expanding exports, rising agricultural prices, and increasing costs of maintaining a sustainable degree of armed presence to protect its interests. These three, while constituting a composite whole, also, paradoxically, tended to work against each other. Rising prices raised the price of procurement, which would negatively impact the scale of military deployment, whereas raising the investments in military deployment would tend to adversely impact commercial investments. Therefore, contrary to the commonsensical understanding about its surpluses, the Company, as Marshall says, was actually faced with a perennial shortage of funds in Bengal (Marshall 1976). These cross-cutting indispensables necessitated a constant search for resources, which guided its fiscal policies and also helped in contextualising its interface with 'native' finances in the late eighteenth century. This opens up for scrutiny the question of whether colonialism, which was undoubtedly foisted from the outside, could actually consolidate because it was supported from the inside. In other words, while colonial rule generated tensions and conflicts, it also enjoyed the fruits of collaboration and cooperation from within. The prime locations of this collaboration were in commerce and financial dealings with the Company.

There is another dimension to this interface when viewed from inside out. This was the perception amongst indigenous business groups that the new regime had opened up fresh opportunities for them. By the Company's own admission, its economic policies after 1765 had 'exceedingly enlarged the demands for the market of Bengal'.[2] In other words, the global reach of Bengal's products had increased considerably since the Company took over the reins of the province. This understanding was indeed justified. As Figure 11.1 shows, exports from Bengal on the Company account reached an unprecedented high after 1757. Customs receipts collected by the Board of Trade in the late 1790s showed that Bengal's exports from the port of Calcutta tripled between 1777 and 1797, and that most of it was still based on an exchange of textiles, foodstuffs, and other raw materials for precious metals and certain manufactured goods.[3] The prices of agricultural commodities were also rising in tandem with exports (see Table 11.1).

Rising exports pushed up costs, which needed more investments, and the evidence points to the fact that the capital which the Company could raise on its own was proving to be inadequate for its requirements, despite the devastating famine of 1769–1770. Commercial reports from the Company's Bengal manufactories (*aurangs*) in 1773 revealed that the combined investments of the English, the Dutch, and the French companies and those made by private European merchants 'exceed double the quantity [of piece goods] which can possibly be made in the year'.[4] Nevertheless, one fundamental problem faced by the British in Bengal was shortage

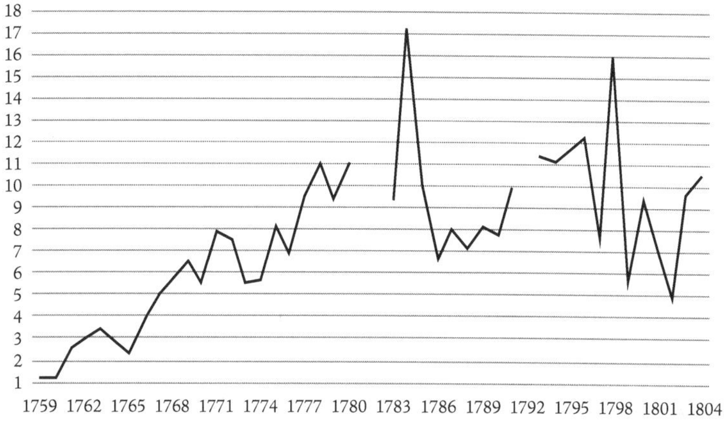

FIGURE 11.1: Exports of Bengal Goods by the English East India Company, 1759–1804 (in Rupee Million)

Source: OIOC, India Office Library, Ms. EUR D. 282. fol. 8.

TABLE 11.1: Quinquennial Averages of Agricultural Prices in Bengal, 1754–1798 (rupees per maund)

Year	Rice	Sugar	Mustard Oil	Ghee	Jaggery
1754–1758	0.77	7.48	3.5	11.25	2.25
1759–1763	1	7.49	4.5	12	2.51
1764–1768	1.03	7.49	5.5	12.55	2.5
1769–1773	1.6	16.25	5.55	12.56	2.75
1774–1778	1.2	9.8	6.5	13.25	2.5
1779–1783	1.15	7.5	6.8	15.7	2.53
1784–1788	1.29	9	6.8	13.95	2.57
1789–1793	1.35	9	6.5	14.75	2.58
1794–1798	1.06	8	7.25	15.5	2.59

Source: Prices derived from the relevant volumes of the Bengal General Ledgers and Journal and Ledgers, OIOC, P/174/80 to P/176/57, with those given by J. Herklotts (1829) and W. B. Bayley (1816).

of liquidity. The finances of the East India Company after 1765 were often stymied by erratic flows of revenues,[5] and the private enterprise of its officials and of private traders was often hit by elusive investments. From Rs 2.94 million in the years 1767–1768, the Company's investment fund in Bengal had dropped to Rs 0.6 million in the years 1784–1785, and was pegged at Rs 2 million in 1791–92.[6] The Company was thus faced with a serious deficit and was in desperate need of funds to carry on with its procurements. They therefore tapped the local money market to tide over, a mode of raising capital which, as we have noticed, continued a longstanding arrangement between local financiers and the Mughals, and also with the Nizamat after 1707.

The East India Company and Bengal's Money Market

The nexus between indigenous finance and the Company's enterprise in Bengal was not a new development that originated after 1757. It had a much longer past and operated around the advance contracts (*dadni*) given to Indian merchants for the procurement of the Company's goods, particularly silk.[7] Loaning money on interest to the Company for commercial requirements was another dimension of this nexus. The banking houses of Jagat Seth were recognised as the chief providers of cash and credit to the European trading companies operating out of Bengal. Between 1733 and 1750, this house loaned 4,232,278 sicca rupees at an interest of 9 per cent to the Company's factory at Kasimbazar.[8] However, the scale of such operations appears to have been lower compared to the amounts contracted as dadni. For instance, merchant Kissenpersaud Biswas took a dadni of Rs 7,52,000 for silk in 1733, but this appears to have been an unusually high amount as, in 1736–1737, he entered into a contract for a more modest sum of Rs 29,750.[9] Profits were good, but uncertainties were equally pervasive. The Maratha depredations between 1741 and 1746 ruined many substantial merchant families of Kasimbazar. Khusal Chand and Raghunath said that they had been 'entirely ruined' and forced to 'live on the charity and benevolence of friends' or 'obliged to serve as under Banian [sub-contractor] for his livelihood', whereas Kissenpersaud Biswas just about managed to stay afloat after suffering huge losses owing to the plunder of their 'money and goods'.[10] Subsequently, high prices of raw silk and the consequent uncertain quality of the finished goods placed the dadni merchant in an unenviable position, and by 1756 the dadni system was all but over. The old commercial world of the Asian merchant was already under severe stress on the eve of the British takeover. This would explain, at least partially, their eagerness to latch onto the emerging structures of the Indo-Anglo business interface, not only in eastern India but also in Bombay (Chakrabarti 2006).

Therefore, the close nexus between the State and the bankers, which had become the hallmark of regional polities in the early eighteenth century, continued and even deepened in this post-1757 Bengal. While affluent bankers supported the Company during the Plassey 'revolution', the Nawab had practically no support. Once the Company was in place, many changes occurred. The large banking house of Jagat Seth declined. The dramatic nature of that decline has often hidden the fact that banking became much more dispersed and open-ended in its wake. Upcountry bankers, particularly from Banaras, such as Gopal Das and Bhawani Das, quickly rushed in to fill the vacuum, setting up *kothis* (banking houses) in various places of eastern and western India and putting up £1 million to start their venture (Sinha 1970, 74). Marwari bankers who based themselves in Calcutta combined banking with commercial ventures, and their presence was already becoming strong in the internal markets of the province (Datta 1999, 209–210). Elsewhere, upcountry merchants continued to do robust business. Seven such bankers (*kothiwals*) did lucrative business in Murshidabad in the early nineteenth century (Buchanan-Hamilton 1833, 320–321), combining deposit and remittance banking through bills of exchange (*hundi*) with moneylending and agiotage (Mohsin 1973, 126).

In this connection, Table 11.2, which shows the arrival of fresh silver to the Calcutta mint between 1777 and 1793, is significant. In the 174 documented months between 1777 and 1793, an additional Rs 42.68 million rupees (£4.27 million) worth of silver siccas were freshly minted (as distinct from recoinage) for circulation. Most of this silver was brought into the mint by the shroffs from upper India, through Lucknow in Awadh[11] and Banaras, which was the principal centre of the remittance of bullion 'agreeable to the demand for the specie.'[12]

Table 11.2: New Silver for Coinage at the Calcutta Mint, 1777–1793 (rupees)

Year	Recorded Months	Amount Minted
1777	6 months	800,207
1778	12 months	4,612,017
1779	11 months	2,824,888
1780	12 months	1,539,252
1781	12 months	2,601,603
1782	11 months	5,544,978
1783	10 months	2,002,994
1784	8 months	2,202,562
1785	11 months	1,841,109
1786	10 months	1,044,382
1787	11 months	615,434
1788	11 months	2,317,864
1789	12 months	1,543,356
1790	12 months	1,828,654
1791	12 months	3,837,824
1792	11 months	6,247,828
1793	2 months	1,278,563
Total	**183 months**	**42,683,515**
Average		**2,510,795**

Source: OIOC, Bengal General Journal and Ledgers, P/176/5 to P/176/35 for the relevant years.

With no supporting financial institutions in the provinces, European finance in India depended critically on these upcountry and Bengal bankers for a long time, till the mid-nineteenth century at least (Sinha 1970, 75–76). These bankers cooperated with the Company, but on their own terms, and their 'intransigence' was the main reason why the Company's repeated attempts to reform the currency of Bengal remained unfulfilled till 1835 (Chakrabarti 1997). Bengal was not an isolated instance. Studies of banking in other parts of India have also shown the persistence of the relationship between indigenous capital and the early colonial State (Subramanian 2012).

Who were these sarrafs? They constituted a combination of *kothiwals* located in the cities of Calcutta, Murshidabad, and Banaras. Table 11.3 provides a list of 136 such people handling bullion for the Calcutta mint between 1777 and 1793.

The Making of Indo-Anglian Finance in Eighteenth-century Bengal

The other aspect of the interface was intermediation, which had two major components: buying goods from the Company for sale in Bengal, particularly the Calcutta markets, and loaning money to the Company.

'Broadcloth, flannel, serge, lead, tin, iron, copper and brass cog-wheels'[13] and 'looking glasses, lamps, pictures & ca' to the tune of about £250,000 per annum in the 1790s[14] were among the principal items purchased from the Company by Indian and private European traders. In 1768–1769, such purchases amounted to Rs 578,844.[15] In 1784, purchases amounted to Rs 700,493,[16] while in 1786, they were Rs 345,626.[17] Of the total value of Rs 1,624,463 sold by the Company in these three years, Rs 1,359,394 (84 per cent) were mopped up by local merchants.

Table 11.4 provides a consolidated list of Indian buyers of Company goods in the city of Calcutta in those three years.

TABLE 11.3: Bullion Suppliers to the Calcutta Mint, 1777–1793

Ahmad Zaman	Giridhar Das
Annunchund Seth	Giridhar Shaw
Ayodhyacharan	Gocul Ghose
Baghobat Mandal	Goculcharan Mukherjee
Baghobat Nandi	Golap Chand
Baidyanath Banerjee	Gopal Das
Baidyanath Nandi	Gorachand Basak
Baijanath De	Gorachand Mukherjee
Bancharam Ghosal	Gurjaram Seth
Biroo Dutt	Gurudas Dutt
Brajo Mohan Seal	Hari Mohan Basak
Brindaban Addy	Hari Prasad
Brojo Dutt	Hari Prasad Addy
Bustomcharan Poddar	Harikissen Das
Bustomcharan Seal	Jagat Chund Mukherjee
Chaitanya Charan Pal	Jagmohan Seal
Chaitanya Charan Sen	Joyram Sen
Chetan Addy	Kalicharan Ghose
Dalumchund	Kalimohan Nandi
Damodar Addy	Kaliprasad Chaudhury
Darpanarian Tagore	Kaliprasad Ganguly
Dayaram Bhavani Das	Kashinath
Debicharan Banerjee	Kashmirimal
Debicharan Mitra	Kasinath Baboo
Dharam Das Addy	Kasinath Basak
Dharam Das Addy	Khushal Chand
Dharam Deo Addy	Kissenchund Dutt
Dulal Bose	Kissendeb Ganguly
Dulal Das	Lakhikanta Baral
Dulal Mandal	Lalbani Bhattacharjee
Dulal Nandi	Lalmohan Nandi
Durgacharan Mitra	Laul Mohan Addy
Ganesh Das	Madan Dutt
Gayaram Poddar	Madan Mohun Tagore

(Contd)

Table 11.3 (Contd)

Manik Das	Raghunath De
Manikchand	Raghunath Dutt
Manohar Das	Raicharan Addy
Mathur Mohan	Ram Shaw
Mirza Muhammad Jafar	Ramhari Das
Moti Lal De	Ramkanai Ghosal
Motiram Charan Sen	Ramkissen Poddar
Nandkumar Pal	Ramnarain Adhikari
Nandkumar Poddar	Ramnarsing Gossain
Nandlal Addy	Ramprasad Sen
Nandram Baidnath	Ramsundar Parry (?)
Nanduram	Ramsundar Roy
Nankumar Pal	Ramsundar Sen
Narsing Baboo	Rashbehari Addy
Nayan Adhikari	Sambhunath Ghose
Netramohan Nandi	Samcharan Brahmdas
Nilambar Seal	Sanatan Seal
Niloo Seal	Santiram Ghose
Nimai Chund Addy	Sarup Nandi
Nimaicharan Mallik	Shambhunath Ganesh Das
Nitai Mandal	Shamcharan Das
Paran Pal	Shibcharan Bose
Parbaticharan Seal	Shyamcharan Dharma Das
Poorangir Gosain	Shyamprasad Sen
Prankrishna Sen	Sibprasad Das
Rabi Chand Seth	Sibram Das
Radhakant Pal	Sriram Pandit
Radhakanta Pal	Subbalom Ghose
Radhakanto Pal	Subonail Poddar
Radhakisen Nandi	Surjanath Kasinath
Radhanath De	Surroop Chand
Radhanath Pal	Tilak Chandar
Radhnath Pal	Uday Ram Addy
Raghunath Datta	Wurgoseen (?) Beerbull

Source: OIOC, IOR, BGJL, P/176/5 to P/176/33.

TABLE 11.4: Purchasers of Company Goods, 1768–1769, 1784, and 1786

Name of purchaser	Amount in Rupees
Amarti Lal	6,822
Assaram	4,386
Balaram Mukherjee	2,310
Bisnuram Chakrabarti	4,770
Boobun Possary	24,440
Brajamohan Dutt	2,322
Chuckoo (?) Dutt	2,470
Dayaram Mukherjee	2,330
Debicharan Chaterjee	2,270
Debicharan Mukherjee	7,030
Dukhiram Seal	2,390
Durgachharan Mitra	4,725
Fakirchand Pasari	12,520
Gayaram Ghose	5,070
Giridhar Mitra	38,375
Gocul Das	2,172
Gocul Mukherjee	2,300
Goculchund Cotmah	18,055
Gopal Das	11,638
Gopal Ghose	2,085
Gopal Sen	2,350
Gopimohan Baboo	5
Hara Lal	2,178
Jagannath Haldar	20,844
Jugul Addy	10,430
Kisnanandan Dutt	2,390
Kriparam Das	167,472
Kriparan Nandi	5,050

(Contd)

Table 11.4 (Contd)

Name of purchaser	Amount in Rupees
Krisnakant Sharma	146,238
Lalji	2,184
Madan Cotmah	4,950
Manik Dutt	9,280
Manikchand	2,172
Manohar Tagore	20,844
Mathur Das	8,616
Mohun Lal	2,172
Monohor Mukherjee	21,760
Nandlal Mohta	7,320
Narayan Pasari	2,290
Nimai Ghose	2,280
Nimai Haldar	38,710
Nundcumar Cotmah	5,360
Pachoo Tagore	2,400
Radhabinod Haldar	77,078
Raghu Mullik	2,620
Raghunath Dey	8,696
Ramakant Biswas	2,166
Ramasray Pasari	7,620
Rambudder Ghose	77,545
Rambullub Tagore	6,306
Ramkisno Mullik	14,250
Ramprasad Pasari	4,590
Ramratan Tagore	375,229
Ramtanu Dass	96,836
Roopchund	2,226
Rupram Tagore	2,350

(Contd)

Table 11.4 (Contd)

Name of purchaser	Amount in Rupees
Sakulliram Pal	4,035
Sankar Das	24
Sibaram Basak	27,776
Simul Das	2,184
Sital Singh	2,088

Source: OIOC, BGJL, P/175/83, 48–56; P/176/19, 62–63; P/176/21, 55.

Finally, Table 11.5 provides a list of people who loaned money to the Company at various points between 1753 and 1792.[18] The borrowings, which were somewhat in the nature of a sinking fund, were to tide over various exigencies, both commercial and military, when the Company was forced to raise money in the Indian market at 8–12 per cent interest.[19] War finance certainly played a major role, but the evidence suggests a more complex commercial motive: borrowings were higher in 1753–1754, compared to 1756–1757 during the run-up to the Battle of Plassey. The crucial aspect is that monies raised from private Indian capital occupied a fairly high proportion of the finances raised by tapping the market. Such loans amounted to 61 per cent of the Company's total borrowing in 1758–1759, 57 per cent in 1761–1762, 83 per cent in 1770–1771, and 31 per cent in 1776–1777.[20] By contrast, such loans had contributed 39 per cent of the total in 1756–1757.[21] However, the military logistics of the wars in Mysore and previous hostilities with the French required a massive mobilisation of private funds from the Presidencies, mainly from Bengal, which 'proved a bonus to the rich [and] induced the timid amongst the moneyed men to speculate in these loans'.[22] By 1802, as the pressures of war finance decreased and as interest rates dropped to 8 per cent, 'opulent natives of Bengal' began moving their capital back into trade and servicing the commercial requirements of the Company and other private traders.[23] That the big expansion of Agency Houses occurred precisely around this time is far from coincidental (Singh 1966).

Table 11.5: Money Borrowed from Private Indian Capital (sicca rupees, selected years)

1753–1754	Money Loaned	1756–1757	Money Loaned	1764–1765	Money Loaned
Aminul Khan	22,110	Aminul Khan	6,048	Anandram Addy	15,000
Anupchund	19,637	Anupchund	8,008	Anandroy Mitra	1,080
Anunderam Kapuriya	800	Anundram Kaporiya	800	Anupchund	2,596
Brijoo Ram De	2,045	Brijoo Ram De	2,045	Biswanath Bose	20,000
Chandan Narain	7,169	Chandan Narain	7,169	Brajo Dulal Seal	15,000
Cheton Das	1,425	Cheton Das	1,425	Brindaban Basak	2,000
Doorga Majumder	34,880	Dulal Cotmah	63,500	Chiticharan Adddy	6,250
Dulal Cotmah	63,500	Durga Majumdar	34,880	Cheton Das	10,518
Dwaraka Das	1,295	Dwaraka Das	1,295	Dayachand	72,449
Gangaram	21,245	Gangaram	1,188	Goculchand Cotmah	14,286
Garib Das	6,832	Garib Das	6,567	Goculkishore Seth	29,482
Gobindram Basak	4,905	Gobindram Basak	4,905	Gourcharan Mallik	160,253
Goculcharan Sen	22,555	Goculcharan Sen	20,459	Huzuri Mal	4,500
Golap Das	5,798	Golap Das	2,000	Joynarain Ghose	7,000
Gopal Haldar	12,008	Gopal Haldar	12,008	Kalicharan Mitra	15,000
Gopimohan Basak	60,819	Gopimohan Basak	43,306	Kaliprasad Ghose	17,990
Gourcharan Mallik	263,477	Gourcharan Mallik	265,477	Kasinath Tagore	42,000

(Contd)

Table 11.5 (Contd)

1753–1754	Money Loaned	1756–1757	Money Loaned	1764–1765	Money Loaned
Harimohan Basak	31,035	Harimohan Basak	31,035	Kirtichand Cotmah	40,301
Jagamohan	7	Jagamonah	8	Kisnacharan Haldar	6,400
Jagannath	65,282	Jagannath	65,282	Lakhichandar	41,985
Janakiram	3,179	Janakiram	3,179	Lalchund	4,000
Kisna	3,558	Kisna	696	Madam Mitra	6,214
Madan Mohan Cotmah	5,096	Madan Mohan Cotmah	5,096	Madan Cotmah	19,713
Narahari	3,706	Narhari	3,706	Mohammad Taqi	23,300
Ominchund	17,560	Ominchund	17,560	Nabakisore Set	2,250
Radhacharan	38,850	Otta (?)	2,557	Narahari	2,332
Radhakissen Basak	13,485	Radakissen Basak	12,340	Narain Basak	8,000
Raghumitra Samji	9,060	Radhacharan	38,850	Nemoo Mallik	3,500
Ramchand	14,191	Raghumitra Samji	9,060	Niloy Das	3,000
Ramcharan	22,016	Ramchand	14,191	Nimaichran Mallik	141,266
Ramjibon Cobrass (?)	12,540	Ramcharan	6,540	Parbaticharan Chakrabarti	4,000
Rasik Lal	3,245	Ramgobind Das	12,540	Radhacharan Mallik	143,787

(Contd)

Table 11.5 (Contd)

1753–1754	Money Loaned	1756–1757	Money Loaned	1764–1765	Money Loaned
Roopchand	5,180	Rasik Lal	5,798	Ramakanta Basak	7,000
Sitaram	86,279	Roopchund	5,180	Ramhari	5,000
Hinga (?)	5,031	***Total for 1756–1757***	***714,698***	Ramlochun Roy	20,000
Otta (?)	2,557			Ramlochun Tagore	27,010
Saib Ali	5,546			Rammohun Roy	30,000
Sam	89			Ramsunder Roy	10,000
Ramkissen	7,725			Ramtanu Dutt	8,000
Durgaram Bose	8,937			Ramtanu Sur	6,000
Ramgobind Das	12,540			Rasik Lal	7,000
Total for 1753–1754	***927,194***			Sibram Ghose	6,000
				Sibu Chakrabarti	9,000
				Tilakram Mallik	19,718
				Udayram Addy	26800
				Total for 1764–1765	***1,066,980***

(Contd)

Table 11.5 (Contd)

1767–1768	Money Loaned	1780–1781	Money Loaned	1791–1792	Money Loaned
Durgacharan Mitra	1,384	Ajodharam Basak	11,8487	Anundehundee (?) Singh	11600
Goculchand Cotmah	39,291	Balaram Haldar	84,330	Baranasi Ghose	700
Gourcharan Mallik	50,328	Bishambar Mallik	126,755	Bishambar Mallik	230600
Jagannath Addy	1,703	Brajamohan Dutt	20,853	Chaitanyacharan Basak	2400
Kalicharan Mitra	25,759	Brindaban Basak	48,361	Choyton Mallik	2600
Kirticharan Cotmah	24,265	Chandar Saw	20,431	Darpanarain Tagore	20,000
Kriparam Dutt	4,401	Darpanarain Tagore	103,960	Debicharan Chatterjee	2,300
Madan Cotmah	3,556	Durgacharan Mitra	81,213	Gayaprasad Mukherjee	1,500
Nimaicharan Mallik	50,328	Giridhar	20,433	Gobindchand Basak	5,400
Radhacharan Mallik	81,842	Goculchand Cotmah	65,928	Gokulchandra Banerjee	4,600
Raghuchunder Roy	13,500	Goculchand Dutt	25,716	Gopimohan Ghose	26,600
Raghunath Sirkar	1,597	Gourcharan Mallik	347,555	Gourcharan De	1,000
Rambhadra Chaudhury	4,660	Jagamohan Mallik	40,862	Guruprasad	1,200
Ramcharan Roy	5,000	Jugal Addy	138,065	Haralal Dutt	500
Ramkrishna Choudhury	4,872	Kasinath Tagore	140,956	Hridayram Banerjee	3,500
Ramlochan Roy	27,000	Kissenchand Sharma	10,173	Jagannath Kar	11,000
Sibnarain Cotmah	6,500	Kriparam Das	10,616	Jagannath Prasad	6,100

(Contd)

Table 11.5 (Contd)

1767–1768	Money Loaned	1780–1781	Money Loaned	1791–1792	Money Loaned
Sibram Basak	15,000	Lakhikant Basak	38,658	Kalicharan Mitra	5,000
Sukhmoy Roy	40,000	Mirza Mubarak	10,331	Kasinath Tagore	98,500
Sukhdeb Poddar	3,432	Nandkumar Biswas	12,980	Kebalram Bagchi	600
Swarupchand Addy	2,000	Nilochand Basak	123,689	Kishnoprosad Haldar	52,100
Total for 1767–1768	***406,418***	Nimacharan Mallik	347,555	Krisnakanta Sen	29,000
		Prabhuram Mallik	52,305	Lalbehari Shaw	500
		Radhacharan Mallik	334,400	Madan Dutt	1,300
		Ramlochun Mallik	102,222	Madan Gopal Bose	21,600
		Ramratan Tagore	118,564	Nandkishore Kundu	11,220
		Sibram Mallik	30,000	Nilmani Haldar	8,000
		Sudam Haldar	80,165	Nimaicharan Mallik	12,000
		Zainab Khanum	10,331	Nimaicharan Tagore	6,000
		Total for 1780–1781	***2,665,894***	Paddalochan	12900
				Panchanan Mukherjee	2,600
				Radhacharan Mallik	3,000
				Rambani Tagore	29,320
				Ramdulal Dey	5,600

(Contd)

Table 11.5 (Contd)

1767–1768	Money Loaned	1780–1781	Money Loaned	1791–1792	Money Loaned
				Ramhari Rakshit	5,300
				Ramhari Tagore	42,740
				Ramkissen Mallik	154,800
				RamnarainDutt	500
				Ramnarain Ghose	44,100
				Ramnarain Tagore	30,800
				Ramnath Tagore	37,500
				Ramratan Chakrabarti	8,000
				Ramsankar Majumder	4,900
				Ramsunder Mitra	44,600
				Roopcharan Roy	11,000
				Sookhomy Roy	108,000
				Srimati	3,972
				Taranicharan Bose	1,100
				Tilakchand Basak	29,000
				Total for 1791–1792	***1,157,152***

Source: Calculated from OIOC, BGJL, P/175/66 for 1753–1754, 54; P/175/60 for 1756–1757; P/175/77, for 1765–1766; P/175/83 for 1767–1768; P/176/11 for 1780–1781; and P/176/33 for 1791–1792.

Such borrowings were not insignificant. They were also important in the Company's fiscal structure. Table 11.5 shows that post 1761, depending on the exigency and availability, such private borrowings, at their lowest, comprised 10 per cent of the Company's fisc; they could go up to 50 per cent on occasion, but on an average hovered around 20 per cent. Therefore, the connections between indigenous finance and British rule in eighteenth-century Bengal are indisputable and appear more diversified compared to the situation before 1757. No wonder it was being claimed in 1802 that 'respectable native stockbrokers' in Calcutta could now negotiate 'the purchase and sale of stock [government loans of any description] to any amount required' in the course of one day's trading.[24]

For such people, the late eighteenth century was certainly a period of expanding commercial opportunities. Here, the Company effectively intervened to free the internal trade of the multiple tariff impositions levied by zamindari customs houses (*chowkis*), as was done under the Mughals and the Nawabi regime. The combined result of these policies was a proliferation of marketplaces all over Bengal. The increase in their numbers or their establishment in previously deficient areas enabled the peasantry to relate more easily to wider markets, and merchants could also move smoothly through them with their networks of credit (Datta 1999, 202–206). Landed proprietors, who set up markets in the interior areas, provided loans to cultivators, and generally underwrote the finances for agricultural reclamation, also joined the commercial bandwagon. Landed magnates also tried their hand at the direct cultivation of indigo when markets looked favourable, but most of them preferred to latch on to opportunities opened by the newly expanding horizons in indigo and opium by routing some of their monies and supplying the agency houses which, at least in the initial stages, raised a part of their capital locally.

As European, especially British, private capital expanded in the triangular trade between Britain, India, and China,[25] the dependence on earlier forms of 'native' financial intermediation lessened because of the huge profits that began to accrue from opium and indigo exports. By 1803, twenty-nine of them had already come into existence. By the 1820s, six of the bigger ones were financing the indigo enterprise to the tune of Rs 20,000,000 (Singh 1966, 24). Although primarily a European private enterprise, these agency houses were seen as opportunities by many of the moneyed locals. 'Large capitals possessed by natives' came into these agency houses, and *banias* (middlemen) were entrusted to take charge of the security and safety of goods in exchange for customary commissions. People like Raghunath Gossain of Serampore and Matilal Seal of Calcutta were the banias of the Agency House Cockerel & Co. Gossain deposited a security of Rs 100,000 at 7 per cent interest with the Company. Seal had a favourable balance of Rs 350,000 in the books of the Company when his account was closed in November 1847 (Sinha 1970, 106–107). Palmer and Company, perhaps the most important among these houses, was held in high esteem by Indians and enjoyed the highest investment of Indian capital among the houses which had, by the 1830s, invested about Rs 4,000,000 in its ventures (Webster 2007, 48). The amounts invested were likely larger, but were never made a part of the official accounts of this house because 'Indian merchants had their own strategies and mechanisms for conducting agency house business which were separate and hidden from the European decision making processes,' and thus not available for scrutiny in the house's official, legal records (ibid., 49). This probably also explains why so many of them were wiped out, as they could not recover their outstanding balances when these agency houses collapsed with the massive slump in the global market for Indian indigo in the 1830s.

Indo-Anglian Finance: Some Reflections

It is an article of faith among Indian historians that the establishment of British rule in the second half of the eighteenth century in Bengal was a massive disjuncture in every respect, forgetting the fact that there were many continuities as well, including the interface between Indian finance and British financial requirements. These provided a far more secure foundation for British rule in eighteenth-century Bengal than the sporadic acts of aggression on an effete Nizamat. Anxieties about the failures or the atrophy of Indian business and finances in the eighteenth century also appear somewhat excessive as older patterns of trading and money supplies had not been discarded or replaced. The high levels of commercial growth, which had been the hallmark of the earlier century, were carried on uninterruptedly in the eighteenth century, too. Despite the changed political circumstances, merchant families still accumulated vast fortunes and continued investing in money-dealing, government bonds, landed properties, and internal trade (Sinha 1970, 88–90). 'The formerly timid Hindoo,' says a commercial report of 1802,

> Now lends money (or respondentia) on distant voyages, engages in speculation to various parts of the world, and is an underwriter in the different insurance offices, erects indigo works in various parts of Bengal, and is just as well acquainted with the principles, and British laws respecting commerce, as the generality of European Merchants; and enjoys two very great advantages over the latter, the first, the trading in his own, instead of borrowed capital, and secondly of living and conducting his business at probably one-tenth of the expense of the European.[26]

The connections between Indian finances and British rule therefore appear to be much more than a simple tale of subjugation to metropolitan capital, of which there was not enough around to invest in eighteenth-century Bengal. Private trade was beset with a shortage of capital and high rates of interest, and had to depend in almost all respects on Indian financial providers. Borrowing was a matter of personal interaction in the absence of institutionalised arrangements of credit in eighteenth-century Bengal's Anglo-Indian finance, which was also made up of commissioned agents (banias) who often amassed huge fortunes while working for their patrons (Marshall 1976, 55; 1993). Banias remained vital throughout and despite all their efforts to control the money marker, the local money-changer (sarraf) remained 'intransigent', up to 1835 at least

(Chakrabarti 1997). Far from being a saga of helpless obliteration, Indian money and British enterprise in the eighteenth century displayed various modes of cooperation and collaboration in the midst of rapidly changing commercial environments. Nor was Bengal alone in this respect. The commercial world of eighteenth-century Bombay was similarly poised. Here, too, the interactions between the 'seths and sahibs' was one of pragmatic accommodation, which allowed Gujarati and Parsi entrepreneurship to flourish. Respondentia and insurance were under the control of the bania caste of merchants, and these were still two very powerful instruments of control (Subramanian 2012, 316).

Furthermore, there are some other points of significance which the information regarding this financial interface throws up for scrutiny, and these lie in what these data tell us about the social composition of the moneyed people in early British Bengal. Whether that money came from land or went back into land is a moot point. Money, like water, finds its own level. What these lists show is that while the commercial community of Bengal overwhelmingly belonged to a particular community, namely the Vaisya, it was composed of various sub-castes who belonged to the more subaltern *jatis*. While such a traditional varna framework of business, both upcountry and local, continued to operate well into the nineteenth century (Chakrabarti 2006; Cook 1863, 11–13), there was also a considerable expansion in social participation with the incorporation of high-caste literate jatis, Brahmins, and Vaidyas, along with the scribal, the Kayastha caste, within the commercial sector.[27] Brahmins moved through markets as buyers, as creditors, and as bullion-handlers in the company of their more traditional 'subaltern' bania fellow travellers, like the *sahas*, the *cotmahs*, and the *basaks*.

How did this come about? This process had an earlier genesis, linked directly, it would seem, to the expansion of European commerce in Bengal from the middle of the seventeenth century[28] when several lower and intermediate jatis benefitted from the economic opportunities this expansion proffered to them (Sanyal 1971). Lists of dadni merchants in pre-1757 Bengal available in the Company's Kasimbazar factory records clearly demonstrate the substantial presence of purely commercial castes like the *telis*, *baniks*, *sahas*, *poddars*, *cotmahs*, and *tantis*.[29] Interspersed with these were 'upcountry' merchants, mainly from Rajasthan, Gujarat, and Multan,[30] and a motley group of high-caste participants: Brahmins with patronyms like Sarma, Ghoshal, and Tagore, along with the Kayastha, who bore patronyms such as Dutt or Bose, among others. Therefore, one tends to see a broadening of the social composition of the mercantile community beyond the traditional prescription of the normative varna framework. As the detailed lists of those who lent money or traded or invested in the Company's enterprise show, the post-1757 era continued, widened, and deepened this social expansion.

One would therefore be quite justified in saying that a significant feature of the eighteenth century in Bengal was the considerable expansion in the commercial participation of traditionally land-based, literate, and service groups, thereby attenuating the caste-oriented restrictions on commercial activities and professions. One would consider this a very significant social development, and also be justified in saying that eighteenth-century British rule had been unable to stifle Indian businesses or subvert their fundamental modes. 'Traditional' forms of doing business, respondentia, moneylending, insurance, and local trade were not disrupted. The joint family remained the nucleus of the business house, as it had been in the past. Some went bust and insolvencies occurred, but new ones came up and portfolios which combined landed property and business ventures, like the one operated by Krishnakanta Nandi (better known as Cantoo Babu) of Kasimbazar, also prospered. Impressive amounts of mercantile wealth continued to be accumulated by prominent business families of Calcutta and other cities, many of whom belonged to the subordinate castes. Despite all the travails it was facing, Indian finance and business was not crushed or left bereft of dynamism, not only in Bengal but also elsewhere (Leonard 1981), although whether Indian businesses indeed had such dynamic possibilities prior to colonialism remains a moot point. The existence of potentialities in India's business environment, despite the impressive levels of economic expansion in the seventeenth century, has been forcefully rejected (Habib 1971), and to look for it to perform otherwise in the eighteenth century might be a case of great expectations. But the debate is far from over.

Endnotes

1. Hereafter referred to as the Company.
2. Report of Commercial Occurrences, 9 August 1789. Oriental and India Office Collections (OIOC), India Office Records (IOR), Home Miscellaneous (HM), Vol. 393, 279–280.
3. West Bengal State Archives (WBSA), Proceedings of the Board of Trade, Customs, Vol. 8, 3 January–29 December 1797, 31 July 1797.
4. WBSA, Proceedings of the Comptrolling Committee of Commerce, Vol. 3, 2 January–30 November 1773, 26 May 1773.
5. This runs contrary to the widely held belief that post-1765, the Company had succeeded in bringing about an unprecedented maximisation of revenue.
6. OIOC, India Office Library (IOL), Mss. Eur.D. 281, f. 34.
7. There is copious information on such merchants in OIOC, Factory Records, Kasimbazar (KFR) G/23/4/ to G/23/13, covering the period 1684–1789. For a recent use of these sources to reconstruct the changing fortunes of the silk merchants in Kasimbazar, see Mukherjee (2006).
8. OIOC, IOR, KFR, cited in Mukherjee (2006).
9. OIOC, IOR, KFR, G/23/5, 26 March 1733 and 9 March 1736.
10. Ibid., G/23/1, Consultation of February 1752.
11. OIOC, IOR, Bengal General Journal and Ledgers (BGJL), P/176/7, 523, P/1176/9, 102–103.
12. OIOC, IOR, Bengal Commercial Reports, External Commerce (BCTRC), P/174/14, 63.
13. OIOC, IOR, BGJL, P/176/19, 63.
14. OIOC, IOR, BCREC, P/174/14, 9.
15. OIOC, BGJL, P/175/83, 48–56.
16. Ibid., P/176/18, 62–63.
17. Ibid., P/176/21, 55.

18. These lists are of fresh loans raised in the current year and do not include loans and repayments carried over from previous years, nor do they show the considerable amounts raised from private European and British capital.

19. OIOC, BCREC, P/174/13, 4. There was a third aspect of intermediation. Many Indian merchants acted as agents (*bania*) for Company officials and other private traders. This feature is not being considered here. However, for a comprehensive discussion on *bania*s and the Company, see Basu (1973) and Marshall (1993).

20. OIOC, BGJL, P/175/63 for 1758–1759, P/175/69 for 1761–1762, P/175/87 for 1770–1771, and P/176/3 for 1776–1777.

21. Ibid., P/175?60.

22. OIOC, BCREC, P/174/14, 3.

23. Ibid., 6.

24. OIOC, BCREC, P/174/14, 7.

25. One of the best accounts of this shift still remains Furber (1948).

26. OIOC, BCREC, P/174/14, 7.

27. The significant expansion in numbers can also be seen from the fact that there were only fifteen listed merchants buying Company goods in Calcutta in 1757–1758 (OIOC, BGJL, P/175/61, 60).

28. For an overall view of this unfolding, see Prakash (1998).

29. I base myself on the lists of *dadni* merchants available in OIOC, KFR, G/23/5 for 1733 and 1736–1737, G/23/6 for 1740, and G/23/11 for 1752.

30. Ibid., G/23/6, 9 December 1741 and G/23/12, 20 September 1757.

Select References

Barnett, Richard. 1980. *North India between Empires: Awadh, the Mughals, and the British, 1720–1801*. Berkeley: University of California Press.

Bayley, W. B. 1816. *Asiatick Researches*, Vol. XII, 560–561. Calcutta: Calcutta Gazette Office.

Buchanan-Hamilton, Francis. 1833. *A Geographical, Statistical and Historical Description of the District or Zilla of Dinajpur in the Province or Soubah of Bengal*. Calcutta: Baptist Mission Press.

Chakrabarti, Shubhra. 1997. 'Collaboration and Resistance: Intransigent *Shroffs* and the English East India Company's Currency Reforms in Bengal, 1757–1800'. *Indian Economic and Social History Review* 54 (1).

———. 2006. 'Colonized Trade: Major Shifts in India's Trade and Commercial Organizations, 1700–1860'. In B. B. Chaudhari (ed.), *Economic History of India from Eighteenth to Twentieth Century*. New Delhi: Pearson.

Chatterjee, Kumkum. 1996. *Merchants, Politics and Society in Early Modern India: Bihar, 1733–1820*. Leiden: E. J. Brill.

Chaudhuri, B. B. (ed.). 2006. *Economic History of India from Eighteenth to Twentieth Century*. New Delhi: Pearson.

Cook, C. N. 1863. *Rise, Progress and Present Condition of Banking in India*. Calcutta: P. M. Cranenburgh.

Datta, Rajat. 1999. *Society, Economy and the Market: Commercialization in Rural Bengal, ca. 1760–1800*. New Delhi: Manohar.

———. 2003. 'Commercialization, Tribute and the Transition from Late Medieval to Early Colonial in India'. *The Medieval History Journal* 6 (2), 259–291.

Furber, H. 1948. *John Company at Work: A Study of European Expansion in India in the Late Eighteenth Century*. Cambridge, Mass.: Harvard University Press.

Habib, Irfan. 1971. 'Potentialities of Capitalistic Transformation in the Economy of Mughal India'. *Enquiry (n.s.)* 5 (3).

Herklotts, J. 1829. 'Table Showing the Market Price of Grain etc. in Lower Bengal from the Year 1700 to 1813', in *Gleanings in Science*, Vol. 1, 369. Calcutta: Baptist Mission Press.

Leonard, Karen. 1979. 'The "Great Firm" Theory of Mughal Decline'. *Comparative Studies in Society and History* 21 (2), 151–167.

———. 1981. 'Banking Firms in Nineteenth-Century Hyderabad Politics'. *Modern Asian Studies* 15 (2), 177–201.

Little, J. H. 1967. *House of Jagat Seth*. Calcutta: Calcutta Historical Society.

Marshall, P. J. 1976. *East Indian Fortunes: The British in Bengal in the Eighteenth Century*. Oxford: Clarendon Press.

———. 1993. 'Masters and Banias in Eighteenth Century Calcutta'. In P. J. Marshall (ed.), *Trade and Conquest: Studies on the Rise of British Dominance of India*. Aldershot: Variorum.

Mishra, K. P. 1973. 'Banaras Bankers in the Eighteenth Century'. In *Proceedings of the Indian History Congress*, 34th Session, Chandigarh.

Mohsin, K. M. 1973. *A Bengal District in Transition, Murshidabad, 1765–1793*. Dacca: Dacca University Press.

Mukherjee, Rila. 2006. *Merchants and Companies in Bengal: Kasimbazar and Jugdia in the Late Eighteenth Century*. New Delhi: Pragati Publications.

Prakash, Om. 1998. *European Commercial Enterprise in Pre-colonial India*. Cambridge: Cambridge University Press.

Richards, J. F. 1981. 'Mughal State Finance and Pre-Modern World Economy'. *Comparative Studies in Society and History* 23 (2), 285–308.

Sanyal, Hitesranjan. 1971. 'Continuities of Social Mobility in Traditional and Modern Society in India: Two Case Studies of Caste Mobility in Bengal'. *Journal of Asian Studies* 30 (2), 315–339.

Singh, S. B. 1966. *European Agency House in Bengal, 1783–1833*. Calcutta: Firma KLM.

Sinha, N. K. 1970. *The Economic History of Bengal, 1793–1848*, Vol. III. Calcutta: Firma KLM.

Subramanian, Lakshmi. 2012. 'Seths and Sahibs: Negotiated Relationships between Indigenous Capital and the East India Company'. In H. V. Bowen, Elizabeth Mancke, and John G. Reid (eds), *Britain's Oceanic Empire: Atlantic and Indian Ocean Worlds, c. 1550–1850*. Cambridge: Cambridge University Press.

Webster, Anthony. 2007. *The Richest East India Merchant: The Life and Business of John Palmer of Calcutta, 1767–1836*. Suffolk: The Boydell Press.

12

Nitya Gopal Mukherji
An Agricultural Enthusiast in Colonial Bengal

Bipasha Raha

Social Thinking in Nineteenth-century Bengal

Exposure to Western thoughts and ideas informed the worldview of a section of Bengali society, comprising primarily the Hindu upper castes, in the nineteenth century. It was in Bengal that the first Western-educated intelligentsia emerged. Opportunities for trade and prospects of service under the colonial rulers afforded avenues for the creation of a Hindu literati. The meteoric rise of and position acquired in contemporary society by Raja Rammohun Roy and Dwarkanath Tagore initiated a new trend.

Rammohun Roy, who was instrumental in ingraining colonial modernity in the Bengali psyche and was unquestionably the forerunner of the newly emergent literati, introduced the agrarian question into public discourse when he discussed how colonial rule had impacted Bengal's rural society and economy in his response to the questionnaire sent to him by the Select Committee appointed by the British House of Commons in 1831. This was in connection with the renewal of the English East India Company's Charter, due in 1833 (Raha 2012, 44). Henceforth, agrarian thought became a major concern of the Bengali intelligentsia. This trend was continued by his successors in the course of the nineteenth century, and even later. The increasing poverty of the rural masses, intermittent peasant rebellions, and the occasional attempts of the government to intervene in agrarian relations through legislations served to sustain an interest in the rural countryside. Besides, from the 1860s, many of the literati were associated with government service, which entailed rural postings and hence acquainted them with an experience of life in the village. Some members of the intelligentsia also had rural roots. As the anti-colonial movement acquired momentum and a critique of colonial rule was sought to be prepared, the Bengali intelligentsia strove to establish their claim of being the natural leaders of society (Raha 2018, 275–306). Rural society could not be ignored and the agrarian question acquired varied dimensions. Famines, too, necessitated a quest for remedies. The attempts of Joykrishna Mukherjee, the erstwhile zamindar of Uttarpara, to initiate agrarian innovations also left a deep imprint on contemporary agrarian thinking. The literati also expressed their ideas through various means, ranging from literary genres, to speeches and debates in the legislature, to journalistic expositions.

From the Rent Act of 1859 to the Bengal Tenancy Act of 1885, there was a prolonged discourse on tenurial rights for ryots. This kept the agrarian issue alive in the public psyche. It is in this context that the work of Nitya Gopal Mukherji needs to be explained. This chapter will assess his work through a reading of two books authored by him, *Handbook of Indian Agriculture* (1901) and *Handbook of Sericulture* (1912).

Educated Youth and Agriculture

By the 1870s, the literati had been concerned for a while about agrarian relations and the rights and conditions of different sections of ryots. But the arduous task of agriculture was something they felt was better left to peasants and rustic village dwellers. It was the response to the initiatives undertaken by the colonial masters, along with an economic critique of colonial rule and theorisations on India's impoverishment that highlighted the backward nature of Indian agriculture and led to a gradual shift in focus to the inputs and outputs of agriculture. It may be argued that the introduction of agricultural education in different provinces of India was one of the outcomes of the deliberations of the Famine Commission, which had been sent out to India upon the instance of the British Parliament in 1878. The Commission submitted its report in 1880. Subsequently, systems of land and police administration underwent certain modifications, which extended some security of possession to cultivators and obtained correct statistics and information regarding agricultural conditions and depressions (Mukherji 1901, 1). Through agricultural experiments and education, the produce of land was sought to be improved upon and increased, and agricultural knowledge disseminated amongst the cultivating classes (ibid.). This led to the subsequent establishment of the Pusa Research Institute, and attempts were made to set up a College of Agriculture in each province, as well as a practical system of agricultural education in villages. Over the years, the establishment of semi-official agricultural associations in the districts was a further attempt to familiarise the cultivators with the results of the agricultural experiments carried out in experimental farms.

These events prompted an interest among the educated youth to pursue higher studies in agriculture, which began to be seen as a viable career option. Opportunities for financial support for training in agricultural sciences in England was also often followed by absorption in government service. Even in the 1880s, as the anti-colonial struggle acquired new dimensions and social reform came to occupy a backseat, the literati's interest in agricultural issues continued to be sustained. The introduction of the Bengal Tenancy Act put to rest, for the time being, any contestation over the differential rights of various classes of the Bengal peasantry. However, as a productive activity, agriculture continued to hold the interest of the Bengali literati.

Many from Bengal, like Ambika Charan Sen and Syed Sakhawat Hossein, were sent to the Royal Agricultural College Cirencester, the first agricultural college in the English-speaking world. Sen and Hossein were among the first to be sent to the College by the Bengal government. Subsequently, Byomkesh Chakravarty, Girishchandra Bose, Atul Krishna Roy, and Bhupalchandra Bose were also sent to Cirencester during 1882–1883.[1]

Later, the eminent poet and lyricist Dwijendralal Roy went to Cirencester in 1884 on a government scholarship. He cleared the examination and was enrolled as a member of the Royal Agricultural College and the Royal Agricultural Society. On his return from England in 1886, he was appointed as a Deputy Magistrate and took up various government assignments.[2]

Roy's close contemporary was Nitya Gopal Mukherji, who went to England in 1884 for higher education in agricultural knowledge,[3] securing an annual stipend of £200 as well as a travel allowance.[4] On his return, he was appointed in 1886 by Wood Mason on a monthly salary of Rs 150, which was subsequently enhanced by Rs 50 in April 1887, to investigate diseases in silkworms.[5] In 1887, he was sent to Europe to study the French system of determining diseases in silkworms and cattle, and their treatment, on a monthly salary of Rs 250.[6] After he returned, he was appointed Deputy Magistrate on a salary of Rs 200. Later, he was inducted into the Silk Committee on a monthly salary of Rs 300.[7]

Meanwhile, two significant developments took place in the closing decade of the nineteenth century that strengthened the focus of the Bengali intelligentsia on agriculture. The first was the visit of John Augustus Voelcker, an English agricultural chemist and consulting chemist to the Royal Agricultural Society. In 1889, he was requested by the Secretary of State for India to examine improvements in Indian agriculture (Raha 2012, 157). He travelled across the country for a long period of time and produced a manuscript covering more than 400 pages, which was published in 1893. It contained his notes on Indian agriculture and techniques of production, and his recommendations for their improvement. In the subsequent period, the Indian government accepted and implemented many of them. Second, leading luminaries of the urban Bengali literati reiterated the importance of rejuvenating agriculture for rural reconstruction and economic recovery; for example, Rabindranath Tagore's work at Shilaidaha and the publication of Romesh Chandra Dutt's two volumes on the economic history of India.

Nitya Gopal Mukherji and Agricultural Knowledge

A gold medallist of the Royal Agricultural College, Cirencester, Fellow of the Royal Highland and Agricultural Society, Scotland, and Professor of Agriculture and Agricultural Chemistry, Civil Engineering College, Shibpur, Nitya Gopal Mukherji exhibited his knowledge and expertise on all aspects of agriculture. This knowledge was all-comprehensive, as evident in his two masterly works, *Handbook of Indian Agriculture* and *Handbook of Sericulture*. The latter was the fruit of years of experiments on silkworms, their rearing and diseases. The former established his claim as the leading agricultural scientist of his time in the country. *Handbook of Indian Agriculture* discusses agricultural inputs and agrarian techniques and practices, and also explores pertinent issues relevant to contemporary Indian agriculture.

In the Preface to the first edition, published in 1901, the author justifies its publication in the form of a handbook by stating: '... Handbook was found necessary owing to the want of a text-book on the whole subject of Indian Agriculture suitable for the use of advanced students' (Mukherji 1901). However, he warned that mere reading from a textbook would never suffice to equip one with knowledge in agriculture:

> It is not possible to learn agriculture from a text-book, apart from a farm, and to learn the subject in a systematic manner, a museum and a laboratory are also necessary. Even one passing out of an agricultural college which is equipped with a farm, laboratory, and museum, and possessing a thorough knowledge of a text-book, must be prepared to buy his experience, either by apprenticeship in another person's farm, or by losing money on his own, for a year or two, before he can expect to acquire confidence in himself, his crops and his methods. (ibid., Preface)

Mukherji stressed that practical experience was indispensable: 'Book-knowledge and college-education must be supplemented by detailed experience in that particular department of agriculture which one chooses to take up, in any particular locality, before one can expect to be a successful farmer' (ibid.).

However, the author was emphatic in his assertion that the book was a valuable aid to both the student and the person engaged in planting or farming. He stated that he had used facts 'scattered in hundreds of Reports, Notes, Monographs, Ledgers and Journals [that] have been brought together here in one volume and treated in a systematic manner' (ibid.). He informs his readers that he had endeavoured to fill the lack of a textbook by publishing a book on agriculture in Bengali and Oriya that would be suitable for use among the cultivating classes (ibid., 1).

Seventy per cent of the Indian population, he writes, lived directly by farming. The author made it clear at the beginning that the agricultural condition of India was not especially depressed, compared to some other countries of Europe. Mukherji begins his handbook by underscoring the importance of agricultural education and lauds the government for its successful enterprise in Madras. He did not subscribe to the view that native agricultural practices were the best for India, or that they were incapable of improvement; rather, he saw great scope for improvement for Indian cultivators with regard to agricultural practices. His successive tours across the length and breadth of the country brought home the realisation that the native agricultural practices of the Madras, Bombay, and Central Provinces were far in advance of those of Bengal and the United Provinces of India. Agricultural education had also benefitted peasants in Madras Presidency. Indian agriculture, he wrote, could only benefit through contact with the West. It was the European planters who had acted as the agents of transmission of Western agricultural knowledge:

> In the most out-of-the-way places of India we find European planters imperceptibly and noiselessly carrying on agricultural experiments and improvements. We find them growing the most delicate English vegetables even during the hot weather by cultivating them in trenches. Some of our commonest articles of food and fodder have been introduced by Europeans. Maize, oats, potatoes, cabbages… the superior

> varieties of plantains... guinea-grass are all exotics. Indeed, there are few English cereals... vegetables and fruits that have not been introduced with success into India, and European farm implements are in common use in some plantations. (Mukherji 1901, 2)

Even the steam-plough, which was still considered an expensive luxury in Europe, had been introduced, Mukherji asserts, in some of the plantations.

Among the issues pertinent to fruitful agriculture that he addressed included: how soils could be made to yield more than they did; how irrigation could be made possible for the poor ryot; how to extend the cultivation of drought-resistant crops; the preservation of food and fodder; and organising measures of protection against famine. The focus was on food, or what could become food for the masses (Mukherji 1901, 2). Agricultural implements that could be used by the ryots, individually or collectively, were also explained (ibid., 120–141). The book discusses manures and fertilisers within easy reach of the ryots, and means of getting rid of pests and parasites that were so destructive for ordinary crops (ibid., 3). Mukherji paid particular attention to soil: the classification of soils in Bengal, their properties, barrenness, and fertility, so crucial for productive agriculture, are discussed at length (ibid., 11–68). Farmers are advised on how to ascertain soil types and readers are informed of ways to increase the fertility of soil and make it conducive for necessary crops. Theories underlying cultivation (ibid., 70–78) and irrigation are analysed (ibid., 114–119).

Mukherji devoted more than 200 pages to the discussion on crops. This includes botanical (ibid., 143–146) and economic classifications (ibid., 147–148) as well as the chemical composition of the principal crops (ibid., 149–150). The most effective methods of cultivating these crops are suggested. Agricultural statistics, systems of farming, and rotation of crops are other issues that the author focussed upon. The most interesting insertion is the provision of an agricultural calendar for Lower Bengal:

> January—Sugar-cane harvesting and *gur*-making. Sowing of *kuli begun* and *deshi* onion seeds. Planting of *ol* for the August

> to September crop. Final irrigation of potatoes, cabbages and other English vegetables.... Arrowroot and cassava harvesting.
>
> February—Harvesting linseed, mustard, *mung* and *til*.... Sale of English vegetables. Picking of cotton.
>
> ...
>
> December—*Aman* harvest... Sale of *palval* may commence, while sale of brinjal continues.
>
> Note—The operations for *kharif* crops generally take place a month earlier in Eastern Bengal districts, and a month later in Bihar and Chhota Nagpur. In the hill districts the time for different operations varies with the elevation, and in high elevation only *rabi* crops can be grown in the *kharif* season, the sowing time being February and March and the harvesting time, August to October. In the lower hills and valleys, the Eastern Bengal system is applicable. In the Bihar, Chhota Nagpur, and Sonthal Pergana districts, the *rabi* operations take place a month earlier and in the Eastern Bengal districts a month later. (ibid., 393–394)

Such an agricultural manual is unprecedented. Mukherji's knowledge of local conditions was formidable. His exposure to agricultural practices in the West had convinced him of the need for scientific agriculture. This was also a logical corollary to the quest for scientific knowledge in the colonial period. It was being increasingly perceived by the intelligentsia that a relationship existed between the modernisation of agriculture, that is, the application of modern scientific knowledge about agriculture, and the socioeconomic context of agricultural production.

As soil is the most important input of agriculture, Mukherji discusses manures, their uses and applications, and methods of analysis. Animal herding and livestock and dairy farming and their products are included in the narrative. He suggests methods of goat and poultry-keeping, the cultivation of fodder crops, and also sheep farming (Mukherji 1901, 474–529). Insects and pests, the bane of peasant life, are not ignored; the author suggests general remedies against pests and parasites (ibid., 530–532). Insects injurious to Indian crops, their nature, and methods of control are elaborated, as are zymotic diseases and their remedies (ibid., 566–572). Agricultural, dairy, and soil bacteriology is attended to (ibid., 573): Mukherji details how the decay of food substances may be prevented in various ways—this, according to him, was one of the most important applications of bacteriology in the field of agriculture and its allied arts, viz., the use of vinegar and spirits of wine for pickling and preserving medicinal substances (ibid., 573). In the section on soil bacteriology, Mukherji underlines the application of the Western knowledge of microbes and bacteria for increasing soil fertility (ibid., 582–583). He claims that one of the most important results of the study of bacteriology applied to agriculture had been the methods devised to protect farm animals by vaccination against several virulent diseases, and then proceeds to enumerate their preparation (ibid., 586).

A sound knowledge of these technicalities, the author hoped, would facilitate effective agricultural production. With an eye to enabling the ryots to supplement their income, he suggested the cultivation of products such as mushrooms, which were in demand in cities like Calcutta, where there was a considerable European population.

Mukherji was an expert on sericulture with years of experience. His *Handbook of Sericulture* bears testimony to his expertise. Here, he provides an in-depth discussion on varieties of mulberry; the rearing of silkworms; diseases that afflict silkworms; and processes and techniques of silk manufacture. He dwells at length on the silk trade and how Indians can benefit from the production and trade of silk (Mukherji 1912, 599). The author hoped that his handbook would be 'a guide, philosopher and friend to the actual tiller of the soil and be the means of ameliorating his condition' (ibid.).

On Peasantry and Famines

Two of the most crucial issues of the time were the condition of the Bengal peasantry and the recurrent famines. The former had held centre-stage in the public discourse on agrarian issues since the 1840s, when Akshay Kumar Dutt in *Tattvabodhini Patrika* and the Young Bengal in *Bengal Spectator* stepped in to carry forward the legacy of Rammohun Roy (Raha 2012, 43–62). This was a recurrent theme in the creations of litterateurs, from Ishwarchandra Gupta to Bankimchandra Chattopadhyay, Meer Masarraf Hussain, and others till the closing decade of the nineteenth century, and in journalistic expositions, from Harishchandra Mukherjee in *Hindoo Patriot* to Harinath Majumdar in *Gramvarta Prakashika* (ibid.). Recurrent famines continued to disrupt the social fabric of the rural countryside. The government was forced to adopt measures to combat the devastation, which left a trail of suffering and adversely impacted agrarian productivity. Indian leaders consistently raised this issue in their dialogue with colonial rulers.

While alluding to this, Mukherji held that the recent famines did not match the severity of those that had occurred during the reigns of Shah Jahan, Aurangzeb, or even Akbar:

> The most recent of serious famines, viz., that prevailing in some part of India or other from 1896 to 1901, was severer than the famine of 1874–78, but neither of these two famines which are within our living memory can be compared in destructiveness of human life to the famines which prevailed more than one hundred years ago. (Mukherji 1901, 602)

Yet, Mukherji cautioned, there was much to be worried about and no scope for complacency. It was a fact, he argued, that more land had been put to the plough than before; on the whole, there had been steady progress in the export of foodstuff from India; there was no need yet for India to look to foreign countries for means of livelihood; and the agricultural population 'appear to be generally better off now than they ever were before'. Therefore, 'there is nothing to fear from the steady increase of population and the necessary limit there is to extension of cultivation' (ibid.). Already, he observed, the extension of cultivation in populous localities had reached such a pass that there was no longer any sufficient pastureland left for the cattle. Barring the occasional famine, there was actually not much to worry about regarding food supply in India (ibid., 601).

However, Mukherji advocated, unless agricultural improvements kept pace with the increasing population in the next two decades or plague decimated the population at an even greater rate than earlier, the scenario would change drastically, and India would have to look to foreign sources for food supply or resort to 'emigration on a more wholesale scale' (ibid.). The area under foodgrains and their production, though sufficient at present, would not suffice if the population expanded further. For the time being, the difficulty could be met by the conversion of non-food areas into food-growing areas; but, he cautioned, there was a limit to this source of expansion also (Mukherji 1901, 602).

In view of the increasing population and as a safeguard against famines, Mukherji advocated the adoption of improved methods of cultivation, whereby production would increase. He also called for attention to be directed towards commerce and manufactures, which would reduce pressure on land; suggested that India should start importing foodstuff from those parts of the Empire where meat and corn were produced cheaply when a famine seemed imminent; and also that India 'must learn to send out her superfluous population voluntarily and willingly to those parts of the Empire' (Mukherji 1901, 602). He suggested that India should learn to keep herself free of want in the matter of food supply. The stress of the population, he said, was not usually felt in normal years because the allotment of 3 acres per individual of the populace on an average was quite sufficient. However, where cultivators readily converted their surplus food into cash in a good year and where this surplus food was sent out to foreign countries, a bad year caused great distress. There was no relief in India, unlike in other, more civilised countries, by the 'indigenous commercial enterprise bringing food-stuffs in from foreign sources' (ibid.). In a bad year, the grain-dealer, like the cultivator, depended on the government for means of subsistence. Mukherji was emphatic that although the need for emigration had still not made itself felt except in special localities, over the next two decades, it would become necessary:

> But in another twenty years, the question of emigration into other parts of the Empire may have to be more seriously taken up, and then India must make common cause with England and try to be recognized as an integral part of the Empire, looking upon the sparsely populated portions of the Empire as the natural field for her expansion. (ibid., 603)

Mukherji attributed famines to the failure of the monsoons. The canal-irrigated tracts and regions of heavy rainfall, viz., Assam and parts of eastern Bengal, the Cis-Himalayan regions of northern Bengal, Eastern and Western Ghats, and Southern Burma, that is, all those tracts where the normal rainfall was 70 inches per annum or more, were protected from famines during the failure of the monsoons. The rest of India was to be looked upon as 'precarious tracts' (Mukherji 1901, 603). The question of famines in India, he said, was mainly a question of irrigation, and to manage irrigation properly, one needed a solid knowledge of engineering and agricultural science. Canals were the best protection, in his opinion, against famine.

Mukherji refused to link famines to land revenue. He said that the present land revenue systems of India were a 'direct heritage' from former governments; the British had introduced very few modifications (Mukherji 1901, 604). However, he observed that the Permanent Settlement was saddled with three serious mistakes: no survey of estates or holdings was done and the revenue was fixed forever, irrespective of the extent or the possibilities of the estate; the rights of the cultivators were not safeguarded and almost no limit was placed on rent demands; and in fixing the land revenue forever, the government was hampered in the matter of taxation—zamindars, for instance, were exempt from the payment of income tax at the expense of their fellow-subjects (ibid., 605). So the burden of revenue was much less in permanently settled areas than it was on estates that were not permanently settled (ibid., 606).

He asserted categorically that when famine or distress of any kind occurred in the country, the blame had to be laid squarely on the government; to blame poverty on an over-assessment of land revenue was absurd. The high rent actually paid by cultivators in non-government estates was due to the existing provisions that allowed for the creation of intermediate proprietorship and tenures between the government and the cultivator. This system could be altered only with the dismantling of the Permanent Settlement. Mukherji did not accept that Bengal suffered more from famines than other parts of India, or even that the ryots in the permanently settled estates were worse-off than those in the Central Provinces. He claimed significantly that the more settled rainfall on the Gangetic plain secured Bengal against famines. However, the cultivator was burdened with larger demands in the form of rent by their immediate landlords (Mukherji 1901, 606–607).

Mukherji suggested measures to protect against famines and provide relief during their occurrence. The government should introduce certain legislative measures to help the cultivators. This would include the prohibition of exports of new rice and oilseeds and fixing forever the minimum proportion between land revenue and rent paid by the actual occupier, who was also a cultivator. All cultivating ryots, he advocated, should be compelled by law to maintain one food or fodder-yielding tree per acre of land held. A list of such trees should be published from time to time, and nurseries maintained in connection with District Engineers' offices and inspection bungalows, whence planting on road, river, and canal sides may also proceed systematically. Each Village Union, he suggested, should be compelled to maintain a conservancy establishment and allotted fields for the burial of dead animals, night soil, and refuse matter, where trees yielding food and fodder may be systematically grown and the fuel and fodder sold from this miniature forest after ten years. Here, he was reiterating Dr Voelcker's recommendation regarding the propagation of fuel and fodder reserves (Mukherji 1901, 606–607).

As for the departmental measures, the Agricultural Department, he suggested, could teach ryots how to store grains by having stores of superior varieties of seeds at certain recognised centres for sale. This department was to be entrusted with the task of procuring high-quality seeds. The ryots should be discouraged from procuring low-quality seeds from the *mahajans*. The latter's stranglehold over the rural economy should be weakened. Mukherji also suggested that the Agricultural Department organise a system through village unions and *pulwaries*, which would rent out irrigation and other machinery and high-quality farm animals. Mukherji believed that the fruits of agricultural science could filter down to the actual cultivators only by means of an organised agency. This was particularly so in a country where the ryots were either illiterate or very poorly educated, and were not accustomed to innovations. Other protective measures against famines included the extension of canals and railways at the behest of the government. Better communication with the interior would guard against famines (ibid., 608–609).

The Famine Code, observed Mukherji, had outlined in detail the relief programme to be adopted in case of famines. He had only one further suggestion to offer: by the end of September or mid-October, it becomes apparent if a famine is imminent. If the general yield of *Bhadoi* and *Aman* crops estimated for the whole province by the Agricultural Department fell short of 50 per cent, a famine could be anticipated (Mukherji 1901, 608–609). Relief work should be started in each *thana* where the estimated crop was 25 per cent or less. All works, Mukherji advised, should be arranged from October to January, but the actual opening of test-works should be delayed as long as possible and the programme of works should include only those calculated to increase the produce of land, directly or indirectly. He strongly criticised the practice of setting the famine-stricken populace to labour on public works such as building roads, for which they were most ill-equipped. They should rather be employed more usefully in irrigating lands on canal and riversides, and excavating canals, irrigation channels, tanks, and even wells (ibid., 608–609). Mukherji also suggested that the ryots be imparted the object lesson of growing a crop by irrigation during the driest season of the year, from February to May. This, he said, would have a permanent effect on the ryots, teaching them how to avoid famines for all times to come. February to May was a slack period; if, at this time, the ryots could produce a food crop by artificial methods of irrigation, its benefit would be immense (ibid., 610).

Mukherji also mentioned agricultural banks. He believed that these should fall under government supervision, and the government could guarantee an interest of 3 per cent per annum and transfer to the banks the duty of granting *takavi* loans on interest. The banks should invest the money in securities approved by the government. However, he also suggested that speculations of an agricultural character approved by the government be allowed. A scheme worked out along such lines would impart lessons on economy to the ryots as well, and could also lay the foundation for many pertinent agricultural improvements that would benefit the vast multitude of the peasantry. If the government, he concluded, guaranteed an interest of 3 per cent and controlled the banks, there would be no dearth of shareholders and capital (Mukherji 1901, 610).

Mukherji was a part of the administrative cadre. Much of what he suggested was included in the policy undertaken by the government. However, not all his recommendations were accepted. Cooperative credit societies were gradually coming up and his more famous contemporary, Rabindranath Tagore, would soon be iterating the need for 'krishibanks' in his programme for rural reconstruction. In the absence of such banks, rural moneylenders were the sole source of credit in most areas.

Like his more illustrious senior contemporary Romesh Chandra Dutt, Mukherji too dwelt at length on the issues of famine and irrigation. Both were convinced that these functioned as crucial determinants of the existence of the ryots, since these had a direct bearing on their impoverishment. However, the underlying premise of Mukherji's submission was that the agricultural condition in India could not be considered as being in an especially depressed state, as it was, for instance, in some European countries. Except for the periodic recurrence of famines, local or general, which had always occurred and continued to occur in India, particularly in recent years, the agricultural population of India could be regarded as being in a prosperous condition. This was borne out by the fact that the area under cultivation had been steadily increasing, as had the export of foodgrains, which represented surplus stocks. In spite of the increasing population, the rental and revenue from land had registered an increase (Mukherji 1901, 3).

Agricultural Education

Agricultural education was a recurrent theme in Mukherji's long narrative. While admitting that it worked slowly, he believed that education was ultimately the surest and principal means to overcome famines. While the foundations had already been laid in Bengal, he bemoaned the fact that the arrangements formerly made at Sibpur only enabled the government to impart agricultural education of a high standard, to just a few individuals every year. However, if these men, who were mostly Science graduates from Calcutta University, 'had been judiciously employed, they might have been able to supply all the special agricultural agency needed for developing the educational and experimental works under Government' (Mukherji 1901, 611). He observed:

> A much larger scheme of superior agricultural education has, however, now been carried out, involving the establishment of an agricultural college at Bhagalpur, which may ultimately turn out fifty or sixty trained men each year. The passed men from this college might be employed in charge of farms attached to the Normal Schools, which should form the centres of that form of agricultural education which should be imparted in the different vernaculars of the province. The practical work of the farms can then be conducted under those conditions under which agriculturists have to work in the different parts of these Provinces. The methods or staples that may be introduced with success at Sibpur or Bhagalpur may not answer for Hazaribagh, or for Kalimpong, or for Cuttack. (ibid.)

Men trained in the scientific principles of agriculture would, he said, be able to adopt new methods better suited to the conditions of and environment in which they worked. He advised that village school teachers also be taught, not principles or theories, but concrete facts regarding improvements that were feasible in their own particular localities. The knowledge communicated through textbooks by means of object lessons in the school garden was bound to spread in a real, sustainable manner (ibid.).

Nitya Gopal Mukherji strongly believed that the spread of literary education had been antagonistic to the advancement of the arts and industries. He wrote:

> If the school-going son of a cultivator can be of help to his father in his own difficulties, the father and the son will both begin to find out that education and farming are not necessarily antagonistic to each other. If the village schoolmaster can be of help to the *raiyat* in his own business the *raiyat* will think more highly of his own business also than he is accustomed to think at present. The tendency among cultivators and artisans who attain to some amount of prosperity by following their own ancestral craft is to shun their craft, to take to money-lending, and to make clerks of their sons. (Mukherji 1901, 612)

It was important, Mukherji observed, for children to have such an education from an early age, which would enable them to pursue their ancestral occupations with greater facility and interest. It would also deter them from shifting to occupations that were considered 'genteel' when compared to their ancestral ones (ibid.).

While making his case for agricultural education, Mukherji offers a glimpse of the existing system and condition of contemporary education. He suggested that the principle already recognised for primary and secondary schools could be applied to high schools and colleges as well. Permission should be granted to all *mofussil* schools and colleges to teach agriculture in place of physics or chemistry. It costs much less, he said, to organise gardens and farms here than it does to make adequate arrangements for teaching science. Students who had passed out of the Sibpur agricultural classes could be employed by mofussil schools and colleges:

> However meagre the arrangement that may be made by a mofussil school or college for teaching agriculture, this subject cannot possibly be worse taught than physics or chemistry is at present. Facts of agricultural science abound in the mofussil, and if the teacher employed has been taught himself in a practical manner, he will not need much outlay of money to impart sound knowledge of such facts and the principles underlying them, to his pupils. (Mukherji 1901, 612)

The study of agricultural science, Mukherji claimed, is given due importance in all advanced countries of the West.

The author acknowledges that in the initial stages, he doubted how useful high-caste Bengalis could be in the sphere of practical agriculture. But over the years, and with experience, he had reason to modify his opinion. The number of students seeking admission to agricultural courses in Sibpur Engineering College, students who were really interested in agriculture, increased steadily. Those who had completed the course and were employed in agricultural jobs were doing commendable work. In view of this, Mukherji concluded, 'English education will have as much influence in remodelling and improving the agricultural condition of the country, as it has had in other walks of Indian life' (Mukherji 1901, 613).

Nitya Gopal Mukherji was, however, emphatic that agriculture would not be a profitable occupation for a 'gentleman'. It was only by dint of hard labour that the Indian cultivator could make agriculture pay well. However, these same cultivators, so industrious when working for themselves, would shirk work when employed as labourers, that is, if they were hired by the 'gentlemen' to work on the fields of the latter:

> He can never compete with the actual cultivators in ordinary agriculture, as by their frugality and industry they will be able to get their outturn at a smaller cost and thus undersell him. He may succeed with a new crop but only for a time. When the cultivator finds out how he grows it, and where he sells it, he (the cultivator) will grow it at a smaller cost and put it on the market at a smaller price. (Mukherji 1901, 4)

Speaking from experience, Mukherji observed that he had taught scientific methods of sericulture to many; however, it was only the actual cocoon-rearers who were still persevering and making a profit, while all the educated men who had embarked on the venture had lost money and left. In a climate like India, Mukherji believed that only those who could work in the fields with their labourers were best suited for the agricultural industry.

The only viable alternative was a partnership. Capitalists and educated men could derive profit from agriculture by acting as middlemen. They would arrange for land, seed, manure, and implements for cultivators, and use their labour and cattle on a profit-sharing basis. If trained agriculturists adopted this practice, the system would greatly benefit by way of the introduction of superior staples and methods of cultivation. This system would yield good results if applied to dairy, fruit, and vegetable farming too.

On Empire

Authored by a man who enjoyed considerable repute in official circles, this handbook also gives us an understanding of his political beliefs. While talking about emigration, he opined that its need would be felt in another two decades. The question of emigration to other parts of the Empire would have to be considered seriously. India would have to make common cause with England and attempt to be recognised as an integral part of the Empire. She would have to consider the sparsely populated areas of the Empire as the natural field for expansion. India, Mukherji observed, could aspire for recognition as an important centre of the Empire, with equal rights and privileges as England, only by assisting in the foreign wars waged by the Empire and by political sympathies that had the interests of the Empire at heart. The encouragement of merely national or racial feelings would not help (Mukherji 1901, 603).

The time would come, Mukherji assured, when the right political attitude would be forced 'by necessity' upon the

> intellects and consciences of the leaders of Indian thought who can still afford to indulge in the idea that India's resources make her quite independent of the ideas of colonial expansion by which the nations of Europe are perforce guided, compelling them to seek fresh fields and pastures new in sparsely populated regions of the globe. (Mukherji 1901, 603)

According to him, what was perceived as 'imperial feeling' was neither a byword nor a mistake, but 'a concrete necessity' that English politicians 'of all schools of thought are beginning to realize and it must be the solid foundation of that vast Empire to which we have the privilege to belong' (ibid.).

This was written at the height of the nationalist movement. An official career and the social standing that went with it informed his political beliefs. But this did not conflict with his mission to foster agricultural development in the country. As he said, in no other country in the world does such a large proportion of the population depend on agriculture (ibid., 3).

Conclusion

Agricultural science was a colonial product. But it did not entrench itself in a pre-existing system of production with no consideration of the conditions specific to Indian localities. The object of agriculture was the production of food and other essential requirements, and the aim of the science of agriculture was the production of the greatest amount of produce in the best possible condition, in the shortest span of time, at the lowest cost, and with the least deterioration of land (Mukherji 1901, 9). According to Mukherji, the sciences helpful to this end were Geology, Mineralogy, Mechanics, Hydrostatics, Botany, Chemistry, Veterinary Science, Zoology, Bacteriology, and Political Economy—for an understanding of soils, crops, agricultural implements, manures, livestock, and pests and parasites (ibid., 10).

Knowledge of scientific agriculture would not only benefit agrarian production but it would also be of great value to revenue officers and district engineers. They would be able to help the administration and policymakers by compiling and providing agricultural statistics, drawing up famine programmes, reading local conditions, and sundry other administrative work. The 'proverbially conservative' ryots, too, would be influenced by agrarian innovations and new scientific knowledge, an influence that would be slow but lasting. The ryot was obliged to be conservative on account of his poverty; he could not afford to lose money on experiments and speculations (Mukherji 1901, 6). But he would adapt and adopt practicable methods if their benefits were persistently demonstrated.

Mukherji, however, bemoaned the fact that here, agricultural education was being taken advantage of almost exclusively by persons who were not directly interested in agriculture. Neither the farm labourer, nor the farmer, nor even the landed proprietor really cared for agricultural education. He drew attention to another significant fact. In India, he claimed, the caste system had 'ingrained and stamped in different classes, different abilities and disabilities in such an indelible manner, that the priestly and writer castes who generally go in for high education are *ab initio* unfit subjects for agricultural pursuit' (Mukherji 1901, 8). It was therefore important that in India, 'the right classes' of people be encouraged to receive agricultural education. This would ensure that the benefit derived by them could filter down easily to their fellow caste members in rural areas (ibid., 9). It was a little far-fetched to expect the benefits of agricultural education to filter down to the rural tracts 'from the prospective gardens, farms and plantations that the Bengali or the Maratha "gentleman" may establish' after receiving agricultural education (ibid.). The ryots should be taught to help themselves. Mukherji strongly believed that the ryots were capable of receiving a systematic training in agriculture.

Nineteenth-century Bengal saw the emergence of multiple trends in the thought process of the Bengali literati. At one level, colonialism was contested on different fronts. On the other, society and social processes were questioned with a view to defend what was considered relevant, or reform practices whenever necessary. There were also men who attempted to make a difference, yet often went unnoticed and unsung as their work failed to catch the imagination of the age they lived in. Sometimes, their work yielded no immediate results. Nitya Gopal Mukherji was one such man. The site of his concern was a domain and a social category—agriculture and the peasantry—thinking about which was certainly fashionable, but working for which was just as certainly not. It was back-breaking and required immense patience and perseverance, with no immediate results in sight.

Mukherji was in government service, and his exposure to agricultural developments in the West brought home the fact that scientific agriculture, with all its necessary inputs, was a precondition for agrarian development. His magnum opus was certainly not a critique of colonial rule. In fact, he deviated from the nationalist critique on some of the effects of colonialism (Mukherji 1901, 3). He claimed that in spite of periodic famines, there were few cases in India of lands going out of cultivation, and of farmers being ruined and having to emigrate to foreign countries in search of a living (ibid.). There were also no cases of ryots, in spite of their hereditary debts, being alienated from their holdings and being forced to adopt other trades (ibid.). Many crafts and trades had suffered such a fate, but not agriculture.

These claims have been contested by statistical data. But Mukherji's prescriptions for agrarian development and his thorough knowledge of the inputs and outputs of successful agriculture are beyond doubt. Agriculture as a system of production was a neglected subject. This is established by the fact that Nitya Gopal Mukherji has been ignored in the narrative of the developmental discourse of nineteenth-century Bengal (Sartori 2014).

Endnotes

1. Hossein returned to India after getting his degree in agriculture and joined the government service. He went on to become the Deputy Magistrate of Bhagalpur. He was married to the eminent litterateur and educationist, Begum Rokeya Hossein (Government of Bengal, Revenue Department, September 1889, no. 3590–506 Agri., 2, West Bengal State Archives).

2. He worked in the Departments of Survey and Settlement, Excise, Land Records and Agriculture, Administration, and Judiciary in different parts of Bengal, Bihar, and the Central Province. He was made Assistant Director, Land Records and Agriculture Department, in 1898 while being in service under the Director of Agriculture.

3. Government of Bengal, Revenue Department, 1889, No. 3590–506 Agriculture, 2, West Bengal State Archives.

4. Ibid.

5. Ibid.

6. Ibid., March 1887, no. 949–185 Agri., 27, West Bengal State Archives.

7. Ibid., September 1889, no. 3590–506 Agri., 2, West Bengal State Archives.

Select References

Mukherji, Nitya Gopal. 1901. *Handbook of Indian Agriculture*. Calcutta: Thacker, Spink and Co.

———. 1912. *Handbook of Sericulture*. Calcutta: Bengal Secretariat Book Depot.

Raha, Bipasha. 2012. *The Plough and the Pen: Peasantry, Agriculture and the Literati in Colonial India*. New Delhi: Manohar.

———. 2018. 'Agrarian Thinking in Bengal in the Nineteenth Century'. In Arun Bandyopadhyay and Sanjukta Das Gupta (eds), *In Quest of the Historian's Craft: Essays in Honour of Professor B.B. Chaudhuri*, Part I: *The Economy*. New Delhi: Manohar.

Sartori, Andrew. 2014. *Liberalism in Empire: An Alternative History*. California: University of California Press.

13

Prosperity, Dominance, and Social Mobility

Emergence of a Mobile Caste in Colonial Southwest Bengal*

Achintya Kumar Dutta

Caste is an important phenomenon in the social history of colonial India, constituting an important part of social identity and the social fabric. Caste in colonial India gripped historical scholarship for many years and a number of Western scholars, such as H. H. Risley, J. H. Hutton, Bernard S. Cohn, Rosalind O'Hanlon, Susan Bayly, and Nicholas B. Dirks, among others, have investigated the origin, nature, and development of the caste system, caste mobility, and many other significant aspects of the history of caste in India (Bayly 2000; Cohn 1987, 224–254; Dirks 2003; Hutton 1963; O'Hanlon 2010, 172–180; Risley 1981). Similarly, learned Indian scholars like G. S. Ghurye, M. N. Srinivas, K. S. Singh, Jogendra Nath Bhattacharya, and many others have studied various aspects of caste history in modern India (Bhattacharya 1995; Ghurye 1961 [1931]; Singh 1992; Srinivas 1962, 1966).

Caste mobility in Bengal is a well-researched field and the seminal works on it by Hitesranjan Sanyal and Sekhar Bandyopadhyay deserve special mention in this context. Unlike the earlier works, which were more descriptive and informative than

*An earlier version of this chapter was published as 'Social Mobility of an Entrepreneurial Caste: The Ugra Kshatriyas of Rarh Bengal', in Arabinda Samanta, et al. (eds), *Life and Culture in Bengal Colonial and Post-colonial Experiences*. Calcutta: Progressive Publishers, 2011. Permission to publish this version granted by Progressive Publishers.

analytical, these works address various issues related to caste society through an analytical lens and in a rational, objective manner. Sanyal's *Social Mobility in Bengal* (1981), a collection of learned essays, has dealt with the caste structure and caste hierarchy, and the types of social mobility adopted by the Sudras for acquiring higher status and respectability in society. He also discusses the mobility movements of the dissident Gops and Telis for a higher ritual and social rank in the caste hierarchy of Bengal. Through these movements, these castes had risen to the rank of Nabasakh, which is originally said to have been formed by nine branches of 'clean' Sudras and subsequently included fourteen to sixteen castes, from their original position as 'unclean' Sudras (ibid., 38, 115). Bandyopadhyay has explored why and how certain lower ranks of Bengali society organised movements in the nineteenth and twentieth centuries for a new identity in the caste hierarchy, leading to 'limited vertical social mobility' amongst them (Bandyopadhyay 1990; 2010, 181–196). Amitabha Mukhopadhyay has also studied how some of the socially mobile castes in colonial Bengal struggled to elevate their caste status through organising caste movements (Mukhopadhyay 1981, 1–47). In recent times, the origin as well as social mobility of particular castes in colonial Bengal has been, from an anthropo-historical perspective, the subject of academic pursuit for some scholars. We may refer to the studies on pastoral Gops or agricultural and trading Telis by Hitesranjan Sanyal, on the Namasudras by Sekhar Bandyopadhyay, on the Kansaris (bell-metal workers) by Smriti Kumar Sarkar, on the Rajbansis by S. Taniguchi and Swaraj Basu, and so on. These case studies have shed light on why and how these castes sought to change their social and ritual status in the colonial milieu, following new economic opportunities and the model of 'Sanskritisation' (Bandyopadhyay 2004, 11–36).

Undeniably, economic prosperity brought about through occupational changes in the case of the dissident Gops and Telis and other castes had facilitated a rise in their socioeconomic status and their dominance in some regions of Bengal. In this context, we may refer to the Ugra Kshatriyas, locally known as the Aguris, of southwest Bengal, who proved to be the most influential and powerful community in Burdwan district and its adjoining areas. The scope of engaging in a new profession in the nineteenth-century economic milieu helped many of them to make their fortunes. Economic prosperity, in turn, helped them achieve social and cultural prominence. Many of them invested part of their earnings in agricultural land and the grain-lending and moneylending business, thus gradually controlling land and agricultural production in the countryside. This control consolidated their dominance in the rural society, in terms of wealth and landed properties.

This chapter will attempt to unfold the caste status of the Ugra Kshatriyas in the caste hierarchy of Bengal, along with the various dimensions of entrepreneurial competence of the caste that maintained its dominance in the economy and society of Rarh Bengal. It will also shed light on their origins in light of the debate amongst scholars on whether they belong to the Kshatriya community, and will focus on their vertical mobility in the context of their reforming zeal and the process of Kshatriyaisation.

Status in the Caste Hierarchy

Before discoursing on the economic and social mobility of this caste, it would not be out of place to throw some light on their genesis and caste status in the society of Rarh Bengal. Referring to their Kshatriyahood, the caste argued that most of the Ugra Kshatriyas in Burdwan had taken to agriculture instead of the traditional Kshatriya occupation of warfare. Agriculture was not their traditional occupation; they were forced to change their profession under unforeseen circumstances after the English East India Company introduced the 'Resident System' in the 1760s. Before that, many of the troops of the Burdwan Raj belonged to the Ugra Kshatriyas who constituted the bulk of the *nagdees*, a considerable force who were paid in cash. Their annual maintenance cost over Rs 3 lakh (Halder 1982, 53; Hill and Banerjee 1940, 22). About 10,000 nagdee infantry of the Burdwan Raj had joined the battle against the Company's forces under Martin White in 1760 (Halder 1982, 52–53). John Johnstone, the first Resident of the Company, reduced the number of these forces and the consequent maintenance costs in 1763. Thereafter, the nagdees were chiefly employed in preventing the incursions of bands of robbers from the Birbhum and Bankura jungles, a real danger in those days.[1] However, their number was reduced further as the need for their forces declined, although the duty of protecting the Burdwan treasury continued to be entrusted to them even in the 1780s. This arrangement continued till 1809, after which there is no further evidence of their involvement in any public service.[2] Under the Company's rule, the troops of the Burdwan Raj were disbanded and the Ugra Kshatriyas were deprived of their traditional occupation. At this juncture, as lands became their mainstay, agriculture appears to have become a major source of income for them, and they began acquiring large tracts of land or *jote* through various means, including deception and trickery (Banerjee 1983, 2; Halder 1982, 53). In the long run, many of them turned into powerful *jotedar*s who gradually constituted the landed aristocracy, and dominated the rural agrarian society of Burdwan district during the colonial period.

British civil servant William Benjamin Oldham questioned the Aguris' claim to be identified with the Ugra Kshatriyas (Oldham 1894). His theory, which was subsequently accepted without question by J. C. K. Peterson and others, is that the Aguris are the product of illicit unions between the Khetris of the Burdwan Raj family and the Sadgops of the Gopabhum dynasty, and appeared as a distinct caste only around the eighteenth century (Ganguly 1987, 96; Peterson 1910, 65). They are said to have never reached the status of Kshatriya and formed a distinct cultivating caste. But Oldham's theory is hardly reasonable, and stands on neither historical nor ethnological grounds. Jogendra Nath Bhåttacharya has offered cogent arguments refuting Oldham's theory. While Oldham maintains that his theory is based on the admissions of the Aguris themselves with regard to their origin, Bhattacharya believes that it was quite unlikely that any of them would furnish such a humiliating account of their origins. Moreover, according to the principles of the law of evidence recognised by almost every system of jurisprudence, an admission can hardly be treated as conclusive evidence (Bhattacharya 1995, 123).

In fact, Oldham's hypothesis has little ground to stand upon. That the Aguris existed in Bengal before the advent of the Khetris of the Burdwan Raj family is evident from Kabikankan Mukundaram's *Chandimangal,* which seems to have been written in the sixteenth century. Mukundaram writes,

> *Aghari (Aguri) nibase pure*
> *apnar brtti kare*
> *Anuchit nā kare kakhano*[3]
>
> [The Ugra Kshatriyas live in the villages, do their own professional works, and never do any wrong.]

Even earlier, *Ugra* or *Agari* (today's Aguri) had been referred to as a separate non-Brahmin caste in the *Brihaddharmapurana* and the *Brahmavaivartapurana,* which are known to have been composed sometime between the twelfth and the fourteenth centuries (Roy 1993, 211, 245–248). Moreover, there are many families among the Aguris whose history may be traced from a much earlier period than the time of even Abu Roy and Babu Roy, the founders of the Burdwan Raj family (Bhattacharya 1995, 123). All this evidence indicates that the Aguris had been living for centuries in the Rarh region.[4] Again, a consideration of their ethnic and moral characteristics shows that the Aguris are a distinct community, unlike any other caste in Bengal. The Khetris and the Sadgops, whom Oldham considers their progenitors, are very dissimilar to the former (ibid.).

That the Aguris are an established caste in southwest Bengal is acknowledged by the official records of the British India government. The Census of India, 1921 states that the Aguris appear to have been the dominant caste around Burdwan right up to Mughal times.[5] However, some of the Aguris claim to be pure Kshatriyas, whose ancestors had come as military officers from Agra under Man Singha (Mitra 1953, 35). No wonder, then, that

Aguris in the mid-twentieth century did not like being identified with the Ugras who, according to Manu, were cruel (ibid.). In fact, the origin and early history of the Ugra Kshatriyas seem, to a great extent, obscure and even, on occasion, elusive. Some accounts trace their existence to the Hindu period, when many of the Ugra Kshatriyas occupied the position of *Agraharika* (those who supervised the *devottar* lands) (Ghosh 1954 [1361 BS], 22–23). It is also said that they are connected with the *Aghari* tribe of the Central Provinces or the *Aghareahs*/*Agharia* of Hindu peasants in the Tributary Mahals or Madhya Pradesh. Agharia is the corrupt form of Agaria, which means 'those who came from Agra' (Singh 1991, 26). According to tradition, they were Kshatriyas, but having been subjected to persecution by the ruler of Agra, they left and, taking up new lands in a new country, cast aside their sacred thread and took to the plough (Dalton 1960 [1872], 311). The Agharias believed that their ancestors had fled Agra and settled down in the Chhattisgarh region. These accounts, however, are not corroborated by historical evidence. Again, the Aguris are said to have come to Bengal as warriors (and, therefore, as Kshatriyas) in the wake of some military expedition in the Mughal period (Ghosh 1957, 193).[6] Once they were settled in Bengal, they were given the status of Sudra in the *varna*-based social hierarchy as determined by ritual practices.[7]

Interestingly, the four-fold varna system is not prevalent in Bengal. Only two varnas exist in the caste hierarchy of Bengal—Brahmins and non-Brahmins. The Kshatriyas and Vaisyas are not represented as separate varnas in Bengal (Roy 1993, 225, 245–246). Therefore, all non-Brahmins belong to the Sudra or mixed varna. According to the *Brahmavaivartapurana*, Sudras are divided into two groups—*Satsudra* (unpolluted and clean Sudras) and *Asatsudra* (unclean Sudras)—and the Agaris or Aguris are placed within the latter group (ibid., 247–248). However, the Sudras comprise a large number of castes, which are hierarchically arranged. Each caste has its own place in the local variant of the caste hierarchy in Bengal, in addition to its Sudra identity. *Karma* or profession seems to have been associated with the caste system.

But many of these castes might have adopted novel professions instead of continuing with their original ones in the prevailing historical context. This change in profession is seen especially after the advent of the Europeans, an event that dislodged the traditional socioeconomic order. Even the Brahmins adopted the professions of the Vaisyas and the Sudras whenever necessary (Mukhopadhyay 1971, 15–19). Similarly, in the absence of the Kshatriya varna, the Kshatriya occupation of warfare in Bengal was adopted by people of different castes, some of whom belonged to the Sudras and *Antyaja* (the untouchables and others who constituted the lowest stratum of the caste hierarchy). The Aguris were one of them; the fact that they were favourably exposed to both agricultural and military occupations led to their becoming an influential caste in southwest Bengal, particularly in Burdwan (ibid., 19). The issue of whether the Aguris belong to the Kshatriya varna or not remains a vexed question.

While it is impossible to determine the origin of the Aguris, we may refer to circumstances in the past that would signal the possibility of their apparent connection with the warrior castes. That warrior castes came into Bengal in the wake of military invasions is not unknown. Pala records show that Pala rulers employed foreigners from Gauda (Bengal), Khasa and Huna (northwest India), Kulika (west India), Lata (Gujarat), etc., in military service (Majumdar 1984, 221). Pala inscriptions mention them in the list of royal officials, from the time of Devapala down to Madanapala. It is also known that Dharmapala's vassal states in the Punjab, Rajputana, Malwa, Berar, etc., which enjoyed internal autonomy under his suzerainty, paid homage and rendered military assistance. Presumably, some foreign military officials may have settled in eastern India and became powerful in course of time. The Aguris could have been connected to these mercenary groups; their remote descendants might have carried on their military activities and rendered valuable services to the Burdwan Raj. When their traditional occupation gradually lost relevance after the establishment of the East India Company's paramountcy, they switched over to new occupations. As the military power of the local lords declined in the early years of Company rule, they embarked on agricultural and commercial pursuits to make their fortunes. Later, many of them became educated professionals of middle-class society. In some cases, they also held supremacy in the field of education. For example, Rajnarayan Basu writes in his autobiography that the teacher from whom he had received education in his early life in the village of Boral, in the district 24 Parganas, belonged to the Aguri community and came from Burdwan (Mukhopadhyay 1971, 19).

Undeniably, many castes like Sadgop, Teli, and Namasudra changed their occupations during the colonial period and most adopted agriculture and trade as their new professions. In the *East India Gazetteer* (1828), W. Hamilton wrote,

> In practice little attention is paid to the limitations of castes, daily observations showing Brahmins exercising the martial profession of a Khetri, and even the menial one of a Sudra ... every profession, with a few exceptions, being open to every descriptions of persons. (Mukhopadhyay 1971, 24)

The Aguris were no exception to this trend. The question of purity or impurity was not considered so much as the question of earnings when it came to a change in occupation. So it would be difficult to define caste status on the basis of profession. Agriculture appears to have been the primary source of earning, and therefore subsequently a lucrative one to the Aguris.

While describing the caste divisions of Bengal in the contemporary caste hierarchy, Hitesranjan Sanyal shows that the Baidyas and Kayasthas had the same ritual rank as the Nabasakhs, but the social position of the former was much higher than the latter mainly because of their good occupational positions and the privileges that issued from them. This is why Baidyas and Kayasthas were often grouped together with the Brahmins to constitute what is popularly known as the *uchchajati* or higher-caste group. Therefore, Baidyas and Kayasthas never felt the need to make any effort to move upwards within the regional caste hierarchy. Similarly, both the local and the migrant Kshatriyas who settled in the southwestern Bengal districts of Burdwan, Bankura, Purulia, Midnapore, and Hooghly enjoyed a high social position. The Ugra Kshatriyas were found to have settled in these areas, where these castes rank immediately below the Brahmins and are accepted as Kshatriyas; and amazingly, the Baidyas and Kayasthas are ranked below them. These local Kshatriyas may also be lumped together with the Brahmins, Baidyas, and Kayasthas. Collectively, these castes were referred to as the upper castes (Sanyal 1981, 37–38). The Aguris are popularly believed to be the modern representatives of the Ugra or Ugra Kshatriyas mentioned in *Manu*, X, 9: 'From a Kshatriya by a Sudra girl is born a creature called an Ugra (cruel), which has a nature partaking both of Kshatriya and of Sudra, and finds its pleasure in savage conduct' (Risley 1981, 1, 12). In an official note on ethnography in Bengal, H. H. Risley states that the Aguris are a cultivating and trading caste, very numerous in western Bengal, where they wear the sacred thread and have adopted the Brahmanical system of *gotras*.[8]

A great majority of the Aguris, comprising about 75 per cent of the Aguris of Bengal, come from Burdwan district (Basu 1915, 12). The comparative figures in Table 13.1 will help us to understand their majority in Burdwan.

TABLE 13.1: Number of Aguris in Bengal and Burdwan

Year	Total number of Aguris in Bengal	Total number of Aguris in Burdwan
1872	70,606	59,887
1881	78,349	57,272
1911	79,272	66,551
1921	68,816	59,949

Source: Hunter 1973, 44; *Census of India*, 1881, 1911, 1921, relevant volumes and tables.

Their numerical strength in the upper strata of society in Burdwan district was also remarkable, as shown in Table 13.2.

Table 13.2: Comparative Figures of Brahmins, Sadgops, and Aguris in Burdwan

Year	Brahmins	Sadgops	Aguris
1872	1,60,824	1,85,804	59,887
1891	1,03,749	1,06,674	62,249

Source: Hunter 1973, 44; O'Donnell (1891, relevant tables).

Tables 13.1 and 13.2 make it clear that the Aguris occupied the third place, following the Brahmins and the Sadgops. However, the regional distribution of the dominant Aguri families was widespread. By 1881, they were—and still are, albeit in a minority—distributed in a number of districts of Bengal, as well as in a few places of Bihar and Odisha, such as Bankura, Birbhum, Midnapore, Hoogly, 24 Parganas, Nadia, Murshidabad, Dinajpur, Maldah, Jalpaiguri, Dacca, Faridpur, Santal Parganas, Bhagalpur, Patna, Cuttack, Balasore, Hazaribagh, and Dumka (Bandhu 1985 [1392 BS]).

Prosperity, Power, and Dominance

The Ugra Kshatriyas are a dominant and influential caste in the agrarian and commercial economy of Burdwan district. Dominance was determined by numerical preponderance and by economic and political power. Scholars have stated that a large and powerful caste group could easily become dominant if its position in the local caste hierarchy was not too low (Banerjee-Dube 2010, xxiii). The elders in these caste groups commanded respect and wielded economic and political power, thereby exerting influence and establishing their hold over the rural society. The Ugra Kshatriyas came into prominence by dint of their economic prosperity and the influence they had exerted as landholders, merchants, and substantial peasants. Unlike Gobinda Samanta, a poor Ugra Kshatriya *raiyat* and hero of Lal Behari Day's *Bengal Peasant Life,* a large number of people from this caste were prosperous.

Agricultural and commercial pursuits increased their prosperity; they dominated the rural society as landholders, jotedars, and rich peasants, controlling agricultural land in their localities and often consolidating their position further by securing a lower grade of *patni taluqs* (Bandopadhyay 1990, 106).[9]

In the formative years of colonial rule, a stratum of powerful peasants situated between the zamindars and the cultivators rose to power in the agrarian society of Burdwan. Many former nagdee soldiers belonging to the Aguri community constituted a part of this group (Halder 1982, 53). Each of them had a large quantity of jotes or holdings, ranging from 30 to 100 acres. They formed an influential and powerful section in the rural society of Burdwan district. Such an image of the Aguris has been depicted by Tara Krishna Basu, who had visited Lal Behari Day's native village Sonapalasi, near Burdwan town. He writes that in the mid-nineteenth century socioeconomic structure of the village, the zamindar (who held a patni-taluq under His Highness the Maharaja of Burdwan) dominated the scene, while the large peasants belonging to the Sadgops and the Aguris formed the economic backbone of the village (Basu 1962, 41). The moneylending and grain-lending business enabled them to exercise their domination over smallholder peasants and cultivators. Although some of the Aguris were also middle-class farmers and poor peasants, most were fairly well-off in southwestern Bengal districts. Besides enjoying a substantial share in village lands, they exerted power on the poor people in their villages, especially the untouchables and the tribes, who lived in a separate quarter of the village (Roy 1979, 52–53). The Aguris' economic prosperity had undoubtedly raised their position and status in society, which supports the hypothesis that wealthy people *always* have a superior position in the social set-up, at any given place and time. During the British period, the Ugra Kshatriyas were dominant in terms of wealth and possession of landed interests, and this domination was hardly ever challenged.

A great many of them were engaged in trade and commerce, especially trade in foodgrains—they had a monopoly over the paddy/rice trade in Burdwan district—which further added to their riches (Palit 1926 [1333 BS]). Most of the paddy and rice merchants of Katwa, Guskara, Memari, Nadanghat, Manteshwar, and Burdwan town belonged to the Ugra Kshatriya community. The emergence of new market centres at Asansol, Raniganj, Memari, and other places in the late nineteenth and early twentieth century provided commercial opportunities for the entrepreneurs. At the same time, the rise of Burdwan as a market town after the scourge of malaria was reduced and the railway transportation network developed, along with the establishment of the new Raj Palace and new business premises of Nutanganj, Alamganj, and Barabazar, created further economic opportunities. Important business families emigrated to these places and carried on their trade and commerce with the mainstream of Bengal's expanding overseas trade.

A typical example of an Aguri business tycoon was Banwarilal Panja, who came from village Sathinandi, about 15 km west of Burdwan town, in the wake of commercial pursuits. The Panjas were essentially agents commissioned to sell products such as mustard and other oilseeds, grains, poppy-seeds, and tobacco, a calling that brought them an annual income of Rs 50,000–100,000. Surplus profits were reinvested in agricultural lands in Burdwan and Bankura districts, which brought in an almost equivalent annual sum (Ganguly 1987, 84). In this way, trade and commerce led to economic solvency for the entire family, and enabled them to occupy a higher rank in the social hierarchy.

It is through such commercial pursuits that the Aguris acquired huge fortunes, and most reinvested a part of their enormous profits derived from trade in purchasing agricultural lands or other profitable businesses. Some of them took on the lease of patni-taluqs, *darpatni*s (a type of sub-infeudation), and so on, and even rose to the status of zamindar in their respective villages and surrounding areas in Burdwan district. We may refer to the Roy Chowdhurys of Chaitanyapur, the Tahs of Palitpur, the Hazras of Anguna, and the Panjas of Sathinandi in Burdwan district. The prosperity of these families greatly increased under the guidance of the ablest members. Most of them purchased patnis and darpatnis, either from the Burdwan Raj or from the Mukherjees of Uttarpara, Hooghly. Thus, they began collecting rent from the raiyats and thereby raised their social prestige, position, and power.

The entrepreneurial activities of the Ugra Kshatriyas also deserve mention. A large number of them are found to have prospered as small and medium-scale entrepreneurs in coal mines, rice mills, and mica mines. Men like Nagendranath Samanta, Janaki Nath Samanta, and others belonging to the Ugra Kshatriya caste were pioneers in the rice milling industry of Burdwan district,[10] and a large number of rice mills are still owned by this community. The Hazras of Anguna in the trans-Damodar region were involved in both rice milling and coal mining in Burdwan, and acquired solvency.

Another significant example of an enterprising Ugra Kshatriya family was that of Satya Kinkar Sahana, the great zamindar of Bankura. Satya Kinkar Sahana's grandfather had augmented the family's cultivating and moneylending activities with a small trans-shipment and warehousing business at Raniganj, shortly after the railway from Calcutta reached there in 1854 (Broomfield 1982, 176). When the line was carried further west into southern Bihar, his two sons—Prankrishna and Rajkrishna—extended the business to Giridi, Pachamba, and some other places (ibid.; Sahana 1960 [1367 BS], 2). They were remarkably successful, and not long after Satya Kinkar was born in 1874, they began investing their profits in coal and mica mines. Such industrial activities substantiate the claim that Indian peasants were not un-enterprising, and neither were Bengalis entrepreneurially inept (Broomfield 1982, 176). The management of his family business fell on Satya Kinkar from 1908 onwards with the death of his father Prankrishna and uncle Rajkrishna. Satya Kinkar continued their policy of investing a large part of the mining profits in Bankura lands, and in 1917, after communications improved largely due to the railway network and particularly the opening of the Bankura Damodar River Railway in 1913, he settled down in Bankura permanently. Before that, he had lived in Burdwan and Giridi (ibid.; Sahana 1960 [1367 BS], 8). Satya Kinkar Sahana was a moneylending landlord and also the *aratdar* or grain dealer, who had seven zamidaris and eight houses scattered throughout Bengal and Bihar (Broomfield 1982, 177; Palit 1982, 70). He pioneered the rice-milling industry in Bankura; Sreedhar Rice Mill, established by him, encouraged other Bengali traders to take to the rice-milling enterprise (Sahana 1960 [1367 BS], 9). Thus, besides the business of farming and rent-collecting, the Sahanas' multipurpose enterprises in coal and mica mining and rice milling are symbolic of their riches, prosperity, and social prestige.

This economic prosperity facilitated their modern education; some of them started practising law and became successful advocates at the District Court of Burdwan. Some others who rose to prominence in the legal profession also came from old service families. One such person was Banwari Lal Hati. His grandfather, Kshetramohan Hati, was well-versed in Arabic and Persian and earned his living as a *munsif* (judge) at the Court of Suri. Later, he was appointed *Dewan* (chief treasury official) of the Jamua Raj and moved to Behrampur, where Banwari Lal began to practice law after obtaining his degree in 1857 (Ganguly 1987, 79). After the death of Kshetramohan Hati in 1882, Banwari Lal moved to Burdwan. In 1888, he was appointed munsif of the first order, and in 1889, Public Prosecutor of Burdwan district. He subsequently became the Vice-Chairman of the District Board, a position he held for about twenty-five years (ibid., 150–151). Another well-known member of the Burdwan Bar was Jadabendranath Panja of village Sathinandi, who belonged to a prosperous landowning Ugra Kshatriya family of Burdwan district. Jadabendra's father, Nrisinghamurari, was the first graduate of Burdwan Raj College and a successful teacher at the Burdwan Raj Collegiate School in the last quarter of the nineteenth century (ibid., 84).[11] After receiving his law degree in 1911 from Ripon College, Jadabendra started practising at the District Court of Burdwan. In 1920, he left this profession and devoted himself to the freedom movement of the country.[12]

All of this enhanced the social prestige of the Ugra Kshatriyas and helped them acquire sociopolitical power. Interestingly, many of the prosperous and influential Ugra Kshatriyas moved towards acquiring greater local influence politically through new forums such as the Local and District Boards and Municipalities, in order to consolidate their power and authority and thereby rise in social status. This trend began after the Local Self-Government Act was passed in 1885 and these local bodies became the new source of power; many prosperous individuals in different districts of Bengal contested the elections of 1886 so as to access them (Bandyopadhyay 1990, 112). In fact, they were in search of wider recognition. Of those elected to different Local Boards in Burdwan district, more than 11 per cent were Ugra Kshatriya by caste (ibid.). Many individuals belonging to the Sadgop caste also contested the elections successfully.

Sociocultural Performance

That the Ugra Kshatriyas were a mobile caste and culturally superior to their caste neighbours is evident from their sociocultural activities. With the advent of Western education, they, like the Brahmins and Kayasthas, imbibed the new ideas of liberalism and rationalism. The educated, self-conscious members of the caste devoted their energy to ensuring the progress and welfare of their own community. Like some other castes of Bengal, they tried to organise themselves and for this purpose, established their own association or Samiti, including a journal of their own, edited by educated members. Thus, the Ugra Kshatriya Samiti came into existence in 1888, and is said to be the earliest caste association in Burdwan.[13] A monthly journal, *Ugra Kshatriya Pratinidhi*, was started in 1891, but could not last long.[14] The Samiti also funded the publication of books and organised annual meetings. Its activities continued till about 1913, after which it started declining (Ganguly 1987, 97). More than a decade later, the first successful attempt to reorganise the Samiti was made in 1927. In 1929, the Samiti started a quarterly journal, *Ugra Kshatriya Patrika*, which published articles on both the Ugra Kshatriya society and contemporary socioreligious problems (Bandhu 1985 [1392 BS], 119). Thereafter, the Ugra Kshatriyas held a number of conferences both within and outside Burdwan under the auspices of the Samiti, which continued till 1950 (ibid., 114–118). Caste members from different occupational backgrounds joined this association and attended these conferences. The most influential in Burdwan were the wealthy merchant families such as the Panjas and the Kundus, eminent lawyers like Banwari Lal Hati, Mrityunjay Chaudhury, and Bidhubhushan Sikdar, as well as men like Kumar Behari Samanta and Ganapati Panja, and medical practitioners Pratap Chandra Roy, Haradhan Tah, and Haridas Sain (Ganguly 1987, 97).[15] They presided over various meetings organised by the Samiti in Burdwan and also attended sessions in Calcutta.

The primary purpose of these meetings was to improve the socioeconomic and cultural conscience of the Ugra Kshatriyas. Emphasis was placed on integration and coordination among the different branches of the caste, eradication of social evils and customs like the dowry system, encouragement of widow remarriage, improvement in agriculture through scientific systems, the use of indigenous goods, progress of education within their own community, etc. They were divided into two main branches—*Jana* and *Suta*. The Sutas were subdivided into several sub-classes, for example the *Bardhamaniya*, the *Kashipuri*, *Chagrami*, etc. (Bandhu 1985 [1392 BS], 116).[16] Although the reasons for their division are not exactly known, each regarded itself as superior to the others. The Jana adopted the sacred thread, while the Suta did not. Intermarriage was well-nigh impossible between the two branches, and between the Suta sub-classes too (Bhattacharya 1995, 125). All the branches and sub-classes belonged to the same caste, but there was no coordination among them. The Ugra Kshatriya Samiti aimed at achieving solidarity within the caste and preached the necessity of reforming their lifestyles and purifying their ritual practices. With the introduction of elective institutions, the Samiti campaigned for votes for the Ugra Kshatriya candidates, urging the caste to show its solidarity and enhance its power by withholding votes from the non-Ugra Kshatriyas (Broomfield

1982, 255). Members of the Samiti even advocated reforms in the countryside of Burdwan district. Besides, the Samiti provided financial assistance to the poor and the destitute, particularly for the education of their children.[17]

Another association, the Nikhil Bharat Ugra Kshatriya Yubak Sangha (All India Ugra Kshatriya Youth Association), was organised in December 1938 in Calcutta under the Presidency of Bishnupada Chowdhury. It aimed to introduce sociocultural reforms in Ugra Kshatriya society.[18] None of these organisations was political in nature and did not seek to humiliate other communities. They took the initiative to eliminate prejudices and irrational social customs and social evils that existed amongst the Aguris. The Yubak Sangha also emphasised widow remarriage and fostered the unity and integrity of the Ugra Kshatriya community as a whole, disregarding their class divisions. Thus, the educated members sought to initiate liberal reforms, relax caste restrictions, integrate the different branches and sub-castes, and so on. Efforts were made to establish affinal connections with each other, and intermarriages also took place between the two main groups in the 1920s.[19] Class divisions gradually reduced and widow remarriages took place, one of which was held in April 1938 at Bankura and attended by a handful of reputed and respectable men. The names of the bridegroom and bride were Radhanath Kesh and Mahamaya, respectively.[20] Thus, while this association could not tackle all the problems their members faced, they did seek to raise the status of the caste and uplift the Ugra Kshatriya society.

Many Ugra Kshatriya families and personages were held in great esteem by the people of this region, both for their wealth and influence and for their sociocultural and political activities. The intellectual performance of a handful of people belonging to this community is also believed to have been very impressive. We may mention Pratap Chandra Roy of village Sanko in Burdwan district, an enterprising publisher and a man of rare tact and grace, who earned fame for his translation and publication of the great Sanskrit epic, *Mahabharata* (Bhattacharya 1995, 125), Dr Manohar Roy of Nasigram, the eminent mathematician who was later President of the Indian Science Congress, 1958–1959, and renowned dermatologist Dr Ganapati Panja of Majhigram (Bandhu 1985 [1392 BS], 128–130). Mention must also be made of Satya Kinkar Sahana of Bankura, who deserves special appreciation for his literary excellence. He was well-read and commanded a wide range of knowledge, from *Kadambari* to Leon Trotsky's *Defence* (Palit 1982, 72). An accomplished literary personality of Bengal, Satya Kinkar wrote poetry and published learned discourses on society, politics, and religion. He authored a number of books and articles on literature, religion, and philosophy, such as *Sakuntala Rahasya* and *Hindu Dharma*. Some Ugra Kshatriyas also joined the freedom movement; men like Jadabendranath Panja, Dasarathi Tah, Ananda Prasad Mondal, Benoy Chowdhury, Harekrishna Koner, and Shib Shankar Chowdhury remain alive in the memory of people at the local level for their leadership and political potential. Many of them rose to political prominence after India's independence and dedicated themselves to the cause of communism (De 1963, 19–27). A great many Ugra Kshatriya personalities of Burdwan also demonstrated their creativity in different sociocultural aspects (Bandhu 1985 [1392 BS], 114–133). Thus, the Ugra Kshatriyas of Rarh Bengal exhibited their potential in almost every field of life. A famous contemporary poet of this region, Kalidas Roy, has aptly remarked that the Ugra Kshatriyas in Burdwan, being educationally advanced and self-conscious, played an active role in the development of the district.

Vertical Mobility and Social Position

However, there was a stark incongruity between this prosperity and dominance and the low status of the Ugra Kshatriya caste in this region, where people considered them unclean Sudras because of certain ritualistic practices that they followed. For instance, they performed the *Adya Sradh*, or the first ceremony for the benefit of the soul of a deceased person, on the thirty-first day after death, and not on the thirteenth day as befits true Kshatriyas (Bhattacharya 1995, 125). In public meetings, the Ugra Kshatriya Samiti frequently protested unfavourable accounts of the Ugra Kshatriyas noted in various official and non-official publications, and objected to the term 'cultivating caste' assigned to them.[21] The members of the Samiti considered Kshatriyahood their rightful status. Thus, Kshatriyaisation was used as a model of vertical mobility in the caste hierarchy of Bengal.

The Ugra Kshatriyas demanded a position higher than the one given to them in the caste hierarchy by producing tracts and journals, putting forward various arguments, as well as establishing caste associations. The latter tried to propagate refined social behaviours and the adoption of purer ritual symbols. A similar process was followed by some castes in south India, particularly in Madras, where 'Pallis' or Vanniyars claimed Kshatriya status. For instance, in 1891, T. Ayakannu Nayakar wrote a learned treatise about the status of the Vanniyars, throwing light on their caste origin and identity (Dirks 2003, 223, 238). The Ugra Kshatriyas' claim for Kshatriyahood was reinforced by connecting them with the Rajputs. Sitikantha Smrititirtha and Haricharan Bandhu wrote two learned treatises in 1893 and 1913, respectively, about the status of the Ugra Kshatriyas and ascribed Kshatriyahood to them, arguing that they belonged to the Kshatriya Rajput community while highlighting their vigour, prowess, and fighting spirit in Burdwan in the past (Bandhu 1913 [1320 BS]; Smrititirtha 1883 [1300 BS]).

The process of Kshatriyaisation through Rajputisation was also seen in Rarh Bengal in the case of Bhumij Kshatriyas, a phenomenon studied much earlier by Surajit Sinha (1959). It was observed that, backed by their economic and political power, the largest Bhumij landholders in south Manbhum, such as the zamindars of Barabhum and Baghmundi or the *taraf sardar* of Satrakhani (a fief covering more than 100 villages), aspired to be recognised as Kshatriya. In order to merit such a recognition from the Brahmins, they drew 'clean' Brahmins to serve as priests in their families by giving them *Brahmottara,* that is, large grants of rent-free tenures. These Brahmins in their turn helped them by creating myths of their Rajput-Kshatriya ancestry and by intensifying the 'Sanskritisation' of their way of life—they had to give up meat and alcohol, refuse widow remarriage, employ pure Brahmins in all birth, marriage, and funeral ceremonies, wear the 'sacred thread' as befits Kshatriyas, build temples 'with images of Brahmanical gods and goddesses' and observe major Hindu festivals like Durga Puja and Kali Puja, and establish matrimonial alliances with families long recognised as Rajput-Kshatriya in the neighbouring districts (Sinha 1959, 11–12, cited in Sanyal 1981, 47–48).

Vertical mobility achieved through Rajputisation in some other parts of India has also gripped the attention of scholars. In a recent paper on the Sudra right to rule, Shail Mayaram discussed how Bhatnagar, Dube, and Dube identified Rajputisation as one of the most dynamic modes of upward mobility among various castes in north India. Various Sudra castes in north India, ranging from peasants and lower-caste Sudras to warriors and tribal chiefs, demonstrated their upward mobility through the process of Rajputisation, which has been considered 'unparalleled in traditional Indian society for its inventiveness in ideologies of legitimation and self-invention', thus demonstrating the process of a Kshatriyaisation of sorts (Mayaram 2010, 109–135). The process of peasant Kshatriya-isation in Gangetic India in the late nineteenth and early twentieth century has also been studied by William R. Pinch (1996). He showed that many of the peasants in this area disdained their low Sudra status and claimed to be the 'descendants of divine warrior clans (Kshatriya) firmly rooted in the Indian past'. Pinch argues:

> [T]he articulation of peasant-kshatriya identity differed in significant ways from the kshatriyahood of the colonial elite in that the latter usually combined martial status with landed power, imperial certification, and brahmanical patronage. Peasant kshatriyahood, by contrast, lacked all these assets, but drew on Vaishnava identities and discourses nurtured in part by institutional connections to Vaishnava. (ibid., 16)

However, the Ugra Kshatriya movement differed from the Kshatriya reform movement of the Kurmi and Jadav peasants of the Gangetic region, in which religion played an important role. In the latter, individual monks, on occasion, played a role in reformist campaigns for Kshatriya identity; becoming Kshatriya was, in large part, predicated on being Vaishnava—in behaviour, belief, language, and diet (ibid., 139–140).

With the growth in prosperity, power, and prestige, they may have come to be known as *bhadralok,* that is, prosperous, well-educated, and well-mannered persons.[22] Consequently, they demanded a corresponding higher rank in the caste hierarchy. There were periodic flurries of activity in the Ugra Kshatriya caste association, especially during the Census (Broomfield 1982, 178). Like some other castes, the Aguris also wanted a high rank in the caste schedule during census operations. This was perhaps because the leaders of almost every caste looked upon the Census as an opportunity to receive formal public recognition of their higher social claims, which had been denied by their caste superiors (Bandyopadhyay 1990, 100). Thus, just as the Baidyas had claimed a status next to the Brahmins and the Kayasthas had demanded a position higher than that of the Baidyas, the Aguris, too, wished to be grouped along with the Baidyas and the Kayasthas (ibid., 101). The Census of 1901 reveals that in the caste hierarchy of Bengal, the Brahmins are placed in Group I while Group II included other castes ranked above clean Sudras, such as Khatris and Rajputs among the non-Bengali castes settled in Bengal, as well as Baidyas, Kayasthas, and Aguris.[23] Before the 1931 Census was held, the caste objected to the term 'Aguri', considering it vulgar or a slang term; however, they agreed to return themselves as Ugra Kshatriya.[24]

The Ugra Kshatriyas also fell back on what is called 'Sanskritisation', which M. N. Srinivas discussed in detail in *Social Change in Modern India* (1966) as a determinant to social mobility, as seen in the case of many other castes. Sanskritisation refers to a process by which some low-caste Hindus sought to reform their customs, rituals, and practices by adopting those followed by the upper castes, such as building temples, worshipping deities favoured by the upper castes, wearing particular ornaments and following the system of marriage associated with upper castes, and so on, and thereby claiming higher caste status in the service of upward social mobility. In their religious and ceremonial observances, the Ugra Kshatriyas differed from the higher castes in Bengal. They belong for the most part to the Vaishnava (worshippers of Lord Vishnu) and Sakta (worshippers of Shakti as goddess) sects, and there were even a few Saivas (worshippers of Lord Shiva as the supreme god) among them as well (Risley 1981, 13). In the nineteenth and early twentieth century, they, like some other castes, were found to have adopted some social and ritual practices that had been the hallmark of respectable castes who enjoyed a higher position in the regional caste hierarchy (Bandyopadhyay 1990, 117). For instance, they had started wearing the sacred thread and embraced 'Kulinism', with all its ancillary taboos and customs (ibid.). But only one branch of the Aguris, that is, the Janas, wore it at the time of their marriage. The Suta Aguris did not follow the practice of wearing the sacred thread at the time of marriage. By following this practice, the Janas demonstrated a distinct identity of their rituals, thus marking a difference from the Suta Aguris. Both the Sutas and the Janas belong to the Aguri caste, but the Janas continue to maintain this custom.

Following the marriage customs of higher castes, the Ugra Kshatriyas adopted the system of dowry in the nineteenth century. Among the higher castes, it was usually the bride's father who made a gift of money to the bridegroom, while among the lower castes the practice was reversed, that is, the bridegroom had to pay a bride-price (Bandyopadhyay 1990, 120). From the second half of the nineteenth century, respectable and well-to-do members of the Aguri caste as well as among the Sadgop and Telis adopted the practice of dowry, offering money to the father of the bridegroom as part of the wedding arrangements (ibid.).

As the Aguris were a landowning dominant and influential group, they successfully employed the priestly services of Brahmins and thereby gained social recognition as Satsudra from their caste superiors. Ordinarily, a clean Brahmin would be immediately degraded if he served anyone from a caste that ranks below the Nabasakhs (nine branches of the clean Sudras) (Sanyal 1981, 94). However, this did not happen when they performed religious ceremonies for the Aguris (Risley 1981, 13). In Burdwan, the social status of the Aguris was fairly high, and this was recognised by the Brahmins as well.[25] Not only did the local Brahmins accept their gifts, but they also partook of food in their houses that was cooked by Brahmins (Bhattacharya 1995, 124). The Brahmins also accepted water and certain sweetmeats from the hands of Aguris, although this practice was not uniformly followed. On the whole, they regarded the Aguris as a clean caste. Thus, in Rarh Bengal in general and Burdwan in particular, where the Ugra Kshatriyas were numerous, they seemed to have acquired a higher caste status than their caste neighbours.

Endnotes

1. *SSR Burdwan*, 22.
2. Ibid., 23.
3. Aghari or Agari refers to the Aguri community. See Sen (1993, 82, 135).
4. Rarh is situated in the southwestern part of Bengal. Its eastern side is surrounded by the Ganga-Bhagirathi while the Chhotanagpur plateau extends on its west. According to the present administrative division, the region comprises Birbhum, Burdwan, Bankura, and western part of Midnapore district. The borders of the Rarh region have been stretched, both geographically and politically. In a wider sense, Rarh comprises the entire southwestern Bengal, excluding only the eastern part of Midnapore district (Roy 1993, 118–120).
5. *Census of India 1921*, Vol. V, Pt. I, 350.
6. *Ugra Kshatriya Patrika*, Baisakh–Asad, 1337 BS, 38.
7. Ibid., 37–38.
8. Government of Bengal, Finance Department, Miscellaneous Branch, Progs 47–50, March 1887.
9. After the introduction of the Permanent Settlement, the assessment of land revenue on the estates settled with the Burdwan Raj was very

high. The heavy pressure levied by the East India Company for punctual remittance of that exorbitant amount was the prime concern of the Raja. Any default in the payment of revenue meant an auction sale of part of his zamindari. Therefore, to save his zamindari from dismemberment and for easy and punctual realisation of rent, the Raja had to subinfeudate his estate perpetually. He, however, divided his large estate into thousands of lots and leased them to middlemen in perpetuity, and at a fixed rent. Each lot was known as patni taluq and its holder as the *patnidar*. The patnidars were made proprietors in the same way as government had made the Maharaja of Burdwan a proprietor. The patnidars in turn sublet perpetual leases within their taluqs to others, who again resorted to the same practice, the motive being to reduce the burden and tension of having to pay the dues. Thus, a chain of patnidars, *darpatnidars*, and so on emerged in Burdwan in the nineteenth and twentieth centuries. By this system, the Raja passed on the responsibility of collecting rent directly and became an annuitant. The lease holders or intermediaries under this system had the right to collect rent from the raiyats (Dutta 2002, 45–46).

10. Interview with Debnath Mondal, President, Bengal Rice Mill Association, and Anath Saran De, dated 29 March 1992.

11. *Jadabendra Smarane* by an anonymous writer, n.d., 2.

12. Ibid., 3–4.

13. *Ugra Kshatriya Patrika* I (Baisakh–Asad), 1337 BS, 2.

14. Ibid.

15. Ibid., 2–3.

16. Ibid., 3–4, 51.

17. Ibid., 52.

18. *Bardhaman Barta*, 2 May 1938.

19. *Census of India, 1931*, Vol. V, Pt. I, 440, 445.

20. *Bardhaman Barta*, 2 May 1938.

21. *Ugra Kshatriya Pratinidhi* 1, 1298 BS, 269–74.

22. In twentieth-century Bengali society, in city, town, and village, there was a group of Bengalis who claimed and were accorded recognition as superior in social status to most of their fellows. They were called the bhadralok, literally, the 'respectable people', the 'gentlemen'. They were distinct in their style of living, manners, habits, and so on, and abstained from any sort of manual labour. They were a socially privileged group and economically dependent upon land rents and professional and clerical employment, maintaining a distance from the masses by their acceptance

of their high-caste position and command over education, and imbued with a sense of pride in their language, literary culture, and history (Broomfield 1968, 5–13).

23. *Census of India, 1901*, Vol. VI, Pt. I, 370.

24. *Census of India, 1931*, Vol. V, Pt. I, 455.

25. Government of Bengal, Finance Department, Miscellaneous Branch, Proceedings No. 47–50, March 1887.

Select References

Anonymous. n.d. *Jadabendra Smarane (Remembering Jadabendra)*.

Bandhu, Haricharan. 1913 (1320 BS). *Rajput O Ugrakshatriya (Rajput and Ugra Kshatriya)*. Burdwan.

Bandhu, Sanjib. 1985 (1392 BS). *Ugrakshatriya Parichiti* (*Introduction of Ugrakshatriya*). Burdwan: Bjay Toran Prakashani.

Bandyopadhyay, Sekhar. 1990. *Caste, Politics and the Raj Bengal, 1872–1937*. Calcutta: K. P. Bagchi & Co.

———. 2004. *Caste, Culture and Hegemony Social Dominance in Colonial Bengal*. New Delhi: Sage Publications.

———. 2010. 'Social Mobility in Colonial Bengal: The Namasudras'. In Ishita Banerjee-Dube (ed.), *Caste in History*, 180–196. New Delhi: Oxford University Press.

Banerjee, Diptendra. 1983. 'Vardhaman: The University and the Town (A Socio-Cultural Perspective)'. *Souvenir of Indian History Congress*, XLIV Session, The University of Burdwan, 5–11.

Banerjee-Dube, Ishita (ed.). 2010. *Caste in History*. New Delhi: Oxford University Press.

Bardhaman Barta, 2 May 1938.

Basu, Nagendra Nath. 1915. *Bardhamaner Itikatha* (*History of Burdwan*). Calcutta.

Basu, Tara Krishna. 1962. *The Bengal Peasant from Time to Time*. Calcutta: Asia Publishing House.

Bayly, Susan. 2000. *Caste, Society and Politics in India from the Eighteenth Century to the Modern Age*. New Delhi: Cambridge University Press.

Bhattacharya, Jogendra Nath. 1995. *Hindu Castes and Sects*. New Delhi: Munshiram Manoharlal.

Broomfield, J. H. 1968. *Elite Conflict in a Plural Society: Twentieth-century Bengal*. Bombay: Oxford University Press.

———. 1982. *Mostly About Bengal*. New Delhi: Manohar Publications.

Census of India. 1901. Vol. VI, Pt. I.

———. 1921. Vol. V, Pt. I.

———. 1931. Vol. V, Pt. I.

Cohn, Bernard S. 1987. 'The Census, Social Structure, and Objectification in South Asia'. In *An Anthropologist among the Historians and Other Essays*, 224–254. New Delhi: Oxford University Press.

Dalton, E. T. 1960 [1872]. *Descriptive Ethnology of Bengal*. Calcutta: Maitra.

Day, Lal Behari. 1969. *Bengal Peasant Life*. Calcutta: Firma K. L. Mukhopadhyay.

De, Barun. 1963. 'Death of Maharani: An Annul of Rural Bengal'. *The Economic Weekly*, 23 November.

Dirks, Nicholas B. 2003. *Castes of Mind: Colonialism and the Making of Modern India*. New Delhi: Permanent Black.

Dutta, Achintya Kumar. 2002. *Economy and Ecology in a Bengal District: Burdwan 1880–1947*. Calcutta: Firma K. L. Mukhopadhyay.

Ganguly, Indrani. 1987. *Social History of a Bengal Town*. Bombay: Himalaya Publishing House.

Ghosh, Benoy. 1954 (1361 BS). 'Bardhamaner Aitihasik Dhara' ('Historical Trend of Burdwan'). *Nutan Patrika*, Saradia Sankhya.

———. 1957. *Paschimbanger Sanskriti*, Vol. 1. Calcutta: Prakash Bhavan, 5e.

Ghurye, G. S. 1961 [1931]. *Caste, Class and Occupation*. Bombay: Popular Book Depot.

Halder, Ajit. 1982. 'Darpane Anya Mukh'. *Bardhaman Raj College Satabarsa 1881–1981*, 51–55, Burdwan Raj College.

Hill, K. A. L., and P. K. Banerjee. 1940. *Final Report on the Survey and Settlement of Operations in the District of Burdwan, 1927–34*. Calcutta: Office of the Superintendent of Government Printing.

Hunter, W. W. 1973. *Statistical Account of Bengal*, Vol. IV. Delhi.

Hutton, J. H. 1963. *Caste in India: Its Nature, Function and Origins*. London: Oxford University Press, 4e.

Majumdar, R. C. 1984. *History of Ancient Bengal*. Calcutta: G. Bharadwaj & Co., rev. edn.

Mayaram, Shail. 2010.'The Sudra Right to Rule: Caste, Clan, Community, and State in Nineteenth-Century Mewat'. In Ishita Banerjee-Dube (ed.), *Caste in History*, 109–135. New Delhi: Oxford University Press.

Mitra, A. 1953. *Census, 1951, West Bengal: The Tribes and Castes of West Bengal*. Calcutta: Office of the Superintendent of Government Printing.

Mukhopadhyay, Amitabha. 1971. *Unish Sataker Samaj O Sanskriti* (*Society and Culture of the Nineteenth Century*). Calcutta: General Printers & Publishers Pvt. Ltd.

______. 1981. *Jatibhedpratha O Unish Sataker Bangali Samaj* (*Caste System and Nineteenth-century Bengali Society*). Calcutta: K. P. Bagchi & Co.

O'Hanlon, Rosalind. 2010. 'Phule and the Inversion of Brahman Myths'. In Ishita Banerjee-Dube (ed,), *Caste in History*, 172–180. New Delhi: Oxford University Press.

O'Donnell, C. J. 1891. *The Lower Provinces of Bengal and their Feudatories*, Census of India, 1891, Vol. 3. Calcutta: Bengal Secretariat Press.

Oldham, William Benjamin. 1894. *Some Historical and Ethnical Aspects of the Burdwan District*. Calcutta: Bengal Secretariat Press.

Palit, Chittabrata. 1982. *Perspectives on Agrarian Bengal*. Calcutta: Papyrus.

Palit, Haridas. 1926 (1333 BS). 'Bardhamaner Bivinna Jaat' ('Different Castes of Burdwan'). *Arthik Unnati* 1 (1).

Peterson, J. C. K. 1910. *Bengal District Gazetteers Burdwan*. Calcutta: Bengal Secretariat Book Depot.

Pinch, William R. 1996. *Peasants and Monks in British India*. London: University of California Press Ltd.

Risley, H. H. 1981. *The Tribes and Castes of Bengal*, Vol. 1. Calcutta: Firma K. L. Mukhopadhyay.

Roy, Niharranjan. 1993. *Bangalir Itihas: Adiparba* (*A History of the Bengali People: Early Period*). Calcutta: Dey's Publishing.

Roy, Ratnalekha. 1979. *Change in Bengal Agrarian Society*. New Delhi: Manohar Publications.

Sahana, Paresh Bijoy. 1960 (1367 BS). *Jibani Satya Kinkar Sahana* (*Biography of Satya Kinkar Sahana*). Bankura: Ananda Kutir.

Sanyal, Hitesranjan. 1981. *Social Mobility in Bengal*. Calcutta: Papyrus.

Sen, Sukumar (ed.). 1993. *Kabikankan Mukundaram's Chandimangal*. New Delhi: Sahitya Academy.

Singh, K. S. (ed.). 1991. *People of India National Series*, Vol. I. New Delhi: Anthropological Survey of India.

———. 1992. *Ethnicity, Caste and People*. New Delhi: Manohar Publishers.

Sinha, Surajit. 1959. 'Bhumij-Kshatriya Social Movement in South Manbhum'. *Bulletin of the Department of Anthropology* VIII (2), 11–12.

Smrititirtha, Sitikantha. 1883 (1300 BS). *Ugrakshatriya Samhita*. Calcutta.

Srinivas, M. N. 1962. *Caste in Modern India and Other Essays*. Bombay: Asia Publishing House.

———. 1966. *Social Change in Modern India*. Berkeley: University of California Press.

Ugra Kshatriya Patrika. 1930 (1337 BS). Baishakh–Asad (April–June).

Notes on the Editor and Contributors

The Editor

Achintya Kumar Dutta is Professor of History, The University of Burdwan, and a former post-doctoral Commonwealth Fellow. He specialises in the areas of socioeconomic history and the history of medicine. He is the author of *Economy and Ecology in a Bengal District Burdwan 1880–1947* (2002) and *Trauma in Public Health: Tuberculosis in Twentieth-century India* (2018).

The Contributors

Arun Bandopadhyay is Historical and Archaeological Secretary of the Asiatic Society, Kolkata, and former Nurul Hasan Professor of History, University of Calcutta. His research interests cover agrarian history, business history, social and cultural history, and the history of science and environment. He is the author of *Nature, Knowledge and Development: Critical Essays on Environmental History of India* (2016).

Varuni Bhatia teaches at Azim Premji University, Bangalore. Her research interests include Bengali Vaishnavism, colonialism and religion, new media technologies, religion in contemporary India, and transnational occult networks in colonial India. She is the author of *Unforgetting Chaitanya: Vaishnavism and Cultures of Devotion in Colonial Bengal* (2017).

Subhayu Chattopadhyay is at the Department of History, Visva-Bharati. His area of research is the history of science and technology, as well as society and culture, in colonial India, with particular reference to the performing arts. He has co-edited *Mapping the Path to Maturity* (2018).

Kailash Chandra Dash served at different Government Colleges under the Government of Odisha Education Service in the capacity of Reader in History. His research interests include traditional narratives of eastern India, Madalapanji, and the Jagannatha Temple. He has authored *Legend, History and Culture of India* (1997).

Rajat Datta was Professor, Centre for Historical Studies, Jawaharlal Nehru University, New Delhi. The main areas of his research, publication, and teaching were the economic history of early modern India; the eighteenth century in Indian history; comparative trajectories of early modern economic development in an Asian perspective; and the nature of globalisation in the early modern world.

Amit Dey is Sir Asutosh (Chair) Professor of Medieval and Modern Indian History, University of Calcutta, and a former Commonwealth Scholar. His area of specialisation is Islam in Medieval and Modern South Asia. He is the author of *The Image of the Prophet in Bengali Muslim Piety, 1850–1947* (2006) and *Islam in South Asia* (2016).

Santanu Dey is Associate Professor, Department of History, Ramakrishna Mission Vidyamandira, Belur Math (affiliated to the University of Calcutta) and also Research Fellow at the Oxford Centre for Hindu Studies, Oxford University, United Kingdom. He has researched and published a number of articles on varied aspects of religion and colonial modernity.

Dipannita Dutta is a Ph.D. scholar at the Department of History, Visva-Bharati. Her research interests lie in the history of science and technology in colonial India.

Ranjeeta Dutta teaches at the Centre for Historical Studies, Jawaharlal Nehru University, New Delhi, and is a former Fellow at Max Weber Kolleg, University of Erfurt, Germany. Her areas of interest lie in the history of religion and ideas of region and spatial histories. She has authored *From Hagiographies to Biographies: Ramanuja in Tradition and History* (2014).

Rila Mukherjee is Professor of History, University of Hyderabad. Her recent co-edited publications include *Cross-Cultural Networking in the Eastern Indian Ocean Realm* (2019) and *Indian Ocean Histories: The Many Worlds of Michael Naylor Pearson* (2020).

Sujata Mukherjee is Professor of History, Rabindra Bharati University, Kolkata and former ICCR Chair for Modern Indian Studies at Victoria University, Wellington, New Zealand. Her research interests include the sociocultural history of modern India and history of science, technology, environment, and medicine. Among her many publications is *Gender, Medicine, and Society in Colonial India: Women's Health Care in Nineteenth- and Early Twentieth-Century Bengal* (2017).

Bipasha Raha is Professor and former Co-ordinator, UGC SAP-DRS, Department of History, Visva-Bharati. She specialises in the agricultural, social, cultural, and intellectual history of colonial Bengal and has authored *The Plough and the Pen: Peasantry, Agriculture and the Literati in Colonial Bengal* (2012) and *Living a Dream: Rabindranath Tagore and Rural Reconstruction* (2014).

Anuradha Roy is retired Professor, Department of History, Jadavpur University. Her research is focused on intellectual and cultural history, with special reference to Bengal. She has authored/edited a dozen books in Bengali and English, most of which are related to the nationalist and communist culture of Bengal.

Index